Contents

KT-442-996

Festivals colour section
following p.80

Hill tribes of Laos
colour section
following p.272

◀◀ Young monks, Thakhek ◀ Sunset over the Mekong, Vientiane

Introduction to

Laos

Often overlooked in favour of its better-known neighbours, landlocked Laos remains one of Southeast Asia's most beguiling destinations. Caught in the middle of the two Indochina wars and long isolated from the rest of the world, the country retains a slow, rather old-fashioned charm, and its people – incredibly laidback and friendly, even by Asian standards – are undoubtedly one of the highlights of any visit.

Laos's lifeline is the Mekong River, which runs the length of the country, at times bisecting it and at others serving as a boundary with Thailand; the rugged Annamite Mountains historically have acted as a buffer against Vietnam, with which Laos shares its eastern border. Most people visit the country as part of a wider trip in the region, often entering from Thailand and following the Mekong further south. However, Laos alone rewards further exploration, and with a little more time it's not hard to feel like you're visiting places where few Westerners venture. Stretching from the forest-clad mountains of the north to the islands of the far south, there's enough here to keep you occupied for weeks, and still feel as though you'd barely scratched the surface.

For such a small country, Laos is surprisingly diverse in terms of its people. Colourfully dressed hill tribes populate the higher elevations, while in the lowland river valleys, coconut palms sway over the Buddhist monasteries of the ethnic Lao. The country also retains some of the French influence it absorbed during colonial days: the familiar smell of freshly baked bread and coffee mingles with exotic local aromas in morning markets, and many of the old shophouses of its larger towns now (appropriately) house French restaurants.

The effects of the wars, and of its communist government, are unmistakable – it remains completely inadvisable to strike out into the countryside without following paths for fear of UXO (unexploded ordnance) – and the country remains heavily dependent on its neighbours for all manner of products; indeed in some parts of the country, the local markets stock more Chinese and Vietnamese goods than Lao. However, whether you're riding through the countryside on a rickety old bus crammed with sacks of rice, more people than seats, and blaring tinny Lao pop music, leisurely sailing down the Mekong past staggeringly beautiful scenery, or being dragged by a stranger to celebrate a birth over too much Beer Lao and *lào-láo*, it's hard not to be won over by this utterly fascinating country and its people.

▶ Fresh chillies at Vientiane morning market

Fact file

• The Lao People's Democratic Republic, whose capital is **Vientiane**, is Southeast Asia's only landlocked country. Modern Laos covers more than 236,000 square kilometres, yet has a **population** of just under 7 million.

• A constitutional monarchy until 1976, Laos is today a one-party dictatorship and one of the world's last official **communist** states. It is also one of the world's poorest countries, heavily reliant on aid.

• **Life expectancy** is a rather paltry 57 years, and there's a young population, with the average age just 19.5 years.

• **Lowland Lao** (Lao Loum) comprise approximately seventy percent of the population, **upland Lao** (Lao Theung) and **highland Lao** (Lao Soung) roughly twenty and ten percent respectively; within these broad definitions, there are many smaller divisions. **Chinese** and **Vietnamese** are a small but economically significant portion of the population.

• The national **language** is Lao, a tonal language closely related to Thai, although the written scripts differ. English is the most spoken European language.

• Laos is a predominately **Buddhist** country and follows the Theravadan school of Buddhism, in common with neighbouring Thailand, Burma and Cambodia. Around thirty percent of the population, particularly those in the highlands, follow **animist** beliefs.

5

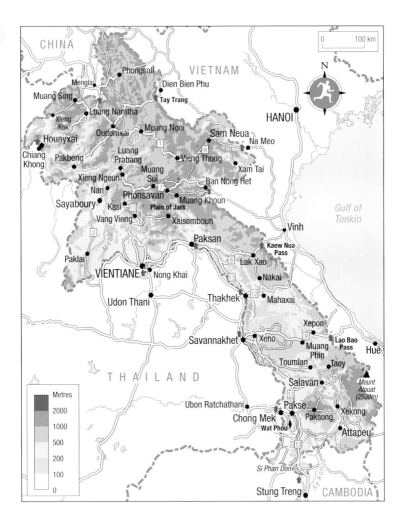

Where to go

S et on a broad curve of the Mekong, **Vientiane** is perhaps Southeast
Asia's most modest capital city. Yet, although lacking the buzz of
Ho Chi Minh City or Bangkok, Laos's capital has been transformed
since the 1990s, with a string of cosmopolitan restaurants and
cafés to complement its charming rows of pale yellow French–Indochinese
shophouses. Robbed of its more splendid temples in battles with Siam long
ago, Vientiane is more a place for adjusting to the pace of Lao life, and
indulging in herbal saunas and sunset drinks on the banks of the Mekong, than

one for breakneck tours of monuments and museums. Few tourists passing through the capital miss a chance for a half-day journey out to **Xieng Khuan**, its riverside meadow filled with mammoth religious statues, one of Laos's most arresting and bizarre sights.

From Vientiane, it makes sense to head north to **Vang Vieng**, a town set in a landscape of glimmering green paddies and sawtoothed karst hills. A great spot for caving, kayaking, rock climbing and long walks in the countryside, the town is best known for its wild tubing scene, and is undoubtedly the country's party capital for young backpackers. From here the mountainous old Royal Road to Luang Prabang rollercoasters through some of Laos's most stunning scenery. The more intrepid can indulge in a road-and-river expedition through Laos's northwestern frontier, stopping off in the remote outpost of **Sayaboury**, home to a large portion of the country's diminishing elephant population.

Despite the ravages of time, the gilded temples and weathered French–Indochinese shophouses of tiny, cultured **Luang Prabang** possess a spellbinding majesty that make this Laos's most enticing destination. Though increasingly touristy, the dusty side streets, Mekong views and quiet mornings still lend the city plenty of charm. Most visitors combine a stay here with a couple of day-trips, to the sacred **Pak Ou Caves**, two riverside grottoes brimming with thousands of Buddha images, and to beautiful **Kouang Si waterfall**, the perfect spot for a refreshing dip on a hot day.

A few hours north up the emerald **Nam Ou River** from Luang Prabang is the quiet town of **Nong Khiaw**, picturesquely surrounded by towering limestone peaks and a great base for trekking and kayaking in the region.

▲ The Tat Lo waterfall, Bolaven Plateau

Just a little further up the river, and only accessible by boat, **Muang Ngoi** is a popular travellers' spot, where it's hard to drag yourself away from the temptation of spending your days soaking up the views from a hammock. Following the river even further north is one of the greatest highlights of a trip to Laos, passing through stunning scenery on resolutely local boats to get to **Phongsali**, from which you can explore further into the isolated far north, or join an overnight trek to local hill-tribe villages.

Improved roads means that it's now a lot easier to explore the **far north**, an often spectacular region that is home to a patchwork of upland tribal groups. **Luang Namtha** and the easy-going village of **Muang Sing** are both centres for treks to nearby hill-tribe villages, while the former also offers kayaking opportunities. Downriver from here is **Houayxai**, on the Thai border, from where you can join a slow boat down the Mekong for the picturesque journey south to Luang Prabang.

Lost in the misty mountains of the far northeast, **Hua Phan** province was the nerve centre of communist Laos during the Second Indochina War, and remains well removed from the Mekong Valley centres of lowland Lao life. The provincial capital, **Sam Neua**, has a resolutely Vietnamese feel (hardly surprising when you consider its proximity to the border), and though it has a rather limited tourist infrastructure, there's a certain charm about the place once you dig a little deeper. The main reason for a stay here is to visit **Vieng Xai**, where the communist Pathet Lao directed their resistance from deep within a vast cave complex, and where the last Lao king was exiled until his untimely demise. South along Route 6 from Hua Phan is **Xieng Khuang** province, the heartland of Laos's **Hmong** population. **Phonsavan**, a dusty rather nondescript town, is the starting point for trips out to the mystical **Plain of Jars**.

Morning markets

Markets remain a mainstay of daily life in Laos, crammed full of stalls selling everything from pigs' heads, congealed blood and pungent *pa dàek* to bamboo baskets for sticky rice and imported toiletries from Vietnam. They're also a great place for a quick meal – even in the smallest you'll be able to find someone selling *fõe* – though you'll generally need to get there early to see the best of them.

To the **south**, the tail of Laos is squeezed between the formidable Annamite Mountains to the east and the Mekong River as it barrels towards Cambodia. **Thakhek** is a good base from which to visit the **Mahaxai Caves** and **Khammouane Limestone NBCA**, the highlight of which is **Tham Lot Kong Lo**, an underground river that can be navigated by canoe. Genial **Savannakhet** is the south's most famous town, almost as culturally Vietnamese as it is Lao, a pleasant urban retreat with an architectural charm second only to Luang Prabang. The cool and fertile **Bolaven Plateau**, where most of Laos's **coffee** is grown, makes a refreshing stop during the hot season, not least to try a cup of the famous brew. To the southwest lies diminutive **Champasak**, with its red-dirt streets and princely villas. The ruins of **Wat Phou**, the greatest of the Khmer temples outside Cambodia, perch on a forested hilltop nearby.

Anchoring the tail of Laos, the countless river islands of **Si Phan Don** lie scattered across the Mekong, swollen to 14km from bank to bank, all the way to the Cambodian border. One of the most significant wetlands in the country, Si Phan Don is the perfect spot to while away lazy days, and harbours scores of long-established fishing communities as well as centuries-old lowland Lao traditions.

When to go

November to January are the most pleasant months to travel in lowland Laos, when daytime temperatures are agreeably warm, evenings are slightly chilly and the countryside is green and lush after the rains. However, at higher elevations

▼ Brightly painted tuk-tuk

temperatures are significantly cooler, sometimes dropping to freezing point. In February, temperatures begin to climb, reaching a peak in April, when the lowlands are baking hot and humid. During this time, the highlands are, for the most part, equally hot if a bit less muggy than the lowlands, though there are places, such as Paksong on the Bolaven Plateau, that have a temperate climate year-round. Due to slash-and-burn agriculture, much of the north, including Luang Prabang, becomes shrouded in smoke from March until the beginning of the monsoon, which can at times be quite uncomfortable, and of course doesn't do your photographs any favours. The rainy season (generally May to September) affects the condition of Laos's network of unpaved roads, some of which become impassable after the rains begin. On the other hand, rivers which may be too low to navigate during the dry season become important transport routes after the rains have caused water levels to rise. Note that the climate in some northern areas – notably Phongsali and Hua Phan (Sam Neua) – can be surprisingly temperamental, even in the hot season, so you could have one scorcher of a day, followed by a cold, wet day that's enough to convince you you're no longer in Southeast Asia.

Average daily maximum temperatures and monthly rainfall

	Jan	Feb	Mar	Apr	May	Jun	Jul	Aug	Sep	Oct	Nov	Dec
Vientiane												
°C	28	30	33	34	32	32	31	31	31	31	29	28
mm	5	15	38	99	267	302	267	292	302	109	15	3
Luang Prabang												
°C	28	32	34	36	35	34	32	32	33	32	29	27
mm	15	18	31	109	163	155	231	300	165	79	31	13

18

things not to miss

It's not possible to see everything that Laos has to offer in one trip – and we don't suggest you try. What follows is a selective and subjective taste of the country's highlights: stunning temples, colourful festivals and great activities. They're arranged in five colour-coded categories to help you find the very best things to see, do, eat and experience. All highlights have a page reference to take you straight into the Guide, where you can find out more.

01 A slow boat down the Mekong Page **201** • The lifeline of this landlocked nation, the Mekong figures in every visit to Laos, supplying the fish for dinner, a stunning array of sunsets and a route to travel along.

02 **Phongsali** Page **180** • Head into the far north to this untouristy town, from where you can explore the beautiful surrounding countryside.

03 **Plain of Jars** Page **153** • Ancient funerary urns, the remnants of a lost civilization, lie scattered across the heart of the northeast.

04 **Waterfalls of the Bolaven Plateau** Page **251** • A series of spectacular waterfalls set among lush forest.

05 **Luang Prabang** Page **113** • At the confluence of the Mekong and the Nam Khan, Laos's most enchanting city boasts atmospheric temples and a variety of excursions.

06 **Lao food** Page **33** • Fiery and crammed with herbs, Lao food is a delight to discover – and there's excellent Beer Lao to wash it down.

07 **Vang Vieng**
Page **97** • Best known for its tubing and backpacker scene, Vang Vieng is also a great place for outdoor adventures.

08 **Trekking** Page **45** • Rugged mountain forests set the scene for hikers seeking to explore the remote hill villages of the north.

09 **The Nam Ou** Page **172** • This tropical waterway in the mountainous north passes through some of the country's most inspiring scenery.

10 **Vieng Xai** Page **164** • A dusty village, beautifully set among stunning limsestone karsts, which were home to the Pathet Lao during the second Indochina War.

11 **Colonial shophouses** Page **215** • French–Indochinese shophouses add character to city streets in Mekong River towns, such as Savannakhet.

12 That Luang Page **81** • The country's most important religious building is best seen at sunset when the golden stupa seems to glow in the fading light.

13 Si Phan Don Page **243** • This picturesque collection of Mekong islands, close to the Cambodian border, is dotted with rustic fishing villages and is the perfect place to relax.

14 Wat Phou Page **236** • The most evocative Khmer ruin outside of Cambodia, this rambling mountainside complex dates from the sixth to twelfth centuries.

15 Lao massage Page **48** • A traditional massage at a Lao sauna is the best way to wind down and rejuvenate after a long trek. The herbal mixtures in the steam bath (and the tea) are jealously guarded secrets.

15

16 **Wat Xieng Thong** Page 128 • Spared wars, fires and overzealous restorations, the jewel of temple-rich Luang Prabang is as elegant as it is historic.

18 **Nong Khiaw** Page 174 • Straddling the Nam Ou, this is the perfect place for a few days, relaxing in a hammock or exploring the surrounding area on foot or by kayak.

17 **Textiles** Page **52** • Weavers plying their craft still work the looms under their homes in the countryside, where each ethnic group is known for having its own style of textiles.

Basics

Basics

Getting there

As Laos is often part of a wider trip to the region, many people choose to travel there overland, with the crossings from Thailand near Vientiane and at Houayxai the most popular options. There are currently no direct flights to Laos from outside of Asia – most visitors fly via Bangkok, from where it takes just over an hour to reach Vientiane, and just under two hours to Luang Prabang. Connections are also possible from Chiang Mai and Udon Thani (Thailand), Ho Chi Minh City and Hanoi (Vietnam), Siem Reap (Cambodia), Kunming (China) and Kuala Lumpur (Malaysia). Due to the lack of direct flights, it can be quite expensive to fly to Laos, though this is more than compensated for by the low cost of living and travelling once in the country.

The **high season** for flights to Southeast Asia is from the beginning of July through to the end of August and also includes most of December, during which period fares can be twenty percent higher than at other times of year. If Laos is only one stop on a longer journey, you might want to consider buying a **Round-the-World (RTW) ticket**, which can be tailored to the destinations you want to visit. Also worth considering if you live in Australia, New Zealand or the west coast of North America are **Circle Pacific** tickets, which feature Bangkok as a standard option.

Package tours to Laos, some of which take in the country as part of a wider Indochina trawl, are inevitably more expensive and less spontaneous than if you travel independently, but are worth investigating if you have limited time or a specialist interest. Booking through a tour company in Laos will undoubtedly save you money compared to booking in your home country – see p.21 for details of recommended tour operators.

Flights from the UK and Ireland

Most flights from the UK and Ireland to Laos will involve a change of plane at Bangkok; an alternative route is via Vietnam, though this requires a change of plane in France or Germany first. In total, flying to Laos from the UK will take at least fifteen and a half hours, though this varies greatly according to connection times – flying on Thai Airways to Vientiane is usually the quickest option.

Flying from Ireland will involve changing planes at least twice – once in London or another European hub, and again at Bangkok or Ho Chi Minh City – with a journey time of at least eighteen and a half hours.

Because of the lack of direct flights, prices are generally high throughout the year. Expect to pay at least £750 from London and €900 from Dublin, though prices often rise over £1000/€1500 respectively. With flights to Bangkok alone significantly cheaper (from £450/€600), it's worth considering travelling overland between the Thai capital and Vientiane by train (see p.70 for more details).

Flights from the US and Canada

Flying to Laos from North America usually involves one stop, in Bangkok, if travelling from the west coast, and two stops, often Hong Kong and Bangkok, from the east coast. Expect journey lengths of at least nineteen and twenty-three hours, respectively.

Fares from the west coast start at around $1200, while you should expect to pay upwards of $1500 from the east coast. From Canada, prices begin at Can$1300 for Vancouver departures, Can$1700 from Toronto.

Six steps to a better kind of travel

At Rough Guides we are passionately committed to travel. We feel strongly that only through travelling do we truly come to understand the world we live in and the people we share it with – plus tourism has brought a great deal of **benefit** to developing economies around the world over the last few decades. But the extraordinary growth in tourism has also damaged some places irreparably, and of course **climate change** is exacerbated by most forms of transport, especially flying. This means that now more than ever it's important to **travel thoughtfully and responsibly**, with respect for the cultures you're visiting – not only to derive the most benefit from your trip but also to preserve the best bits of the planet for everyone to enjoy. At Rough Guides we feel there are six main areas in which you can make a difference:

• Consider what you're contributing to the **local economy**, and how much the services you use do the same, whether it's through employing local workers and guides or sourcing locally grown produce and local services.

• Consider the **environment** on holiday as well as at home. Water is scarce in many developing destinations, and the biodiversity of local flora and fauna can be adversely affected by tourism. Try to patronize businesses that take account of this.

• Travel with a purpose, not just to tick off experiences. Consider **spending longer** in a place, and getting to know it and its people.

• Give thought to how often you **fly**. Try to avoid short hops by air and more harmful night flights.

• Consider **alternatives to flying**, travelling instead by bus, train, boat and even by bike or on foot where possible.

• Make your trips "**climate neutral**" via a reputable carbon offset scheme. All Rough Guide flights are offset, and every year we donate money to a variety of charities devoted to combating the effects of climate change.

Flights from Australia, New Zealand and South Africa

Flights from Perth to Laos are via Bangkok, while those from elsewhere in Australia may go via Vietnam or Hong Kong (the latter requiring an additional change at Bangkok); average journey time is around thirteen hours from Perth and sixteen hours from Sydney, depending on connections. Flights from Perth start at around Aus\$1000, Aus\$1200 from Sydney; a cheaper alternative could be to fly the budget airline Air Asia to Kuala Lumpur, from where you can connect to Vientiane. From New Zealand, flying to Laos involves at least two stops, usually in Australia, Hong Kong, Vietnam or Bangkok; the journey takes around nineteen hours and fares start at around NZ\$1900.

Expect a journey upwards of nineteen hours if flying from South Africa, with at least two stops en route. Prices start at around R8500.

Getting there from neighbouring countries

Landlocked Laos is easily accessed from most of its neighbouring countries, either overland or by flying. Note that visa on arrival is not available at all overland entry points – see the box on p.23 for details and check locally for the most up-to-date information.

From Thailand

Lao Airlines operates flights from Bangkok to Vientiane, Luang Prabang and Savannakhet, from Chiang Mai to Vientiane and Luang Prabang, and from Udon Thani to Luang Prabang. In addition, Bangkok Air has twice-daily flights to Luang Prabang. All flights take between one hour and one hour forty minutes.

As of the time of writing, there are six routes across the Thai border into Laos: Chiang Khong–Houayxai (see p.197); Nong Khai–Vientiane (see p.70); Nakhon

Phanom–Thakhek (see p.210); Mukdahan–Savannakhet (see p.217); Chong Mek–Pakse (see p.233); and Beung Khan–Paksan (see p.209). Visas on arrival are available at all but the last crossing, but check locally before travelling as the situation can change. It's possible to get visas in advance from the Laos Embassy in Bangkok (see p.24).

From Vietnam

Vietnam Airlines flies from **Hanoi** to Vientiane and Luang Prabang, and from **Ho Chi Minh City** (Saigon) to Vientiane (all 3hr); both routes are also served by Lao Airlines. It's also possible to travel **overland** into Laos at six border points: Tay Trang–Sop Hun (see p.180); Nam Xoi–Na Meo (see p.159); Nam Khan–Nam Can (see p.153); Cau Treo–Nam Phao (see p.210); Lao Bao–Dansavanh (see p.224); Ngoc Hoi–Bo Y (see p.260). Visas on arrival are available at all of these crossings.

From Cambodia

Lao Airlines operates direct **flights** from **Siem Reap** to Luang Prabang (1hr 30min) and Pakse (1hr 45min), and to Vientiane via Pakse (3hr). The only way to cross overland into Laos is at the Dom Kralor–Veun Kham crossing, where it's possible to get a visa on arrival. It's also possible to cross here by boat. You will probably have to pay a small "fee", usually around $1–2, to the immigration officials at the checkpoint, in addition to your visa fee.

From China

It's possible to travel by road or air into Laos from China's southwestern **Yunnan** province. Lao Airlines operates **flights** from Kunming to Vientiane (1hr 20min). The only border crossing is at Mengla–Boten, from where buses run to Luang Namtha and Oudomxai (see p.185 & p.184) – it's best to travel first thing in the morning in order to be able to connect to either town.

Airlines

Air Asia ⓦ www.airasia.com.
Air Canada ⓦ www.aircanada.ca.
Air New Zealand ⓦ www.airnewzealand.com.
Bangkok Airways ⓦ www.bangkokair.com.
British Airways ⓦ www.britishairways.com.
Cathay Pacific ⓦ www.cathaypacific.com.
China Airlines ⓦ www.china-airlines.com.
Emirates ⓦ www.emirates.com.
Eva Airways ⓦ www.evaair.com.
Korean Airlines ⓦ www.koreanair.com.
Laos Airlines ⓦ www.laosairlines.com
Northwest/KLM ⓦ www.klm.com.
Qantas ⓦ www.qantas.com.
Singapore Airlines ⓦ www.singaporeair.com.
Thai Airways ⓦ www.thaiair.com.
United Airlines ⓦ www.united.com.
Vietnam Airlines ⓦ www.vietnamairlines.com.

Agents and Operators

Abercrombie & Kent Australia ☏ 1300/851 800, New Zealand ☏ 0800/441 638, UK ☏ 0845/618 2200, US ☏ 800/554-7016; ⓦ www.abercrombiekent.com. Luxury tour operator with a couple of Indochina offerings.
Adventure World Australia ☏ 1300/295 049, ⓦ www.adventureworld.com.au; New Zealand ☏ 0800/238 368; ⓦ www.adventureworld.co.nz. A good range of tours, ranging from two to seventeen days.
Adventures Abroad US ☏ 1-800/665-3998, ⓦ www.adventures-abroad.com. Small-group tour specialists with several regional tours that include Laos on their itinerary, plus one trip out of Bangkok that concentrates exclusively on Laos.
Buffalo Tours Vietnam ⓦ www.buffalotours.com. Vietnam-based tour operator with a range of options for Laos, including luxury hotels and culinary tours.
Exodus UK ☏ 0845/863 9600, ⓦ www.exodus.co.uk. Various Indochina packages from this specialist in cultural and adventure tourism, including a cycling trip in Laos and northern Vietnam.
Exotissimo Vientiane ☏ 021/241861 Luang Prabang ☏ 071/252879; ⓦ www.exotissimo.com. Well-established tour operator with branches throughout Indochina offering tours catered to a range of holidays, from honeymoons and family trips to hotel bookings and treks.
Explore Worldwide UK ☏ 0845/0131537, ⓦ www.exploreworldwide.com. A number of Laos options, most combining the country with Vietnam and Cambodia.
Journeys International US ☏ 1-800/255-8735, ⓦ www.journeys-intl.com. Specialists in small-group nature and culture explorations, offering a couple of week-long trips in Laos or an extended trip in the region.
North South Travel UK ☏ 01245/608 291, ⓦ www.northsouthtravel.co.uk. Friendly, competitive travel agency, offering discounted fares worldwide.

Profits are used to support projects in the developing world, especially the promotion of sustainable tourism. **Selective Asia** UK ☎ 501273/ 670 001, ⓦ www .selectiveasia.com. Helpful and knowledgeable staff and an excellent range of Laos trips, all of which can be tailor-made and to suit a range of budgets.

STA Travel Australia ☎ 134 782, New Zealand ☎ 0800/474 400, South Africa ☎ 0861/781 781, UK ☎ 0871/2300 040, US ☎ 1-800/781-4040; ⓦ www .statravel.co.uk. Worldwide specialists in independent travel; also student IDs, travel insurance, car rental, rail passes, and more. Good discounts for students and under-26s.

Symbiosis UK ☎ 0845/123 2844, US ☎ 1-866/723 7903; ⓦ www.symbiosis-travel .com. An environmentally aware operator that aims to reduce the negative impact of tourism. Tours include "Laos Ancient and Wild", which encompasses trekking, hill-tribe visits, kayaking and a stay in Luang Prabang.

Trailfinders Australia ☎ 1300/780 212, Ireland ☎ 01/677 7888, UK ☎ 0845/058 5858; ⓦ www .trailfinders.com. One of the best-informed and most efficient agents for independent travellers.

Travel CUTS Canada ☎ 1-866/246-9762, US ☎ 1-800/592-2887; ⓦ www.travelcuts.com. Canadian youth and student travel firm.

Travel Indochina Australia ☎ 866/892 9216, ⓦ www.travelindochina.com. An excellent range of tours that take in Laos – either on its own or in conjunction with Thailand, Vietnam or Cambodia.

Trips Worldwide UK ☎ 0800/840 0850, ⓦ www .tripsworldwide.com. A range of tailor-made trips to Laos, including "Off the beaten track", which takes in Luang Namtha, Akha hill tribes and Nong Khiaw.

USIT Ireland ☎ 01/602 1906, Northern Ireland ☎ 028/9032 7111, ⓦ www.usit.ie. Ireland's main student and youth travel specialists.

Wendy Wu Tours South Africa ☎ 011/394 1660, ⓦ www.wendywutours.co.za. Short tours just focusing on Laos or a 28-day "Grand tour of Indochina".

World Expeditions Australia ☎ 1300/720 000, Canada ☎ 613/241-2700, New Zealand ☎ 09/368 4161, UK ☎ 020/8545 9030, US ☎ 1-613/241-2700; ⓦ www.worldexpeditions.com. An interesting array of group trips, including an "Eco Tourism Development Project".

Entry requirements

Unless you hold a passport from Japan or one of the ASEAN member states, you'll need a visa to enter Laos. The good news is that you probably won't need to arrange it in advance; thirty-day visas are now available on arrival at most international borders. Note that all visitors must hold a passport that is valid for at least six months from the time of entry into Laos.

Visas on arrival take just a few minutes to process, cost around $35, and are available to passengers flying into Luang Prabang Airport, Pakse Airport and Wattay Airport in Vientiane. Those travelling to Laos from Thailand can pick up visas on arrival at any of the border crossings open to foreign tourists, as can those entering from certain places in Vietnam (Nam Khan, Bo Y, Tay Trang, Cau Treo and Lao Bao) and China (Mo Han). Only US dollars are accepted as payment and a passport-sized photo is required. If you forget the photo, border officials will usually turn a blind eye for an extra $1. Note that passport holders from a number of countries, including Pakistan, Turkey and Zambia, are not eligible for visas on arrival and must obtain one in advance – for a comprehensive list see ⓦtinyurl.com/3ykrvyy. To cross into Laos from all other points, including Cha Lo in Vietnam, you'll need to arrange a visa

before arriving at the border. Like visas on arrival, **pre-arranged tourist visas** allow for a stay of up to thirty days. Prices are generally a little higher though – especially if you pay a tour operator to help you out – so avoid buying one unless your border crossing demands it. If it does, visas can be obtained directly from Lao embassies and consulates. At the Lao embassy in Bangkok (see p.24), thirty-day visas cost 1,400 baht for nationals of the UK, US and Ireland, 1,200 baht for those from Australia, New Zealand and South Africa, and 1,680 baht for Canadians. You'll need to take two passport-sized photos with you but, provided you apply before noon, processing can usually be done on the same day. **Advance visas** can also be obtained at the Lao consulate in Khon Kaen, in the northeast of Thailand, or through one of the many travel agents concentrated on or around Khao San Road. However,

Lao visas

Visa on arrival: Thirty days. Available at Wattay International Airport (Vientiane), Pakse Airport, Luang Prabang International Airport, and all Thai–Lao border crossings open to foreigners. Also available at border crossings with Vietnam (Nam Khan, Bo Y, Tay Trang, Cau Treo and Lao Bao) and China (Mo Han).

Tourist visa (T): Thirty days. Required for all border crossings where visa on arrival is not available. Can be arranged in advance at Lao embassies and consulates, or through tour operators in Thailand, Vietnam and Cambodia.

Visitor visa (B3): One-month stay. Extendable for two further months. Lao guarantor required, and intended for those visiting relatives who work in Laos.

Transit visa (TR): Allows for a maximum of five days' stay and intended to help travellers who wish to make a short stopover in Laos. The visa is only valid for one province, and takes three working days to process. To qualify you must have proof of an onward journey within five days.

Business visa (B2): One-month stay, but can be extended until the end of your business term. Requires a Lao sponsor.

Multiple entry visa: Only issued by the Ministry of Foreign Affairs, Consular Department.

prices (and processing fees) can vary wildly. Wherever you choose to get your visa, bear in mind that Lao visa regulations and prices are subject to frequent change.

The Lao embassy in Hanoi, and consulates in Ho Chi Minh City and Da Nang, can also issue visas but it's important to note that the prices charged vary from place to place, and the regulations and conditions change frequently. Lao visas issued in Vietnam are also significantly more expensive than those issued in Thailand.

Extending visas

Visa **extensions** are fairly easy to obtain, but you'll need to plan ahead if you want to avoid overstaying your visa (there's currently a $10 penalty for each extra day you spend in the country). The cheapest option is to visit the immigration office on Hatsady Road in Vientiane before your visa expires. Here, visa extensions are issued at the cost of $2 per day and the maximum length of extension is fifteen days. Alternatively you could leave the country and enter again (which might work out cheaper if you're planning to extend by twenty days or more) or pay a local travel agent to arrange the visa extension for you. Generally this is more expensive, with most vendors charging around $4 per extra day required. Thirty-day business visas that have the potential to be extended can also be arranged in advance at the Lao embassies and consulates listed below.

Australia 1 Dalman Crescent, O'Malley, Canberra ☎02/6286 4595, ⓦwww.laosembassy.net.

Cambodia 15–17 Mao Tse Tung Blvd, Phnom Penh ☎23/982632.

China 11 E 4th St, Sanlitun, Chaoyang, Beijing ☎010/5321224; Camelia Hotel, Suite 3226, 154 E Dong Feng Rd, Kunming ☎0871/3176624.

Hong Kong Room 1002 Arion Commercial Centre, 2–12 Queen's Rd West, Hong Kong ☎2544 1186.

India Panchsheel Park, New Delhi ☎011/642 7447, ⓕ642 8588.

Indonesia 33 Jalan Kintamani Raya, Kuningan Timur, Jakarta ☎021/520 2673, ⓕ522 9601.

Japan 3-3-22, Nishi-Azabu, Minato-ku ☎03/54112291, ⓕ54112293.

Malaysia 25 Jalan Damai, Kuala Lumpur ☎03/4251 1118, ⓕ4251 0080.

Myanmar (Burma), Diplomatic Headquarters, Taw Win Road, Yangon (Rangoon) ☎01/22482, ⓕ27446.

New Zealand Contact embassy in Canberra.

Philippines 34 Lapu-Lapu St, Magallanes, Makati, Manila ☎02/852 5759.

Singapore 479-B Gold Hill Centre, Thomson Rd ☎6250 6044, ⓕ6014.

Thailand 502/13 Ramkhamhaeng Soi 39, Bangkapi, Bangkok ☎02 539 3642; 19/1–3 Phothisan Rd, Khon Kaen ☎043 223 698, ⓦwww.bkklaoembassy.com

US 2222 S St NW, Washington DC ☎202/332-6416, ⓕ332-4923 ⓦwww.laoembassy.com

Vietnam 22 Rue Tran Bing Trong, Hanoi ☎04/942 4576, ⓕ822 8414; 93 Pasteur St, District 1, Ho Chi Minh City ☎08/829 7667.

Getting around

Getting around on Laos's transport system is an adventure in itself, what with its barely seaworthy boats, aged jalopies with hard seats and hot, crowded buses. Don't be fooled by maps and distance charts – seemingly short rides can take hours, as tired vehicles slow to a crawl in their uphill battle against muddy, mountainous roads. Take heart though, in knowing that many visitors have their best encounters with the people of Laos amid the adversity of a bad bus ride.

Laos's road system has improved significantly over the last few years. Roads have been upgraded, and getting around is easier than ever, though often still challenging. Keep in mind, however, that a newly graded and paved road this year may get no maintenance, and after just two or even one rainy seasons the road will revert to being nothing but a potholed track. Some roads are only built to last a season, being washed away each year by the monsoon.

The country's main thoroughfare is **Route 13**, which stretches from Luang Prabang to the Cambodian border, passing through Vientiane, Savannakhet and Pakse. Route 13 sees a steady flow of bus traffic, and it's usually possible to flag down a vehicle during daylight hours provided it's not already full. Off Route 13, you'll encounter a wide range of road conditions – from freshly paved carriageways to bone-rattling, potholed tracks. With the improved road conditions, **buses** have largely supplanted **river travel**, the traditional means of getting around.

You only need to travel for a week or two in Laos before you realize that **timetables** are irrelevant: planes, buses and boats leave on a whim and estimated times of arrival are pointless. Wherever you go in Laos, the driver does not seem to be in any hurry to arrive.

For an idea of frequency and duration of bus services between towns, check the **travel details** at the end of each chapter. Given the poor condition of many roads and buses, as well as the many unscheduled stops en route, all travel times in these sections should be taken as rough estimates.

Inter-town transport

Visitors hoping to see rural Laos can expect hours of arduous, bone-crunching travel on the country's motley fleet of lumbering jitter-boxes. Buses link only larger towns, and on many routes can be few and far between, a fact which makes a number of attractions, such as ruins and waterfalls, difficult to reach. Even when there is transport, you may find that the limited bus timetable will allow you to get to a particular site, but not make a same-day return trip – something of a problem given the dearth of accommodation in far-flung spots. In the rainy season, some unpaved roads dissolve into rivers of mud, slowing buses to a crawl or swallowing them whole. Even vehicles in reasonably good condition make painfully slow progress, as

drivers combat **mountainous roads** and make frequent (and at times long) stops to pick up passengers, load goods and even haggle for bargains at roadside stalls.

Buses

Ordinary buses provide cheap transport between major towns and link provincial hubs with their surrounding districts. Cramped, overloaded and designed for the smaller Lao frame, these buses are profound tests of endurance and patience. Seats often have either torn cushions or are nothing more than a hard plank. Luggage – ranging from incontinent roosters to sloshing buckets of fish and the inevitable fifty-kilo sacks of rice – is piled in every conceivable space, filling up the aisle and soaring skywards from the roof. **Breakdowns** are commonplace and often require a lengthy roadside wait as the driver repairs the bus on a lonely stretch of road. Typical fares are of the order of 100,000K for Vientiane to Luang Prabang or Pakse, though fares could rise rapidly if fuel prices increase.

Operating out of Vientiane, a fleet of blue, **government-owned buses** caters mostly to the capital's outlying districts, although it does provide a service to towns as far north as Vang Vieng and as far south as Pakse. While newer than most vehicles in Laos, these Japanese- and Korean-built buses are not air-conditioned and have cramped seats, a situation that worsens as rural passengers pile in. Buses plying **remote routes** tend to be in worse shape: aged jalopies cast off from Thailand or left behind by the Russians, which reach new lows in terms of discomfort and are even more prone to breakdowns. These vehicles range in style from buses in the classic sense of the word to souped-up tourist vans. Converted Russian flat-bed trucks, once the mainstay of travel in Laos, still operate in remote areas.

In most instances, **tickets** should be bought from the town's bus station – it's best to arrive with plenty of time in order to buy your ticket and grab a seat, especially in towns that are busy transport hubs, such as Oudomxai. In larger towns with an established tourist infrastructure, you'll often be able to buy your tickets from a travel agent; this will usually be a little more

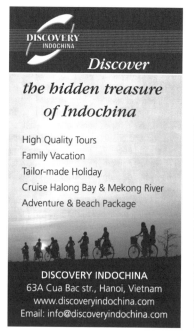

expensive, but will include transport to the bus station. In more rural areas, you'll pay for your ticket once on board.

At the other end of the spectrum you'll find air-conditioned **VIP buses**, such as the daily $15 coach service from Vientiane to Luang Prabang. These services leave from their own private "stations", and reservations, which can be made through guesthouses and travellers' cafés, are recommended.

Additionally, you'll find a number of **van** and **minibus** services in the more touristy towns, connecting to other popular tourist destinations, such as Vang Vieng and Si Phan Don. Prices for these services are higher than for the local bus alternative and the journey time will usually be a fair bit quicker, though you may find yourself just as crammed in as on a regular bus, and of course you miss out on the opportunity to meet local people. The situation changes rapidly at this end of the market, so check with travel agents for the latest information on routes and bookings. It's also worth shopping around if booking minibus tickets – regardless of how much you pay for your ticket, and where you buy it, you're likely to end up on the same minibus.

Reliable timetables only exist in regional hubs like Vientiane, Luang Prabang and Savannakhet; elsewhere it's best to go to the bus station the night before you plan to travel to find out the schedule for the next day. Most departures are usually around 8 or 9am, and very few buses leave after midday. Many drivers will sit in the bus station long after their stated departure time, revving their engines in an attempt to lure enough passengers to make the trip worthwhile.

Sawngthaews

In rural areas, away from the Mekong Valley, the bus network is often replaced by **sawngthaews** – converted pick-up trucks – into which drivers stuff as many passengers as they possibly can. Passengers are crammed onto two facing benches in the back ("sawngthaew" means "two rows"); latecomers are left to dangle off the back, with their feet on a running board, an experience that, on a bumpy road, is akin to inland windsurfing.

Sawngthaews also ply routes between larger towns and their satellite villages, a service for which they charge roughly the same amount as buses. They usually depart from the regular bus station, but will only leave when a driver feels he has enough passengers to make the trip worth his while. Some drivers try to sweat extra kip out of passengers by delaying departure. Your fellow passengers may agree to this, but most often they grudgingly wait. In some situations, you can save yourself a lot of trouble and waiting by getting a few fellow travellers together and flat-out **hiring the driver** to take you where you want to go; the fares being so ridiculously low as to make this quite affordable. To catch a sawngthaew in between stops, simply flag it down from the side of the road and tell the driver where you're headed so he knows when to let you off. The fare is usually paid when you get off. If the driver is working without a fare collector, he will tend to stop on the outskirts of his final destination to collect fares.

City and town transport

With even the capital too small to support a local bus system, transport within Lao towns and cities is left to squadrons of motorized **samlaw** (literally, "three wheels") vehicles, more commonly known as jumbos and tuk-tuks. Painted in primary reds, blues and yellows, the two types of samlaw look alike and both function as shared taxis, with facing benches in the rear to accommodate four or five passengers. **Jumbos** are the original Lao vehicle, a home-made three-wheeler consisting of a two-wheeled carriage soldered to the front half of a motorcycle, a process best summed up by the name for the vehicle used in the southern town of Savannakhet – Skylab (pronounced "sakai-laeb"), after the doomed space station that fell to earth, piece by piece, in the late 1980s. **Tuk-tuks**, offspring of the three-wheeled taxis known for striking terror in Bangkok pedestrians, are really just bigger, sturdier jumbos, the unlikely product of some Thai factory, which take their name from their incessantly sputtering engines. Lao tend to refer to these vehicles interchangeably.

Although most northern towns are more than manageable on foot, the Mekong towns tend to sprawl, so you'll find tuk-tuks particularly useful for getting from a bus station into the centre of town. To flag down a tuk-tuk, wave your hand, palm face down and parallel to the ground. Tell the driver where you're going, bargain the price and pay at the end.

Tuk-tuks are also on hand for inner-city journeys. Payment is usually per person, according to the distance travelled and your bargaining skills. Rates vary from town to town and are prone to fluctuate in step with rising petrol prices, but figure on paying around 5000K per kilometre. In some towns, tuk-tuks run set routes to the surrounding villages and leave from a stand, usually near the market, once full. Chartering tuk-tuks is also a good way to get to sites within 10 to 15km of a city.

Boats

With the country possessing roughly 4600km of navigable **waterways**, including stretches of the Mekong, Nam Ou, Nam Ngum, Xe Kong and seven other arteries, it's no surprise to learn that rivers are the ancient highways of mountainous Laos. Road improvements in recent years, however, have led to the decline of river travel between many towns, with buses and sawngthaews replacing the armada of boats that once plied regular routes.

The main **Mekong route** that remains links Houayxai to Luang Prabang. Since the upgrading of Route 13, boats very rarely ply the stretches of river between Luang Prabang, Pakse and Si Phan Don. Aside from the larger, so-called "slow boats" on the Mekong routes, smaller passenger boats still cruise up the wide Nam Ou River (Muang Khoua–Hat Sa), the Nam Tha (Luang Namtha to Pak Tha), and a few others, provided water levels are high enough.

Slow boats and passenger boats

The diesel-chugging cargo boats that lumber up and down the **Mekong routes** are known as "**slow boats**" (*heua sa*). Originally hammered together from ill-fitting pieces of wood, and powered by a jury-rigged engine that needs to be coaxed along by an on-board mechanic, these boats once offered one of Asia's last great travel adventures, but you'll need to speak Lao to arrange a trip. Much easier is to take advantage of the **passenger boats** with seating for a couple of dozen people, which have been introduced on the river journey most popular with Western visitors, namely Houayxai to Luang Prabang.

On smaller rivers, river travel is by long, narrow boats powered by a small outboard engine. Confusingly, these are also known as "slow boats", although, unlike the big Mekong cargo boats, they only hold eight people and never attempt major Mekong routes. They never have a fixed schedule and only leave if and when there are enough passengers.

Addresses and street names

Lao addresses can be terribly confusing, firstly because property is usually numbered twice – when numbered at all – to show which lot it stands in, and then to signify where it is on that lot. To add to the confusion, some cities have several conflicting address systems – Vientiane, for example, has three, although no one seems to use any of them. To avoid confusion, numbers are often omitted from addresses given in the Guide, and locations are described using landmarks instead.

Only five cities in Laos actually have **street names** – and that's just the start of the problem. Signs are few and far between and many roads have several entirely different names, sometimes changing name from block to block. If you ask for directions, locals most likely won't know the name of a street with the exception of the three or four largest avenues in Vientiane. Use street names to find a hotel on a map in the Guide, but when asking directions or telling a tuk-tuk driver where to go you'll have better luck mentioning a landmark, monastery or prominent hotel. Fortunately, Lao cities, even Vientiane, are relatively small, making it more of a challenge to get lost than it is to figure out where you're going.

Due to the casual nature of river travel in Laos, the best way to deal with uncertain departures is to simply **show up early** in the morning and head down to the landing and ask around. Be prepared for contradictory answers to questions regarding price, departure and arrival time, and even destination. Given variations in currents and water levels and the possibility of breakdowns and lengthy stops to load passengers and cargo, no one really knows how long a trip will take. On occasion, boats don't make their final destination during the daytime. If you're counting on finding a guesthouse and a fruit shake at the end of the journey, such unannounced stopovers can take you out of your comfort zone, as passengers are forced to sleep in the nearest village or aboard the boat. It's also a good idea to bring extra water and food just in case.

The **northern Mekong and Nam Ou** services (Houayxai–Pakbeng–Luang Prabang, and Luang Prabang–Nong Khia–Muang Ngoi–Muang Khoua–Hat Sa) are somewhat better managed, with **tickets** sold from a wooden booth or office near the landing (buy tickets on the day of departure). Fares are generally posted, but foreigners pay significantly more than locals. Always arrive early in the morning to get a seat. **Southern Mekong** services (Pakse–Champasak–Don Khong) have now all but stopped thanks to the improved state of Route 13, and most trips south now combine a bus journey along this road with a quick ferry ride across the water.

Travelling by river in Laos can be dangerous and reports of boats **sinking** are not uncommon. The Mekong has some particularly tricky stretches, with narrow channels threading through rapids and past churning whirlpools. The river can be particularly rough late in the rainy season, when the Mekong swells and uprooted trees and other debris are swept into the river.

Speedboats

On both the Mekong and its tributaries, **speedboats** (*heua wai*) are a faster but more expensive alternative to slow boats. Connecting towns along the Nam Ou and

the Mekong from Vientiane to the Chinese border, these five-metre-long terrors are usually powered by a 1200cc Toyota car engine and can accommodate up to eight passengers.

Donning a crash helmet and being catapulted up the Mekong River at 50km an hour may not sound like most people's idea of relaxed holiday travel, but if you're up for it, speedboats can shave hours or days off a river journey and give you a thrilling spin at the same time. It's by no means safe, of course, although captains swear by their navigational skills. The boats skim the surface of churning whirlpools and slalom through rapids sharp enough to turn the wooden hull into toothpicks.

Speedboats have their own **landings** in Vientiane, Thadua, Paklai, Luang Prabang, Pakbeng and Houayxai, and depart when full. Seating is incredibly **cramped**, so you may want to consider paying for the price of two seats. **Crash helmets** are handed out before journeys – to spare your hearing from the overpowering screech of the engine. Although the roar of the engine is less annoying on board than it is from the banks, consider bringing along **ear plugs**. For safety's sake, insist on being given a life jacket to wear before paying.

Tickets cost as much as two to three times what you might pay to take a slow boat: the journey from Luang Prabang to Pakbeng, for example, is around $12. Speedboats can also be **chartered** for around $50 per hour – Luang Prabang to Phongsali, for example, costs around $200, Luang Prabang to Houayxai $100.

Cross-river ferries

Clunky metal car **ferries** and **pirogues** – dug-out wooden skiffs propelled by poles, paddles or tiny engines – are both useful means of fording rivers in the absence of a bridge. Both leave when they have a sufficient number of passengers and usually charge 3000–5000K, unless you're taking a vehicle across, in which case you can expect to pay 7000–10,000K. If you don't want to wait, pirogues are always open for hire. In the outback, fishermen can usually be persuaded to ferry you across to the opposite bank for a small sum.

Planes

The government-owned **Lao Airlines** (ⓦwww.laoairlines.com), the country's only domestic carrier, once had a dubious safety record. These days, however, standards are up and the airline is on a par with other regional carriers. Domestic routes have diversified in recent years, with destinations like Oudomxay and Luang Namtha now well connected with Vientiane.

You'll need to remain flexible, though reliability increases on key routes: Vientiane–Luang Prabang, Vientiane–Pakse and Vientiane–Savannkhet. Given the popularity of such routes in the peak season it's even wise to **book ahead**. On other routes, you may find it better to reconfirm the departure of your flight by stopping by the Lao Airlines office.

Sample one-way **fares** are Vientiane to Luang Prabang $82; Vientiane to Savannakhet $104; Vientiane to Oudomxay $140; Vientiane to Luang Namtha $150.

Vehicle and bike rental

Renting a **private vehicle** is expensive, but is sometimes the only way you'll be able to get to certain spots. Self-drive is an option, and cars can be rented from a couple of agencies in Vientiane only. However, it's usually easier and cheaper to hire a **car and driver**. Tour agencies will rent out air-conditioned vans and 4WD pick-up trucks as well as provide drivers. Prices are inflated by the rates paid by UN organizations, and can be as high as $80–100 per day, sometimes more if you're hiring a car to head upcountry from Vientiane. When settling on a price, it's important to clarify who is responsible for what: check who pays for the driver's food and lodging, fuel and repairs, and be sure to ask what happens in case of a major breakdown or accident.

Motorbikes

One of the best ways to explore the country-side is to rent a **motorbike**. Unfortunately, this is only an option in tourist-friendly places like Vientiane, Vang Vieng, Luang Prabang, Thakhek and Pakse, and even then you're often limited to smaller bikes, usually 100cc step-throughs such as the Honda Dream.

Rental prices for the day are generally $8–10, depending on the age and condition of the bike. More powerful 125cc **dirt bikes** suitable for cross-country driving are available only in Vientiane and cost $20 a day.

A licence is not needed, but you'll be asked to leave your passport as a deposit and may be required to return the bike by dark. Insurance is not available, so it's a good idea to make sure your travel insurance covers you for any potential accidents.

Before zooming off, be sure to **check the bike** thoroughly for any scratches and damaged parts and take it for a test run to make sure the vehicle is running properly. As far as **equipment** goes, a helmet offers essential protection, although few rental places will have one to offer you; bear in mind it's illegal to ride without a helmet. **Sunglasses** are essential in order to fend off the glare of the tropical sun and keep dust and bugs out of your eyes. Proper shoes, long trousers and a long-sleeved shirt are all worthwhile additions to your biking outfit and will provide a thin layer of protection if you take a spill.

Bicycles

Bicycles are available in most major tourist centres; guesthouses, souvenir shops and a few tourist-oriented restaurants may keep a small stable of Thai- or Chinese-made bikes (though rarely mountain bikes) to rent out for $1–2 per day.

Organized tours

Although less spontaneous and consider-ably more expensive than independent travel, **organized tours** are worth looking into if you have limited time or prefer to have someone smooth over the many logistical difficulties of travelling in Laos. Although the government encourages travellers to visit Laos through an authorized tour company, the tours aren't bogged down in political rhetoric and guides tend to be easy-going and informative.

About a dozen **tour companies** have sprung up in Vientiane, all offering similar tours in roughly the same price range, although it never hurts to shop around and bargain. A typical multi-day package might include a private cruise down the Mekong River on a slow boat operated by the tour company, with guided day-tours around Luang Prabang and other towns. While some tours include accommodation, meals and entry fees, others don't, so check what you're getting before paying.

Organized **adventure tours** are rapidly gaining popularity in Laos. These can be single- or multi-day programmes and usually involve hill-tribe trekking or river kayaking, or a combination of both. Rafting tours are also available and organized rock climbing is just starting to take off. The main centres for adventure tours are Vientiane, Vang Vieng, Luang Prabang, Luang Namtha and Muang Sing.

All Laos's tour companies are authorized by the Lao National Tourism Administration, which ensures that you won't be dealing with a fly-by-night organization.

Guides are generally flexible about adjusting the itinerary, but if you want more

freedom, an alternative is to set up your own custom-made tour by gathering a group of people and renting your own vehicle plus driver.

Local tour operators

Diethelm Travel Laos Nam Phou Place, PO Box 2657, Vientiane ⓣ021/215920, ⓕ217151. In Bangkok ⓣ02 255 9150, ⓦwww.diethelmtravel.com.
Green Discovery 54 Setthathilat Rd, Vientiane ⓣ021/251564, ⓦwww.greendiscoverylaos .com. Branches in Luang Nahtha, Luang Prabang, Thakhek, Pakse and Vang Vieng.
Savannakhet Eco Guide Unit Latsaphanit Rd, Savannakhet ⓣ041/214203 ⓦwww .savannakhet-trekking.com.
Exotissimo 44 Pangkham Rd, Vientiane ⓣ021/241861 or 241862 ⓦwww.exotissimo.com.
Lao National Tourism Administration ⓦwww .ecotourismlaos.com.
Sodetour 16 Fa Ngum Rd, PO Box 70, Vientiane ⓣ021/216314, ⓕ216313.

Accommodation

The influx of foreign visitors has meant a rapid increase in hotels and improved standards in tourist centres, although out in the boondocks change comes more slowly and comfort can be harder to come by. Expect to find higher standards of accommodation, as well as the greatest variety, in larger towns. Provincial towns, with the exception of popular stopovers on backpacker routes, tend to lag far behind, with small towns on well-travelled highways offering at best one or two rather rustic guesthouses.

Outside Luang Prabang, Pakse, Vang Vieng and the capital, finding a place to stay is a far simpler process than in most Southeast Asian countries – often because there are only one or two places in town and they're just a short walk from one another. Few towns have touts or taxi drivers trying to influence your decision.

Once you've found a spot, ask to see a number of rooms before reaching a decision, as standards and room types can vary widely within the same establishment.

En-suite showers and flush toilets are increasingly available in budget accommodation, though squat toilets are still common at the very cheapest places.

Establishments that do not quote their prices in dollars or baht keep a close eye on the volatile exchange rate and change their prices frequently, keeping the room rate at roughly the same dollar value. Many establishments will allow you to pay in Lao kip, US dollars or Thai baht, regardless of which currency their rates are quoted in; exchange rates are generally fairly close to the official rate. Count on being able to use credit cards only at higher-end establishments in cities.

Prices for the most basic double room start at around 30,000–40,000K in the provinces and 40,000–70,000K in Vientiane and Luang Prabang. Dorm beds (only usually found in the main tourist areas) can be had for as little as 25,000K per night. At these prices rooms can be pretty shabby, although there are a few diamonds in the rough.

For 100,000–200,000K you can buy yourself considerably more comfort, whether it's the luxuries of a standard hotel or the cosiness and hospitality of an upmarket guesthouse with a garden, tucked away in a quiet side street. If you're willing and able to spend around $25, you can actually get something quite luxurious, with wi-fi and a flat-screen TV.

Moving further up the scale, a whole host of expensive hotels has appeared on the scene, and with many of them struggling to fill rooms, managers can be amenable to discounts, especially in low season. Before settling on a price at mid-range and high-end hotels, check whether service charge and tax are included in the quoted price.

Most places are open to **negotiation**, especially in the low season, so it's a good idea to try and bargain; your case will be helped if you are staying for several days.

Not all accommodation places have **phones**, which is why some listings in this Guide don't have numbers alongside. Online booking services include ⓦwww.laos-hotels .com and ⓦwww.laos-hotel-link.com.

Budget accommodation

The distinction between a **guesthouse** and a **budget hotel** is rather blurry in Laos.

Either can denote anything ranging from a bamboo-and-thatch hut to a multistorey concrete monstrosity. There's very little that's standard from place to place – even rooms within one establishment can vary widely – although in tourist centres the cheapest bet is generally a fan room with shared washing facilities. As you tack on extra dollars, you'll gain the luxury of a private bathroom with a hot-water shower and an air conditioner. In small towns in remote areas you'll find that the facilities are often rustic at best – squat toilets and a large jar of water with a plastic scoop with which to shower, though this is rapidly changing. The further off the beaten track you go the greater the chances are that you'll be pumping your own water from a well or bathing in a stream.

Mid-range accommodation

Mid-range hotels have been opening up in medium sized towns all over Laos over the last few years, greatly improving the accommodation situation. Most of these hotels are compact, of up to five storeys, and offer spacious rooms with tiled floors and en-suite bathrooms with Western-style toilets for between 100,000–200,000K. The mattresses are usually hard – but at least the sheets and quilts are consistently clean. The bathroom fittings in such hotels are usually brand new but a few don't have water heaters. Because the standard of construction is poor and there is no concept of maintaining buildings, such hotels tend to age quickly.

Upmarket hotels

Once you've crossed the $25 threshold, you enter a whole new level of comfort. In the

---

Accommodation price codes

Accommodation throughout the Guide has been categorized according to the following price codes, reflecting the minimum you can expect to pay for a double room:

❶ 40,000K and under
❷ 40,500–80,000K
❸ 80,500–120,000K
❹ 120,500–200,000K
❺ $25–40
❻ $41–60
❼ $61–100
❽ $101–200
❾ $201 and over

In cases where an establishment charges per bed the price is given in the text rather than indicated by a price code.

former French towns on the Mekong this level of expense translates into an atmospheric room in a restored colonial villa or accommodation in a recently built establishment where rooms boast some of the trappings of a high-end hotel, such as cable television, fridge, air conditioning and a hot-water shower.

Colonial-era hotels often have a limited number of rooms, so **book ahead** if you want to take advantage of them – well in advance if you plan to visit during the peak months (Dec & Jan). Many of these places are firmly ensconced on the tour-group circuit, so push for a discount if you're travelling independently.

Thanks to foreign investors, a raft of **top-end hotels** have opened their doors in Vientiane and Luang Prabang, charging upwards of $80 a night. The best hotels in the capital, such as the *Settha Palace Hotel* and the *Novotel Belvedere*, have international-class facilities, including business centres and gyms. At the moment, there's a glut of high-end hotel accommodation in the capital, so don't hesitate to ask for discounts, especially for longer-term stays.

Staying in villages

Should you find yourself stuck in a small town for the night, a victim of the tired machinery of Laos's infrastructure or the yawning distances between villages, villagers are usually kind enough to find space for you in the absence of a local guesthouse. Don't expect much in the way of luxuries: you'll most likely find yourself bathing at the local well or in the river and going to the bathroom under the stars. Many small towns don't have so much as a noodle shop, so you'll also need to prepare yourself for some very authentic cooking. Before leaving, you should offer to remunerate your host with a sum of cash equivalent to what you would have paid in a budget guesthouse.

If there's a local **police station**, you should make yourself known to them, otherwise ask for permission to stay from the **village headman**; the government doesn't encourage foreigners to spend the night at a villager's house.

Food and drink

Fiery and fragrant, with a touch of sour, Lao food owes its distinctive taste to fermented fish sauce, lemongrass, coriander leaves, chillies and lime juice. Eaten with the hands along with the staple, sticky rice, much of Lao cuisine is roasted over an open fire and served with fresh herbs and vegetables. Pork, chicken, duck and water buffalo all end up in the kitchen, but freshwater fish is the main source of protein in the Lao diet. Many in rural Laos, especially in the more remote mountainous regions, prefer animals of a wilder sort – mouse deer, wild pigs, rats, birds or whatever else can be caught. Though you may not encounter them on menus, you're likely to see them being sold by the side of the road when travelling in these parts.

Closely related to Thai cuisine, Lao food is, in fact, more widely consumed than you might think: in addition to the more than two million ethnic Lao in Laos, Lao cuisine is the daily sustenance for roughly a third of the Thai population, while more than a few Lao dishes are commonplace on the menus of Thai restaurants in the West. Although Lao cuisine isn't strongly influenced by that of its other neighbours, Chinese and Vietnamese immigrants have made their mark on the culinary landscape by opening

For a food and drink glossary,
see p.317.

restaurants and noodle stalls throughout the country, while the French introduced bread, pâté and pastries.

Vientiane and **Luang Prabang** are the country's culinary centres, boasting excellent Lao food and international cuisine. Towns with a well-developed tourist infrastructure will usually have a number of restaurants serving a mix of Lao, Thai, Chinese and Western dishes, usually of varying standards, but once you're off the well-beaten tourist trail it can be hard to find much variety beyond fried rice and noodle soup.

Where to eat

Food is generally very inexpensive in Laos, with the cheapest options those sold by hawkers – usually fruit, small dishes like papaya salad, and grilled skewered meat – and the most expensive being the upmarket tourist restaurants (usually French or European) in Luang Prabang and Vientiane. Though hygiene standards have improved over recent years, basic food preparation knowledge in many places still lacks behind other countries in the region. However, though a little caution is a good idea, especially when you first arrive in the country in order to allow your stomach time to adjust to the change of cuisine, it's best just to exercise common sense. Generally, noodle stalls and restaurants that do a brisk business are a safe bet, though you may find that this denies you the opportunity to seek out more interesting, less touristy food.

Markets, street stalls and noodle shops

Morning markets (*talat sâo*), found in most towns throughout Laos, remain open all day despite their name and provide a focal point for noodle shops, coffee vendors and fruit stands. In Luang Prabang, Vientiane and Luang Namtha, vendors hawking pre-made dishes gather towards late afternoon in **evening markets** known as *talat láeng*. Takeaways include grilled chicken (*pîng kai*), spicy papaya salad (*tam màk hung*) and in some instances a variety

of dishes, displayed in trays and ranging from minced pork salad (*larp mu*) to stir-fried vegetables (*khùa phák*).

Most market vendors offer only takeaway food, with the exception of noodle stalls, where there will always be a small table or bench on which to sit, season and eat your noodle soups. Outside of the markets, **noodle shops** (*hân khãi fõe*) feature a makeshift kitchen surrounded by a handful of tables and stools, inhabiting a permanent patch of pavement or even an open-air shophouse. Most stalls specialize in one general food type, or, in some cases, only one dish; for example a stall with a mortar and pestle, unripe papayas and plastic bags full of pork rinds will only offer spicy papaya salad and variants on that theme. Similarly, a noodle shop will generally only prepare noodles with or without broth – they won't have meat or fish dishes that are usually eaten with rice.

Restaurants

Proper **restaurants** (*hân ahãn*) aren't far ahead of noodle shops in terms of comfort; most are open-sided establishments tucked beneath a corrugated tin roof. Ethnic **Vietnamese** and **Chinese** dominate the restaurant scene in some parts of Laos; indeed it can be downright difficult to find a Lao restaurant in some northern towns. Most towns that have even the most basic of tourist infrastructure will have at least one restaurant with an English-language menu – even if the translation can lead to some amusement. Away from the larger tourist centres, dishes will usually encompass variations on fried rice and noodle dishes, often with a few Lao, Chinese or Thai options intended to be eaten with sticky or steamed rice.

Tourist restaurants in larger centres usually offer a hotchpotch of cuisine – often encompassing standard Lao dishes like *larp* and *mók pa* alongside sandwiches, pastas and steaks. The most upmarket restaurants in Vientiane and Luang Prabang generally serve French cuisine, often in very sophisticated, un-Lao surroundings, but at very reasonable prices – a meal for two, including wine, is unlikely to stretch past $40.

When it comes to **paying**, the normal sign language will be readily understood in most restaurants, or simply say *"khāw sék dae"* ("the bill, please"). You'll generally only be able to use **credit cards** at upscale establishments in Vientiane and Luang Prabang. **Tipping** is only expected in the most upmarket restaurants – ten percent should suffice.

What to eat

So that a variety of tastes can be enjoyed during the course of a meal, Lao **meals** are eaten communally, with each dish being served at once, rather than in courses. The dishes – typically a fish or meat dish and soup, with a plate of fresh vegetables such as string beans, lettuce, basil and mint served on the side – are placed in the centre of the table, and each person helps him- or herself to only a little at a time. When ordering a meal, if there are two of you it's common to order two or three dishes, plus your own individual servings of rice, while three diners would order three or four different dishes.

The staple of Lao meals is **rice**, with **noodles** a common choice for breakfast or as a snack. Most meals are enjoyed with **sticky rice** (*khào niaw*), which is served in a lidded wicker basket (*típ khào*) and eaten with the hands. Although it can be tricky at first, it's fairly easy to pick up the proper technique if you watch the Lao around you. Grab a small chunk of rice from the basket, press it into a firm wad with your fingers and then dip the rice ball into one of the dishes. Replace the lid of the *típ khào* when you are finished eating or you will be offered more rice.

Plain steamed **white rice** (*khào jào*) is eaten with a fork and spoon – the spoon and not the fork is used to deliver the food to your mouth. If you're eating a meal with steamed white rice, it's polite to only put a small helping of each dish onto your rice at a time. Chopsticks (*mâi thu*) are reserved for **noodles**, the main exception being Chinese-style rice served in bowls.

If you are **dining with a Lao family** as a guest, wait until you are invited to eat by your host before taking your first mouthful. While dipping a wad of sticky rice into the main dish, try not to let grains of rice fall into it, and dip with your right hand only. Resist the temptation to continue eating after the others at the table have finished. Custom dictates that a little food should be left on your plate at the end of the meal.

Flavours

In addition to chillies, coriander, lemongrass and lime juice, common ingredients in Lao food include ginger, coconut milk, galangal, shallots and tamarind. Another vital addition to a number of Lao dishes is *khào khùa*, raw rice roasted in a wok until thoroughly browned and then pounded into powder; it's used to add both a nutty flavour and an agreeably gritty texture to food.

The definitive accent, however, comes from the fermented fish mixtures that are used to salt Lao food. An ingredient in nearly every recipe, *nâm pa*, or **fish sauce**, is made by steeping large quantities of fish in salt in earthen containers for several months and then straining the resulting liquid, which is golden brown. Good fish sauce, it has been said, should attain the warm, salty smell of the air along a beach on a sunny day. Most Lao use *nâm pa* imported from Thailand.

While *nâm pa* is found in cooking across Southeast Asia, a related concoction, **pa dàek**, is specific to Laos and northeastern Thailand. Unlike the bottled and imported *nâm pa*, thicker *pa dàek* retains a home-made feel, much thicker than fish sauce, with chunks of fermented fish as well as rice husks, and possessing a scent that the uninitiated usually find foul. However, as *pa dàek* is added to cooked food, it's unlikely that you'll really notice it in your food, and its saltiness is one of the pleasurable qualities of the cuisine.

Use of **monosodium glutamate** (MSG) is also common. The seasoning, which resembles salt in appearance, sometimes appears on tables in noodle shops alongside various other seasonings – it's generally coarser and shinier than salt.

Standard dishes

If Laos were to nominate a national dish, a strong contender would be *larp*, a "**salad**" of minced meat or fish mixed with garlic, chillies, shallots, galangal, ground sticky rice and fish sauce. Traditionally, larp is eaten raw (díp), though you're more likely to encounter it súk (cooked), and is often served with lettuce, which is good for cooling off your mouth after swallowing a chilli. The notion of a "meat salad" is a common concept in Lao food, although in Luang Prabang you'll find Lao salads closer to the Western salad, with many falling into the broad category of yam, or "mixture", such as yam sin ngúa, a spicy beef salad.

Another quintessentially Lao dish is tam màk hung, a spicy **papaya salad** made with shredded green papaya, garlic, chillies, lime juice, pa dàek and, sometimes, dried shrimp and crab juice. One of the most common street-vendor foods, tam màk hung, is known as tam sòm in Vientiane; stalls producing this treat are identifiable by the vendor pounding away with a mortar and pestle. Each vendor will have their own particular recipe, but it's also completely acceptable to pick out which ingredients – and how many chillies – you'd like when you order. One of several variants on tam màk hung is tam kûay tani, which replaces shredded papaya with green banana and eggplant.

Usually not far away from any tam màk hung vendor, you'll find someone selling pîng kai, basted **grilled chicken**. Fish, pîng pa is another grilled favourite, with whole fish skewered, stuffed with herbs and lemongrass, and thrown on the barbecue.

Soup is a common component of Lao meals and is served along with the other main courses during a meal. Fish soups, kaeng pa (or tôm yám paw when lemongrass and mushrooms are included), frequently appear on menus, as does kaeng jèut, a clear, mild soup with vegetables and pork, which can also be ordered with bean curd (kaeng jèut tâo hû).

A speciality of southern Laos and Luang Prabang, well worth ordering if you can find

it, is **mók pa** or fish steamed in banana leaves. Other variations, including mók kheuang nai kai (chicken giblets grilled in banana leaves) and mók pa fa lai (with freshwater stingray), are also worth sampling, though they appear less frequently on restaurant menus.

Restaurants catering to travellers can whip up a variety of **stir-fried dishes**, which tend to be a mix of Thai, Lao and Chinese food, and are usually eaten with steamed rice. **Fried rice** is a reliable standby throughout the country, as are Chinese and Thai dishes such as pork with basil over rice (mû phát bai holapha), chicken with ginger (khùa khing kai) and mixed vegetables (khùa phák).

Noodles

When the Lao aren't filling up on glutinous rice, they're busy eating fõe, the ubiquitous **noodle soup** that takes its name from the Vietnamese soup pho. Although primarily eaten in the morning for breakfast, fõe can be enjoyed at any time of day, and in more remote towns you may find that it's your only option.

The basic bowl of fõe consists of a light broth to which is added thin rice noodles and slices of meat (usually beef, water buffalo or grilled chicken). It's served with a plate of fresh raw leaves and herbs, usually including lettuce, mint and coriander. Flavouring the broth is pretty much up to you: containers of chilli, sugar, vinegar and fish sauce (and sometimes lime wedges and MSG) are on the tables of every noodle shop, allowing you to find the perfect balance of spicy, sweet, sour and salty. Also on offer at many noodle shops is mi, a yellow wheat noodle served in broth with slices of meat and a few vegetables. It's also common to eat fõe and mi softened in broth but served without it (hàeng), and at times fried (khùa).

Vegetarian food

Although very few people in Laos are vegetarian, it's usually fairly easy to persuade cooks to put together a vegetable-only rice or vegetable dish. In many places that may be your only option unless you eat fish. If you don't eat fish, keep in mind that most Lao cooking calls for fish sauce so, when ordering a veggie-only dish, you may want to add "baw sai nâm pa" ("without fish sauce").

Many other types of noodle soup are dished up at street stalls. *Khào biak sèn* is another soup popular in the morning, consisting of soft, round rice noodles, slices of chicken and fresh ginger and served in a chicken broth, though it's hard to find outside bigger towns. More widely available, and a favourite at family gatherings during festivals, is *khào pûn*, a dish of round, white, translucent flour noodles, onto which is scooped one of any number of sweet, spicy coconut-milk based sauces. These noodles also find their way into several Vietnamese dishes, such as barbecued pork meatballs (*nâm néuang*) and spring rolls (*yáw*), in which they are served cold with several condiments and a sauce. There's also a Lao incarnation of *khào soi*, the spicy noodle curry eaten throughout northern Thailand and the Shan States of Myanmar; the version common in Laos (in Luang Prabang and certain northwestern towns) consists of rice noodles served in almost clear broth and topped with a spicy meat curry.

Fruits and desserts

The best way to round off a meal or fill your stomach on a long bus ride is with **fresh fruit** (*màk mâi*), as the country offers a wide variety, from the more commonly known bananas, papayas, mangoes, pineapples, watermelons and green apples imported from China to more exotic options: crisp green guavas; burgundy lychees, with tart, sweet white fruit hidden in a coat of thin leather; wild-haired, red rambutans, milder and cheaper than lychees; dark purple mangosteen, tough-skinned treasures with a velvety smooth inside divided into succulent sweet segments; airy, bell-shaped green rose apples; pomelos, gigantic citruses whose thick rinds yield a grapefruit without the tartness; fuzzy, brown sapodillas, oval in shape and almost honey-sweet; large, spiky durian, notoriously stinky yet divinely creamy; oblong jackfruit, with sweet, yellow flesh possessing the texture of soft leather; and rare Xieng Khuang avocados, three times the size of those available in the West, with a subtle perfumed flavour. Restaurants occasionally serve fruit to end a meal, and, throughout the country, handcart-pushing hawkers patrol the streets with ready-peeled segments.

Desserts don't really figure on many restaurant menus, although some tourist restaurants will usually have a few featuring **coconut milk** or cream, notably banana in coconut milk (*nâm wãn màk kûay*). Markets often have a food stall specializing in inexpensive coconut-milk desserts, generally called *nâm wãn*. Look for a stall displaying a dozen bowls, containing everything from water chestnuts to corn to fluorescent green and pink jellies, from which one or two items are selected and then added to a sweet mixture of crushed ice, slabs of young coconut meat and coconut milk. Also popular are light Chinese **doughnuts**, fried in a skillet full of oil and known as *khào nõm khu* or *pá thawng ko*, and another fried delight, crispy bananas (*kûay khaek*).

Sticky rice, of course, also turns up in a few desserts. As **mangoes** begin to ripen in March, look for *khào niaw màk muang*, sliced mango splashed with coconut cream served over sticky rice; those who don't mind the smell of durian can try the durian variant on this dessert. *Khào lãm*, another treat, this one popular during the cool season, is cooked in sections of bamboo, which is gradually peeled back to reveal a tube of sticky rice and beans joined in coconut cream. Another thing to look out for at street stalls is *kanom krok* – delicious, soft little pancakes made with rice flour and coconut.

Soft drinks and juices

Brand-name **soft drinks**, such as 7-Up, Coca-Cola and Fanta, are widely available. Most vendors will pour the drink into a small plastic pouch packet (which is then tied with a string or rubber band and inserted with a straw) for taking away.

A particularly refreshing alternative, available in most towns with tourist restaurants, are fruit shakes (*màk mâi pan*), made from your choice of fruit, blended with ice, liquid sugar and condensed milk. Even more readily available are freshly squeezed **fruit juices**, such as lemon (*nâm màk nao*), plus coconut water (*nâm màk phao*) enjoyed directly from the fruit after it has been dehusked and cut open. Also popular is the exceptionally sweet sugar-cane juice, *nâm oi*.

Hot drinks

Laos's best **coffee** is grown on the Bolaven Plateau, outside Paksong in southern Laos, where it was introduced by the French in the early twentieth century. Most of the coffee produced is robusta, although some arabica is grown as well. Quality is generally very high, and the coffee has a rich, full-bodied flavour. Some establishments that are accustomed to foreigners may serve instant coffee (*kafeh net*, after the Lao word for Nescafé, the most common brand); if you want locally grown coffee ask for *kafeh Láo* or *kafeh thông*, literally "bag coffee", after the traditional technique of preparing the coffee.

Traditionally, hot coffee is served with a complimentary glass of weak Chinese tea or hot water, to be drunk in between sips of the very sweet coffee, though you're unlikely to experience this in many places. If you prefer your coffee black, and without sugar, order *kafeh dam baw sai nâm tan*. A perfect alternative for the hot weather is *kafeh yén*, in which the same concoction is mixed with crushed ice.

Black and Chinese-style **tea** are both served in Laos. Weak Chinese tea is often found, lukewarm, on tables in restaurants and can be enjoyed free of charge. Stronger Chinese tea (*sá jin*) you'll need to order. If you request *sá hâwn*, you usually get a brew based on local or imported black tea, mixed with sweetened condensed milk and sugar; it's available at most coffee vendors.

Alcoholic drinks

Beer Lao, the locally produced lager, is regarded by many as one of Southeast Asia's best beers, and is the perfect companion to a Lao meal. Containing five percent alcohol, the beer owes its light, distinctive taste to the French investors who founded the company in 1971, although the company was later state-owned, with Czechoslovakian brewmasters training the Lao staff, until it was privatized in the mid-1990s. Nearly all that goes into making Beer Lao is imported, from hops to bottle caps, although locally grown rice is used in place of twenty percent of the malt. Also available is the stronger Beer Lao Dark, which has a smooth, malty flavour

Lào-láo and other rice spirits

Drunk with gusto by the Lao is *lào-láo*, a clear rice alcohol with the fire of a blinding Mississippi moonshine. Most people indulge in local brews, the taste varying from region to region and even town to town.

Drinking *lào-láo* often takes on the air of a sacred ritual, albeit a rather boisterous one. After (or sometimes during) a meal, the host will bring out a bottle of *lào-láo* to share with the guests. The host begins the proceedings by pouring a shot of *lào-láo* and tossing it onto the ground to appease the house spirit. He then pours himself a measure, raising the glass for all to see before throwing back the drink and emptying the remaining droplets onto the floor, in order to empty the glass for the next drinker. The host then pours a shot for each guest in turn. After the host has completed one circuit, the bottle and the glass are passed along to a guest, who serves him- or herself first, then the rest of the party, one by one. Guests are expected to drink at least one shot in order not to offend the house spirit and the host, although in such situations there's often pressure, however playful, to drink much more. One polite escape route is to take a sip of the shot and then dump out the rest on the floor during the "glass emptying" move.

Another rice alcohol, *lào hái*, also inspires a festive, communal drinking experience. Drunk from a large earthenware jar with thin bamboo straws, *lào hái* is fermented by households or villages in the countryside and is weaker than *lào-láo*, closer to a wine in taste than a backwoods whisky. Drinking *lào hái*, however, can be a bit risky as unboiled water is sometimes added to the jar during the fermentation process.

and is generally more expensive than regular Beer Lao.

In Vientiane, **draught** Beer Lao, known as *bia sót* and sometimes appearing on English signs as "Fresh Beer", is available at bargain prices by the litre. Often served warm from the keg, the beer is poured over ice, though some establishments serve it chilled. There are dozens of *bia sót* outlets in the capital, most of which are casual outdoor beer gardens with thatch roofs. You can usually get snacks here too, known as "**drinking food**" or *káp kâem* – typical dishes include spicy papaya salad, fresh spring rolls, omelette, fried peanuts (*thua jeun*), shrimp-flavoured chips (*khào kiap kûng*) and grilled chicken.

Other Asian beers, including Tiger and Singha, are often available (sometimes on tap in Luang Prabang), and closer to the Chinese border you'll find cheaper and less flavousome Chinese lagers on many menus.

In Vientiane, Luang Prabang and other larger, more touristy, towns, you'll find a good range of Western spirits and liquors, and more upmarket restaurants usually have imported wine available by the glass or bottle.

Health

Healthcare in Laos is so poor as to be virtually nonexistent; the average life expectancy is just 57. Malaria and other mosquito-borne diseases are rife, and you'll need to take a number of precautions to avoid contracting these, especially if you plan on spending long periods of time in rural regions. The nearest medical care of any competence is in neighbouring Thailand; if you find yourself afflicted by anything more serious than travellers' diarrhoea, it's best to head for the closest Thai border crossing and check into a hospital.

Plan on consulting a doctor at least two months before your travel date to discuss which diseases you should receive immunization against. Some antimalarials must be taken several days before arrival in a malarial area in order to be effective. If you are going to be on the road for some time, a dental check-up is also advisable.

Vaccinations

While there are no mandatory vaccinations for Laos (except yellow fever if you are coming from an infected area), a few are recommended. Hepatitis A, typhus, tetanus and polio are the most important ones, but you should also consider hepatitis B, rabies and Japanese encephalitis. All shots should be recorded on an International Certificate of Vaccination and carried with your passport when travelling abroad.

Hepatitis A is contracted via contaminated food and water and can be prevented by the Havrix vaccine which provides protection for up to ten years. Two injections two to four weeks apart are necessary, followed by a booster a year later. The older one-shot vaccine only provides protection for three months. Hepatitis B is spread via sexual contact, transfusions of tainted blood and dirty needles. Vaccination is recommended for travellers who plan on staying for long periods of time (six months or more). Note that the vaccine can take up to six months before it is fully effective.

Rabies can be prevented by a vaccine that consists of two injections over a two-month period with a third a year later and boosters every two to five years. If you haven't had shots and are bitten by a potentially rabid animal, you will need to get the jabs immediately.

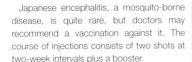
Japanese encephalitis, a mosquito-borne disease, is quite rare, but doctors may recommend a vaccination against it. The course of injections consists of two shots at two-week intervals plus a booster.

Medical resources for travellers

ⓦ www.istm.org Website of the International Society for Travel Medicine, with a full list of clinics specializing in international travel health.
ⓦ www.tripprep.com Travel Health Online provides an online-only comprehensive database of necessary vaccinations for most countries, as well as destination and medical service provider information.
ⓦ www.fitfortravel.scot.nhs.uk UK NHS website carrying information about travel-related diseases and how to avoid them.

Travel medicine

US and Canada

ⓦ www.cdc.gov/travel The US government's official site for travel health
MEDJET Assistance ☎ 1-800/863-3538, ⓦ www.medjetassistance.com. Annual membership programme for travellers which, in the event of illness or injury, will fly members home or to the hospital of their choice in a medically equipped jet.
Travel Medicine ☎ 1-800/872-8633, ⓦ www.travmed.com. Sells first-aid kits, mosquito netting, water filters, reference books and other health-related travel products; the website includes a list of US travel clinics.
ⓦ www.csih.org The website of the Canadian Society for International Health contains an extensive list of travel health centres in Canada.

UK and Ireland

Hospital for Tropical Diseases Travel Clinic 2nd floor, Mortimer Market Building, Capper St, London WC1E 6JB ☎ 020/7388 9600, ⓦ www.thehtd.org (Mon–Fri 9am–4.30pm except Wed, 10am–4.30pm, by appointment only). A consultation costs £15, which is waived if you have your injections or buy your malaria pills here.
Well Travelled Clinics An offshoot of the Liverpool School of Tropical Medicine, offering pre-travel advice and vaccinations. Pembroke Place, Liverpool L3 5QA ☎ 0151/705 3223, ⓦ www.welltravelledclinics.co.uk.
MASTA (Medical Advisory Service for Travellers Abroad) ☎ 0330/100 4224, ⓦ www.masta.org. Travel clinics around the UK.

Trailfinders Immunization clinic (no appointment necessary) at 194 Kensington High St, London (Mon–Fri 9am–5pm except Thurs to 6pm, Sat 10am–5.15pm; ☎ 020/7938 3999, ⓦ www.trailfinders.com/travelessentials/travelclinic.htm).
Travel Medicine Services PO Box 254, 16 College St, Belfast 1 ☎ 028/9031 5220. Offers medical advice before and after trips.
Tropical Medical Bureau Grafton Buildings, 34 Grafton St, Dublin 2 ☎ 01850/487 674, ⓦ www.tmb.ie. Travel clinics in Dublin and elsewhere across the Republic of Ireland.

Australia and New Zealand

Travel Doctor Australia ☎ 1300/658844, ⓦ www.tmvc.com.au; New Zealand ☎ 09/373 3531, ⓦ www.traveldoctor.co.nz. Clinics in major Australian and New Zealand cities; travel health factsheets available online.

General precautions

The average traveller to Laos has little to worry about as long as they use common sense and exercise a few precautions. The changes in climate and diet experienced during travel collaborate to lower your resistance, so you need to take special care to maintain a healthy intake of food and water and to try to minimize the effects of heat and humidity on the body. Excessive alcohol consumption should be avoided, as the dehydrating effects of alcohol are amplified by the heat and humidity.

Good **personal hygiene** is essential; hands should be washed before eating, especially given that much of the Lao cuisine is traditionally eaten with the hands. Cuts or scratches, no matter how minor, can become infected very easily and should be thoroughly cleaned, disinfected and bandaged to keep dirt out.

Most health problems experienced by travellers are a direct result of something they've eaten. Avoid eating uncooked vegetables and fruits that cannot be peeled. Dishes containing raw meat or fish are considered a delicacy in Laos but people who eat them risk ingesting worms and other parasites. Cooked food that has been sitting out for an undetermined period should be treated with suspicion.

Stomach trouble and viruses

Most travellers experience some form of **stomach trouble** during their visit to Laos,

What about the water?

The simple rule while travelling in Laos is not to drink river or tap water. Contaminated water is a major cause of sickness due to the presence of pathogenic organisms: bacteria, viruses and microscopic giardia cysts. These microorganisms cause diseases such as diarrhoea, gastroenteritis, typhoid, cholera, dysentery, polio, hepatitis A, giardia and bilharzia, and can be present even when water looks clean.

Safe **bottled water** is available almost anywhere, though when buying, check that the seal is unbroken as bottles are occasionally refilled from the tap. Water purifying tablets, carried with you from home, are an environmentally friendly alternative as they help to reduce the number of plastic bottles left behind after your travels.

Chinese **tea** made from boiled water is generally safe, but travellers should shun **ice** that doesn't look factory-made. Some of the fanciest hotels have filtration systems that make tap water safe enough to clean your teeth with, but as a general rule, you're best off using purified or bottled water.

simply because their digestive system needs time to adapt to the local germs. To deal with travellers' diarrhoea, it is usually enough to drink lots of liquids and eat lightly, avoiding spicy or greasy foods in favour of bland noodle soups until your system recovers. The use of Lomotil or Imodium should be avoided, as they just prevent your body clearing the cause of the diarrhoea, unless long-distance road travel makes it absolutely necessary. Diarrhoea accompanied by severe stomach cramps, nausea or vomiting is an indication of **food poisoning**. As with common diarrhoea, it usually ends after a couple of days. In either case, be sure to increase your liquid intake to make up for lost fluids. It's a good idea to bring **oral rehydration salts** with you from home. If symptoms persist or become worse after a couple of days, consider seeking medical advice in Thailand.

Blood or mucus in the faeces is an indication of dysentery. There are two types of dysentery and they differ in their symptoms and treatment. **Bacillary dysentery** has an acute onset, with severe abdominal pain accompanied by the presence of blood in the diarrhoea. Fever and vomiting may also be symptoms. Bacillary dysentery requires immediate medical attention and antibiotics are usually prescribed. **Amoebic dysentery** is more serious: the onset is gradual with bloody faeces accompanied by abdominal pain. Symptoms may eventually disappear but the amoebas will still be in the body and will continue to feed on internal organs,

causing serious health problems in time. If you contract either type of dysentery, seek immediate medical advice in Thailand.

Hepatitis A, a viral infection contracted by consuming contaminated food or water, is quite common in Laos. The infection causes the liver to become inflamed and resulting symptoms include nausea, abdominal pains, dark-brown urine and light-brown faeces that may be followed by jaundice (yellowing of the skin and whites of eyes). Vaccination is the best precaution; if you do come down with hepatitis A, get plenty of rest and eat light meals of non-fatty foods.

Another scatological horror is **giardia**, symptoms of which include a bloated stomach, evil-smelling burps and farts, and diarrhoea or floating stools. As with dysentery, treatment by a physician in Thailand should be sought immediately.

Occasional outbreaks of **cholera** occur in Laos. The initial symptoms are a sudden onset of watery but painless diarrhoea. Later nausea, vomiting and muscle cramps set in. Cholera can be fatal if adequate fluid intake is not maintained. Copious amounts of liquids, including oral rehydration solution, should be consumed and urgent medical treatment in Thailand should be sought.

Like cholera, **typhoid** is also spread in small, localized epidemics. The disease is sometimes difficult to diagnose, as symptoms can vary widely. Generally, they include headaches, fever and constipation, followed by diarrhoea.

Mosquito-borne illnesses

Malaria, caused by the plasmodium parasite, is rife in much of Laos. **Symptoms** include chills, a high fever and then sweats, during which the fever falls; the cycle repeats every couple of days. These symptoms aren't so different to those of flu, making diagnosis difficult without a blood test; if you think you've contracted malaria, check into a Thai hospital immediately.

Vientiane is said to be malaria-free, but visitors to other parts of Laos should take all possible precautions to avoid contracting this sometimes fatal disease. Night-feeding mosquitoes are the carriers, so you'll need to take extra care in the evening, particularly at dawn and dusk. High-strength mosquito **repellent** that contains the chemical compound DEET is a necessity, although bear in mind that prolonged use may be harmful. A natural alternative is citronella oil, found in some repellents. Wearing trousers, long-sleeved shirts and socks gives added protection.

If you plan on travelling in remote areas, bring a **mosquito net**. Most guesthouses provide nets but some of these have holes; gather up the offending section of net and twist a rubber band around it. Many hotels have replaced nets with screened-in windows, which is fine if the room door remains shut at all times, but doors are usually left wide open when maids are tidying up the rooms between guests. If you can't get hold of a mosquito net, try pyrethrum **coils** which can be found in most markets and general stores in Laos.

For added insurance against malaria, it's advisable to take **antimalarial tablets**. Though **doxycycline** and **mefloquine** are the most commonly prescribed antimalarials for Laos, the plasmodium parasites are showing resistance to the latter drug. While none of the antimalarials guarantees that you will not contract malaria, the risks will be greatly reduced. Note that some antimalarials can have unpleasant side effects. Mefloquine in particular can sometimes cause dizziness, extreme fatigue, nausea and nightmares. Pregnant or lactating women are not advised to take mefloquine.

Day-feeding mosquitoes are the carriers of **dengue fever**. The disease is common in urban as well as rural areas, and outbreaks occur annually during the rainy season. The symptoms are similar to malaria and include fever, chills, aching joints and a red rash that spreads from the torso to the limbs and face. Dengue can be fatal in small children. There is no preventative vaccination or prophylactic. As with malaria, travellers should use insect repellent, keep skin covered with loose-fitting clothing and wear socks. There is no specific treatment for dengue other than rest, lots of liquids and paracetamol for pain and fever. Aspirin should be avoided as it can aggravate the proneness to internal bleeding which dengue sometimes produces.

Sun-related maladies

The Lao hot season, roughly March to May, can be brutal, especially in the lowlands. To prevent **sunburn**, fair-skinned people should wear sunblock and consider purchasing a wide-brimmed straw hat. UV protective sunglasses are useful for cutting the sun's glare, which can be especially harsh during river journeys. The threat of **dehydration** increases with physical exertion. Even if you don't feel thirsty, drink plenty of water. Not having to urinate or passing dark-coloured urine are sure signs that your system is not getting enough liquids.

Heat exhaustion, signified by headaches, dizziness and nausea, is treated by resting in a cool place and increasing your liquid intake until the symptoms disappear. **Heatstroke**, indicated by high body temperature, flushed skin and a lack of perspiration, can be life-threatening if not treated immediately. Reducing the body's temperature by immersion in tepid water is an initial treatment but no substitute for prompt medical attention. Heat and high humidity sometimes cause **prickly heat**, an itchy rash that is easily avoided by wearing loose-fitting cotton clothing.

Critters that bite and sting

In Laos the **bugs** are thick, especially during the rainy season when they swarm round light bulbs and pummel bare skin until you feel like the trampoline at a flea circus. Fortunately, most flying insects pose no threat and are simply looking for a place to land and rest up.

Visitors who spend the night in hill-tribe villages where hygiene is poor risk being infected by **scabies**. These microscopic creatures are just as loathsome as their name suggests, causing severe itching by burrowing under the skin and laying eggs. Scabies is most commonly contracted by sleeping on dirty bedclothes or being in prolonged physical contact with someone who is infected. More common are **head lice**, especially among children in rural areas. Like scabies, it takes physical contact, such as sleeping next to an infected person, to contract head lice, though it may also be possible to contract head lice by wearing a hat belonging to someone who is infected.

The **leeches**' most commonly encountered in Laos are about the size and shape of an inchworm, and travellers are most likely to pick them up while trekking through wooded areas. Take extra care when relieving yourself during breaks on long-distance bus rides. The habit of pushing deep into a bush for privacy gives leeches just enough time to grab hold of your shoes or trousers. Later they will crawl their way beneath clothing and attach themselves to joint areas (ankles, knees, elbows) where veins are near the surface of the skin. An anaesthetic and anticoagulant in the leeches' saliva allows the little vampires to gorge themselves on blood without the host feeling any pain. Tucking your trouser-legs into your socks is an easy way to foil leeches. Wounds left by sucking leeches should be washed and bandaged as soon as possible to avoid infection.

Laos has several varieties of poisonous **snakes**, including the king cobra, but the Lao habit of killing every snake they come across, whether venomous or not, keeps areas of human habitation largely snake-free. Travelling in rural areas greatly increases the risk of snakebite, but visitors can lessen the chances of being bitten by not wearing sandals or flip-flops outside urban areas.

While hiking between hill-tribe villages especially, take the precaution of wearing boots, socks and long trousers. If you are bitten, the number-one rule is not to panic; remain still to prevent the venom from being quickly absorbed into the bloodstream. Snakebites should be washed and disinfected and immediate medical attention sought – a challenge in most parts of Laos, making avoidance of the problem vital. Huge, black **scorpions** the size of large prawns lurk under the shade of fallen leaves and sting reflexively when stepped on, another solid reason to restrict flip-flop-wearing to urban areas. While the sting is very painful, it is not fatal and pain and swelling usually disappear after a few hours.

Animals that are infected with **rabies** can transmit the disease by biting or even by licking an open wound. Dogs are the most common carriers but the disease can also be contracted from the bites of gibbons, bats and other mammals. Travellers should stay clear of all wild animals and resist the urge to pet unfamiliar dogs or cats. If bitten by a suspect animal, wash and disinfect the wound with alcohol or iodine and seek urgent medical help; the disease is fatal if left untreated.

Sexually transmitted diseases

Prostitution is on the rise in Laos, and with it the inevitable scourge of **sexually transmitted diseases** (STDs). Gonorrhoea and syphilis are common but easily treated with antibiotics. Symptoms of the former include pain or a pus-like discharge when urinating. An open sore on or around the genitals is a symptom of syphilis. In women symptoms are internal and may not be noticed. The number of cases of **AIDS** is also rising in Laos, mostly the result of Lao prostitutes contracting HIV in Thailand.

Bring **condoms** from home; most sold in Laos are imported from Thailand, and are often defective.

The media

Tightly controlled by the communist party since the Pathet Lao came to power in 1975, Laos's minuscule media struggles to compete with flashy Thai TV gameshows and the multitude of channels offered by satellite dishes. With only one-tenth of the population of its neighbour, it's very hard for Laos to compete with Thailand.

Newspapers and magazines

Laos has only one **English-language newspaper**, the *Vientiane Times*, established in 1994. Despite being somewhat thin, self-censored and nearly impossible to find outside the capital, it is nonetheless a good window on Laos. Published by the Ministry of Information and Culture, the *Vientiane Times* focuses primarily on business and trade issues, although interesting cultural pieces do slip in from time to time, and the occasional column showcasing people's opinion on a selected social topic is a worthwhile read. You'll also find ads for restaurant specials and local teaching jobs.

There are two **Lao-language dailies** and five weeklies. Of the two dailies, *Wieng Mai* and *Pasason*, the latter is more widely read. Both get their international news from KPL, the government news agency, and, for the most part, have their own reporters who file domestic news. Neither is known for independent-minded reportage. In fact it's fair to say you'll find much more news about Laos online (a list of recommended websites appears below) than you can in the country.

Foreign publications are extremely difficult to find outside Vientiane, and even in the capital there are scant copies. *Newsweek*, *The Economist*, *Time* and the *Bangkok Post* are all sold at minimarkets in Vientiane.

Online news about Laos

ⓦ **www.vientianetimes.org.la** The official website of the Vientiane Times contains most of the stories from Laos's only English-language newspaper.
ⓦ **www.laosguide.com** News gathered from around the world, with a strong bias towards issues affecting Laos.

ⓦ **www.laosnews.net** Daily news updates from Laos, including links to stories about its economy and tourist industry.
ⓦ **www.muonglao.com** An online magazine running articles that focus on the people and culture of Laos.
ⓦ **www.bangkokpost.net** The website of Thailand's leading English-language daily, which often runs stories about Laos.
ⓦ **www.asianobserver.com** This lively web forum has news and debates on all things Laos.

Television and radio

Lao television's two **government-run channels** broadcast a mix of news, cultural shows and Chinese soaps for several hours a day, with no English programming. Reception is poor, however, in rural areas. One of the oddest sights in Laos is that of rickety bamboo and thatch huts and houses all over the country with huge, modern satellite dishes attached to the roofs. Many mid-range and top-end hotels provide **satellite TV** – though often these show only a handful of channels – as do a few coffee shops and bakeries in Luang Prabang and Vientiane.

Lao radio thrives, helped along by the fact that newspapers and TV stations are not available to many people in the countryside. The main radio station, **Lao National Radio**, can be picked up in the vicinity of Vientiane or on shortwave in roughly seventy percent of the country. LNR gets its international news from a number of sources, including CNN, BBC, Xinhua and KPL, and broadcasts news in English twice a day. Tuning into LNR will also give you a chance to hear traditional **Lao music**, which you otherwise may only get to hear at festivals.

Sports and outdoor activities

Laos is one of the better outdoor-adventure destinations in Southeast Asia: there are excellent trekking opportunities, vast cave systems to be explored and crashing whitewater rivers to be rafted. With the emergence of a number of specialized travel companies offering inexpensive, organized, adventure tours in previously remote reaches, it's now easier than ever to experience the wild side of Laos.

Over seventy percent of the country comprises high terrain, with chains of **mountains** reaching heights of over 2800m running its entire length. Covering many of these ranges are expanses of virgin **rainforest**. And from these highlands run steep, narrow valleys through which **rivers** rush down from the mountain heights to join the "Mother of Waters", the mighty Mekong River, which flows the entire length of Laos.

Trekking

The easiest and most popular adventure sport in Laos is **trekking**, with new routes opening up across the country all the time. Trekking is rapidly becoming a major money-earner for Laos, with a range of one- to five-day treks (usually with an environmentally conscious twist) attracting visitors from around the world.

The **far north** has mountain scenery, forest areas and colourful ethnic hill tribes living in traditional villages. There are excellent **tourist facilities** available in many northern towns, and **Guide Service Offices** are gradually being opened throughout the north to support tourists who want to take part in guided treks that are both environmentally friendly and have a low impact on the local peoples.

For visitors interested in hill tribes and **organized trekking**, the best towns to head for are Luang Namtha, Muang Sing, Luang Prabang and Vang Vieng, all of which have developed programmes for travellers wanting to make a series of day-trips based out of town or take part in multi-day treks involving camping and village stays.

If you want to take a more independent, DIY approach, other towns highly suitable for **independent trekking** opportunities using self-hired local guides include Muang Long, Xieng Kok, Houayxai, Vieng Phoukha, Muang Khoua and Nong Khiaw, all of which have guesthouses and are close to tribal areas.

In **South Central Laos**, new companies have been set up to allow visitors to discover sacred lakes, trek through ancient forests and interact with diverse local tribes. The tours (see p.212 and p.217) have been built to foster development and improve the lives of local people without destroying the region's natural beauty.

NBCAs and eco-tours

A handful of Lao companies organize **eco-tours** to wilderness areas featuring rare and exotic flora and fauna. Here, nature lovers and birdwatchers will find some of the rarest species on the planet and vast forest canopies. Although Laos does not have any national parks in the Western sense, since 1993 the government has established twenty **National Biodiversity Conservation Areas (NBCAs)**, many still with villagers and hill tribes living within their boundaries. Unfortunately, though NBCA status means government recognition of their biodiversity, this status has not conferred any real protection (see p.300).

The NBCAs are scattered around the country, often in remote border areas without roads. While many of the parks are inaccessible short of mounting a professional expedition, several have been developed for eco-tourism and have **visitor centres** and **guided walks**. The best developed NBCAs for tourists are Phou Khao Khouay (see p.93), Nam Ha (see p.190) and Phou Hin Poun (see p.215), all of which can be reached by road.

Boules and blood sports

One of the quirkiest legacies of French colonial rule is surely *petang* – a form of boules you'll see being played in dusty front yards and side streets right around the country.

Like boules, the aim is to throw a small wooden ball, or *cochonnet*, into the centre of a hard gravel court, and then take it in turns to toss larger metal balls towards it. Players are awarded a point for each time their ball lands nearer to the *cochonnet* than their opponent's, and the game ends when one of the players scores thirteen points.

Official rules state *petang* should be played in teams of two or three, but in practice it's usually a casual affair, giving people the chance to chat and while away an afternoon.

Team sports aren't played too often in Laos, simply because equipment is prohibitively expensive. The honourable exception is *kataw*. Played with a grapefruit-sized woven wicker ball, it's thought to have originated in the Malay Archipelago, but is also quite popular in Thailand. *Kataw* is a hands-free hotchpotch of volleyball, football and tennis, played both with and without a net. Players have to use their feet, legs, chests and heads to keep the ball aloft, and the acrobatics involved are simply astounding. Games are played just about anywhere, but are commonly seen in schoolyards or in monastery grounds.

Another sport you might encounter in Laos is *Muay Lao*, also known as Lao boxing, which sees fighters striking each other with their fists, knees, elbows and feet. The sport is essentially the same as *Muay Thai* kickboxing, Thailand's national sport, but in Laos professional bouts are held fairly infrequently.

As with the rest of Southeast Asia, cockfighting is a celebrated diversion in Laos – no surprise, as the blood sport originated in this region. Betting is, of course, the whole point. Cockfights take place on Sundays and the local cockpit can usually be found by wandering around and listening for the exuberant cheers of the spectators. Unlike in some Southeast Asian countries, knives are not attached to the rooster's legs in Laos, which means that cockfights last much longer and the birds don't usually die in the ring.

Another sport that relies on a wager to sharpen excitement is **rhinoceros beetle fighting**. Although it is difficult to say just how far back the tradition of beetle fighting goes, it is known to be popular among ethnic Tai peoples from the Shan States to northern Vietnam. The walnut-sized beetles hiss alarmingly when angered and it doesn't require much goading to get them to do battle. Pincer-like horns are used by the beetles to seize and lift an opponent, and the fight is considered finished when one of the two beetles breaks and runs. The fighting season is during the rains when the insects breed. They are sometimes peddled in markets tethered to pieces of sugar cane.

Watersports

While most river-journey enthusiasts are satisfied with a slow boat down the Mekong between Houayxai and Luang Prabang, many opportunities exist for exploring Laos's faster waterways. Several companies offer **whitewater-rafting** trips out of Luang Prabang on a number of northern rivers, including the Nam Ou, the Nam Xuang and the Nam Ming.

Even more popular are **river-kayaking** adventures ranging from easy day-trips for beginners to multi-day adventures down rivers with grade 5 rapids. Professional guided kayaking tours are currently operated on a regular basis on eight northern rivers as well as the Ang Nam Ngum Reservoir (near the capital) and in Si Phan Don. The best bases for kayaking tours are Vientiane, Vang Vieng, Luang Prabang and Luang Namtha. Another fantastic region for kayaking is the Khammouane Limestone NBCA (see p.215). Among other scenic wonders, this NBCA features a 7km-long natural river-tunnel through the heart of a mountain, and is becoming popular for organized tours out of Vientiane.

Caves and rock climbing

With its great forests of limestone karst scenery receding into the distance like an image in a Chinese scroll painting, Laos is a great destination for cave exploring, spelunking and rock-climbing. Prime areas for limestone karst scenery in Laos include Vang Vieng, Kasi, Thakhet and Vieng Xai. For most tourists, **cave exploring** is limited to climbing up to and wandering around in caves that are fairly touristy and have clearly defined pathways. Serious spelunkers can find vast cave and tunnel systems to explore in the Khammouane Limestone NBCA and the Hin Nam No NBCA, but should seek local permission before launching any major expeditions as many caves have yet to have archeological surveys done. With so many awesome unclimbed and unnamed peaks, **rock climbing** is one sport that seems to have a huge future in Laos. At present the sport is still in its infancy, but new routes continue to be opened up around Vang Vieng.

Mountain biking

With some of the best untamed scenery in Southeast Asia, many unpaved roads, and little traffic, Laos is becoming a very hot destination for cross-country **mountain-bike touring**. A lot of independent travellers do self-organized mountain-bike touring in northern Laos, bringing their bikes with them from home. **Route 13** from Luang Prabang to Vientiane seems to be the most popular route, but be warned that despite the beautiful scenery, the route is also extremely mountainous, crossing several large ranges before reaching the Vientiane Plain. There are much better routes in **Houa Phan** and **Xieng Khuang** provinces where you'll find fantastic landscapes, plenty of remote villages and paved roads with very few vehicles on them.

It's a good idea to plan carefully. What appear to be very short distances on the map can often take many hours, even in a vehicle. One good thing about bicycle touring in Laos is that should things get too difficult, you can always flag down a passing sawngthaew and throw the bike on the roof. Another alternative is to join an **organized cycling tour**. There are plenty to choose from but London-based Red Spokes (☎020/7502 7252, ⓦwww.redspokes .co.uk) runs a popular two-week tour that takes in Luang Prabang, Vang Vieng and Vientiane, as well as some rural stretches with spectacular scenery.

Alternative therapies

During their period of colonization, the French regarded traditional Lao therapies as quaint and amusing, and this attitude was passed on to the Lao elite who studied in France. In an essay about traditional Lao medicine written in the 1950s by a former Minister of Health, the traditional Lao doctor is repeatedly referred to as "the quack". But renewed interest, partially fuelled by a similar rekindling of enthusiasm in neighbouring China, has seen a resurgence of confidence in traditional techniques.

Tourism has been partially responsible for renewed interest in traditional massage and herbal sauna, though these alternative therapies are generally limited to larger towns and cities. Besides the obvious physical benefits the Lao massage and sauna afford the recipient, administering massage and sauna to others is believed to bring spiritual merit to those who perform the labour, making Lao massage and sauna a win-win proposition for all involved.

Lao massage

Lao massage owes more to **Chinese** than to Thai schools, utilizing medicated balms and salves which are rubbed into the skin. Muscles are kneaded and joints are flexed while a warm compress of steeped herbs is applied to the area being treated. Besides massage, Lao doctors may utilize other "exotic" treatments that have been borrowed from neighbouring countries. One decidedly Chinese therapy that is sometimes employed in Laos is **acupuncture** (*fang khem*), in which long, thin needles are inserted into special points that correspond to specific organs or parts of the body. Another imported practice is the application of **suction cups** (*kaew dut*), a remedy popular in neighbouring Cambodia. Small glass jars are briefly heated with a flame and applied to bare skin; air within the cup contracts as it cools, drawing blood under the skin into the mouth of the cup. Theoretically, toxins within the bloodstream are in this way brought to the surface of the skin.

Lao herbal saunas

Before getting a massage, many Lao opt for some time in the **herbal sauna**. This usually consists of a rustic wooden shack divided into separate rooms for men and women; beneath the shack a drum of water sits on a wood fire. Medicinal herbs boiling in the drum release their juices into the water and the resulting steam is carried up into the rooms. The temperature inside is normally quite high and bathers should spend no more than fifteen minutes at a time in the sauna, taking frequent breaks to cool off by lounging outside and sipping herbal tea to replace water that the body so profusely sweats out. The **recipes** of both the saunas and teas are jealously guarded but are known to contain such herbal additives as carambola, tamarind, eucalyptus and citrus leaves.

Culture and etiquette

While history may have given them ample reason to distrust outsiders, the Lao are a genuinely friendly people and interacting with them is one of the greatest joys of travelling through the country. Always remember, though, that Laos is a Buddhist country and so it's important to dress and behave in a way that is respectful.

Because of the sheer diversity of **ethnic groups** in Laos, it is difficult to generalize when speaking of "Lao" attitudes and behaviour. The dominant group, the so-called "Lao Loum", or **lowland Lao**, who make up the majority in the valleys of the Mekong and its tributaries, are Theravada Buddhists and this has a strong effect on their attitudes and behaviour. The focus here is on dos and don'ts within that culture; customs among the **hill-tribe peoples** are often quite different from those of the lowlanders (see the "Trekking Etiquette" box on p.192 for more).

Dress and appearance

Appearance is very important in Lao society. **Conservative dress** is always recommended, and visitors should keep in mind that the Lao dislike foreigners who come to their country and dress in what they deem a disrespectful manner. This includes men appearing shirtless in public, and women bearing their shoulders and thighs. Be aware also that dreadlocks, tattoos and body-piercing are viewed with disfavour by lowland Lao, although hill-tribe people are usually more accepting. Dressing too casually (or too outrageously) can also be counterproductive in dealings with Lao authorities, such as when applying for visa extensions at immigration.

When in urban areas or visiting Buddhist monasteries or holy sites, visitors should refrain from outfits that would be more suited to the beach. Women especially should avoid wearing anything that reveals too much skin or could be conceived of as provocative – this includes shorts and sleeveless shirts. Sandals or flip-flops can be worn for all but the most formal occasions; in fact, they are much more practical than shoes, since footwear must be **removed** upon entering private homes, certain Buddhist monastery buildings or any living space. The habit of leaving your footwear outside the threshold is not just a matter of wanting to keep interiors clean, it is a long-standing tradition that will cause offence if flouted.

Manners

Lao **social taboos** are sometimes linked to Buddhist beliefs. **Feet** are considered low and unclean – be careful not to step over any part of people who are sitting or lying on the floor, as this is also considered rude. If you do accidentally kick or brush someone with your feet, apologize immediately and smile as you do so. Conversely, people's **heads** are considered sacred and shouldn't be touched.

Besides dressing conservatively, there are other conventions that must be followed when visiting **Buddhist monasteries**. Before entering monastery buildings such as the *sim* or *wihan*, or if you are invited into monks' living quarters, footwear must be removed. Women should never touch Buddhist monks or novices (or their clothes), or hand objects directly to them. When giving something to a monk, the object should be placed on a nearby table or passed to a layman who will then hand it to the monk.

All Buddha images are objects of veneration, so it should go without saying

that touching Buddha images disrespectfully is inappropriate. When sitting on the floor of a monastery building that has a Buddha image, never point your feet in the direction of the image. If possible, observe the Lao and imitate the way they sit: in a modified kneeling position with legs pointed away from the image.

Greetings

The lowland Lao traditionally **greet** each other with a *nop* – bringing their hands together at the chin in a prayer-like gesture. After the revolution the *nop* was discouraged, but it now seems to be making a comeback. This graceful gesture is more difficult to execute properly than it may at first appear, however, as the status of the persons giving and returning the *nop* determines how they execute it. Most Lao reserve the *nop* greeting for each other, preferring to shake hands with Westerners, and the only time a Westerner is likely to receive a *nop* is from the staff of upmarket hotels or fancy restaurants. In any case, if you do receive a *nop* as a gesture of greeting or thank you, it is best to reply with a smile and nod of the head.

The Lao often feel that many foreign visitors seem to be a bit aloof. They have obviously spent a lot of time and money to get so far from home, but once they get to Laos they walk around briskly, looking at the locals, but rarely bothering to smile or greet those they have come so far to see. Foreign visitors who are not grin-stingy will find that a smile and a *sabai di* (hello) will break the ice of initial reservation some locals may have upon seeing a foreigner, and will invariably bring a smile in response.

It's worth bearing in mind that, as in the rest of Asia, showing anger in Laos is rather futile – it'll more likely be met with amusement or the swift departure of the person you're talking to, in order to save face.

Social invitations

Lao people are very **hospitable** and will often go out of their way to help visitors. Especially in rural areas, you may find people inviting you to join them for a meal or to celebrate a birth or marriage. This is a real privilege, and even if you don't wish to stay for long, it's polite to join them and to accept at least one drink if it's offered to you. More than anything, it gives you a chance to experience local life, and gives Lao people a good impression of the tourists that come to their country, and an opportunity to learn more about the world.

Sexual attitudes

Public displays of affection – even just hugging – are considered tasteless by the Lao and is likely to cause offence. Though the gay scene remains very underground in Laos, gay travellers are unlikely to be threatened or hassled. Sexual relations between an unmarried Lao national and a Westerner are officially illegal in Laos – in Vientiane especially, the law prohibiting Lao nationals from sharing hotel rooms with foreigners is sometimes enforced.

Crime and personal safety

Laos is a relatively safe country for travellers, although certain areas remain off-limits because of unexploded ordnance left over from decades of warfare. As a visitor, however, you're an obvious target for thieves (who may include your fellow travellers), so do take necessary precautions.

Carry your passport, travellers' cheques and other valuables in a concealed **money belt** and don't leave anything important lying about in your room, particularly when staying in rural bungalows. A few hotels have safes which you may want to use, although you should keep in mind that you never know who has access to the safe. A **padlock** and chain, or a cable lock, is useful for doors and windows at inexpensive guesthouses and budget hotels and for securing your pack on buses, where you're often separated from your belongings. It's also a good idea to keep a reserve of cash, photocopies of the relevant pages of your passport, insurance details and travellers' cheque receipts separate from the rest of your valuables.

As tranquil as Laos can seem, petty theft and serious crimes do happen throughout the country – even on seemingly deserted country roads. Petty crime is more common in **Vang Vieng** than just about anywhere else in Laos, with drunk (or stoned) tourists often leaving themselves open to theft and robbery. Although crime rates in **Vientiane** are low,

be on your guard in darker streets outside the city centre, and along the river. Motorbike-borne thieves ply the city streets and have been known to snatch bags out of the front basket of other motorbikes that they pass.

If you do have anything stolen, you'll need to get the **police** to write up a report in order to claim on your insurance: bring along a Lao speaker to simplify matters if you can. While police generally keep their distance from foreigners, they may try to exact "fines" from visitors for alleged misdemeanours. With a lot of patience, you should be able to resolve most problems, and, if you keep your cool, you may find that you can bargain down such "fines". It helps to have your passport with you at all times – if you don't, police have greater incentive to ask for money and may even try to bring you to the station. In some instances police may puzzle over your passport for what seems like an awfully long time. Again, such situations are best handled with an ample dose of patience. If your papers are in order, you shouldn't have anything to worry about.

Drugs

In recent years Laos has seen a steady rise of drug tourism. Ganja (marijuana) is widely available in Laos, although it's illegal to smoke it. Tourists who buy and use ganja risk substantial "fines" if caught by police, who do not need a warrant to search you or your room. As in Thailand, there have been many instances of locals selling foreigners marijuana and then telling the police. In Vang Vieng, mushrooms and weed are offered at most backpacker bars – either straight up or baked into a dizzying array of "happy" pizzas – but you should bear in mind that plenty of travellers get sick, or robbed, after indulging.

In northern towns, tourists are sometimes approached by **opium** addicts who, in return for cash, offer to take the visitors to a hut or some other private place, where opium pipes will be prepared and smoked. Many Westerners feel the romanticism of doing this all-but-extinct drug is just as appealing as the promise of intoxication, but the opium prepared for tourists is often not opium at all, but **morphine**-laden opium ash that has been mixed with painkillers. The resulting "high" is, for many, several hours of nausea and vomiting. While real **opium** is not as addictive as its derivative, heroin, withdrawal symptoms are similarly painful. Visitors caught smoking opium (or even opium ash) face fines, jail time and deportation.

In addition, it's important to consider the local implications of using drugs in Laos. There remains a serious problem with drug addiction in some rural communities, which local organizations are working hard to address, and using drugs while in the country can encourage local people to do the same, thus undoing a lot of hard work.

Banditry

With far more serious consequences than petty theft, **banditry** is still a possible threat in some parts of Laos. In the past, buses, motorcyclists and private vehicles on certain highways have been held up, their passengers robbed and, in some instances, killed. Because information in Laos is tightly controlled, no one knows exactly if rumoured bandit attacks have actually occurred or if other incidents have happened and gone unreported. Therefore it's always good to ask at a Western embassy in Vientiane for any **travel advisories** before heading out into remote regions.

Security has improved greatly in recent years along **Route 13** between Kasi and Luang Prabang, though the insurgent/bandit group generally thought to be responsible for the attacks in this area in the mid-1990s, the **Chao Fa**, is still active in parts of Xieng Khuang province (see p.149). Back in 2004 two European tourists were killed, along with six Lao, when a shadowy group attacked a bus on Route 13 just north of Vang Vieng. After punitive attacks on nearby Hmong villages by the Lao army in 2004 and 2005, the road fell quiet. Though in February 2007 the US embassy in Vientiane reported small

skirmishes just north of Vang Vieng, the situation didn't escalate, and the road is now considered safe once again – bus drivers in the area have stopped carrying guns.

Although the chances of getting caught up in an incident are very small indeed, it's a good idea to be aware of the potential risks, especially when travelling on Route 7 or the northern stretch of Route 13. Locally based expats in both Vientiane and Luang Prabang will often have the best idea of whether or not the routes are safe to travel.

Unexploded ordnance

The **Second Indochina War** left Laos with the dubious distinction of being the most heavily bombed country per capita in the history of warfare. The areas of the country most affected by aerial bombing are along the border of Vietnam – especially in southern Laos where the border runs parallel to the former Ho Chi Minh Trail; also heavily targeted was Xieng Khuang province in the northeast. Other provinces, far from the border with Vietnam, were the site of land battles in which both sides lobbed artillery and mortar shells at each other. A fair quantity of this ordnance did not explode.

These dangerous relics of the war, known as **UXO** (unexploded ordnance), have been the focus of disposal teams since the 1980s. According to the Lao government, most areas that tourists are likely to visit have been swept clean of UXO. That said, it always pays to be cautious when in rural areas or when trekking. UXO unearthed during road construction can be pushed onto the shoulder, where it becomes overgrown with weeds and forgotten. Disposal experts say that fast-growing bamboo has been known to unearth UXO, lifting it aloft as the stalk grows and then letting it fall onto a trail that was previously clean. Consequently, it's best to stay on trails and beware any odd-looking metallic objects that you may come across. Picking something up for closer inspection (or giving it a kick to turn it over) can be suicidal. When taking a toilet break during long-distance bus journeys, it's not a good idea to penetrate too deeply into the bush looking for privacy.

In some southern towns locals use old bombs, bomb cases, mortar shells etc for a variety of functions, from demarcating plots of land to decorating. These will have been checked by UXO disposal experts, and should pose no threat. Still, it pays to have a healthy respect for all UXO. After all, these are weapons that were designed to kill or maim.

Shopping

One of the pleasures of shopping in a non-industrial country like Laos is the availability of hand-crafted goods. Because items made by hand can only be produced in limited quantities, they are usually sold or bartered in the village in which they were made, and seldom get very far afield. Handmade baskets, bolts of cloth and household utensils are best acquired at village level, as everything is cheaper at the source, though it's not all that easy for non-Lao-speaking visitors to turn up and make known what they're after. Provincial markets are the obvious alternative; prices here are usually just a bit more than what you would pay were you to buy directly from village artisans. Of course, if village-made objects make it all the way to the boutiques of Vientiane, their "value" will have multiplied many times over.

As with the rest of Southeast Asia, merchandise often has no price tag and the buyer is expected to make a spirited attempt at **haggling** the quoted price down. Even if an item is sporting a price tag, it's still perfectly acceptable to ask for a discount. Bargaining takes patience and tact, and knowing what an item is really worth is half the battle. The first price quoted will usually be inflated. If you feel the price is way out of line, it is better to just smile and walk away than to squawk in disbelief and argue that the price is unfair – no matter how loud or valid your protestations, nobody will believe that you cannot afford to buy.

On the whole, **Luang Prabang** is better for shopping than Vientiane, as much of what is for sale in Luang Prabang is produced locally, meaning you get a better selection of goods and at better prices.

Textiles

A surprisingly large number of the ethnic groups that make up the population of Laos produce cloth of their own design, which is turned into men's and women's sarongs, shoulder bags, headscarves and shawls. Traditionally, most textiles stayed within the village where they were woven, but the increasing popularity of Lao textiles with visitors has led urban textile merchants to employ buyers to comb isolated villages for **old textiles** that might be resold at a profit. The result is that many merchants have only a vague idea of where their old textiles are from or which group made them. This doesn't seem to deter foreign buyers, however, and sales are brisk, which has given rise to the practice of boiling new textiles to artificially age them. Some of these so-called antique textiles sell for hundreds of dollars.

To some shopkeepers "old" can mean ten years or so and most will have little idea what the age of a certain piece is, but if you persist in asking, they will often claim an item has been around for a couple of centuries. As textiles are difficult to date, it's best to take such claims with a pinch of salt. All in all, though, it is rare for the local merchants to go to great lengths to deceive customers.

These days, though, the vast majority of the textiles for sale are **new textiles** specifically made for the tourist market. These may have the same patterns and motifs as the traditional sarongs and so forth, but are cut and sewn into items such as pillowcases. If you're after antique textiles you have to ask; unless you are an expert or have money to burn, it is a good idea to stick to new textiles, which can be had for as little as $5 and are just as pleasing to the eye as the older pieces.

Lao weavers have a long tradition of combining **cotton** and **silk**: a typical piece may have a cotton base with silk details woven into it. Modern pieces of inferior quality substitute synthetic fibres for silk, and some vendors have been known to try to pass off hundred-percent synthetic cloth as silk. Lastly, the synthetic dyes used by most weavers are not colourfast, something to bear in mind when laundering newly purchased textiles.

Silver

Although Thai antique dealers have made off with quite a bit of old Lao **silver** (and marketed it in Thailand as old Thai silver) there is still a fair amount of the stuff floating around. Items to look out for are paraphernalia for **betel chewing**: egg-sized round or oval boxes for storing white lime,

cone-shaped containers for holding betel leaves and miniature mortars used to pound areca nuts. Larger silver boxes or bowls with human or animal figures hammered into them were once used in religious ceremonies. C-shaped **bracelets** and anklets are found in a variety of styles. Bracelets and anklets of traditional Lao style, as opposed to hill-tribe design, have a stylized lotus bud on each end.

Hill-tribe silver jewellery (traditionally made by melting down and hammering silver French piastres) is usually bold and heavy – the better to show off one's wealth. With few exceptions, the hill-tribe jewellery being peddled in Laos is the handiwork of the Hmong tribe. In **Luang Prabang**, the old silversmith families that once supplied the monarchy with ceremonial objects are again practising their trade, and their silver creations represent some of the best-value souvenirs to be found in Laos.

Antiques

Thai merchants regularly scour Laos for **antiques** so there are probably more authentic Lao antiques for sale in the malls of Bangkok and Chiang Mai than anywhere in Laos. Conversely, many of the "antiques" for sale in Laos are actually reproductions made in Thailand or Cambodia. This is particularly true in the case of metal Buddhist or Hindu figurines.

Wooden **Buddha images** are often genuine antiques, but were most likely pilfered from some temple or shrine. Refraining from buying them will help discourage this practice. Prospective buyers should also be aware that there is an **official ban** on the export of Buddha images from Laos. Although this is aimed primarily at curbing the theft of large Lao bronze Buddhas from rural monasteries, small images are also included in the ban. That said, it is highly unlikely that Lao officials will confiscate new Buddhas from foreign visitors. The Lao, when acquiring a Buddha image, pay particular attention to the expression on the Buddha's face. Does the Buddha look serene? If so, the image is considered auspicious.

Antique brass weights, sometimes referred to as "**opium weights**", come in a variety of

Shipping

It is not advisable to ship anything of value home from Laos. If you're planning to travel onwards to **Thailand**, it would be a good idea to wait and ship it from there.

sizes and shapes. Those cast in zoomorphic figures (stylized birds, elephants, lions, etc) are an established collectable and command high prices, sometimes selling for hundreds of dollars. Weights of simpler design, such as those shaped like miniature stupas, are much more affordable and can be bought for just a few dollars in provincial towns.

Opium pipes come in sundry forms as well. Although very few are genuine antiques, the workmanship is generally quite good as they are produced by pipemakers who once supplied Vientiane's now-defunct opium dens. A typical pipe may have a bamboo body, a ceramic bowl and silver or brass ornamentation, and should sell for about $50. During the past few years Laos has been flooded with reproduction opium pipes from Vietnam. These are more colourful and ornate than the Laos-made pipes, but aren't worth spending more than $10 or so to buy.

Royalist regalia

With the memories of the war that divided Laos fading, paraphernalia associated with the defunct kingdom is less likely to offend officials of the present regime, though wearing such memorabilia in public would be considered poor form. Brass buttons, badges and medals decorated with the Hindu iconography of the Lao monarchy are sometimes found in gold or silver jewellery and antique shops. Royal Lao Army hat devices depicting Shiva's trident superimposed on Vishnu's discus and brass buttons decorated with Airavata, the three-headed elephant, are typical finds.

Woodcarving, rattan, wicker and bamboo

Until tourism created a demand for souvenirs, nearly all examples of Lao **woodcarving** were religious in nature – for example, the small, antique, wooden Buddha images which are finding their way into curio shops (see p.53). For those who have bought a stunning, hand-woven textile but are unsure of how to display it, there are ornately **carved hangers** made expressly for this purpose. Workmanship varies, however, so inspect carefully to ensure that there are no splinters or jagged edges which may damage the textile. Keep in mind also that large woodcarvings sometimes crack when transported to less humid climes.

That **baskets** are an important part of traditional Lao culture is reflected in the language: Lao has dozens upon dozens of words for them, and they're used in all spheres of everyday life. Many different forms of basket are used as **backpacks**; those made by the Gie-Trieng tribe in Xekong province are probably the most expertly woven. Baskets are also used for serving food, such as sticky rice. These mini-baskets come with a long loop of string so they can be slung over the shoulder when hiking, as sticky rice is the perfect snack on long treks, road or boat trips. **Mats** made of woven grass or reeds can be found in sizes for one or two people. The one-person mats are dirt-cheap, easily carried when rolled up and make a lot more sense than foam rubber mattresses. Woven mats are especially handy when taking a slow boat down the Mekong, as the passenger holds are often not the cleanest of places. Ordinary sticky rice baskets and mats can be found at any provincial market and should cost no more than a couple of dollars.

Travelling with children

Travelling through Laos with children can be both challenging and fun, but the rewards far outweigh any negatives. The presence of children can help break the ice with locals, especially as the Lao people are so family-focused, but long, bumpy journeys and poor sanitation can make things a struggle at times.

Laos' s lack of adequate healthcare facilities is a major concern for parents, so sufficient travel insurance (see p.57) is a must for peace of mind. It's worth taking a first aid set with you, as well as a rehydration solution in case of diarrhoea, which can be quite dangerous in young children. Rabies is a problem in Laos, so explain to your children the dangers of playing with animals and consider a rabies vaccination before departing.

In tourist areas it should be no problem finding food that kids will **eat**, and dishes like spring rolls, fried rice and *fõe* (see p.33), where chilli is added by the diner, are a good choice for those who may not be used to the spiciness of Lao cuisine.

A major consideration will be the long journeys that are sometimes necessary when travelling around the country – these can be bone-numbing at the best of times,

and young children may find them excruciatingly boring. That said, bus journeys are a real "local" experience that can make more of an impression than wandering around temples. It is easy, however, to see a fair amount of the country by sticking to journeys of less than six hours.

Most hotels and guesthouses are very accommodating to families, often allowing children to stay for free in their parents' room, or adding an extra bed or cot to the room for a small charge.

If you're travelling with babies, you'll have difficulty finding **nappies** (diapers) throughout Laos. For short journeys, you could bring a supply of nappies from home; for longer trips, consider switching over to washables.

For more **advice** on travelling with children, consult *The Rough Guide to Travel with Babies and Young Children*.

Travel essentials

Customs

Lao customs regulations limit visitors to 500 cigarettes and one litre of distilled alcohol per person upon entry, but in practice bags are rarely opened unless a suspiciously large amount of luggage is being brought in. A customs declaration form must be filled out along with the arrival form, but typically nobody bothers to check that the information is correct. There is no limit on

the amount of foreign currency you can bring into Laos.

Costs

Laos is one of the world's poorest nations, and consequently one of the cheapest Asian countries to travel in. Your largest expense is likely to be transport, with journeys usually costing between 60,000 and 120,000K; accommodation and food are very inexpensive.

By eating at noodle stalls and cheap restaurants, opting for basic accommodation and travelling by public transport, you can travel in Laos on a **daily budget** of less than $20. Staying in more upmarket hotels and resorts, and eating in the best restaurants will push your budget up to a very reasonable $40–60 a day – though you'll struggle to find upmarket accommodation and restaurants in much of the country. Note, however, that prices are significantly higher in Vientiane and Luang Prabang.

While restaurants and some shops have fixed prices, in general merchandise almost never has price tags, and the lack of a fixed pricing scheme can take some getting used to. Prices, unless marked or for food in a market, should usually be negotiated, as should the cost of chartering transport (as opposed to fares on passenger vehicles, which are non-negotiable). Hotel and guesthouse operators are usually open to a little bargaining, particularly during off-peak months.

Bargaining is very much a part of life in Laos, and an art form, requiring a delicate balance of humour, patience and tact. It's important to remain realistic, as vendors will lose interest if you've quoted a price that's way out of line, and to keep a sense of perspective: cut-throat haggling over 1000K only reflects poorly on both buyer and seller. As the Lao in general – with the exception of drivers of vehicles for hire and souvenir sellers in Vientiane and Luang Prabang – are less out to rip off tourists than their counterparts in Thailand and Vietnam, they start off the haggling by quoting a fairly realistic price and expect to come down only a little. It's worth bearing in mind that the country's dependence on imported goods from its neighbours does push prices up – whether for food, toiletries or transport.

Electricity

Supplied at 220 volts AC. Two-pin sockets taking plugs with flat prongs are the norm. Many smaller towns, including several provincial capitals, have power for only a few hours in the evening or none at all, so it's worth bringing a torch.

Information

Good, reliable information on Laos is hard to come by and, because everything from visa requirements to transport routes are subject to frequent change, your best bet is often to get the latest advice from internet forums, guesthouses and fellow travellers.

The government-run Lao National Tourism Administration (LNTA for short; ⓦwww .tourismlaos.org), which has offices around Laos, including Vientiane and Luang Prabang, should be able to supply decent brochures and maps, including *Destination Laos*, a free mini-guidebook published annually.

Privately owned travel companies such as Green Discovery and Diethelm Travel can provide reliable tourist information in provincial capitals, as well as some free fold-out maps. For more detailed maps of the country, try one of the bookshops in Vientiane or Vang Vieng.

Online resources

ⓦ **www.destination-laos.net** Attractive province-by-province guide to Laos, featuring maps, pictures and plenty of useful information.

ⓦ **www.vientianetimes.com** Features news, accommodation listings and links to hundreds of other websites on Laos.

ⓦ **www.mekongexpress.com** Huge general info site.

ⓦ **www.laoembassy.com** Website of the Lao embassy to the United States features tourist info and updated visa regulations.

ⓦ **www.ecotourismlaos.com** A slick, award-winning website by the Lao National Tourism Administration that features helpful tips on exploring Laos's national parks.

ⓦ **www.laos-travel.itgo.com** Useful site (if a little dated) with province-by-province info.

ⓦ **www.laosglobe.com** Laos-related news from around the world is collated on this regularly updated site.

ⓦ **www.tripadvisor.com** User-generated reviews of hotels, guesthouses and tourist attractions in Laos.

ⓦ **www.muonglao.com** This locally run website includes travel tips and a list of tourist highlights.

ⓦ **www.theboatlanding.laopdr.com** An excellent site on travel in Northern Laos. Features information on independent trekking and eco-tourism.

Insurance

It is important to purchase a good travel insurance policy before travelling that covers against theft, loss and illness or injury. Good medical coverage is particularly important in Laos where the poor healthcare system means that any serious accident or illness while there would most likely require you to travel to Thailand for treatment.

Internet access

Internet cafés are increasingly common in Laos, though there are still a fair few towns that don't have access. Prices range between 6000 and 15,000K per hour; in most places, connections can be excruciatingly slow. Numerous cafés and many hotels and guest-houses in Vientiane and Luang Prabang now offer wi-fi – outside of these places wi-fi is limited to more upmarket accommodation and occasionally cafés in more touristy towns.

Laundry

Most guesthouses and hotels offer a same-day laundry service, and in larger towns a few shops offer laundry service which can be cheaper than what you'll be charged at your accommodation. In either situation, the charge is usually per kilogram. Your clothes will take a beating, so it's best not to entrust prized articles to these services. If you want to wash clothes yourself, you can buy small packets of detergent in many general stores and markets around the country. Hang out your underwear discreetly – women should take particular care, as women's undergarments are believed to have the power to render Buddhist tattoos and amulets powerless.

Money

Lao currency, the kip, is available in 50,000K, 20,000K, 10,000K, 5000K, 2000K, 1000K and 500K notes; there are no coins in circulation.

Although a law passed in 1990 technically forbids the use of foreign currencies to pay for goods and services in local markets, many tour operators, and upmarket hotels and restaurants quote their prices in dollars (especially common when the price is above 350,000K). Many shops, especially those in more touristy towns, and tourist services will accept Thai baht or US dollars in place of kip, usually at a fairly decent exchange rate, though it makes little sense unless you're paying for something that would require a large amount of kip.

Due to the high denominations of Lao money, it can be rather cumbersome to carry even relatively small amounts of money in kip. It's far easier to carry large sums of money in dollars or baht and to change them as you need to – bear in mind though that larger US notes will get you better exchange rates. It's not possible to convert money to or from kip outside of Laos.

Banks and exchange

Banking **hours** are generally Monday to Friday 8.30am to 3.30pm. Exchange rates are fairly uniform throughout the country, though marginally better in larger towns and cities. Most towns have a bank with at least the most basic of exchange facilities – usually dollars and baht – though travellers' cheques (US dollars) are now accepted at many banks and a wide variety of international currencies can often be changed,

---

Rough Guides travel insurance

Rough Guides has teamed up with WorldNomads.com to offer great **travel insurance** deals. Policies are available to residents of over 150 countries, with cover for a wide range of **adventure sports**, 24hr emergency assistance, high levels of medical and evacuation cover and a stream of **travel safety information**. Roughguides.com users can take advantage of their policies online 24/7, from anywhere in the world – even if you're already travelling. And since plans often change when you're on the road, you can extend your policy and even claim online. Roughguides.com users who buy travel insurance with WorldNomads.com can also leave a positive footprint and donate to a community development project. For more information go to Ⓦ www.**roughguides.com/shop**.

Kip and dollars

Prices in the Guide are predominantly given in kip throughout, with the exception of anything over $25 (around 210,000K at the time of writing). This reflects the way things are priced in country – although you will, of course, come across some exceptions to the rule – with more expensive goods, services and accommodation priced in dollars rather than kip. Unless you're staying in high-end accommodation, most of your transactions will be in kip.

including euros and sterling. Moneychangers are common in larger towns, and rates are generally a little lower, though not disproportionately so, than the banks.

Travellers' cheques, cash and cards

The most convenient way to carry money in Laos is to take a good supply of US dollars or Thai baht with you. Travellers' cheques are the safest way to carry larger amounts of money, and as they are now accepted at banks throughout the country they are a good option if you're travelling for a few weeks, though cashing them will incur a charge of around $1 per cheque. ATMs are becoming more prevalent, but are still fairly rare, and even so it's best not to rely on them. In addition, some travellers have had problems with receiving funds from ATMs, with reports that their accounts were debited despite not receiving cash at the end of the transaction. In such a situation, contact your bank as soon as possible.

Major **credit cards** are accepted at upmarket hotels and restaurants in Vientiane and Luang Prabang, and in a limited number of other tourist centres. **Cash advances** on Visa cards, and less frequently Mastercard, are possible in some banks in larger towns, though minimum amounts and commission are likely to be imposed. Bear in mind that electricity supply in much of the country can be somewhat temperamental, so paying by credit card or getting a cash advance on a card is not always possible even when the service is advertised – it's important not to rely on plastic in Laos and to always have some cash as a fall-back option.

Mail

The Lao **postal system** can be slow and unreliable – mail takes seven to fourteen days in or out of Laos, depending on where you

are. **Post offices** are open Monday to Friday from 8am to 5pm, sometimes with an hour break at lunchtime. When sending parcels, keep the package open for inspection.

Poste restante services are available in Vientiane and Luang Prabang. Post offices in both towns charge a small fee for letters (postcards received this way are free) and keep mail behind the counter for two or three months. Bring your passport on the off chance that you're asked to show identification when picking up your mail. Mail should be addressed: name, GPO, city, Lao PDR.

Opening hours and public holidays

Hours for government offices are generally Monday to Friday from 8am to noon and from 1 to 5pm. Private businesses usually open and close a bit later, with most opening on Saturday but almost all closed on Sunday. Details of banking and post office hours are given on p.57 and above respectively.

The posted hours on **museums** are not always scrupulously followed outside of the major cities and on slow days (almost every day) the curators and staff are often tempted to pack up and head home. Unless a festival

Public holidays

January 1 New Year's Day
January 6 Pathet Lao Day
January 20 Army Day
March 8 Women's Day
March 22 Lao People's Party Day
April 13–15 Lao New Year
May 1 International Labour Day
June 1 Children's Day
August 13 Lao Issara
August 23 Liberation Day
October 12 Freedom from France Day
December 2 National Day

is taking place (see the *Festivals* colour section), **monasteries** should only be visited during daylight hours as monks are very early risers and are usually in bed not long after sunset.

Government offices, banks and post offices close for public holidays – a lot of shops, especially in smaller towns, also close for the day.

Phones

The majority of internet cafés now have facilities for international calling, usually through Skype. Alternatively, international calls can be made at the local Telecom Office, though prices are generally quite high.

Regional codes are given throughout the Guide: the "0" must be dialled before all long-distance calls. Some hotels have consecutively numbered phone lines – thus ☏021/221200–5 means that the last digit can be any number between 0 and 5.

GSM or Triband **mobile phones** can be used in Laos, though call and text charges will be high, so if you're planning on using your phone it's worth buying a local SIM card. These are readily available from shops and markets and cost 20,000–30,000K, which will also give you an initial amount of credit to use. Mobile phone coverage is limited in more remote provinces – at the time of writing, the most comprehensive network was ETL. Top-up cards can be purchased in most towns and villages that have even the most basic shop – just look for the flag displaying the network's name.

Showers

Most hotels and guesthouses in Laos now claim to have hot-water showers – though in reality the water is often disappointingly cold. Traditional Lao showers, sometimes found in accommodation in rural areas, consist of a large, ceramic jar or a cement tub resembling an oversized bathtub without a drain. Standing next to the tub, you use the plastic scoop provided to sluice water over your body. While it may look tempting on a hot day, don't get into these tubs or try to use them for doing your laundry, as the water has to be used by others. In many towns villagers opt for an even more traditional technique – the river. Men usually bathe in their underwear, women in sarongs.

Tampons

Hard to find outside Vientiane's minimarkets, which have a very limited selection. Bring supplies.

Time zone

Ignoring daylight-saving time abroad, Laos is 7 hours ahead of London, 15 hours ahead of Vancouver, 12 hours ahead of New York, 3 hours behind Sydney and 5 hours behind Auckland.

Toilets

Squat toilets are the norm throughout Laos, although almost all hotels and guesthouses have Western-style porcelain thrones. Public toilets are not common in Laos though you'll find them at airports and most bus stations; at the latter a small fee is usually collected. Not all toilets will have toilet paper, so it's worth carrying some with you. Most squat toilets require manual flushing – you'll find a bucket of water with a scoop floating on the surface for this purpose. In some small, rural villages people tend to take to the woods because of a lack of plumbing. On long road trips this is also a perfectly acceptable way to relieve yourself, though keep in mind that many parts of Laos have UXO (see p.51), so it's not wise to wade too far into the bush when the bus stops for a bathroom break.

Travellers with disabilities

For anyone with limited mobility, Laos is a difficult country to explore. Even in the big tourist cities of Luang Prabang and Vientiane, you'll be met with uneven pavements, which lack ramps, and small sets of stairs leading into most restaurants and guesthouses. In smaller towns the situation is even worse – there are often no pavements and most of the roads are dirt tracks.

However, a handful of the newer hotels in Laos (especially in cities) have been built with some regard for disabled guests. The best places have ramps at the front of the building, lifts to all floors of the hotel, and wider doorways that at least allow wheelchair users to pass from one part of the building to another. That said, your chances of getting a room that's been specially adapted for a wheelchair user, complete with grab-rails and a roll-in shower, are close to zero.

Hotels that do make specific allowances for disabled guests include the *3 Nagas* by Alila in Luang Prabang (see p.117) and the *Lao Plaza* (see p.73) in Vientiane.

The best way to alleviate transport difficulties is to take internal flights and hire a private minibus with a driver. You should also consider hiring a local tour guide to accompany you on sightseeing trips – a Lao speaker can facilitate access to temples and museums. Flying an international carrier whose planes are suited to your needs is also helpful. Keep in mind that airline companies can cope better if they are expecting you, with a wheelchair provided at airports and staff primed to help.

When preparing for your trip, it's a good idea to pack spares of any clothing or equipment that might be hard to find. If you use a wheelchair, you should have it serviced before you go and carry a repair kit. If you do not use a wheelchair all the time but your walking capabilities are limited, remember that you are likely to need to cover greater distances while travelling (often over rougher terrain and in hotter temperatures) than you are used to.

Contacts for travellers with disabilities

The following organizations can provide general advice though little by way of specific advice on the country itself.

US and Canada

Access-Able Ⓦ www.access-able.com. Online resource for travellers with disabilities.
Directions Unlimited 123 Green Lane, Bedford Hills, NY 10507 914/241-1700. Tour operator specializing in customized tours for people with disabilities.
Mobility International 451 Broadway, Eugene, OR 97401, voice and TDD ☏ 541/343-1284, Ⓦ www.miusa.org. Information and referral services, access guides, tours and exchange programmes.
Society for the Advancement of Travelers with Handicaps (SATH) 347 5th Ave, New York, NY 10016 ☏ 212/447-7284, Ⓦ www.sath.org. Non-profit educational organization that has actively represented travellers with disabilities since 1976.

UK and Ireland

Tourism For All Shap Road Industrial Estate, Shap Road, Kendal, Cumbria LA9 6NZ, ☏ 0845/1249971 Ⓦ www.tourismforall.org.uk. Provides general advice and information for disabled travellers.
Irish Wheelchair Association Blackheath Drive, Clontarf, Dublin 3 ☏ 01/818 6400, Ⓦ www.iwa.ie. Useful information provided about travelling abroad with a wheelchair.

Australia and New Zealand

National Disability Services P33 Thesiger Court, Deakin, ACT, 2600 T02/6283 3200, Ⓦ www.nds.org.au. Provides lists of travel agencies and tour operators for people with disabilities.
Disabled Persons Assembly 4/173–175 Victoria St, Wellington, New Zealand ☏ 04/801 9100, Ⓦ www.dpa.org.nz. Resource centre with lists of travel agencies and tour operators for people with disabilities.

Guide

Guide

Vientiane and
the northwest

CHAPTER 1 # Highlights

✴ **Lao National Museum** Learn about the heroes of Laos's class struggle as you walk the halls of this crumbling treasure-trove. See p.75

✴ **Wat Sisaket** Vientiane's oldest wat, the only temple spared by the invading Siamese in their 1828 sack of the city. See p.78

✴ **That Luang** Laos's most important religious site, the golden stupa is also the national symbol. See p.81

✴ **Riverside bars** Kick back with a drink and watch the sun sink over the Mekong. See p.87

✴ **Xieng Khuan** The highlight of Vientiane's most popular day-trip destination is a stunning 40m-long reclining Buddha. See p.91

✴ **Ang Nam Ngum Reservoir** There's fishing, boating and island-hopping in this vast lake north of Vientiane. See p.94

✴ **Vang Vieng** Party till you drop in Laos's backpacker capital, or save your strength for caving, mountain biking, rafting and rock climbing in the surrounding countryside. See p.97

▲ "Buddha park", Xieng Khuan

Vientiane and the northwest

Without doubt, **Vientiane** is one of Southeast Asia's quietest capital cities. Hugging a wide bend of the Mekong River, it looks more like a rambling collection of villages, dotted with a few grandiose monuments, than the engine room of a nation. However, in the mere two decades since Laos reopened its doors to foreign visitors, the city has changed with dizzying rapidity. At the beginning of the Nineties, Vientiane wallowed in an economic stupor brought about by a fifteen-year near-ban on free enterprise and a heavy reliance on Soviet aid. But with the collapse of the Soviet Union in 1991, economic restrictions were relaxed; soon afterwards, Vientiane's collection of billboards proclaiming the glories of socialism were outnumbered by advertisements for Pepsi, and the hammer and sickle that had been erected atop the abandoned French cultural centre was removed. Shophouses that had long been padlocked and disused were opened up and transformed into minimarts and pizza parlours. Now, the city has a shopping mall, a thriving tourist economy, and some excellent places to stay. That said, Vientiane remains quaint and easy-going, and the people have managed to retain their hospitality and sense of humour.

Two days is enough to see Vientiane's sights, and if the small-town atmosphere of the capital gets too claustrophobic, there's plenty to see nearby. The most popular **day-trip** is to Xieng Khuan or the "**Buddha Park**", a concrete-cluttered meadow that's home to more than 200 Buddhist and Hindu statues, including a 40m-long reclining Buddha. North of Vientiane, the **Ang Nam Ngum Reservoir** attracts locals and foreign visitors alike for relaxing weekend retreats, offering hiking and camping and boat trips to small, half-sunk islands. Off the beaten track and a bit more of an effort to reach is the resort of **Ban Pako**, on the banks of the Nam Ngum River, which offers a rural Lao experience within relatively easy distance of the capital.

Slightly further afield but still within day-tripping range of Vientiane is **Vang Vieng,** the home of tubing and Laos's most notorious backpacker hotspot. Set amid spectacular scenery on Route 13, Vang Vieng is a natural wonderland providing the perfect environment for hiking, kayaking, climbing and caving, and is also a convenient stopover en route from Vientiane to Luang Prabang, Laos's second city. An alternative route to Luang Prabang involves road and river travel through **Sayaboury,** a remote left-bank province that's famed for its wild elephants.

Vientiane and around

High on the list of any visitor to **VIENTIANE** should be **Wat Sisaket**, the city's oldest temple, and **Wat Simuang**, which is the most popular temple with worshippers. Another top attraction is **That Luang**, Laos's most important religious building, best viewed at sundown when its golden surface glows like a lamp. Aside from temples and stupas, the **museum of Lao art**, housed in the former royal temple of **Haw Pha Kaew**, and the socialist-era **Lao National Museum** are also worth a visit.

As with other urban centres in the region, the majority of Vientiane's merchant class are ethnic Chinese and Vietnamese, whose forefathers emigrated to Laos during the French era. Foreign expatriate workers comprise a significant percentage of the capital's population, which adds a **cosmopolitan** touch to the place and has given rise to a surprisingly wide choice of places to eat.

Some history

Vientiane's history has been turbulent, as its meagre collection of old buildings suggests. An old settlement, possibly dating back to the eighth century, Vientiane was occupied and subsequently abandoned by the Mon and then the Khmer long before the Lao king Setthathilat moved his **capital** here from Luang Prabang in 1560. Vientiane is actually pronounced "Wiang Jan" (the modern Romanized spelling is a French transliteration), *wiang* being Lao for a "settlement with a stockade", while *jan* means "sandalwood". The wooden ramparts of the "City of

Sandalwood" were evidently no match for invaders, for Vientiane was overrun or occupied several times by the Burmese, Chinese and, most spectacularly, by the **Siamese**. During one punitive raid in 1828, the Siamese levelled the entire city. For the next four decades, Vientiane was almost completely abandoned. When **French explorers** arrived in 1867, they found the city all but reclaimed by the jungle.

Within a few decades, the French controlled most of what is now Laos, Cambodia and Vietnam. When Vientiane was chosen by the French to be the capital of an administrative division of French Indochina, they rebuilt the city and laid out its system of roads. It is from this period, roughly 1899 to 1945, that the city's crumbling collection of French colonial mansions dates.

The end of the First Indochina War between France and Vietnam in 1954 saw a flood of **Vietnamese refugees** enter Vientiane from Ho Chi Minh's newly independent Democratic Republic of Vietnam. As North Vietnamese troops began to infiltrate into South Vietnam while simultaneously occupying large areas of northeastern Laos, the United States started pouring massive amounts of unregulated aid into Vientiane, causing widespread corruption among government and military officials. In August 1960, a disgruntled army captain who resented the vast difference in lifestyles between his high-living superiors and his hard-bitten troops staged a successful **coup d'état**. Four months later during the Battle of Vientiane two Lao factions (one supplied by the US and the other by the USSR) managed to level whole blocks of the city with mortars and artillery.

As the **war in Vietnam** steadily escalated with growing US involvement, Laos was pulled deeper into the conflict, but for most of the war, Vientiane was like an island of calm surrounded by violent seas. A steady influx of refugees arrived from the outer provinces, the population of the capital swelled, and rows of squatters' shanties appeared along the tree-lined avenues, contrasting sharply with the Mercedes-Benz automobiles of wartime profiteers.

After the fall of Saigon in 1975, the **Lao communists** suddenly gained power and, with coaching from the Vietnamese, set out to create the Lao People's Democratic Republic. Thieves, prostitutes and other undesirables were rounded up and held captive on two small islands in the nearby Ang Nam Ngum Reservoir and, although revolutionary fervour never reached the extremes seen in China or Cambodia, a large percentage of the population of Vientiane found it necessary to escape across the Mekong. These were replaced by immigrants from the former "liberated zone" in northeastern Laos, further changing Vientiane's ethnic make-up.

The 1980s were a time of quiet stagnation. Soviet aid eased the transition to **socialism**, but the majority of Lao with any education were in some form of exile, either attending "re-education camps" or squatting in Thai refugee camps, awaiting resettlement in a third country. Grand plans for progress were announced by the communist government and then promptly forgotten. Not until the collapse of the Soviet Union in 1991 and the suspension of Soviet aid was the government forced to rethink its opinions of capitalism. A number of **economic reforms** were implemented, leading to an explosion of new ventures and businesses.

In 1994, the first bridge to span the Mekong River between Laos and Thailand was completed. Dubbed the **"Friendship Bridge"**, it marked a new era of cooperation between the former enemies. Thai entrepreneurs were soon arriving in Vientiane to search for economic potential. French colonial mansions were restored for use as offices, and scores of venerable old trees were cut down in road-widening projects to accommodate the ever-multiplying number of cars and motorbikes.

Officials know trade with Thailand is working – and vital for the country – but they're determined to preserve Lao culture. This means you'll occasionally see

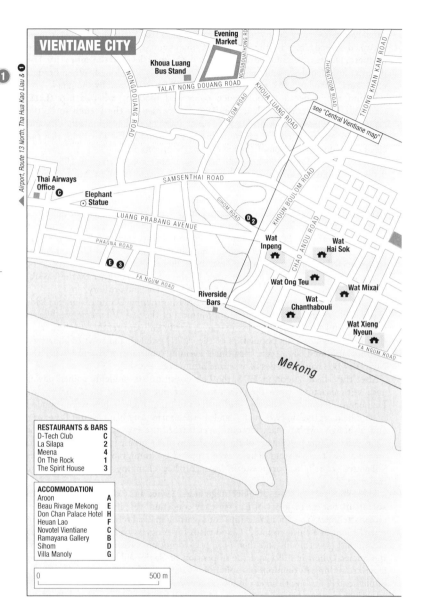

VIENTIANE CITY

Evening Market

Khoua Luang Bus Stand

NONGBOUA THONG RD

TALAT NONG DOUANG ROAD

NONGDOUANG ROAD

SILOM ROAD

KHOUA LUANG ROAD

see "Central Vientiane map"

THONGTOUM ROAD

THONG KHAN KAM ROAD

Thai Airways Office ⦿

Elephant Statue

SAMSENTHAI ROAD

LUANG PRABANG AVENUE

SIHOM ROAD

KHOUN BOULOM ROAD

CHAO ANOU ROAD

❶ 2

PHAGNA ROAD

Wat Inpeng 卍

Wat Hai Sok 卍

❸ 3

FA NGUM ROAD

Wat Ong Teu 卍

Wat Mixai 卍

Riverside Bars

Wat Chanthabouli 卍

Wat Xieng Nyeun 卍

FA NGUM ROAD

Mekong

RESTAURANTS & BARS
D-Tech Club	C
La Silapa	2
Meena	4
On The Rock	1
The Spirit House	3

ACCOMMODATION
Aroon	A
Beau Rivage Mekong	E
Don Chan Palace Hotel	H
Heuan Lao	F
Novotel Vientiane	C
Ramayana Gallery	B
Sihom	D
Villa Manoly	G

0 — 500 m

police snaring motorbike-racing youths, or cracking down on bars and nightclubs that flout the midnight curfew.

However, the Lao inability to sustain enthusiasm for anything *baw muan* ("no fun") ensures any closures are short-lived.

In 2009 Vientiane hosted the 25th Southeast Asian Games, attracting more foreign investment and renewing debate about the city's rampant development.

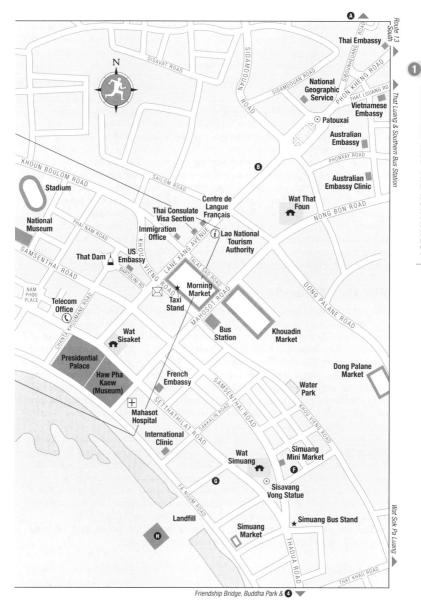

Friendship Bridge, Buddha Park & ▼

Arrival

However you arrive, there's no need to panic if you don't have Lao kip for your trip into town, as taxi drivers will happily accept Thai baht or American dollars. A useful reference point is a humble fountain in the middle of a square known as **Nam Phou** (actually Lao for "fountain"), which marks the heart of **downtown Vientiane**, though grandiose monuments elsewhere may suggest otherwise.

Situated in a quarter built by the French, Nam Phou lies at the heart of a cosmo-politan, commercial district populated by Vietnamese, Chinese and a smattering of Indians, as well as Lao. Here, you'll find the city's greatest concentration of accommodation, restaurants and shops catering to visitors.

By air

Wattay International Airport, Vientiane's main airport and the terminus for most internal flights, is located on Luang Prabang Avenue, roughly 6km west of downtown Vientiane. Here you can get a 30-day **visa on arrival**, and there are a wide range of facilities inside the building, including an ATM, restaurant, duty-free shop, and a desk for **exchanging currency**. The easiest way to get to the city centre is by taxi ($6 for a car; $8 for a minivan) – the official booking desk is straight ahead as you emerge from immigration. The helpful staff should be able to provide you with a free map of Vientiane. Taking a tuk-tuk or jumbo from across the street (they're not allowed to pick up from the terminal) can be a little cheaper, but you'll need to haggle to save any real cash. If money is really tight, just walk a few hundred metres from the terminal out to Luang Prabang Avenue, and hail a sawngthaew coming from the north (5000K) which will drop you off at the main bus station next to the Morning Market in the city centre.

Via the Friendship Bridge

The vast majority of tourists still enter Laos using the original **Thai–Lao Friendship Bridge** (daily, 6am–10pm). Completed in 1994, the 1240-metre-long bridge spans the Mekong River at a point 5km west of Nong Khai in Thailand, and 20km east of Vientiane. **Minibuses** (20 baht) shuttle passengers across the bridge, leaving every fifteen to twenty minutes. The minibuses stop at Thai immigration control at the base of the bridge, where passengers must clear Thai customs before reboarding and continuing on to Lao immigration on the opposite side of the river. An "overtime fee" of $1 may be charged if you cross at the weekend or after 4.30pm. **Motorcycles** may cross the bridge, but you should have the registration papers with you. Nearby facilities include duty-free, an exchange booth and a post office.

It's now also possible to cross into Laos using the local **train** that connects Nong Khai in Thailand with Tha Naleng Station, 20km east of downtown Vientiane. You can buy a single ticket in Nong Khai for the 15-minute chug across the Friendship Bridge (20 baht), or have this leg added to a standard Bangkok–Nong Khai rail ticket. Two trains leave Nong Khai for Laos each day (9.30am & 4pm), but they can be held back if northbound trains from Bangkok are running late. Trains running in the other direction leave at 10.30am and 5pm.

Visas on arrival are available at the Lao immigration booth, and tuk-tuks (10,000K) are on hand for the 25-minute run into Vientiane.

By bus

Most public buses from the south arrive at Vientiane's compact **main bus station,** next to the Morning Market (Talat Sao) on Khou Vieng Road, about 1500m from Nam Phou fountain. From here it's only a short tuk-tuk ride to all the central hotels and guesthouses. VIP buses from the south, however, usually drop off at the **southern bus station**, about 9km northeast of the centre. From here, a shared tuk-tuk into town costs 20,000K, and drivers will usually drop you right outside your guesthouse. Most **buses from the north** arrive at the **northern bus station**, near the Evening Market, about 2km northwest of the city centre. Shared tuk-tuks from here to the centre cost around 5000K.

By boat

Speedboats and slow boats from the north arrive at **Tha Hua Kao Liaw pier**, located on the Mekong River 10km west of the centre of Vientiane. The only way to get to the city centre from here is by tuk-tuk (60,000K). No regular boat traffic arrives in Vientiane from points south.

Information and city transport

The **Lao National Tourism Administration** (LNTA) operates out of a nondescript building on Lane Xang Avenue (Mon–Fri 8am–noon & 1–5pm; ℡021/212248 or 212251), just north of the Morning Market. Apart from handing out free pamphlets and the latest bus times, however, the office and staff aren't of much assistance to tourists; you'll get better information from talking to other travellers. For maps and reading material on Laos it's better to stock up in Thailand if possible, but in Vientiane itself the best bets are Monument Books and Book Café (see p.83). Some of the more popular coffee shops, such as the *Scandinavian Bakery* and *Le Croissant D'Or* (see map, p.85), maintain notice boards, displaying information on everything from film festivals to language classes.

There are a few free city **maps** available. *The Vientiane Tourist Map*, published by the LNTA, offers a decent citywide orientation, a list of sights and a map of Vientiane Prefecture, but the best and most accurate is the official tourist map (published by the Vientiane Capital Tourism Department), which you can pick up at shops and hotels across town.

For "**what's on**" **info** check out the *Vientiane Times* (published daily), which also carries advertisements for restaurant specials.

City transport

Vientiane is a very walkable city, but **bicycles** are an excellent way of getting around, and can be rented at many guesthouses and shops around town. If you don't fancy pedalling about in the tropical heat, you can easily find a **motorbike or scooter** to rent (you'll be required to leave your passport as a deposit). Motorbikes come in especially handy for exploring the areas around Vientiane. Details can be found in the "Listings" section on p.90. Although travel speeds are relatively slow, negotiating Vientiane's cluttered roads at rush hour can take some getting used to at first.

Otherwise, **tuk-tuks** and **jumbos** can be a quick and efficient way of getting around. These often operate as a kind of bus system within the city (picking up people heading in vaguely the same direction), and charge per person according to how far you're going. Shared tuk-tuks generally ply frequently travelled routes, such as Lane Xang Avenue between the Morning Market and That Luang, and Luang Prabang Avenue; they charge a flat fee of 5000K. Tuk-tuks can also be flagged down for private hire like taxis, though you'll need to bargain with the drivers a bit. Many drivers inflate their prices for foreigners, but figure on paying 10,000K per person for distances of 1–2km, and adding 2000K per kilometre beyond that.

Downtown Vientiane is too small to support a metropolitan public transport system, but **bus routes** originating at the main bus station, next to the Morning Market, do connect Vientiane with nearby places on the Vientiane Plain, such as the Buddha Park and Ban Pako. For destinations further afield, a fleet of **unmetered taxis**, consisting of banged-up old Toyotas, gathers outside the Morning Market, in the car park on Khou Vieng Road. Prices are negotiable and drivers will accept Lao kip, Thai baht, or American dollars. Hiring a driver for a day-tour of sights within the city will cost in the region of $15; for trips out to Ang Nam Ngum, expect to pay double that.

Accommodation

Vientiane has a wide range of tourist **accommodation**, from cheap backpacker dives to five-star behemoths like the *Don Chan Palace*. Most of the city's hotels and guesthouses are located near Nam Phou in the centre of town but others, especially mid-range hotels, continue to open up beyond this area – particularly in the vicinity of Patouxai and on Luang Prabang Avenue, a quick tuk-tuk ride into the centre.

Budget hotels in the central area are generally housed in renovated older buildings. Rooms at the best budget places, like the *MOIC* or *Saybaidee*, tend to fill up very quickly, even in low season. It's not uncommon to see late arrivals desperately pounding the pavements looking for a reasonably priced room, as what's left by that time tends to be towards the top end of the budget range without meriting the price. It's therefore a good idea to check in by noon, when people start checking out. Guesthouses and budget hotels rarely take advance bookings unless they know you already. As a general rule, better deals can be found in the **mid-range** establishments.

Hotels listed under "Central Vientiane" below appear on the map on pp.76–77 unless otherwise stated; for hotels listed under "Outside the centre", see the Vientiane City map on pp.68–69.

Central Vientiane

Auberge Sala Inpeng 063 Inpeng Rd ☎021/242021, ⓦwww.salalao.com. These traditional Lao-style bungalows, built on a secluded plot between much larger buildings, offer a chance to escape the hustle of Vientiane's streets without moving too far from the action. After a quiet night's sleep in the a/c rooms, you can enjoy breakfast on your own balcony overlooking the gardens. Friendly staff. ❺

City Inn Pangkham Rd, north of Nam Phou Place ☎021/218333, ⓦwww.cityinnvientiane.com. The best of Vientiane's mid-range options. Expect warm smiles, floors you can see your face in, and bath-tubs big enough to ease away those post-journey aches. Every room in this spotless new hotel has TV, a/c, phone, satellite TV and free wi-fi. Popular with the package tour crowd, so make sure you book ahead. ❻

Day Inn 059/3 Pangkham Rd, behind the *Lao Plaza Hotel* ☎021/223848, ⓔdayinn@laopdr.com. This friendly, well-run hotel is still first choice for volunteers working in Laos (and is often fully booked) but it is starting to look a little tired. Unless you're planning a lengthy stay, when discounts may be available, you could probably find better value for money at the newer hotels across the street. ❺

Douang Deuane 6 Nokeo Koummane Rd ☎021/222301, ⓕ222300. Rooms in this centrally

located hotel have enormous beds and big-screen TVs, but the bathrooms can be a bit grubby. Still, good value considering its location. Motorbike and bicycle rental, as well as airport pick-up. ❹

Family Hotel Pangkham Rd, opposite *Day Inn* ☎021/260448, ⓦwww.familyhotellaos.com. Another of the gleaming new mid-range hotels to crop up in the quiet street just north of Nam Phou Place. *Family Hotel* is a tall, skinny building, which means rooms can be a bit poky, but the lack of space inside is made up for by flat-screen TVs and the funky, marble-clad reception areas. Pop into the textile shop downstairs for a quick lesson in weaving, Lao style. ❺

Khampiane (KP) Hotel 059 Heng Boune Rd ☎021/223762 ⓦwww.khampianehotel.com. This new, wood-panelled hotel is tucked away on a quiet road near the Lao National Cultural Hall. Rooms are cosy, with brilliant white sheets and big dressing tables, and there are added luxuries like minibars and LCD TVs in every room. Good value. ❺

Lane Xang Fa Ngum Rd ☎021/214102, ⓦwww .lanexanghotel.com.la. Once Laos's premier hotel, this place is starting to look a bit rough around the edges. That said, it has a charming retro appeal, and the rooms are large, clean and quirky, with impressive bedsteads. Facilities include tennis courts, a snooker parlour and an inviting, kidney-shaped pool. The only real drawback is the noise on weekends and some weekdays, when the hotel is a popular venue for wedding receptions. ⑤

Lani I Setthathilat Rd, opposite Wat Ong Teu ☏021/216103, ⓦwww.laniguesthouse.com. Supremely pleasant accommodation in a centrally located house, decorated with antiques and handicrafts, with the added attraction of a terrace dining area. All twelve rooms have hot water and wireless internet, but the rooms at the back are gloomy and overpriced. It's worth the extra kip to upgrade to the priciest rooms for the light and space. Reservations recommended. ⑤

Lao Plaza 63 Samsenthai Rd ☏021/218800, ⓦwww.laoplazahotel.com. This gleaming, Thai-built business hotel is just a block from the quaint guesthouses of Nam Phou Place, but to look at it you'd think it came from another planet. The rooms are superb though, with fluffy pillows, giant armchairs and all the mod cons you'd expect from an international-class hotel. For the ultimate upgrade, consider checking into the two-storey Setthathinath Suite ($550), which features its own dining area with commanding views over the city. Free airport transfers. ⑧

MOIC (Ministry of Information and Culture) Manthatoulat Rd ☏021/212362. This fifteen-room guesthouse is the budget travellers' perennial favourite. The stairwells hold all the appeal of a long-derelict building, but the rooms, all with attached bathrooms, are reasonably clean. Comfort-enhancing extras include TV, a/c and a complimentary bottle of water. If full, you can always try to get in at *Saybaidee* and the *Mixok*, which are both very close by. ②

Mixay 039 Nokeo Koummane Rd ☏021/217023. Probably the cheapest place in town, with spartan rooms ranging from fan singles to triples with either attached bathrooms or shared facilities. There's hot water and a reception room with TV. Two rooms have balconies overlooking the street. Fills up very quickly. ①

Mixok 188 Setthathilat Rd, next door to ITIC Computer ☏021/251606. Backpacker hostel similar to the *Mixay*, with singles, doubles, triples and dorms (42,000K) with shared facilities. Rock-bottom prices and a terrific location on the city's prettiest street, but the rooms are a little grotty. ②

Sabaidy Setthathilat Rd, next door to *True Coffee*. This centrally located guesthouse is one of the cheapest places in town, which might explain why it's almost constantly full – just be careful not to trip up on the pile of trainers that appears outside the front door. The dorm rooms (20,000K) are basic, but great for meeting fellow backpackers. ②

Santisouk 77/79 Nokeo Koummane Rd ☏021/215303. This compact guesthouse above the *Santisouk Restaurant* has nine a/c rooms and an upstairs balcony. It's run-down, and certainly no great shakes, but competition for a room here is still hot during busy periods. Rooms with a/c and a private bathroom cost $2 more. ③

Saysouly 23 Manthatoulat Rd ☏021/218383 ⓦwww.saysouly.com. A cheap standby option with a range of singles and doubles, some with shared facilities. The rooms upstairs at the front of the building are the best value, as they have direct access to the shared balconies. ③

🏃 **Settha Palace Hotel** 6 Pangkham Rd ☏021/217581, ⓦwww.setthapalace.com. Until recently, Vientiane was the only Southeast Asian capital without a historic colonial-era hotel. This palatial 1932 building is filled with French period furniture, but the hotel's 29 rooms have all the mod cons, including mini-bar and safe. Elsewhere, you'll find an outstanding pool, beautiful landscaped gardens and a well-run business centre. The published rate is around $200 for a double, though discounts may be available. ⑧

Sihom Sihom Rd, along the alley to the west of *La Silapa* restaurant, see "Vientiane City" map. ☏021/219081. Tastefully decorated rooms fitted out with rattan double beds, a/c, refrigerator and satellite TV. Great value, and particularly recommended for couples on a budget. ③

Soukxana 013 Pangkham Rd ☏021/264114 ⓔsoukxana_guest_house@yahoo.com. Basic double and twin rooms with en-suite bathrooms and TV. The room rate goes up by $4 if you go for a/c. Free tea and coffee in the restaurant downstairs. ③

Syri Saigon Rd ☏021/212682, ⓕ217252. A large house on a quiet lane in the Chao Anou residential district, with spacious double and triple a/c rooms and a nice balcony. The TV area downstairs is a good place to retreat to when you're tired of pounding the pavements. ④

Syri 2 63/67 Setthathirat Rd ☏021/241345, ⓔsyri2@hotmail.com. This old colonial-era building is just a five-minute walk from the centre of town, and the staff are friendly enough. Just don't let the slumped mattresses and gloomy rooms get you down. A popular budget option. ③

Tai-Pan 2–12 François Nginn Rd, near the Mekong ☏021/216906–9. Once Vientiane's best-value small business hotel, the *Tai-Pan* is now facing stiff competition from newly built rivals. The rooms are still in good nick though, with all mod cons, and guests have free rein of the on-site fitness room, sauna and swimming pool. ⑦

Vayakorn Guesthouse Nokeo Koummane Rd, just opposite Carol Cassidy Lao Textiles ☏021/214911.

Still one of the best guesthouses in downtown Vientiane, *Vayakorn* goes above and beyond for cleanliness and efficiency. All rooms have satellite TV, wi-fi and en-suite bathroom, and are decorated with more attention to detail than is usual for rooms in this bracket. Good value. ⑤

Vayakorn Inn 19 Hengbounnoy St. Not to be confused with the *Vayakorn Guesthouse*, which is owned by the same friendly people, this brand-new hotel is far more luxurious. There are beautiful wooden floors and furnishings throughout, and the rooms feature a/c, TV and big corner showers. The only letdown is the size of the private balconies, which don't leave much room for stretching out. Highly recommended. ⑤

Youth Inn 029 Fa Ngum Rd ☎ 021/217130 ⓔ youthinn@hotmail.com. Good, clean accommodation right on the riverfront. There are en-suite doubles, as well as dorm-style rooms sleeping up to six people (180,000K for the room), which are ideal for solo travellers who can find other people to split the cost with. ③

Outside the centre

Aroon Asean Rd ☎ 021/219912, ⓦ www .aroonhotel.com. Ornate chairs adorn the reception areas of this modern hotel on a busy junction just north of the Patouxai monument. Inside the spotlessly clean rooms, you'll find coffee- and tea-making facilities, loungers and bright white bathrooms. For the best night's sleep, go for a room at the back of the hotel. ⑥

Beau Rivage Mekong Fa Ngum Rd ☎ 021/243350, ⓦ www.hbrm.com. Wonderfully stylish rooms in a fresh, minimalist-style hotel right on the riverfront. wi-fi, TV and a/c come as standard, but panoramic views of the Mekong cost $10 more. The adjoining restaurant, *The Spirit House* (see p.87) is one of Vientiane's best spots for sunsets. ⑥

Don Chan Palace Hotel Fa Ngum Rd ☎ 021/244288, ⓦ www.donchanpalacelaopdr .com. Built on a sandbar in the middle of the Mekong, this massive eleven-storey hotel is perhaps the beginning of the end of Vientiane's

reign as Southeast Asia's most low-rise capital, and is the tallest building in Laos at the time of writing. As a consequence, the luxurious rooms in this five-star giant have the best views in town. Deluxe rooms come with enormous beds, lavish rugs and massive TVs. Facilities include a health spa, swimming pool and, you guessed it, karaoke bar. A big shopping mall looks set to be built next door. ⑧

Heuan Lao Off Samsenthai Rd, near Wat Simuang ☎ 021/216258, ⓕ 216258. This friendly upmarket guesthouse is located on a quiet lane opposite a park and offers singles, doubles and triples, all en suite. ④

Novotel Belvedere Vientiane Samsenthai Rd ☎ 021/213570–1, ⓦ www.novotel.com. The four-star *Novotel* is still one of the best modern hotels in Vientiane, but its location on the edge of town definitely counts against it. It is well equipped though, with a pool, sauna, gym and nightclub all on site. The 172 rooms all have a minibar, a/c and satellite TV but, unless you're staying in one of the suites, you'll have to shell out extra for internet access. Good breakfast buffets. ⑦

Ramayana Gallery Lane Xang Ave, near Patouxai (formerly the *Royal Dokmaideng*) ☎ 021/214455, ⓦ www.ramayana-gallery-hotel.com. Although renamed and under new management, the outside of the old *Dokmaideng* building still looks a little gloomy. The inside has been completely refreshed, however, and the intriguing paintings and sculptures hanging from the walls give it a bit more character than most business hotels in town. If you can ignore the lurid green murals in the corridors, the rooms are actually pretty nice, and there's a swimming pool. ⑥

Villa Manoly Ban Simuang, next to Honour International School and around the corner from Wat Simuang ☎ & ⓕ 021/218907, ⓔ manoly20 @hotmail.com. Indeed a villa and an attractive place too, with a pleasant upstairs terrace and spacious grounds. The singles and doubles are pretty basic, but with high ceilings and en-suite hot showers. Just a short walk from the river, it also has a lovely outdoor swimming pool. ⑤

The City

Three main streets run parallel to the river to form the backbone of the city centre, cutting across narrower streets to form an easily deciphered grid. Tree-lined **Setthathilat Road**, just south of Nam Phou, is unarguably the city's most scenic thoroughfare, particularly the west end, with its four monasteries. Further north runs **Samsenthai Road**, Vientiane's principal commercial district and site of the massive *Lao Plaza Hotel*, as well as the **Lao National Museum**, an anachronistic hangover from the days of banner-hoisting socialism. **Fa Ngum Road**, fronting the river, is set to feature a waterfront park by early 2011. For now, though, the makeshift refreshment stands here are still perfect for watching the sunsets.

Fa Ngum Road follows the river as it bends southeast and skirts behind the Presidential Palace. The palace is off-limits to visitors, but the **Haw Pha Kaew**, which occupies the western corner of the palace compound, has been converted into a museum, housing the largest collection of Lao art and antiquities in the country. Roughly opposite the Haw Pha Kaew, across Setthathilat Road, stands **Wat Sisaket**, a picturesque Buddhist monastery containing what is thought to be the oldest structure in Vientiane.

The eastern edge of the city centre is defined by Vientiane's principal thoroughfare, **Lane Xang Avenue**, which begins at the Presidential Palace and marches away from the river past the **Talat Sao Mall** (Morning Market). The broad avenue terminates at **Patouxai**, a massive victory arch, around which are scattered numerous embassies, international organizations and government buildings. Just beyond the Patouxai monument, the road forks, its right branch leading off towards **That Luang**, the golden-spired Buddhist stupa and national symbol of Laos.

Nam Phou

The fountain of **Nam Phou Place** was once the centre of a roundabout, but the renovation of the fountain and the blocking off of half the roundabout created a pleasant public space in which both locals and visitors congregate to cool off after the sun sets. The square is dominated by one of Vientiane's tallest buildings, the semi-abandoned French Cultural Centre. With a few exceptions, most of Vientiane's sights are within comfortable walking distance of here.

The district surrounding the fountain, also known as **Nam Phou**, is the city's oldest. Although the roads and grid system of the district were devised by the French, most of the buildings were hastily constructed during the free-wheeling days of American aid in the 1950s. Many of the oldest buildings have been remodelled in the last decade, and their facades are plain and uninteresting; an exception is the **National Library**, located due south of the square, which was carefully restored with Australian assistance.

Lao National Museum

Just north of Nam Phou, on Samsenthai Road, the **Lao National Museum** (daily except public holidays 8am–noon & 1–4pm; 10,000K) is housed in the former mansion of the French *résident supérieur* and set in overgrown grounds with a hideous fountain and plumeria (frangipani) trees, the delicate blossoms of which are the national flower of Laos. Previously known as the Lao Revolutionary Museum, the institution deals primarily with the events, both ancient and recent, that led to the "inevitable victory" of the proletariat in 1975. Inside, Laos's ancient past is crudely depicted on canvas, with scenes such as crimson-clad Lao patriots of yore liberating the motherland from Thai and Burmese "feudalists". Upstairs there are more crude oils: "French colonialists" are depicted as hair-faced ogres bullwhipping tightly trussed Lao villagers or tossing Lao tots down a well. Black-and-white **photographs** take over to tell the story of the struggle against "the Japanese fascists" and "American imperialists". Most of the best artefacts on display, including a wonderfully detailed **Khmer sculpture of Ganesh** and a bronze frog-drum, possibly used in ancient rain-making rituals, didn't fit neatly into the official socialist story line, and were, until recently, very neglected. Some of the exhibits are currently only labelled in Lao, but a project is underway to ensure English translations are made available.

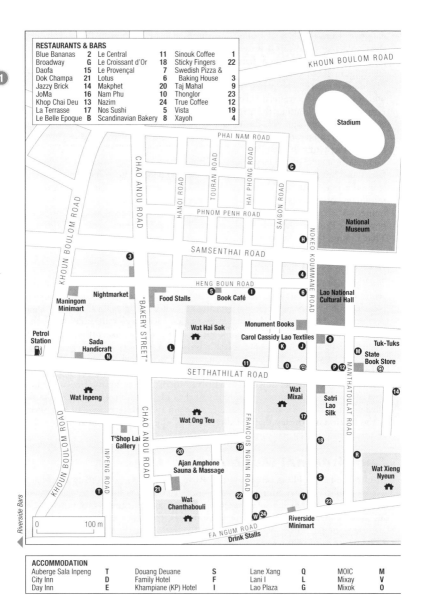

RESTAURANTS & BARS

Blue Bananas	2	Le Central	11	Sinouk Coffee	1
Broadway	G	Le Croissant d'Or	18	Sticky Fingers	22
Daofa	15	Le Provençal	7	Swedish Pizza &	
Dok Champa	21	Lotus	6	Baking House	3
Jazzy Brick	14	Makphet	20	Taj Mahal	9
JoMa	16	Nam Phu	10	Thonglor	23
Khop Chai Deu	13	Nazim	24	True Coffee	12
La Terrasse	17	Nos Sushi	5	Vista	19
Le Belle Epoque	B	Scandinavian Bakery	8	Xayoh	4

ACCOMMODATION

Auberge Sala Inpeng	T	Douang Deuane	S	Lane Xang	Q	MOIC	M
City Inn	D	Family Hotel	F	Lani I	L	Mixay	V
Day Inn	E	Khampiane (KP) Hotel	I	Lao Plaza	G	Mixok	O

The Lao National Cultural Hall

Across from the museum, as if you could miss it, is the gargantuan **Lao National Cultural Hall**. This love-it-or-hate-it building, opened in 2000, houses a giant 1,500-seat auditorium and occasionally hosts art exhibitions or performances by dance troupes and circuses. It's not always clear what will be happening at the hall until a few days beforehand, so keep your eyes peeled for the adverts that spring up around town or in the *Vientiane Times*.

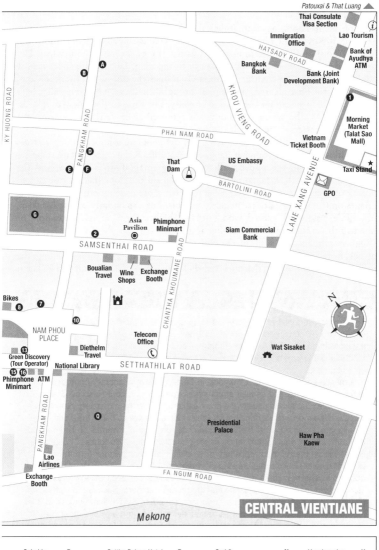

Patouxai & That Luang ▲

CENTRAL VIENTIANE

Sabaidy	P	Settha Palace Hotel	B	Syri 2	N	Vayakorn Inn	K
Santisouk	H	Soukxana	A	Tai-Pan	U	Youth Inn	W
Saysouly	R	Syri	C	Vayakorn Guesthouse	J		

Setthathilat Road

Running parallel to and one block south of Samsenthai Road is **Setthathilat Road**, with its shady trees and monasteries. Not all of the monasteries are particularly deserving of attention, however. If time is limited, the four at the street's western end – wats Ong Teu, Mixai, Inpeng and Hai Sok – can be skipped in favour of **Wat Sisaket** and **Wat Simuang** at the eastern end.

Wat Sisaket

East of Nam Phou, on Setthathilat Road, **Wat Sisaket** (daily 8am–noon & 1–4pm; 5000K) is the oldest wat in Vientiane. Constructed by King Anouvong (Chao Anou) in 1818, the monastery was the site of a ceremony in which Lao lords and nobles swore an oath of loyalty to the king. During the 1828 sack of Vientiane by the Siamese, this was the only monastery not put to the torch and, once the smoke had cleared, the Siamese brought the surviving Lao nobility here and made them swear another oath of loyalty, this time to their new overlords. Later, in 1893, the whole ceremony was repeated again at this very same wat before new masters – the French.

Surrounded by a tile-roofed cloister, the *sim* contains some charming **murals** similar in style to those found at Bangkok's Wat Phra Kaew. The murals, together with the niches in the upper walls containing small Buddha images, and the ornate ceiling, are best taken in while kneeling on the floor (taking care not to point your feet towards the altar – see p.48 for more on etiquette). The Buddha images on the altar are not particularly notable, but a splendidly ornate *hao thian*, or candle holder, of carved wood situated before the altar is an example of nineteenth-century Lao woodcarving at its best.

Outside, the interior walls of the **cloister** echo those of the *sim*, with countless niches from which peer diminutive Buddhas in twos and threes. Lining the galleries are larger images that survived the destruction of 1828 and, in a locker at

---

Wat is that?

The **wat**, or Buddhist **monastery**, is the centrepiece of most villages populated by ethnic Lao. A contingent of monks and novices lives in each wat, providing the laypeople with an outlet for **merit-making** (see p.288). The wat also serves as a hub for social gatherings and, during annual festivals and Buddhist holy days, a venue for entertainment.

Sometimes referred to as a "temple" in English, a wat is actually composed of a number of religious and secular structures, some of which could also be described as a temple. The **sim** is usually the grandest structure in the monastery grounds, as it houses the monastery's principal Buddha images, as well as being the place where monks are ordained. The *that*, or **stupa**, is generally a pyramid or bell-shaped structure which contains holy relics, usually a cache of small Buddhas. Occasionally, a *that* will be the reputed repository of a splinter of bone belonging to the historic Buddha himself, while miniature stupas, or *that kaduk*, contain the ashes of deceased adherents. The *haw tai* is a solid structure, usually raised high off the ground, for storing palm-leaf manuscripts, and *kuti* are monks' quarters. Because the latter two buildings are not considered as important as other religious structures in the monastery grounds, they are not as frequently restored, and are thus most likely to exude that "timeless Asia" charm. Minor buildings sometimes found at a wat include a bell tower and a **sala**, or open-air pavilion. Many monasteries also have a venerable specimen of a bodhi (*Ficus religiosa*), a wonderfully shady tree of spade-shaped leaves that is said to have sheltered the Buddha while he meditated his way to enlightenment.

Because the wat and resident monks depend on adherents for support, the extravagance of a monastery's **decoration** is directly related to the amount of cash flow in the host village or town. In poor villages, the wat may consist of just a *sim*, which will be a large but simple hut-like structure, raised on stilts without any ornamentation. The only clue to the outsider that this is a monastery will be the freshly laundered monks' robes hanging out to dry alongside a piece of junk metal or war scrap, such as an old artillery-shell casing, which when struck serves as a bell to wake the monks or call them to assemble.

the western wall, a heap of Buddhas that did not. The shaded galleries are a cool and pleasant place to linger and soak up the atmosphere. Breaching the wall that runs along Lane Xang Avenue, the structure with the multi-tiered roof is the monastery's former **library** (closed to the public), where its palm-leaf manuscripts were once kept.

Haw Pha Kaew

Opposite Wat Sisaket stands the **Presidential Palace**, a rather unimpressive French Beaux Arts-style structure, built to house the French colonial governor, and nowadays used mainly for government ceremonies. Just west of the palace, the **Haw Pha Kaew** (daily 8am–noon & 1–4pm; 5000K) was once the king's personal Buddhist temple, but now functions as a **museum of art and antiquities**. Said to date from the mid-sixteenth century, the structure was destroyed by marauding Siamese during the sack of Vientiane in 1828 and was later earmarked for restoration by the French. The temple is named for the **Emerald Buddha**, or Pha Kaew, which, along with the Pha Bang (see box, p.126), the most sacred Buddha image in Laos, was pilfered by the Siamese in 1779 and carried off to their capital. The Pha Bang was eventually returned to Laos and is enshrined in its namesake city of Luang Prabang, but the Pha Kaew remains in Bangkok to this day, much to the resentment of Lao Buddhists.

The museum houses the finest collection of Lao art in the country. **Bronze Buddhas**, many looted of the inlay that once decorated their eyes, line the terrace surrounding the building. Inside are some exquisite works, one of the most striking being a Buddha in the "Beckoning Rain" pose (standing with arms to the sides and fingers pointing to the ground) and sporting a jewel-encrusted navel. Also of note are a pair of eighteenth-century terracotta *apsara*, or celestial dancers, and a highly detailed "naga throne" from Xieng Khuang that once served as a pedestal for a Buddha image. Next to the throne stands an elaborate candle holder of ornately carved wood and almost identical to one still in use at Wat Sisaket. An arched metal rod attached to the wood is where the lighted candles were placed.

Outsized bronze **statues** of a kowtowing Lao boy and girl on the lawn outside the museum were once part of a tableau that included the statue of explorer Auguste Pavie. The Frenchman's statue is now located inside the French embassy compound across the street. Sheltered under an adjacent pavilion is a sample stone urn from the Plain of Jars, but this small, broken jar is a rather poor specimen and not really typical of those at the site.

Wat Simuang

Roughly 500m east of Haw Pha Kaew, down Setthathilat Road, sits **Wat Simuang**. While Vientiane has its share of Buddhist monasteries, this wat stands out in terms of the number of worshippers it receives. Numerous pavement stalls stationed outside the walls give some indication of its popularity and sell all the ingredients for a proper tray of offerings (flowers, fruit, incense and candles). The monastery itself was built on an ancient Khmer site, the ruins of which are piled behind the *sim* and consist of laterite bricks with traces of stucco ornamentation. The *sim* of Wat Simuang houses the city's *lak meuang*, a sacred stone pillar. It is believed that the guardian spirit of Vientiane inhabits the pillar, which was consecrated with a human sacrifice at the time of the city's founding. Covered with gold leaf and wrapped in sacred cloth, the pillar is the centrepiece of an altar crowded with Buddha images. That great multitudes of worshippers come here is evident from a glance at the ceiling, coal-black with a thick coating of soot, which is constantly rising from sputtering candles and smouldering joss sticks.

By quietly taking a seat on the floor you can observe the **rituals** of devotees seeking answers or favours. Two baby-sized, crude images resting on their own pillows are the main focus of the worshippers' attention. After a question is posed or a favour requested, the devotee attempts to lift one of the images while kneeling towards the altar. Being able to lift the image three times over one's head is considered an auspicious sign. Worshippers whose wishes are granted must return and appease the guardian spirit with an offering; marigolds, coconuts and bananas are particularly popular tokens of gratitude. The **monastery grounds** surrounding the *sim* contain a dozen or so brightly painted sculptures of animals, Buddhist–Hindu deities and mythological figures from Lao legends, making this a favourite playground for local kids.

On a small wedge of land outside the south wall of the monastery towers a monolithic **statue of King Sisavang Vong**, who reigned from 1904 to 1959. The statue survived the revolution, having been executed by a Soviet sculptor and presented to the Lao government in 1972 after a visit to the Soviet Union by King Sisavang Vatthana. Ironically, within a few short years of the statue being erected in 1974, the royalist government collapsed, and the newly installed communist government banished King Sisavang Vatthana and his family to a cave near the Vietnamese border, where they all perished. A plaque that was once attached to the pedestal has long been missing and, if asked, many locals will only be able to say that the massive statue depicts "an old king".

Patouxai

It has been said that, along with coffee and baguettes, the Lao inherited a taste for pompous town planning from the French. **Lane Xang Avenue**, leading off north from Setthathilat Road, was to be Vientiane's Champs Elysées and **Patouxai**, 1km from the Presidential Palace, its Arc de Triomphe. While it would be impossible to mistake seedy Lane Xang Avenue for Paris's most famous thoroughfare, if you were to stand at a fair distance and squint, you might be able to convince yourself that Patouxai resembles its Parisian inspiration. Popularly known as *anusawali* (Lao for "monument"), this massive reinforced concrete monument (daily 8am–5pm;

▲ Patouxai monument

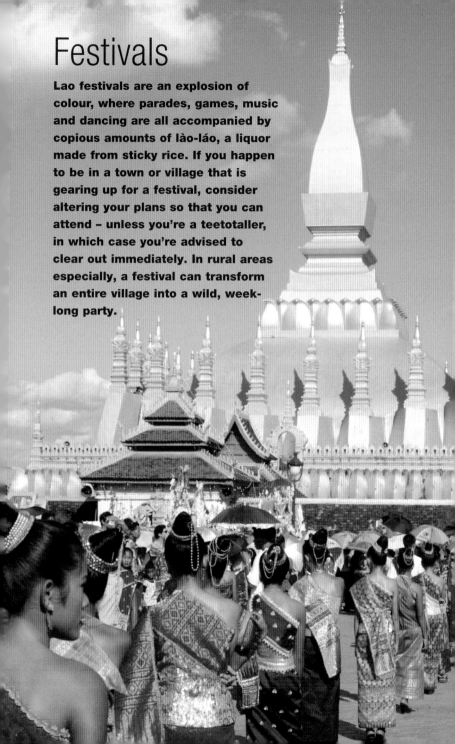

Festivals

Lao festivals are an explosion of colour, where parades, games, music and dancing are all accompanied by copious amounts of lào-láo, a liquor made from sticky rice. If you happen to be in a town or village that is gearing up for a festival, consider altering your plans so that you can attend – unless you're a teetotaller, in which case you're advised to clear out immediately. In rural areas especially, a festival can transform an entire village into a wild, week-long party.

Major festivals

Because the Lao calendar is dictated by both solar and lunar rhythms, the dates of festivals change from year to year, and even just a few days prior to a parade or boat race, there is sometimes confusion over just when it will take place. For the Lao this is not really a problem, as the days leading up to and immediately following large festivals are equally packed with celebrations.

The Makkha Busa Buddhist holy day, observed under a full moon in February, commemorates a legendary sermon given by the Buddha after 1250 of his disciples spontaneously congregated around the enlightened one. Lao New Year, or *pi mai lao*, is celebrated all over Laos between April 15–17, most stunningly in Luang Prabang. There, the town's namesake Buddha image is ritually bathed; a procession led by the guardian spirits of Luang Prabang, and the Seven Daughters of Brahma is held; sand stupas are erected in monastery grounds; and Buddhists make a pilgrimage to nearby caves.

In villages and small towns, the lunar new year is marked with *basi* ceremonies (see p.142) and merrymaking. If you're in the right place at the right time, you may be ambushed by young people carrying pails of water and armed with squirt guns. After being forced to down a few shots of *lào-láo*, you will be given a thorough drenching followed by a liberal dusting with talcum powder and frenzied smearing with blood-red lipstick.

Lai Heau Fai, on the full moon in October, is a festival of lights most magically celebrated in Luang Prabang. In the days leading up to the festival residents build large floats and festoon them with lights. Then, under the full moon, the floats are paraded through the streets, where they are judged for aesthetic

Lights illuminate Pha That Luang at Makkha Busa ▲

Soaking passers-by with water, lunar new year ▼

A float carrying a venerated Buddha icon ▼

merit, and carried down to the Mekong and set atop boats for a second procession on the river. All evening, vendors offer saucer-sized floats made from banana stalks and leaves and containing flowers, incense and a candle. After selecting one, celebrants take the little offerings down to the river and launch them on the current. Lai Heua Fai is celebrated concurrently with Awk Phansa, the end of the three-month "rains retreat", a time when laypeople donate new robes and other offerings to Buddhist monasteries.

In the days leading up to the full moon in November, the great That Luang stupa in Vientiane comes to resemble the centerpiece of a fairground, with street vendors setting up booths in the open spaces around it. The week-long That Luang Festival then kicks off with a mass alms-giving to hundreds of monks and

Bun Bang Fai

Also known as the rocket festival, this **rain-making ritual** predates Buddhism in Laos, and is a madcap combination of fireworks and firewater. In May, crude **rockets** are fashioned from stout bamboo poles stuffed with gunpowder and, after being blessed, are propped up on wooden launch platforms that resemble rickety ladders to heaven. As villagers dance and cheer, the rockets are shot skywards. The thundering noise and clouds of smoke reassuringly simulate rainy season conditions, which are in turn supposed to inspire the spirits to produce the real thing. Celebrations in the south can be wonderfully bawdy: men brandishing foot-long, **wooden phalluses** give the local girls something to giggle about. The rocket festival is also very popular with the ethnic Lao in northeastern Thailand, where it has evolved into more of a sporting event, with participants wagering on what heights the rockets will attain.

▲ Launching a Bang Fai rocket, Oudomxai province

▼ Decorative boat for Awk Phansa, Luang Prabang

Boat races

Lao boat races are rooted in ancient beliefs that predate the arrival of Buddhism in the country. To this day, many lowland Lao believe the Mekong and other local waterways are home to **naga**, serpent-like creatures that leave the river during the rainy season and inhabit the flooded paddy fields (see box on p.244). The **boat races**, held between October and December, seek to lure the naga out of the fields and back into the rivers, so that ploughing may begin.

A Lao boat race ▲

Lighting candles, That Luang, Vientiane ▼

a **procession** from Wat Simuang to That Luang. Over the next few days, bands and performances occupy a stage near the stupa, and *tikhi*, a game resembling field hockey, is played. On the last evening, the whole city shows up to process with offerings around That Luang.

In December or January, **Bun Pha Wet**, which commemorates the Jataka tale of the Buddha's second-to-last incarnation as Pha Wet, or Prince Vessantara, takes place at local monasteries. In larger towns, expect live bands and dancing.

Getting involved

Visitors are most likely to encounter the festivals of the Buddhist **lowland Lao**. On certain Buddhist holy days, the faithful **make merit** by walking clockwise around a stupa or a *sim* three times while holding offerings of incense, lotus blossoms and candles in a prayer-like gesture. Visitors are free to take part in this picturesque ritual, called *wian thian* in Lao, and may even be encouraged to do so. Hill-tribe festivals are less open to outsider participation. If you do happen to come across one, watch from a distance and do not interfere unless it is clear that you are being invited to join in.

3000K), situated in a roundabout at the end of Lane Xang Avenue, was built in the late 1950s to commemorate casualties of war on the side of the Royal Lao Government. The structure, said to have been completed with concrete donated by the US government for the construction of an airport, has been jokingly referred to as "the vertical runway". If the story is true, then Patouxai is also the most notable structure left to show for the millions of dollars of aid that were pumped into Laos during the early years of American involvement in Indochina. After the revolution, the arch was given its current name, which literally means "Victory Gate", and partially redecorated – some Hindu iconography symbolic of the defunct Lao monarchy was chipped away – so the communists could feel more comfortable with this behemoth reminder of the detested royalists in their midst.

Patouxai is best visited in the early morning before the structure has had time to absorb much heat from the sun's rays. A handful of vendors selling souvenirs and refreshments are sheltered by a ceiling adorned with **reliefs** of the Hindu deities – Rahu devouring the sun, Vishnu, Brahma, and Indra on Airavata, the three-headed elephant. Decorating the walls just below the ceiling are characters from the Ramayana. Up close, the structure looks somewhat crude and unfinished, but the **view** of Vientiane from the top is worth the climb. Halfway up, in a dingy two-storey hallway, there's a market selling textiles, T-shirts and tourist trinkets.

That Luang

One and a half kilometres east of Patouxai stands the Buddhist stupa, **That Luang** (daily except Mon & public holidays 8am–noon & 1–4pm; 5000K), Laos's most important religious building and its national symbol. The present building dates from the 1930s and is a reconstruction; the original That Luang is thought to have been built by King Setthathilat in the mid-sixteenth century, and it is his statue that is perched jauntily on a pedestal in front of the stupa.

Archeological evidence suggests that, like most central and southern Lao Buddhist structures of significance, That Luang was built on top of an ancient Khmer site. What the original Buddhist stupa looked like is a mystery, but a Dutch trader, Gerrit van Wuysthoff, who visited Vientiane in 1641, left an awestruck account of the gold-covered "pyramid" he saw there. Between then and the early nineteenth century, the stupa was embellished and restored periodically, but this ceased after the 1828 Siamese raid which left the capital deserted. When French explorers Francis Garnier and Louis Delaporte stumbled upon That Luang in 1867, it was overgrown by jungle, but still largely intact. A few years later, Chinese-led bandits plundered the stupa looking for gold, and left it a pile of rubble. A photo on display in the National Museum, taken in the late 1800s to commemorate the visit of a group of Frenchmen, gives some indication of the extent of the devastation.

A French attempt at **restoration** was made in 1900, after which the stupa was disparagingly referred to as the "Morin Spike", a snipe at the architect, whose idea of a Buddhist stupa resembled a railroad spike turned on its head. Dissatisfaction with the design eventually led to another attempt in the 1930s. Using sketches done by Delaporte as a model, a re-restoration in brick and stucco was carried out over four years, and what you see today are the results of this effort.

The tapering **golden spire** of the main stupa is 45m tall and rests on a plinth of stylized lotus petals, which crowns a mound reminiscent of the first-century BC Buddhist stupa at Sanchi, India. The main stupa is surrounded on all sides by a total of thirty short, spiky stupas, which can be reached via any of four gates in the crenellated walls that support the monument. The whole is in turn surrounded by a cloistered wall, vaguely Chinese in style. Within the **cloisters** is a collection of very worn Buddha images, some of which may have been enshrined in the original Khmer

Nong Chanh Water Park

A good, half-day escape from the tropical heat is the new **Nong Chanh Water Park**, 500m east of the Morning Market on Khou Vieng Road (entry 10,000K, plus 30,000K for a slide pass). There are three waterslides, a handful of cafés, plus the obligatory lazy river. Don't expect the glitz of water parks in Bali or Thailand, though – this place really isn't in the same league.

temple that once occupied the site. Until just a few years ago, only the stupas' spires were "gilded", but with the passing years, more and more gold paint has been applied, so that now even the inner walls and their crenellations are gold. The effect is best seen just before sunset or during the evenings leading up to the **That Luang Festival** (see *Festivals* colour section), when the stupa is festooned with strings of lights, and moths the size of sparrows circle and cling to its glowing surface.

Wat Sok Pa Luang

The majority of Vientiane's most famous temples are found close to the Mekong – there are twenty temples between the riverbank and the length of Setthathilat Road from Wat Simuang to Wat Tainiai, an area that roughly corresponds to the old city. That said, there are over a dozen other temples scattered across the city in an east–west arc to the north that seldom see any tourists, and which make a great excuse for a bicycle ride through Vientiane's quiet outer neighbourhoods.

One example of a worthwhile outlying temple is **Wat Sok Pa Luang**, famous for its **herbal sauna** and **traditional massage**. Originally outside the city limits and surrounded by forest, the wat now lies approximately 3km southeast of central Vientiane in a suburb that spreads out from the highway south to the village of Thadua. The easiest way to get here is by tuk-tuk (15,000K). Wood-fired saunas envelope bathers in clouds of healing steam; impurities are sweated out and the vapours of medicinal herbs soak in. Traditional Lao massage is available as well and is said to interact with the effects of the sauna. Visitors should dress modestly and bring a sarong to wear into the sauna. A soak in the sauna is $1, and $3 pays for forty minutes of massage. You can also join the meditation sessions that take place here at 4pm on Saturdays.

Shopping

Around twenty years ago, immediately after Laos opened its doors to visitors, bargain-hunting in Vientiane was an experience. Capitalism had been stifled for over a decade, and in the Morning Market and the handful of shops around town, antique textiles and silver could be had for a song, while staples such as rice and cooking oil were unbelievably expensive. The situation has since stabilized and Vientiane's merchants now know the correct value of antiques and handicrafts.

Vientiane's **Morning Market** (Talat Sao) is the best place to begin a shopping tour of the capital. Outside, there are still covered shop stalls selling Chinese electronics and cheap consumer goods, but most of these have been swallowed up by the ugly new **Talat Sao Mall**, which houses a variety of shops, restaurants and cafés. The "real" market round the back of the mall is a good place to start when it comes to homespun cotton clothing and handicrafts. Most of the other textile, souvenir and antique shops are found on **Samsenthai** and **Setthathilat roads** and along the lanes running between them.

Vientiane's other markets are either "wet" markets selling produce, "dry" markets selling manufactured goods, or, more commonly, a mixture of both.

Other significant markets close to the centre include Talat Khouadin, Talat Dong Palane, Talat Nongduang and Talat Thong Khan Kham.

Antiques and reproductions

Antique shops can be found in the Morning Market and elsewhere in the centre of Vientiane. As ever, virtually all metal images or figurines of Buddhist or Hindu deities are reproductions from Thailand and Cambodia, though vendors won't admit this. **Opium weights**, usually seen in antique stores but also found in upscale textile shops, are priced at levels way out of line when compared to the rest of Laos, with merchants asking two to five times more for weights than their counterparts in Luang Prabang and the other provinces. Reproduction **opium pipes** can be found in the antique shops on Samsenthai Road. The cheapest are gaudy things made in Vietnam from tusk-shaped bone, but if you look patiently you may come across bamboo and brass or silver pipes made locally by a couple of craftsmen who are the sole remaining pipemakers in Southeast Asia. Local pipes may go for as much as $100, but newly made Vietnamese pipes can be bought for as little as $10.

Books

Monument Books (☎021/243708) on Nokeo Koummane Road, opposite Carol Cassidy Lao Textiles, sells Vientiane's largest selection of **English-language books.** It also offers a subscription service for glossy magazines, and a wide range of detailed maps. If you're looking for books with added feel-good factor, check out Book Café on Heng Boun Road. The small, English-owned shop has a whole section devoted to novels set in Laos – and the proceeds from some books go to victims of UXO.

Rattan, wicker and bamboo

Check the antique stores of the Morning Market and the downtown area for old or rare **baskets** made by the tribal peoples of Laos, which can sell for as much as $200. Sticky rice baskets and mats costing $1–3 can be found on market stalls near Talat Sao bus station.

Textiles

Once a tremendous bargain, antique Lao weavings are now more expensive in Vientiane than in Thailand. If you're determined to buy **old textiles** in Vientiane, the Morning Market is your best bet. **New textiles**, however, are another matter. Lao silk and cotton textiles can be purchased in bolts of plain coloured cloth or as ready-made clothing for $2–5 per item. If you're looking to make a smart purchase without shelling out too much cash, Lao shoulder bags, or *nyam*, are a cheap and functional choice. Hand-woven *pha biang*, a long, scarf-like textile, can be found in a wide variety of colours and patterns, and chequered *pha khao ma*, the knee-length men's sarong, are also good buys. The Morning Market has the best selection; the merchants here are used to foreign tourists and enjoy a spirited haggle.

Aside from the markets, Vientiane boasts an increasing number of upmarket **shops** and **boutiques** carrying, and sometimes specializing in, Lao textiles. They often have the best range and most attractively displayed products and, unsurprisingly, the highest prices. Most of these new boutiques and galleries are located **south of Samsenthai Road** between Khoun Boulom and Manthatoulat roads and can be taken in during a single, short walking tour. Perhaps the most impressive of these boutiques is Carol Cassidy Lao Textiles (☎021/212123 ⓦwww.laotextiles .com), housed in a French-era mansion on Nokeo Koummane Road, which produces hand-woven wall hangings tinted with natural dyes under the supervision of an

American designer. Other top-drawer places include Satri Lao Silk, 79/4 Setthathilat Rd (☎021/219295); Lao Gallery, Nokeo Koummane Road (☎021/212943), and T'Shop Lai Gallery, Inpeng Road (☎021/223178, ✉info@artisanslao.com).

Woodcarving

Unlike Chiang Mai in Thailand, Vientiane is not a centre of **woodcarving** and the merchandise on offer tends to be crudely carved and garishly lacquered. An exception is the handicrafts of the T'Shop Lai Gallery on Inpeng Road next to *Le Vendôme* restaurant, which specializes in unique mosaics and other handicrafts made from coconut shell. Prices are fixed, though, and certainly not cheap. Also worth a look is Sada Handicraft, opposite Wat Inpeng on Setthathilat Road, which offers discounts on larger items.

Eating

The **culinary scene** in Vientiane caters to virtually every taste, from sausage and sauerkraut to Korean BBQ. Vientiane also has a large concentration of French and Italian restaurants, the best of which compare favourably to those in Bangkok. If you plan to head out to the remote provinces for a while, take the opportunity to indulge in the capital's Western culinary offerings before hitting the trail.

For cheap eats, the zone around Heng Boun and Khoun Boulom roads is home to a good night market (see below), *mi pét* (duck noodle) restaurants, fruit stands and French bread vendors, and don't miss the ice cream and pastry shops of Chao Anou Road, between Setthathilat and Heng Boun roads.

Food stalls and markets

For cheap, home-style cooking, seek out the outdoor **food stalls** found near any of the city's markets. Riverside food stalls can be found along the Mekong on Fa Ngum Road approximately opposite Wat Chanthabouli, with most offering Lao staples like *tam màk hung* (spicy papaya salad), *pîng kai* (grilled chicken) and refreshing fruit shakes from morning until nearly midnight. These stalls also provide an excellent spot to enjoy sunset over the Mekong.

A **night market** offering similar fare, and with tables on the street, sets up on Khoun Boulom Road and along Heng Boun Road in the early evening and stays open till about 10pm for cheap Chinese, Lao and Vietnamese food with several *fõe* (noodle soup) stalls. A more extensive night market for good Lao food is at **Dong Palane Market** on Dong Palane Road near Wat Ban Fai – you'll find all the Lao standards on offer. For daytime food, try the **market stalls** on Mahosot Road near the bus station: here you'll find good Lao-style *khào pûn* (noodles with sauce), *tam màk hung* and excellent shakes.

Crusty **baguettes** (*khào ji*) are a speciality of Vientiane, and vendors selling these French-inspired loaves, plain or filled with Lao-style pâté, can be found around downtown.

Minimarkets and wine shops

For many travellers, especially Europeans, one of the great pleasures of returning to Vientiane after a long journey upcountry is the availability of cheeses, wine and other imported goods to accompany those crusty baguettes which are a speciality of the capital. There are several **minimarkets** where you can stock up. Maningom Supermarket (corner of Khoun Boulom and Heng Boun), Riverside Minimarket

(Fa Ngum Rd, near the *Orchid Guesthouse*) and Phimphone Minimarket (with outlets on Samsenthai Rd and Setthathilat Rd) all have a selection of cheeses, wine, imported beer and chocolate, as well as imported body-care products you won't be able to find elsewhere in Laos. The best selections of **wine** in Laos can be found at Vinothèque La Cave and VanSom, both on Samsenthai Road, opposite the *Asia Pavilion Hotel*. At either shop it's possible to find a perfectly drinkable bottle of red or white for around $10.

Bakeries and cafés

The legacy of the French is most deliciously apparent in the range of **cafés** and **bakeries** that crop up all over town. The **coffee** served at these places varies, with some offering Lao coffee and some using imported beans. Cafés and bakeries tend to open early and close by 7pm. At a good café on Setthathilat Road you'll pay $3 for a **breakfast** special such as coffee and a couple of croissants. **Brunch buffets** are on offer at the big international-style hotels like *Novotel* and *Lao Hotel Plaza* for roughly $10.

All the places below appear on the "Central Vientiane" map, pp.68–69.

JoMa Bakery Setthathilat Rd, just west of Nam Phou. This Canadian-owned café is Vientiane's answer to the big western coffee chains – right down to the free wi-fi – and its decent breakfasts will set you up nicely for a day of tramping around town. The salads are good too, if a little pricey. Look out for other branches in Luang Prabang and at the Nong Chanh Water Park.

Le Croissant d'Or 96/1 Nokeo Koummane Rd, opposite Wat Mixay. Start your day the Parisian way at this French-style café. You can wolf down reasonably priced pastries and pies in the leafy outdoor seating area.

Scandinavian Bakery Nam Phou. Vientiane's most popular bakery makes huge sandwiches and a wide selection of pastries and doughnuts. It's a relatively expensive place to stop for a snack, but if you get a table out front and the sun isn't too hot, it's a great place to laze away the morning reading and sipping. Great coffee.

Sinouk Coffee Talat Sao Mall, Lane Xang Avenue. A fashionable little place on the edge of the Morning Market serving coffee from its own plantation on the Bolaven Plateau. If you've got time to kill before you catch your bus (and a taste for something new), try the green tea latte. There's another branch in Pakse.

True Coffee Setthathilat Rd, next door to *Sabaidy Guesthouse*. City-sized, American-style café serving all the usual caffeine kicks plus some interesting variations such as English toffee latte and choc-chip twist coffee. There are 10 Skype-ready computers inside, with internet access available by the hour.

Restaurants

Most of Vientiane's **restaurants** open for lunch and then again for dinner, but no-frills places usually stay open throughout the day, closing around 9pm. In most Western restaurants you'll pay on average $4 for each course, and even in more upmarket restaurants you'll rarely spend more than $15 unless you get into the wine.

The restaurants reviewed below are subdivided for convenience into "Asian" and "Western" places, but Laos isn't a place for culinary purism, and thus many supposedly Asian places do offer Western snacks and light meals, while even the fancier, supposedly Western, restaurants often have a Lao noodle dish or two lurking in the menu.

All the restaurants below are on the "Central Vientiane" map, pp.76–77, unless otherwise specified.

Asian

Dok Champa Chao Anou Rd, near Wat Chanthabouli ☏021/251739. Great range of cheap Lao, Korean and Western dishes. The tables, in a quiet garden courtyard, are just a short walk from the main river road. Good value.

Lotus Nokeo Koummane Rd, just across from *Xayoh*, facing the Lao National Cultural Hall. A huge selection of inexpensive Asian dishes, from Indian curries to local noodle soups, and a pleasant outside seating area. The buffet lunch (10.30am–2pm; $2) is excellent value.

Makphet Behind Wat Ong Teu, south of Setthathilat Rd ☏021/260587. Upscale, not-for-profit restaurant on a quiet backstreet in the centre of town offering a modern take on classic Lao dishes. The place is run by former street kids who were trained up for the job. Hugely popular, especially with business crowds, and it's not unusual for all the tables to be full, even at lunchtime. Bookings advised.

Nazim Fa Ngum Rd. Inexpensive Indian restaurant facing the river, with indoor and outdoor seating. Strong on vegetarian dishes and immensely popular with backpackers. It's so packed most evenings that the whole pavement is taken over by its tables.

Nos Sushi Heng Boun Rd, just west of the Green Discovery head office ☏021/265000. Vientiane's stylish new sushi joint is all brushed steel and blue lights, spinning out well-presented fish favourites from a jam-packed menu. Busy most evenings.

Taj Mahal Off Nokeo Koummane Rd, behind the Lao National Cultural Hall ☏020/511003. By far and away the best – and most popular – Indian restaurant in town. It might not have the glossy veneer of Vientiane's more expensive restaurants, but the steady stream of punters in such a quiet street is testament to the quality and value of the food here. Recommended.

Thonglor Fa Ngum Rd. Fill yourself to the brim without busting the budget at this busy haunt on the edge of the Mekong. Lao and Thai dishes are the top picks, and the chef can turn out veggie versions of most dishes on request. The green curry is ludicrously spicy.

Western

Blue Bananas Samsenthai Rd, ☏021/219732. Run by British golf coach Simon Ward, *Blue Bananas* is renowned for its tasty pies with mashed potatoes and onion gravy. A popular hangout for homesick expats, the skinny blue building also has a decent-sized bar area at the front.

Daofa Setthathilat Rd, next door to *JoMa Bakery*. Serves up a hearty selection of western staples like steak, pizza and pasta. Keep your eye out for the little tabletop menus, which feature eight different types of delicious garlic bread. Nightly discounts on cocktails 6–9pm.

La Terrasse Nokeo Koummane Rd, near Wat Mixai ☏021/218550. Fills its tables by offering outstanding steaks, pizzas, Mexican food and salads at prices lower than most of the other Western joints. Seating in a covered courtyard or chic bar/dining area. There's no dessert menu as such, but the chiller cabinet inside is chock-full of treats. Highly recommended. Closed Sun.

Le Belle Epoque 6 Pangkham Rd, in the *Settha Palace Hotel*. The classiest act in town, serving French food in an elegant dining room. There is nowhere else in Vientiane even remotely like this. Even if you don't dine here, you can have a drink at the bar and soak up the colonial atmosphere.

Le Central Setthathilat Rd, opposite Wat Ong Teu. Reasonably priced pizza, chicken, pasta, salads and sandwiches. White tablecloths and proper cloth napkins add a touch of class to the deal, and the $15 set menu, which features three courses, is decent value. Daily 11.30am–2pm & 6.30–10pm.

Le Provençal Nam Phou. Cosy little French place by the fountain that just oozes charm. The pizza is first-rate, and there's a good selection of wine available by the carafe or bottle. Open daily.

Le Silapa 17/1 Sihom Rd, west of the petrol station, see map, p.68 ☏021/219689. French-managed restaurant serving French food (by a French chef) in a beautifully restored colonial shophouse. One of Vientiane's most expensive choices, but the lunchtime set menu (three courses; $12) is a definite winner. Daily except Sun 11.30am–2pm & 6–10pm.

Nam Phu Nam Phou. Gourmet delights like pâté and Camembert cheese feature high on the menu at this French hideaway next to the Nam Phou fountain. The outside seating area, shaded by lofty trees, is big enough to attract a decent crowd some evenings.

Swedish Pizza & Baking House Chao Anou Rd, near the corner with Samsenthai Rd ☏021/215705. Immensely popular bakery serving scrumptious pizzas and good, healthy salads. The chocolate milkshakes are sublime. One of the few consistently busy places in this part of town. Delivery available.

Vista François Ngin Rd ☏021/213576. If you're lured in by the big shady seating area out front, be sure to try the excellent sandwiches. The delicious waffles, pastries and ice creams also justify a visit. wi-fi, plus internet and massage rooms upstairs.

Xayoh Corner of Samsenthai and Nokeo Koummane, facing the Lao National Cultural Hall. One of Vientiane's most reliable restaurants, serving pizzas and salads as well as very cold beer. There's another branch in Vang Vieng.

Drinking, nightlife and entertainment

Many of the **nightclubs** are Japanese-style, with costumed pop singers, dim lighting, hostesses and deep couches, though they're fairly innocuous. The city's larger hotels often have nightspots like this; the one in the *Novotel* is a decent choice. As you might expect, many of these clubs also feature **karaoke** lounges.

Of more interest to Western visitors, a number of **clubs** playing Thai pop and international dance mixes, and catering to well-heeled teenagers, have cropped up along Luang Prabang Avenue, just beyond the *Novotel*. Smaller clubs are sometimes able to bend the rules more and go until the wee hours depending on the political climate. There's usually no cover charge, but if there is it will include a bottle of Beer Lao. Vientiane's **live music** scene is largely derivative, with popular taste being overwhelmed by a flood of Made-in-Thailand pop churned out by the massive music industry across the river.

Bars and clubs

Broadway *Lao Plaza Hotel*, Samsenthai Rd. The dance club in the *Plaza's* basement has been eclipsed by the club at the *Novotel*, but this means that there's less chance of seeing a fight on the dancefloor. There are deep plush sofas to sink into and black lights to make your gin and tonic glow a pale shade of blue.

D-Tech Club *Novotel*, Luang Prabang Ave. Locals and well-to-do hotel guests vie for space on the dancefloor at this weekend favourite tucked away behind the *Novotel's* tennis courts. A five-minute tuk-tuk ride from the bars of Nam Phou.

Jazzy Brick Nam Phou. Don't worry if it's quiet downstairs; this uber-cool jazz bar usually fills up from the top. There's a well-stocked bar, a cocktail list to die for, and a clutch of old-fashioned electrical appliances hanging from the walls, making the vibe more New Orleans than Vientiane.

Khop Chai Deu Nam Phou. This big, French-period house on the corner of Nam Phou is by far the most popular hangout for foreign tourists. Downstairs in the patio bar you can get cheap pitchers of draught beer; up the big spiral staircase you'll find another very pleasant bar on the roof. You can eat here, too – the mixed menu has reasonable Lao and Indian dishes, though the *falang* food (and service) is a bit hit and miss. The most fun place in town.

Meena Thadua Rd, 3km east of centre. When you tire of the inner-city venues, make the 6km trek east to *Meena*, one of the few big discos that has managed to survive sporadic government crackdowns. The deafening Thai hits attract a young local crowd.

On The Rock Just north of Souphanouvong Rd. Quite a jaunt from the centre of town, so you may need to take a tuk-tuk, but worth the effort if you're craving a bit of live music. Expect competent covers washed down with plenty of Beer Lao.

Sticky Fingers François Nginn Rd. With a pleasant outdoor seating area opposite the *Tai Pan* hotel, this small Australian-run bar has picked up a loyal following among expats. A good crowd is almost guaranteed between 6–8pm on

Beer with a view

Vientiane's location along an east–west stretch of the Mekong makes for spectacular **sunsets**, with the fiery orb lighting up the water before slowly descending into Thailand. Taking advantage of this backdrop, makeshift **stalls** selling bottles of Beer Lao and fruit shakes set up along the pavement on Fa Ngum Road opposite Wat Chanthabouli from afternoon till early evening. If you're looking for something even closer to the water and away from the bustle of the city centre, continue west along Fa Ngum Road, where for the next 2km you'll find a long row of over twenty **beer gardens** with wooden terraces overhanging the riverbank. These laidback, open-air venues offering cheap pitchers of golden "Fresh Beer" (*bia sót*) under a thatch roof define the quintessential Vientiane pub experience. The largest and fanciest of these are all in the vicinity of the *Riverview Hotel*.

Wednesdays and Fridays, when the famously good cocktails are half-price.
The Spirit House Fa Ngum Rd, right next to the *Beau Rivage Mekong*. Well-off travellers flock to *The Spirit House* for delectable cocktails (made with hearty 50ml measures) and a splendid riverfront ambience. One of the classiest places to watch the sun set over Thailand.

Cultural entertainment

Four hundred and fifty years after superseding Luang Prabang as the centre of political power, Vientiane still lacks the natural **cultural life** of the old royal capital, but a few venues offer a taste of Laos's heritage, even if just for the entertainment of foreigners. The **Lao National Theatre** on Manthatoulat Road near Wat Xieng Nyeun has performances featuring lowland Lao music, dance and even a mock wedding ceremony. Also colourful are lowland renditions of the music and dance of the hill-tribe peoples. While the costumes and numbers aren't always strictly traditional, the enthusiasm of the performers compensates. Shows are nightly at 8.30pm, except the third Sunday of every month, and cost $7 for adults and $4 for children under 12. Further north, on Khoun Boulom Road, the **Lao National Opera Theatre** (☎021/260300) presents Lao boxing dances (a kind of combat-free dance based around the martial art), masked plays and scenes from the Ramayana between 7 and 8.30pm on Tuesdays, Thursdays and Saturdays.

Moving on from Vientiane

Lao Airlines operates several domestic **flights** out of Vientiane, for details of which, see "Travel details", p.110. International flights from Vientiane include Lao Airlines' services to Bangkok and Chiang Mai, Hanoi, Phnom Penh and Siem Reap.

Buses

The situation regarding bus-stop locations and departure times can only be described as chaotic. Painfully slow local **buses** heading to points **south** leave from the Talat Sao bus station, adjacent to the Morning Market. If you spend a bit more and get an a/c VIP bus to southern destinations (book a day ahead with your guesthouse) such as Thakek, Savannakhet and Pakse, you'll leave from the southern bus station, 9km northeast of the centre on Route 13. It's also possible to charter a twelve-seater a/c minibus to points south from Boualian Lao Travel Company (☎021/219649, see p.91). Buses to the **north** and northeast leave from the northern bus station (Khiw Lot Khoua Luang in Lao) near the Evening Market (sometimes called Nongduang Market or Talat Laeng) on Talat Nongduang Road, 2km northwest of the city centre. Note that you generally have to go first to Luang Prabang and find buses onward from Luang Prabang's northern bus station.

To the Friendship Bridge: Bus #14 departs every 15 minutes from the Talat Sao bus station; a much, much faster alternative is to take a taxi from the lot at the southeast corner of the Morning Market ($10) or charter a tuk-tuk ($8).

To Nong Khai and Udon Thani: Direct buses to Nong Khai and Udon Thani in Thailand are mostly used by Lao and Vientiane-based expats to make shopping runs to Udon, but they are also a convenient way to get over the Friendship Bridge without having to change vehicles. Six buses leave daily for both destinations (roughly every two hours between 7.30am and 6pm) from Talat Sao bus station. From Nong Khai, overnight buses and trains to **Bangkok** leave between 6 and 8pm. If you intend to catch the train, get a taxi to the Friendship Bridge in time for the 5pm rail crossing into Thailand – see p.70 for details.

Vientiane's grassroots cultural life only really reawakens during **festivals**. The best time to get a taste of Lao music is in November during the **That Luang Festival** (see *Festivals* colour section), when the nation's best singers and musicians are featured in a string of performances during the two weeks leading up to the festival.

Listings

Airlines Lao Airlines, Pangkham Rd ☎021/212057, or at the airport ☎021/512000; Thai Airways, Luang Prabang Ave ☎021/222527; Vietnam Airlines, Samsenthai Rd, mezzanine floor of the *Lao Plaza Hotel* ☎021/217562. The Bangkok Airways office is in Luang Prabang, see p.141.
American Express Their representative agent in Laos is Diethelm Travel, on the corner of Setthathilat Rd and Nam Phou (☎021/213833).
Banks and exchange Banks, hotels, guesthouses and shopkeepers all over downtown Vientiane will happily exchange foreign currency. Thai and Lao banks, many of which are located along Lane Xang Ave, can cash travellers' cheques, but a more convenient option for tourists is bank exchange booths, which can be found on Samsenthai Rd as well as on Fa Ngum Rd by the *Lane Xang Hotel*. There are also exchange booths at the Friendship Bridge and the airport. Banque pour le Commerce Extérieur Lao (BCEL), Pangkham Rd, has the best exchange rates and the widest range of services, including changing travellers' cheques into US

To Luang Prabang: Buses north and northeast to Luang Prabang, Phonsavan and Xam Nua leave from the northern bus station. There is also an a/c tourist coach ($15) between Vientiane and Luang Prabang which departs up to three times daily, depending on the season, and can be booked through most guesthouses.

To Vang Vieng: Six government buses ($4) depart from the Talat Sao bus station every day between 7am and 2pm; much more comfortable is the VIP minibus that leaves *Sabaidy Guesthouse* at 10am each morning ($5).

To Vietnam: Daily buses for Hanoi leave from the southern bus station at 7pm, and should arrive in Hanoi 24 hours later. Expect to pay around $25 for the long, uncomfortable journey. There are also daily buses to Vinh, Hue and Da Nang at the same time, but buses to Saigon only run on Mondays, Wednesdays and Fridays. Departure times change frequently, so check before you travel.

Sawngthaews

The main staging area for **sawngthaews** and unmetered **taxis** is the big car park at the southeast corner of the Morning Market just opposite the bus station. Here you'll find both shared sawngthaews for towns around the Vientiane Plain, and vehicles for hire. North of town, about 8km up Route 13, there is a second bus lot for sawngthaews heading north towards Vang Vieng, with departures every thirty minutes until late afternoon.

Boats

There are now only very infrequent boat services to the **northwest** and **north**; most people take the bus nowadays. When they do run, speedboats and slow boats leave from Tha Hua Kao Liaw pier, on the Mekong River 10km west of the centre of Vientiane; tuk-tuks there from the centre cost 60,000K. You will have to make a trip out here to inquire if any boats will be departing soon. By slow boat it takes three days to get to Luang Prabang. There's also an outside chance of catching a speedboat to Paklai, 217km upriver from Vientiane, which costs around $20 per person (or you could charter one for $100).

dollars and dollar cash advances on Visa; for Mastercard head to Siam Commercial Bank, Lane Xang Ave.

Bicycle rental Bicycles are available at rental shops and some guesthouses for $1/day (you'll need to leave a driving licence or cash as a deposit). There are dozens of places to choose from, but Boualian Lao Travel on Samsenthai Rd (℡021/213061) has one of the better selections in town.

Car rental Europcar (℡021/223867, ⊚www.avr.laopdr.com) and Boualian Lao Travel (℡021/213061) both on Samsenthai Rd. Many guesthouses and hotels can make car-rental arrangements that may be cheaper than agencies.

Courier services DHL Worldwide Express ℡021/214868 or 216830; UPS ℡021/314524.

Embassies and consulates Australia, Thadua Rd ℡021/353800 ℻353801; Canada, c/o embassy in Bangkok ℡+66 2/636 0540; Cambodia, near That Khao, Thadua Rd ℡021/314952; China, near Wat Nak Noi, Wat Nak Noi Rd ℡021/315100; Indonesia, Phon Kheng Rd, Ban Phon Sa-at ℡021/413909 or 413910; Ireland, c/o embassy in Kuala Lumpur ℡+60 3/2161 2963; Malaysia, Singha Rd ℡021/414205 or 414206; Myanmar (Burma), Sok Pa Luang Rd ℡021/314910; New Zealand, c/o embassy in Bangkok ℡+66 2 254 2530; Philippines, Unit 18, Ban Sibounheuang ℡021/452490; Singapore, Thadua Rd ℡021/353939; Thailand (visa section), across from the Lao National Tourism Administration building, Lane Xang Ave ℡021/214582; UK ℡021/413606, but most enquiries should go to the embassy in Bangkok ℡+66 2/305 8333; United States, near That Dam, Bartholonie Rd ℡021/267000; Vietnam, near Wat Phaxai, That Luang Rd ℡021/413400–4.

Emergencies Dial ℡190 in case of fire, ℡195 for an ambulance, or ℡191 for police.

Health clubs *Tai-Pan Hotel*, François Ngin Rd ($7.50/day); *Lao Plaza Hotel*, Samsenthai Rd ($15/day).

Hospitals and clinics Australian Clinic, Thadua Rd, in the Australian Embassy building ℡021/353840 (weekdays only); French Clinic, Khou Vieng Rd, ℡021/214150; International Clinic, Mahosot Hospital Compound, Fa Ngum Rd ℡021/214022 (open 24hr); Mahosot Hospital, Mahosot Rd ℡021/214018.

Immigration department Hatsady Rd, not far from the tourist office ℡021/212520 (Mon & Wed–Sat 8–11.30am & 2–4.30pm).

Internet access *True Coffee*, Setthathilat Rd, has the fastest computers in town (8000K per hour), but there are dozens of smaller internet cafés dotted all around the city, each charging around 200K a minute and closing at about 10pm.

Language courses Centre de Langue Française, Lane Xang Ave ℡021/215764. Short-term courses and private tutorials are available, including a 50-hour introduction to the Lao language.

Laundry Most hotels and guesthouses will wash clothes for you; a faster and cheaper alternative is one of the laundries on Heng Boun Rd, near the corner with Chao Anou Rd.

Massage and herbal sauna Ajan Amphone, tucked away behind Wat Chanthabouli on Fa Ngum Rd, offers massage at $3/hr, and a sauna for $1 (Mon–Fri 2–5pm, Sat & Sun 10am–7pm); slightly classier is Champa Spa (two branches on Pangkham Rd), which offers an extensive range of massages from $7.50/hr.

Motorbike rental Rental motorbikes in Vientiane are mostly secondhand 100cc step-throughs like the Honda Dream, imported from Thailand. The asking price is usually around $10 a day, depending on how new the bike looks, but it's possible to bargain this down to $8 a day, especially if you want it for a few days. The *Douang Deuane Hotel*, Nokeo Koummane Rd (℡021/222301–3) and Boualian Lao Travel Company, 346 Samsenthai Rd (℡021/213061), both have small fleets of Honda Dreams. For something quirky, try Jules Classic Rental, Setthathilat Rd (℡020/7600813, ⊚www.bike-rental-laos.com), which has Vespa Sprints ($10) and Suzuki Van Vans ($25) for rent.

Newspapers The *Vientiane Times* is sold at the big hotels and most minimarkets; the *Bangkok Post* is usually available at the Phimphone minimarket on Samsenthai Rd from 4pm.

Pharmacies The best pharmacies are on Mahosot Rd, north of the Talat Sao bus station.

Post office The GPO is located on the corner of Khou Vieng Rd and Lane Xang Ave (Mon–Fri 8am–5pm, Sat 8am–4pm, Sun 8am–noon), opposite the Morning Market. The poste restante counter will hold mail for up to three months with a minimal charge. There's also a counter selling stamps.

Swimming *Tai-Pan Hotel*, Fa Ngum Rd ($7.50/day, including access to the fitness centre); *Lao Plaza Hotel*, Samsenthai Rd ($10); *Lane Xang Hotel*, Fa Ngum Rd ($4); Sok Pa Luang swimming pool, Sok Pa Luang Rd ($1).

Tailors Several good tailors have set up along Pangkham Rd, just north of the fountain. Expect to pay around $150 for a made-to-measure suit.

Telephone services The Telecom office, on the corner of Setthathilat and Chantha Khoumane roads (daily 7am–10pm), handles international calls and faxes; you can place calls through the operators inside or use their card phones just out front. IDD calls can be made from most hotels, and Skype is available at almost every internet café.

Travel/tour agencies Beside the companies listed in Basics on p.31, you can also contact Boualian Lao Travel Company, 346 Samsenthai Rd (℡021/213061); Green Discovery, Setthathilat Rd (℡021/264528 ⓦ www.greendiscoverylaos.com) or Lao Travel Service, Lane Xang Ave (℡021/216603–4).

Visa services Boualian Lao Travel Company (see above) can arrange visas for Vietnam, Cambodia, Thailand and China, as well as Lao visa extensions ($2/day). The proprietor, Mrs Boualian Dangmani, a Vietnamese–Lao, is sharp as a tack and speaks fluent English, French, Vietnamese, Thai and Lao. For visa extensions, see "Immigration department", p.90.

Excursions from Vientiane

If you need a break from Vientiane or have time to kill while your visa is being processed, it's easy enough to get out of the city in under an hour, and shuttle around the expansive Vientiane Plain by public transport or on a private tour. The most popular destination for a half-day jaunt is the other-worldly **Buddha Park**, southeast of town, while those who have never seen a "Buddha's footprint" might consider travelling further east to **Wat Phabat Phonsan**. North of the capital, the huge **Ang Nam Ngum Reservoir** is a pleasant retreat for boating, fishing and swimming, with scores of islands to explore, as well as a casino. At the southern edge of the reservoir is the vast **Phou Khao Khouay NBCA**, which can be visited on an adventure tour from the capital. Downstream on the Nam Ngum River, **Ban Pako** is an eco-tourism lodge that makes a fine day-trip, though most visitors end up staying on to relax for a few days, visiting country villages and exploring nature trails. Of the two state-sanctioned tourist destinations on the edge of the city, the **National Ethnic Cultural Park** and the **Kaysone Memorial Museum**, the latter is the more worthwhile, making an interesting diversion into the personality cults surrounding communist leaders.

Buddha Park and National Ethnic Cultural Park

Situated some 25km southeast of downtown Vientiane on the Mekong River, Xieng Khuan or the "**Buddha Park**" (daily 8am–5pm; 5000K, plus 3000K for cameras) is surely Laos's quirkiest attraction – a tacky tourist trap to some travellers, one of the most interesting sights in Vientiane to others. This collection of massive ferro-concrete sculptures, dotted around a wide riverside meadow, was created under the direction of Luang Pou Bounleua Soulilat, a self-styled holy man who claimed to have been the disciple of a cave-dwelling Hindu hermit in Vietnam. Upon returning to Laos, Bounleua began the sculpture garden in the late 1950s as a means of spreading his philosophy of life and his ideas about the cosmos. After the revolution, Bounleua was forced to flee across the Mekong to Nong Khai, Thailand, where he established an even more elaborate version of his philosophy in concrete. Ironically, the Lao National Tourism Authority chose Bounleua's sculptures as the symbol of their "Visit Laos Year" campaign, and posters depicting the exiled guru's works can be seen in government offices throughout the country.

Besides the brontosaurian reclining Buddha that dominates the park, there are statues of every conceivable deity in the Hindu-Buddhist pantheon and even a handful of personalities from the old regime. Near the park's entrance is a strange edifice that resembles a giant pumpkin with a dead tree sprouting from its crown. Entering the structure through the gaping maw of devouring time, you can explore representations of the "three planes of existence": hell, earth and heaven.

A spiral stairway leads to the roof of the building, which affords good views of the park and river.

Bus #14 from Vientiane's main bus station (every 15min) stops outside the Buddha Park. Alternatively, get a shared tuk-tuk from the stand near the Morning Market to Thadua, and then charter a tuk-tuk for the remaining 3km to the park. Easiest is to charter a tuk-tuk for the round trip (around $10, including a 2hr wait).

National Ethnic Cultural Park and Beer Lao factory

En route to the Buddha Park you'll pass the **National Ethnic Cultural Park** (daily 8am–6pm; 5000K), some 18km from the capital. This is Laos's answer to the tour-the-country-in-one-hour theme park, which almost every Southeast Asian country finds it necessary to construct. You'll find replicas of traditional Lao dwellings that double up as snack stands, some concrete models of dinosaurs, and a squalid little zoo housing a few disgruntled monkeys. Much more interesting is a trip to the **Beer Lao factory**, 12km from Vientiane on the same road. Not many tourists show up here, but those that do will be taken on a free, 15-minute tour of the factory, and then encouraged to gulp down free samples of the nation's favourite drink. If you're heading for the Buddha Park with a rental car or motorcycle, a swing past either of these attractions isn't much trouble.

The Kaysone Memorial Museum

The Kaysone Memorial Museum (Tues–Sun 8–11.30am & 2–4.30pm; 5000K) is the most visible attempt of the Lao government to build a personality cult around the shadowy man who, according to Party legend, led the Thirty Year Struggle (see p.220). It lies on the edge of Vientiane, in the former American compound known during the Second Indochina War as **Six Klicks City** – after its location, 6km from the centre. An oasis during the years that the US embassy was the seat of power in Vientiane, Six Klicks City was a slice of suburban Americana with nicely paved roads lined with ranch-style homes and swimming pools out back. One month after Saigon and Phnom Penh fell in April 1975, Pathet Lao troops surrounded the barbed-wire-enclosed compound, and the American residents inside had nowhere to run. Three days later, the first busload of Americans headed to Wattay Airport, beginning the end of an era. In December 1975, 264 delegates gathered in the compound's gymnasium and proclaimed the formation of the Lao People's Democratic Republic. Having just emerged from their wartime hide-out in the caves of Vieng Xai, the Lao communist party members promptly moved into the American fortress, which was to become Kaysone's headquarters until his death in 1992.

The Memorial Museum is strikingly modest compared to the mausoleum of Kaysone's Vietnamese counterpart, Ho Chi Minh. Opened in 1994, the museum originally consisted only of the tiny ranch house where Kaysone lived, though a more conventional museum was opened next door a year later. The guide will show you Kaysone's exercise bike and the spot where he used to meditate, as well as cabinets containing Buddha images and bottles of Johnnie Walker scotch – so much for communist austerity, though the guide duly notes that they were gifts of the people. Also on display are gifts to Kaysone from the leaders of Indonesia, Thailand, Vietnam and China, as well as the books – many of which, ardent Lao nationalists might note, are in Vietnamese – of his well-stocked library. Next door, the later part of the museum is heavy on the sort of revolutionary photographs common to other Lao museums, but also features objects from various stages of Kaysone's life, his desk from his Savannakhet school, the winnowing tray on which he was placed during the first days of his life, and his mother's bed, along with a model of Kaysone's Vieng Xai cave, his binoculars, revolver and other items from his time with the resistance movement.

Getting to the museum is easiest by rental motorbike or tuk-tuk. Southbound sawngthaews, departing from the main bus station, pass the road leading to the compound, 6km from the city along Route 13 South; the turn-off is on the left just before the Children's Home. The road leads 300m to the gate of an army outpost, at which point you turn left and continue along the road, which curves right, for 1km. The museum entrance is on the right.

Wat Phabat Phonsan

The somewhat isolated monastery of **WAT PHABAT PHONSAN**, 80km east of Vientiane, is best known for its **"Buddha's footprint"** embellished with paint and gold leaf. In ancient times, the sandstone bluff upon which the monastery now sits was submerged by the nearby river and, over time, the swirling currents carved deep bowls into its surface. When the water receded, one of these indentations looked enough like a footprint for it to become enshrined as one of those left behind by the historic Buddha during his wanderings through Laos. Never mind that there is no record of Gautama Buddha ever having got this far east, his footprints have been found all over Laos wherever there is a population of Buddhists.

Any **public transport** bound for Savannakhet, Thakhek or Paksan will pass by Wat Phabat Phonsan, which is roughly halfway between Vientiane and Paksan, about an hour and a half's drive from each. There is no accommodation in the vicinity of Wat Phabat Phonsan, so it's best visited as a day-trip or en route to or from the south.

Phou Khao Khouay NBCA

Located 90km northeast of the city, this huge NBCA straddles three different administrative districts and forms the southern edge of the Ang Nam Ngum Reservoir. Within easy striking distance of the capital, **PHOU KHAO KHOUAY** basically is to Vientiane what Khao Yai National Park is to Bangkok. The NBCA

Ban Pako (Lao Pako) Resort

A quick trip you can make out of the capital is to **Ban Pako**, 50km northeast of Vientiane, which has a rustic resort on a bend in the Nam Ngum River, reached by road and a short river journey. Once there you could easily spend a couple of days soaking up the laidback atmosphere at this woodsy getaway, affording ample opportunity for swimming, tubing, birdwatching and day hikes to nearby villages. You can also follow self-guided nature trails, along one of which is a herbal steam bath, modelled on the wood-fired saunas at Wat Sok Pa Luang (see p.82), and near a refreshingly cool spring.

To get to the resort, you first catch the blue government **bus** bound for Paksap from the main bus station (at 9am, 1.30pm or 4.30pm), getting off at Somsamai, where there's a sign reading "Boat to Lao Pako". From here boatmen will ferry you down the tranquil Nam Ngum River (30min; 15,000K) to the resort (☏021/451970, Ⓦwww.banpako.com; dorms $6, ❺). Alternatively, there's a direct shuttle bus to the resort (one day's notice required; 140,000K each way), which will pick you up from Nam Phou. **Accommodation** ranges from an eight-bed dorm in a Lao-style longhouse with a huge veranda, to more private detached bungalows with en-suite facilities and verandas. Rooms are limited, so it's best to call ahead for reservations. An **open-air restaurant** overlooking the river serves up Lao staples plus a few decent Western dishes.

features several large ranges and includes two peaks of over 1600m, one of which, Phou Xang, at 1666m, towers over the southern end of the Nam Ngum Lake. There are also several large **waterfalls**, including Tad Xay, Tad Leuk and Tad Phou Khao Khouay, which can be reached by road, and a smaller dam and reservoir, Nam Luek Reservoir, which can also be reached by motor vehicle from the east. Highlights include **Asian elephants**, **tigers** and **gibbons**.

There is a **visitor centre** at Tad Leuk and basic **accommodation** at the *T&M Guesthouse* (40,000K) in the town of **Thabok**, where the road into the NBCA meets Route 13. Ask Vientiane **tour agencies** about organized packages to the eleven-metre-high **Ban Na observation tower** (around $100), where you can spend the night keeping watch for the wild elephants that pass by.

Ang Nam Ngum Reservoir

Ninety kilometres north of Vientiane, the vast **Ang Nam Ngum Reservoir** sits above the northern edge of the Vientiane Plain, where the rice-growing flatlands surrounding the capital meet the mountainous terrain of the north. Created when the Nam Ngum River was dammed in 1971, the deep green waters of the reservoir are dotted with scores of forest-clad islands stretching to a dramatic horizon lined with mountains, their peaks lost in mist. Foreign travellers, usually in a rush to head upcountry, tend to bypass Ang Nam Ngum as they make for nearby Vang Vieng, but those who do stop off discover a pretty 250-square-kilometre expanse of water with islands, secluded beaches and swimming spots. There are a number of convenient options for visiting Ang Nam Ngum, either as a day-trip from Vientiane or Vang Vieng or en route between the two; short package trips are also available from travel agents in Vientiane.

Built with foreign expertise and funding, the reservoir is the driving force behind Laos's production of **hydroelectricity** – the country's largest export earner until the late 1980s – and provides power for Vientiane and surrounding villages on the Vientiane Plain. Most of the power, however, flows across the Mekong into Thailand, which has an agreement to purchase Laos's surplus electricity. The reservoir is also slowly being developed for tourism and boasts a huge hotel on the southern shoreline, the **DanSaVanh Nam Ngum Resort** (℡021/217594–6, Ⓦwww.dansavanh.com; ❺), complete with casino, golf courses and a marina. Less brash is *Longngum View Resort* (℡021/214872 Ⓦwww.longngumview.com ❹), on the western shore of the lake, which has bungalows and rooms with good views of the water.

At the time the dam was built, the Royalist government had only just plugged Vientiane into the hydroelectric dam before they were forced to cede power to the communist Pathet Lao. In an all too typical example of poor environmental planning, the builders of the dam had flooded a vast area of valuable forest 50m underwater. The rotting vegetation sucked oxygen out of the water and blocked up the turbines, a problem that was later turned into profit by underwater logging ventures, whose frogmen dropped to the reservoir floor to cut submerged trees with underwater saws. Meanwhile, the new communist government found a novel use for the reservoir. After 1975, prostitutes, thieves and teenagers "infected with foreign ideas" were rounded up from the streets of Vientiane, a Lao Sodom in the eyes of the Pathet Lao, and were confined on islands in the middle of the lake for "re-education".

These days, day-tripping Lao head for Ang Nam Ngum with relaxation in mind, descending on the scenic reservoir in droves at weekends and hiring out wooden boats for picnic cruises. If you visit, you'll find good swimming, peaceful sandy beaches, and floating restaurants serving fresh seafood dishes just above the water.

Fishing is actually one of the main industries at the reservoir, but most of the catch is sold in the markets of Vientiane.

Reaching the reservoir

Getting to Ang Nam Ngum by public transport is easy enough. **From Vientiane**, four government buses depart daily from the bus station near the morning market for **Thalat** (there are also more frequent sawngthaews here, leaving from the stand in front of the bus station). From Thalat, you can get a shared tuk-tuk to the reservoir (30 min; $5) or the regular tuk-tuk shuttle service to **Na Nam**, near the dam on the western shore of the reservoir, and the most logical base for independent travellers to explore the lake by chartering a taxi ($25 return). If you go for this option, you might consider making a scenic detour en route along the quieter **Route 10** via Ban Keun. Southbound sawngthaews **from Vang Vieng** pass right by the town of **Tha Hua** at the northern end of the reservoir, or you can switch vehicles at the Phonhong junction and cut in to Thalat and Na Nam. If you want to use the lake as an alternative route from Vientiane north to Vang Vieng, charter a boat from Na Nam for the five-hour trip to Tha Hua and then continue by road to Vang Vieng.

Travel companies offer one- to three-day **package tours** to the reservoir out of Vang Vieng, which combine hiking, boating and camping, but expect to pay considerably more for the convenience. You can usually arrange a private boat trip on the reservoir by asking around in Na Nam. Guesthouses and hotels mentioned here should also be able to point you in the direction of the best hiking trails.

Na Nam

Although relatively few people live in **NA NAM**, a port of rickety shacks suspended above the water, it does have a clutch of tourist restaurants, basic accommodation, and a fleet of wooden tourist boats – some seating up to forty passengers – for **lake cruises**. Freelance boatmen down at the waterfront restaurants generally ask for $5 per hour but are willing to negotiate day rates in the vicinity of $15. Na Nam guesthouses can also arrange boat tours. Obviously, the more people you have, the more affordable it becomes. Beyond simply touring the reservoir, possibilities for boat trips include Don Dok Khoun Kham, where there's a rustic restaurant; the secluded beach at Don Keng Phou Vieng – the hour-long trip to which passes the scenic Pha Tao or "star cliff" island – or even down to the *DanSaVanh Nam Ngum Resort*. Some of the islands are quite large; Don 516, for instance, supports a community of five hundred families and is connected to Na Nam twice daily by a passenger ferry (almost 3hr).

Eating figures highly in the weekend plans of Lao tourists, and several restaurants have set up shop in and around Na Nam to cater to this demand. *Nam Ngum*, in the port overlooking the water, delivers with freshly caught reservoir fish cooked in a variety of ways, and has an exceptional view of the lake. Just down the hill, *Boathouse*, a ramshackle barge with pleasant views, does good, moderately priced food. When there's an order, fish kept under the boat are netted and pulled right into the middle of the restaurant.

Don Dok Khoun Kham

Just a ten-minute boat ride from Na Nam, small, densely forested **Don Dok Khoun Kham**, the most accessible of the islands, boasts a pleasant restaurant and a rapidly decaying two-storey **guesthouse** (❷) that will be sure hit with horror-film fans. The eight rooms, of varying shapes and sizes, are all a little the worse for wear. During the week, few guests stay here and the house can at times be without water or electricity. If you don't mind roughing it a bit, the island makes for a pleasant, quiet stay. You might want to bring added provisions and a deck of cards, although the guesthouse is well stocked with necessities such as rice, water and Beer Lao, and fresh fish is always on the restaurant menu. Guests are shuttled by pirogue between the guesthouse and the restaurant across a small cove. The islanders will ferry you back to the mainland for significantly less than what the boatmen in Na Nam charge to pick you up.

The northwest

Although Vientiane and Luang Prabang are both on the banks of the Mekong River, the land between them is extremely mountainous, while the opposite left bank of the Mekong, composed of huge ranges separating Laos and Thailand, forms its own remote province of **Sayaboury**. As almost everyone's itinerary in Laos includes the journey between Vientiane and Luang Prabang, you're highly likely to cross this stunning terrain at some point, and there are three main options to choose from for travel between the two cities.

The quickest option is to follow **Route 13** north from Vientiane through the karst mountains of Vang Vieng and up the **old Royal Road** through the mountains north of **Kasi**. Route 13 was first completed by the French in 1943, and although it was improved in the 1960s with American aid, there was very little maintenance on the road until the mid-1990s, when it was properly sealed. Until that time, this rough track of a road took at best a full 24 hours to traverse, and often as long as three days. The highway was finally completed in 1996 after years of toil by Vietnamese road workers, twenty of whom were killed by guerrillas in the process. The breathtaking mountain scenery from Kasi to Luang Prabang makes this one of the most **scenic routes** in all Southeast Asia.

If you don't fancy making the ten-hour bus journey from Vientiane to Luang Prabang in one go, **Vang Vieng** makes an ideal stopover and is well worth an extended visit in its own right. Aside from **tubing**, which has earned the town notoriety in recent years, there are beautiful caves, **ethnic minority villages** and a host of outdoor activities to keep you busy. **Phou Phanang NBCA** runs close to Route 13 for 75km, but although two tracks lead into the reserve off Route 13, the NBCA is still fairly inaccessible to tourists. However, if you're prepared to rent a four-wheel-drive vehicle or dirt bike from Vientiane, you could try a dirt track running the entire western boundary of the reserve and linking several villages.

The second route, a detour through **Sayaboury**, the sparsely populated region of rugged valleys and wild elephants on the western side of the Mekong, is more complicated, and takes you along a path well off the banana-pancake backpacker circuit. Unless you have your own four-wheel-drive vehicle, the Sayaboury route is tough, and you'll need to travel at least part of the way by boat along the Mekong – the lack of decent roads west of the capital makes Sayaboury much more remote than it appears on maps. The third route is to travel the whole way by boat (see p.89), an attractive option but requiring at least three days of travel time by slow boat, although speedboats can make the trip in a day.

Vang Vieng

Change comes slowly to Laos, but **VANG VIENG**, the once-sleepy town that reclines on the east bank of the Nam Song River between towering limestone karsts, is something of a rare exception. Just half a decade ago, the main street was a potholed track, crowds were rare, and accommodation was limited to a handful of guesthouses. Then as thousands of party-hungry backpackers descended on the

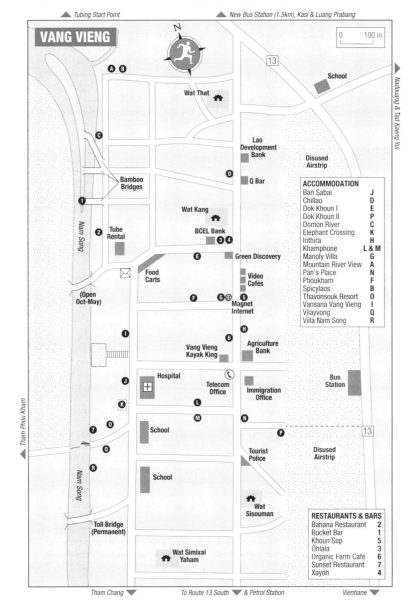

▲ Tubing Start Point   ▲ New Bus Station (1.5km), Kasi & Luang Prabang

VANG VIENG

Naduang & Tad Kaeng Yui

School

Wat That

Lao Development Bank

Disused Airstrip

Q Bar

Bamboo Bridges

Nam Song

Wat Kang

BCEL Bank

Tube Rental

Green Discovery

Food Carts

Video Cafés

(Open Oct–May)

Magnet Internet

Vang Vieng Kayak King

Agriculture Bank

Hospital

Telecom Office

Immigration Office

Bus Station

School

Tham Phou Kham

School

Tourist Police

Disused Airstrip

Nam Song

School

Wat Sisouman

Toll Bridge (Permanent)

Wat Simixai Yaham

ACCOMMODATION
Ban Sabai	J
Chillao	D
Dok Khoun I	E
Dok Khoun II	P
Domon River	C
Elephant Crossing	K
Inthira	H
Khamphone	L & M
Manoly Villa	G
Mountain River View	A
Pan's Place	N
Phoukham	F
Spicylaos	B
Thavonsouk Resort	O
Vansana Vang Vieng	I
Vilayvong	Q
Villa Nam Song	R

RESTAURANTS & BARS
Banana Restaurant	2
Bucket Bar	1
Khoun Sop	5
Ohlala	3
Organic Farm Café	6
Sunset Restaurant	7
Xayoh	4

▼ Tham Chang   ▼ To Route 13 South ▼ & Petrol Station   ▼ Vientiane self-styled "tubing capital of the world", the Lao government found itself struggling to control an inland version of Thailand's Ko Pha Ngan. Today "happy shakes" appear on restaurant menus more often than authentic Lao dishes, and countless bars, internet cafés and market stalls all compete for the backpacker buck.

Arrival and information

At the time of writing, buses to and from Vientiane and Luang Prabang were still using the **old airstrip** just off Route 13, to the east of town and within walking distance of most accommodation. For a long time there have been plans to move all arrivals and departures to the new bus station, 2km north of town, but this has yet to happen, so check arrangements before you travel. If you're heading to Vientiane, sawngthaews are a convenient option, leaving every twenty minutes throughout the day. Heading north to Luang Prabang, you'll need to catch one of the public buses coming up from the capital sometime after 9am, though it's highly unlikely there will be any empty seats, or book one of the VIP buses through your guesthouse. Sawngthaews to surrounding villages leave from the stand at the central market.

Accommodation

Despite its small size, Vang Vieng is one of the best-value spots for accommodation in the country – it's possible to find a perfectly decent en-suite double here for under $10. On the downside, most of the town's **guesthouses** seem to have been built by the same architect, whose forte must be huge, concrete monstrosities with Corinthian columns and absolutely no charm whatsoever. Most visitors seem to end up in these cheap but less-than-atmospheric digs in the centre of town. For something with more character, try one of the boutique hotels or bungalow operations along the river, which have views of the Nam Song and mountains beyond.

Ban Sabai In front of the hospital. Nine well-equipped bungalows on the banks of the Nam Song, built on stilts around a beautiful, deep green fishpond. Rooms come with a/c, comfy beds and spacious balconies. The view from the restaurant, which serves proper oven-baked pizzas, is divine. Visa & MasterCard accepted, and prices include breakfast. ⑤

Chillao Opposite *Q Bar* on the main drag. One of the cheapest places in town, *Chillao* is also gifted with a pretty central location. There are dorms (20,000K) sleeping between 3–7 people, as well as some smaller, private rooms. The pool table, hot water and free wi-fi help to make up for the rather dingy corridors. ②

Dok Khoun I & II Clean, tiled rooms, many en suite and with hot water, in modern multistorey buildings at three locations around town. Very popular, thanks in part to the free bananas and tea downstairs, but despite the good value there's little personality or atmosphere in evidence. ②

Domon River At the northern end of the main river road. A vast new building, fronted by four hideous white pillars, that looks like it's been transported straight from the Las Vegas Strip. The rooms are good value though, but those with the best views (at the back of the building) are also exposed to the nightly racket from *Bucket Bar*. ③

Elephant Crossing At the southern end of the main river road, just south of the hospital, ☏023/511232 ⓦ www.theelephantcrossinghotel .com. Although billed as a boutique hotel, this popular place is actually housed in a large concrete building on the edge of the Nam Song. Its 31 well-equipped rooms all have good views over the river and mountains, and the restaurant downstairs is perfect for a quiet meal after a hard day's exploring. Reservations recommended. ⑥

Inthira Opposite the *Organic Farm Café*, on the main drag ☏023/511070 ⓦ www.inthirahotels.com. A new, wooden building fronted by an attractive street-front restaurant. Upstairs, you'll find spacious rooms with big bathtubs and an excellent shared veranda. The deluxe rooms, off the austere main corridor, offer the best value for money. ⑤

Khamphone ☏023/511062. Two large two-storey houses opposite one another. The house on the south side of the road has eighteen spacious, well-lit rooms with tiled floors and en-suite bathrooms with hot water. A cut above other similar places and a good choice if you're not on too strict a budget. ④

Manoly Villa Just east of *Phoukham*, in the centre of town. Far from being a villa, this is another of Vang Vieng's architectural blunders. That said, the single, double and triple rooms represent quite good value, and the location is central yet reasonably quiet. ❷

Mountain River View In the far north of town, next to the river. One of the few new guesthouses in town with a bit of character, this place has clean, fan-cooled rooms and some, like the name suggests, have excellent views of the distant mountains. Ask to stay on the third floor at the back of the building. ❸

Pan's Place At the southern end of the main road. One of the more popular budget options, *Pan's Place* has a relaxed TV room, a bookswap, and a selection of single, double and triple rooms with shared facilities. For $2 more, you can bag yourself a room with an en-suite bathroom. ❷

Phoukham Directly behind the *Dok Khoun I*. An ugly building with gaudy pillars and rooms that are better value than in similar places, though not great in themselves. Several of the upstairs rooms have nice views of the karsts. ❷

Spicylaos Next door to *Mountain River View*, ⓦ www.spicyhostels.com. *The* place to come if you're on a budget and want to meet new people. *Spicylaos* has a mixed, tree house-style dorm, a sociable dining area with wi-fi and, handily, lockers to stash your valuables in while tubing. Dorm room ❶

Thavonsouk Resort ☎ 023/511096, ⓦ www.thavonsouk.com. At the far end of the main river road, south of the hospital. Mid-range bungalows, some with private balconies, enjoying a prime location on the banks of the Nam Song. There are 35 units to choose from, with prices dependent on the size and quality of the bungalow. Be warned: although this area is usually pretty peaceful, there can be riotous karaoke sessions in the resort's bar. ❺

Vansana Vang Vieng On the main river road, 200m south of the tube hire shops. Vang Vieng's nicest rooms are set in a featureless building off the main river road. The communal areas are spacious and breezy, though, and there's a well-kept outdoor pool. The huge bedrooms come with luxuries like minibar and TV, but expect some of the highest rack rates in town. ❻

Villa Nam Song Far enough out of town to ensure a good night's sleep, these private bungalows are well worth walking to. Each immaculate room has magnificent views of the river, and the whole complex is set in well-maintained gardens away from the main road. ❼

Vilayvong Opposite *Thavonsouk Resort*, down the dirt track just south of the hospital. Skip the main hotel block, which doesn't have much to offer, and go straight for one of the bungalows out front. These are good value, with TV and a/c, and the big, clean bathrooms have hot running water. ❹

▲ Water buffalo make their way home, Vang Vieng

Tubing the Nam Song

Love or hate what it's done to the place, **tubing** is Vang Vieng's premier attraction. In fact, for some people, it's the very reason they ended up in Laos. What started as an inventive way to spend a lazy afternoon floating down the **Nam Song** has rapidly evolved into an all-you-can-drink party on the river, and it's fairly common for people to turn up without tubes and just swim between the first few riverside bars before jumping in a tuk-tuk for the ride back into town. Most of these watering holes lure punters in with free shots of *lào-lào* and, as if to test your mettle, have built giant rope-swings and slides over the river. Naturally it's a lot of fun, but be careful – people have died here.

If you decide to go for the authentic tubing experience, **tubes** are available from shops near the post office for around $14 per day (including a $7 deposit, refundable if you return the tube before 6pm). This includes a tuk-tuk ride upriver to the main launching point, 3km north of town near the Organic Mulberry Farm. A float back into town should take two hours from here, but you could easily spend the whole day dancing, drinking and playing mud volleyball at the bars along the way. It's important to leave enough time to get back before dark however, as it gets cold and it becomes almost impossible to see where you're going in the fast-flowing water. If you're a weak swimmer, wear a life jacket while tubing – the shops supplying the inner tubes should provide them. A good sunblock is also essential if you don't want to come out looking like a lobster; the tropical sun is powerful, even on overcast days.

The town

Despite the tourist droves, Vang Vieng is still jaw-droppingly beautiful, and you could easily spend a week here cycling, cave exploring, tubing, rafting and hiking, or simply relaxing and enjoying the idyllic landscape. There's also no disputing one fact: the place is a lot of fun.

All of Vang Vieng's streets are nameless, but getting around this small town is a fairly simple matter. Bicycles ($2/day) and motorbikes ($10/day) can be rented at many places around town. There's a BCEL **bank** (Mon–Sat 8am–noon & 1–4pm) and ATM on the main street opposite the *Dok Khoun I* guesthouse, a Lao Development Bank on the town's main north–south road, and an Agricultural Promotion Bank on the same street further south. Diagonally across from the latter is the **telecom office** (Mon–Fri 8am–noon & 1–5pm), which handles international calls; the **post office** is right near the tube rental shops in the town centre. **Internet** facilities can be found at about a dozen different places along the main drag. All the usual services are also in supply, including herbal sauna, laundry, massage, photo labs, tour agencies, vehicle rental and DVD hire.

Eating and drinking

Vang Vieng is hardly short of places to eat, but you'll have to search hard to find good food; most restaurants have identical menus featuring bland tourist munchies. The relatively lax regulations and low start-up costs associated with the town mean foreign-run eating and drinking establishments aren't unusual in Vang Vieng – in fact, they're proportionally more common here than in Vientiane or Luang Prabang – and it's possible to find anything from vindaloos to fish tacos. Budget travellers tend to eat at the sandwich and pancake stalls around town, or on the main north–south road where there's a whole strip of cheap restaurants showing *Friends* and *Family Guy* episodes on an endless loop. Most of these places flog "happy" variants of pizzas and shakes that, upon request, are laced with marijuana, mushrooms or, very occasionally, opium. Legal concerns aside, you should be aware of the risks – plenty of travellers have reported freaking out, getting mugged, or ending up ill after indulging. Apart from restaurants in town, there are a few decent places to eat overlooking the river – the best parties happen on the island in the middle.

Banana Restaurant Along the river road, just north of the tube rental shop. Cheap backpacker grub done well. As well as Western staples like pancakes and pizzas, there's a reasonable selection of Lao food - try the spicy fish *larp*. The raised seats at the back have great views over the limestone karsts.

Bucket Bar On the island in the middle of the river. As the name suggests, there's nothing subtle about this huge outdoor bar. Centred around massive, bellowing campfires, it offers cut-price whisky buckets laced with Red Bull and pumping tunes (to the chagrin of nearby hotels) until 1am. The best place to meet fellow travellers after a day on the river.

Khoun Sap Beneath *Khoun Sap Guesthouse*, on the same street as *Q Bar*. The downstairs restaurant in this quaint guesthouse offers a big choice of Lao food (not usually seen in Vang Vieng) and a packed list of fabulous fruit shakes.

Ohlala Right next to the ATM in the centre of town. Very popular with the backpacker crowd, especially after dark, this centrally located bar gets people mingling with the tried and tested combo of Beer Lao and cheesy music. There's a pool table out back and, if you decide to eat here, the Asian food is passable.

Organic Farm Café Opposite the *Inthira* on the main north-south road. One of the best places to get breakfast, and particularly popular with vegetarians. Try the famous mulberry breakfast set, which comes with mulberry pancakes and a mulberry fruit shake.

Sunset Restaurant At *Thavonsouk Resort*. A decent place for a sundowner, boasting a million-dollar view across the Nam Song, and quite good Western and Lao food. If you stick around long enough, you're sure to be treated to some impromptu karaoke.

Xayoh Next to the Green Discovery office in town. A good place for a drink or meal, and boasting a view guaranteed to induce a contented sigh. The thin, crispy pizzas are recommended. You can eat either inside or on the outdoor patio, and there's an attached internet centre.

Around Vang Vieng

The **countryside** surrounding Vang Vieng is full of enough day-trip options to easily fill up a week. Scores of **caves** in limestone karst outcrops, tranquil lowland Lao and minority villages, and **Kaeng Yui Waterfall**, all make worthy destinations for a rewarding day's hike (if walking isn't your thing, you can hire bicycles or motorbikes from various outlets around town), while the Nam Song River makes for a fun afternoon of **tubing**, **kayaking** or **rafting** – tubes can be rented from shops near the post office. Aside from a number of organized tours around Vang Vieng itself, there are also one- to three-day excursions to Ang Nam Ngum Reservoir (see p.94) that can be booked through most guesthouses.

Organized day tours, many of which combine both caving and tubing with lunch in between, are a fast and convenient way for the uninitiated to get into the Vang Vieng groove: once you've done the tour you can go back for more on your own. It's not hard to find a guided tour – just look for signs posted in restaurants and guesthouses. If you do opt to join a tour, be sure to check how many people will be in the group. Some agents have few qualms about stuffing twenty people into a single sawngthaew, which not only spoils a good walk but can seriously hasten the onset of claustrophobia if tramping about several hundred metres underground.

If you decide to visit the caves on your own, it's worth getting hold of one of the hand-drawn **maps** of the Vang Vieng area which show all the **caves** and **trails**;

they're available from several of the restaurants and guesthouses in town. Otherwise just ask around; everyone in Vang Vieng has their favourite cave, swimming hole or countryside getaway. The local people are more than happy to point you in the right direction, and other travellers will also enthusiastically recommend the best places. If you're looking to explore areas north or south of town, there's enough local transport in the form of buses and sawngthaews plying Route 13 to get you up and down the highway cheaply. Or, if you prefer something quick and easy, just hire a tuk-tuk (the stand is at the market), which will gladly wait for you for the right price.

Most of Vang Vieng's attractions lie on the **west bank** of the Nam Song. There's now a permanent toll bridge crossing the river (4000K for pedestrians, 6000K for bikes and 10,000K for motorcycles) or, in the dry season, you can

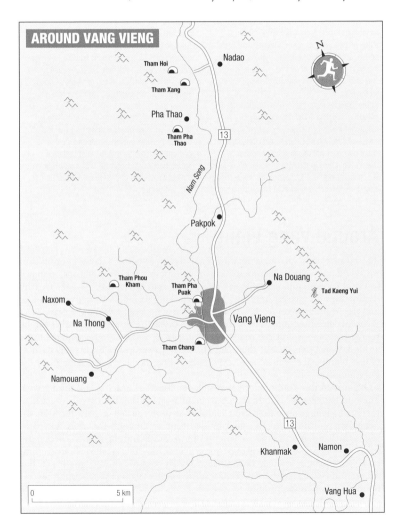

AROUND VANG VIENG

Dress for success in Vang Vieng

The **varied terrain** surrounding Vang Vieng can turn treacherous in a hurry, particularly during the rainy season. **Exercise caution** while wandering through caves and scrambling about on the steep slopes of the karst formations, as serious injuries incurred by foolhardy travellers while tramping about in the area are common. Slippery trails demand that proper shoes be worn – Teva-style sandals with good traction are the best for conquering Vang Vieng's alternately rocky and muddy trails. Bermuda-type shorts are also a good sartorial choice as you may end up knee-deep in water at some point if you intend to enjoy the countryside to the fullest. A re-sealable plastic bag for valuables such as money and your passport is an excellent idea. Do not leave your valuables with local kids or teenagers, who may offer to "look after them for you" while you explore a cave, and make sure you get back to town before dark – robberies have been reported.

Finally, while it may be tempting to wander around in your swimming gear (and it's very common to see travellers walking around town half-naked), always remember that in Laos gratuitous displays of flesh are considered a form of rudeness and disrespect.

---

cross using the rickety bamboo bridge towards the north of town. The pirogues down by *Thavonsouk Resort* will still ferry people across for 5000K. On the other side, Chinese-made tractors trundle along the bumpy paths to nearby villages, acting as makeshift shared taxis that aren't entirely comfortable but are at least faster than walking. You can simply flag them down as you would a bus or tuk-tuk – expect to pay 5000K for journeys of up to 1km, then 2000K for each extra kilometre.

There are several **kayaking** and **rafting** companies operating in Vang Vieng. For more strenuous outdoor activities, Green Discovery (T023/511230, Wwww.greendiscoverylaos.com) has a number of options, including day-trip packages as well as overnight hiking and kayaking excursions. The same company was also behind Laos's first fully operational **rock–climbing** site, featuring fifty different bolted routes – graded from 5b (tricky) to 8c (very difficult) on the internationally recognized French grading system – in the Vang Vieng area. A day's climbing costs $47 with equipment, a guide and lunch.

Chang Cave

Vang Vieng's best-known cave, **Tham Chang**, has been developed for tourism to such an extent that the proprietors of *Vang Vieng Resort*, whose land you have to cross to get to the cave, levy a fee to enter the resort and again at the cave's entrance (10,000K). In the nineteenth century, the cave earned its nom de guerre when it was used for defence during an invasion of Chinese Haw from the north ("chang" means steadfast). Chinese bandits would have an easy run of the place these days, with steep stairs leading up the side of the cliff to the cave mouth. Inside, gaudy coloured lights illuminate cement pathways leading through the cavern, past rock formations that bear an uncanny resemblance to monkeys, frogs, a white elephant and the three-headed elephant, symbol of Lao royalty. Follow the path to the left and you'll wind up at a second cave mouth which affords a bird's-eye view of the valley below. At the base of the cave, cross a stream to find a third cave mouth out of which flows a spring leading into the Nam Song. It's possible to swim up the stream about 50m into this cave, which also has a Buddha image inside. The grassy lawn around the base of the cave is a pleasant spot to catch some rays.

Pha Puak Cave

A little more than 1km north of Ban Houay Nye lies **Tham Pha Puak**, a cave tucked into a karst encircled by Pha Daeng, or the Red Cliffs. Pha Daeng is considered particularly sacred and some locals even maintain that planes flying over the cliff do so at their peril, no doubt a legend with roots in the Second Indochina War, when Vang Vieng was used as an airbase, known to pilots as Lima Site 6. Although in and of itself nothing special, the cave makes a good short walk out of Vang Vieng. To get there, cross the river then follow the signs on the path through the rice fields north of Ban Houay Nye.

Phou Kham Cave

Six kilometres west of Vang Vieng, **Tham Phou Kham** makes a rewarding half-day trip that takes in some fine scenery and affords the chance to visit a cave and enjoy a good swim along the way. Cross the toll bridge south of *Thavonsouk Resort* and follow the road through a pretty valley, ringed by imposing karsts, to **Na Thong**, 4km west. Hop the fence at the bend in the road just past the village schoolhouse and walk through the rice fields towards the cliff face, 1km in the distance. When you see the bizarrely arched bamboo bridge, cross it and you'll reach the path leading to the cave. It's a short steep climb to the entrance and the path is extremely slippery in the rainy season, but there's plenty of bamboo to grab onto on the way up. In the main cavern reclines a bronze Buddha, while there are tunnels branching off the main gallery that you can explore if you have a torch. Outside the cave, the bright blue stream is a great spot for a swim, and you can buy cool drinks and fruit nearby. If you've come by bike, it's best to leave it at the *tam màk hung* stall across from the village school.

Kaeng Yui Waterfall

While it may seem counterintuitive to turn your back on Vang Vieng's majestic karsts, a day spent out east at **Tad Kaeng Yui**, with its twin 30m-high waterfalls, is well worth the trip – especially in the rainy season. Off the beaten track, Tad Kaeng Yui nestles in the forest among the hills protecting Vang Vieng's eastern flank. Besides offering a refreshingly cool picnic spot, with small pools of water directly under the falls to lounge in, it rewards the journey with the sense of being smack in the middle of the tropics, miles from anywhere.

To find the falls, first cross Route 13 just north of the old airstrip, and follow this road, flagged by the secondary school on the corner, 3km east to the village of **Na Douang**. As the path to the waterfall, another 3km from the village, can be completely obscured by bamboo (the falls are rarely visited, even by locals), your safest bet is to pay a villager from Na Douang 10,000K or so to show you the way. From Na Douang, head southeast towards the hills by cutting through the village rice fields; beyond the fields lies a path leading uphill, through scrub forest, across a number of small streams, and then into the woods. Once you've reached the woods, push on for another 300m; the path turns left and the falls become audible.

Plans to exploit the waterfall's tourism potential by building a road out to the falls, which will undoubtedly spoil the spot's secluded beauty, are a sign that times have changed. For now, getting there remains a muddy affair much of the year – even travelling as far as Na Douang. If you plan to do the trip by bicycle, a bit up and bog model ride turning the trip into a Sisyphean feat, but it might be a good splash on a mountain bike.

Pha Thao Cave

A descent into **Tham Pha Thao** is the most satisfying caving trip you can make from Vang Vieng. Stretching for more than 2km, the tunnel-like cave is pitch-black and filled with huge and presumably ancient stalactites and stalagmites. It also contains a **swimming hole**, formed in an underground river that winds through the cave. The cave is best visited near the end of the rainy season, when the water level is perfect for a swim in the subterranean pool 800m into the cave. In the height of the dry season, it's possible to go beyond this point and explore the full length of the cave – not an option during the rains when the water level is too high.

The cave is located in the cliff face behind **Pha Thao**, a smallish village populated by former Hmong refugees. The Hmong living here fled the northern mountains of Laos during the post-revolutionary turmoil of the late 1970s and early 1980s and wound up in a Thai refugee camp where they lived until being repatriated in the mid-1990s. Essentially, they are some of the Hmong who were denied visas to the United States and other Western nations and were forced to go "home". The village lies 13km north of Vang Vieng; to reach it, turn left after the bridge just beyond the Kilometre 10 marker on Route 13 – a road sign points the way to the "Nam Xong-Pha Thao Irrigation Project" – and head for the river. Here, you'll have to ford the river or hail a pirogue to take you across for a few thousand kip. This spot also makes a good launching point for **tubing**. Once you've made it across the river, make your way to the village, which lies at the base of the cliff. Here, you'll find a few simple restaurants serving drinks and Hmong food, and the villagers will be happy to point you in the direction of the cave mouth which, obscured by boulders and trees, isn't terribly apparent. If you explore the cave during the rainy season, you'll be up to your chest in water at times – so travel light and don't bring along anything that you don't want to get wet. A waterproof torch and camera are a good idea. Tour groups often pull through this cave during the morning, so you may want to go in the afternoon.

The Royal Road: Kasi to Luang Prabang

KASI is the northernmost town before Route 13 begins its wild 170-km stretch of highway along steep ridges and around hairpin bends, with headlong views of rugged valleys and remote mountains as far as the eye can see. The road runs right through the centre of town forming the main street, but the town itself lies in the attractive **Nam Lik river valley** surrounded by rice paddies and low hills, with the occasional karst adding an exotic touch to a pretty landscape. Within easy day-tripping distance of Kasi are numerous vast cave systems rumoured to dwarf anything found at Vang Vieng, 60km to the south, but so far plans to develop the Kasi area into a tourist region have come to nought. If the rumours of Olympic-pool-sized cave lakes and caverns large enough to house cathedrals are only half true, then Kasi's hopes of being the next Vang Vieng may some day become a reality.

Buses plying the road between Vientiane and Luang Prabang usually make a lunch stop here, so there are half a dozen decent **places to eat** up and down the street. There are also three guesthouses, including the comfortable *Vanphisith Guesthouse* (❶) near the centre of the strip. If you're staying here, you might want to go down to the sawmill by the river to watch the **elephants** that are still occasionally used to haul logs.

Vieng Kham

Perched on a narrow mountain ridge 39km north of Kasi and just 5km before Phou Khoun, the village of **Vieng Kham** offers good views to the west of one of Laos's most magnificent **peaks** – a gigantic, lone 2097-metre crag that rises like a giant tooth out of the flatlands below. If you're travelling south, Vieng Kham affords the first view of this breathtaking peak and its more distant companion, which stands at an equally impressive 2089m. Just beyond the second peak, out of view, is the Mekong River, and beyond that the distant mountains of Sayaboury. Whether you're travelling north or south on Route 13, it's well worth getting a window seat on the west-facing side of the bus in order to photograph this spectacular peak. South of Vieng Kham there's a long, slow winding descent towards Kasi that provides good photo opportunities of this unforgettable mountain.

Phou Khoun and Route 7 to Phonsavan

A former French outpost, the mountain village of **PHOU KHOUN**, 44km north of Kasi, is the junction of Route 13 and Route 7. The village has sweeping views of the deep valleys below, and is the main market for people living in isolated villages around the area. Given the mountain location, be warned that the weather can get quite chilly here.

From Phou Khoun, **Route 7** branches off from Route 13 and travels due east across the Xieng Khuang Plateau to **Phonsavan** (see p.150) on the Plain of Jars. This road has been greatly improved in recent years, making it possible to get all the way from Vientiane to Phonsavan in around ten hours, but actually catching one of the daily buses that passes through here remains an ordeal. By the time the bus reaches Phou Khoun from Vientiane it is packed, so chances are you'll be standing all the way unless another passenger is prepared to sell you their seat. Should you get stuck at the junction, there are a few guesthouses to choose from, including *Xaiphavong* (❶), near the roundabout, which has clean but basic rooms and a restaurant serving cheap, simple food.

Phou Khoun to Xieng Ngeun

Tiny picturesque villages cling to the mountain ridges every 20km or so for the rest of the journey north, only a few of them providing tables at which to eat a bowl of *fŏe*. If you're travelling by rented or chartered vehicle, you could try the proper noodle shop at **Pha Keng Noi**, a small village perched on a narrow ridge 15km north of Phou Khoun. **Kiou Ka Cham**, 45km north of Phou Khoun, is an even larger town, populated by **Hmong**, and located high up in the mountains. It has several restaurants, tiny pharmacies and general stores selling basic goods and petrol out of old oil drums. There are two very basic guesthouses here as well, one next door to the other: the *Duangvichit* (❶) and the *Kiokajam* (❶). Both have rustic shared facilities. To the north the highway continues to wind through the green-blue mountains, passing ethnic-minority villages and swidden fields cutting bare the hillsides, until it reaches **Xieng Ngeun**, a large settlement 24km south of Luang Prabang. Xieng Ngeun is another important junction: from here **Route 2** heads southwest 110km to the provincial capital of Sayaboury, on the western side of the Mekong River.

The Sayaboury circuit

While the vast majority of visitors use Route 13 between Luang Prabang and the capital, it is possible to swing through Laos's northwestern frontier provided you're willing to allow three to four days for the journey. You can make the entire journey by slow boat, but if you opt for the road-and-river journey, **Paklai** and **Sayaboury** are the best places to make stopovers. As there are still only rugged tracks between Vientiane and the south of Sayaboury province, river travel is the best way to do that section of the trip – if you can find a boat to take you. Route 2, running the length of **SAYABOURY PROVINCE** between Luang Prabang and Kenthao, is especially beautiful, particularly in the rice-growing season (June–Nov), with the electric-green paddies set against a sea of bluish mountains – some as high as 2000m – receding in waves towards Thailand.

Something of a Lao Wild West, this remote, densely forested and mountainous province is home to elephants, tigers and the Sumatran rhino. Recognizing it as the perfect place to disappear, CIA operatives active in the Second Indochina War saw Sayaboury as the escape route for **Vang Pao** and his band of Hmong irregulars (see p.279) should their "secret war" go wrong. They figured the Hmong would be at home in this province peopled by numerous hill tribes, among them Mien, Khamu and Akha, who migrate freely across the western border with Thailand. The untamed nature of the province is perhaps best illustrated by the traditional lifestyle of the **Mabri**, a tribe of nomadic hunter-gatherers numbering only a few hundred, who are known to the Lao as *kha tawng leuang* or "slaves of yellow banana leaves" – the name is derived from the tribal custom of moving on as soon as the leaves of their huts turn yellow.

Some of the villages are so remote that they hardly feel part of Laos, finding it far more convenient to trade with Thai towns across the border, or to simply exist in relatively isolated self-sufficiency. Seizing upon the Lao government's seeming neglect of its far-flung villages, the Thais claimed three Lao villages near the border as their own in a land grab during the 1980s – an incident that sparked two skirmishes between the historic rivals during the course of four years and highlighted the vagueness of the border.

These days the line separating Laos from its larger neighbour has been sketched somewhat more permanently on the map, and it's business as usual for traders on either side, with the bustling border town of **Kenthao** functioning as a gateway for goods flowing across the Nam Huang River. A fair number of smuggled cars, sparkling new and without plates, also pass through here and continue on to Vientiane, where they change hands for a fraction of their tax-heavy cost. Amphetamine production is another thorny cross-border issue, with Thai police accusing clandestine factories on the Lao side of producing *ya ba*, or methamphetamine, which ends up on the streets of the Thai capital Bangkok.

A 150km-long section of the border with Thailand consists of the massive **Nam Phoun NBCA**, Laos's westernmost bio-conservation area. The chain of mountains forming the park's spine includes peaks as high as 1790m. Two significant streams, the Pouy and the Phoun, flow down from heights above and cross the width of Sayaboury province before flowing into the Mekong. Although the town of Nakong on Route 2 sits right on the edge of the park, the NBCA has yet to be developed for trekking.

As you might expect, getting to Sayaboury's remotest corners isn't easy. Secluded caves and waterfalls are out there, but none lie on the tourist route. The region will probably be one of the last places to benefit from the country's improved tourist infrastructure, which is inspiration enough to try this route.

Vientiane to Paklai

Speedboats take about four hours to complete the 217-km journey between Vientiane and the Mekong river-port town of **Paklai**. The boats depart from Tha Hua Kao Liaw pier 10km west of Vientiane (see p.89) – be sure to get to the pier early in the morning, as it's first come first served for space on the speedboat ($20). If there are no other passengers, it's possible to charter a speedboat for $100. A cheaper but less adventurous option is to take one of the daily buses plying the bumpy new route between Vientiane and Paklai (90,000K, including a ferry crossing). Improvements to Route 13 between Vientiane and Luang Prabang have rendered **slow boats** pretty much redundant, and these days they are usually reserved for cargo.

Paklai

PAKLAI, a port town 210km south of Luang Prabang, is the best stopover between Sayaboury and Vientiane. Although not as developed as the border town of Kenthao, 60km to the south, Paklai is bigger, its wooden houses spreading for several kilometres along the riverbank. Speedboats dock at the **boat landing** on the far southern end of town, 3km from the town square, where you'll find a few restaurants and guesthouses. Some captains will take you to Paklai's **port**, which lies in the centre of town near the square and several new guesthouses; failing that, tuk-tuks (2000K) wait at the top of the hill overlooking the pier.

At the town square is Paklai's main **restaurant**, which serves, among a variety of rice dishes, generous helpings of fried rice with a tasty sauce on the side. The best **guesthouse** in town is the friendly *Ban Na* (❶), a short walk upriver on the right, which has clean rooms and a seating area with a nice view of the river. **Moving on**, sawngthaews leave from the market in the morning for the 100km trundle to Sayaboury town (25,000K; 4–5hr), departing when full. Speedboats sometimes leave Paklai for Vientiane and Luang Prabang, but you may have to charter one if they don't have enough passengers.

Sayaboury

SAYABOURY, a dusty, independent-minded town, sits on the Nam Houng River, with the massive grey and white Pha Xang limestone cliffs – so named because they bear a passing resemblance to a herd of elephants in motion – providing a distant backdrop. At the centre of the town, there's a massive thirty-room hotel, an aborted government building begun by a former governor whose political largesse mocks the decidedly rustic atmosphere of Laos's most remote provincial capital.

People from the local **hill tribes** often come down to buy and sell at the town's bustling **market**, spreading out their weird and wonderful range of produce (roots and forest creatures among other things) on swaths of cloth in neat rows around the fringe of the market proper, while members of the Mien tribe run the more established stalls. The textiles available in this section of the market are mostly from Vientiane, so you won't find many treasures here.

Practicalities

Sayaboury has two **bus stations**, one at the southern end of town for pick-ups shuttling the 100km all-weather road between Sayaboury and Paklai, and another at the northern end of town for vehicles making the forty-minute run to the ferry landing at Thadua. Tuk-tuks make the trip into town from the bus stations, stopping at the central market (2000K). From the northern bus station there are sawngthaews to Luang Prabang, though sometimes the trip requires separate sawngthaews for each side of the river. The **airport,** 1km south of town, used to connect Sayaboury with Vientiane, but flights on this route have been suspended indefinitely.

The best guesthouses are *Hong Vilay* (❶), down by the riverfront, which has clean double and triple rooms but grubby shared facilities, and *Mekee* (☎074/399388 ❷), 250m north of the museum, which has large, well-kept rooms, some with TV.

As well as the **noodle shops** in and around the market, there are a few good, inexpensive **restaurants**. The well-run *Nang Noy*, across from the market, is the best bet for rice dishes.

Thadua

Slow boats up and down the Mekong occasionally stop in **THADUA**, 35km northeast of Sayaboury, making this tiny river port, along with Paklai, one of two towns that travellers wind up visiting in Sayaboury province. There's little to recommend here, and most people only make a fleeting visit. **Speedboats** to Luang Prabang take about two hours, but unless there are other passengers you'll have to charter the whole boat. Slow boats for Luang Prabang take nearly four times as long. Pirogues skirt across the river regularly, although if you've come by your own transport you're at the mercy of the Thadua ferry, which can take up to an hour. Large sawngthaews bound for Luang Prabang queue up along the ferry landing ramp on the opposite bank, a gathering of petrol stations and thatch huts known as **Pakkhon**.

Muang Nan and the road to Luang Prabang

At first glance, **MUANG NAN**, around 20km northeast of Thadua on the road to Luang Prabang, seems little more than a dusty truck-stop whose only saving grace is its location in a narrow, pretty valley full of rice fields. But walk off the highway and you'll find a town of traditional homes and old temples hugging the palm-lined banks of the babbling Nan River. The spirited villagers dam up the tiny river annually near the end of the monsoon and hold boat races with long, slender pirogues. While it's difficult to imagine the narrow river offering much sport to a flock of ducks, let alone a fleet of boats, enough city folk from Luang Prabang make the trip down to Nan for the event, held to celebrate Awk Phansa (see *Festivals* colour section), to make it a lively affair.

Sawngthaews in either direction usually pause briefly on their hourly run through the town. From here, it takes two to three hours to reach Luang Prabang, but the gentle roller coaster of a dirt road is scenic, negotiating uneven hills pocked with remote caves.

Travel details

Buses

Pakkhon to: Luang Prabang (5 daily; 3hr).
Paklai to: Kenthao (1–3 daily; 1–2hr); Sayaboury
(1–3 daily; 3–4hr); Vientiane (1 daily; 5hr).
Vang Vieng to: Luang Prabang (5 daily; 5–6hr);
Vientiane (8 daily; 3–4hr).
Vientiane to: Friendship Bridge (every 15min;
45min); Kasi (daily; 5hr); Lak Xao (3 daily; 8hr);
Lao Pako (3 daily; 1hr); Luang Prabang (10 daily;
10–12hr); Oudomxai (4 daily; 15–19hr); Paklai
(1 daily; 5hr); Paksan (5 daily; 2hr); Pakse (14 daily;
10–15hr); Phonsavan (9 daily; 9–11hr);
Savannakhet (10 daily; 7–8 hr); Thakhek (8 daily; 5
–6hr); Thalat (4 daily; 2hr); Vang Vieng (8 daily;
3–4hr); Xam Nua (daily; 22–24hr).

Sayaboury to: Luang Prabang (2 daily; 3–4hr);
Paklai (1–3 daily; 3–4hr); Thadua (4 daily; 40min).

Boats

Thadua to: Luang Prabang (variable; 7–9hr).
Vientiane to: Luang Prabang via Paklai (very
infrequent; 3–4 days).

Domestic flights

Vientiane to: Houayxai (3 weekly; 55min);
Luang Namtha (4 weekly; 1hr); Luang Prabang
(4 daily; 40min); Oudomxai (3 weekly; 50min);
Pakse (up to 11 weekly; 1hr 15min); Phonsavan/
Xieng Khuang (daily; 30min); Savannakhet
(3 weekly; 55min).

Luang Prabang

CHAPTER 2   Highlights

✳ **Wat Xieng Thong** Laos's most historic wat is one of the jewels of Southeast Asian architecture. See p.128

✳ **Traditional Arts and Ethnology Centre** Visit the TAEC for a fantastic introduction to the clothing and traditions of Laos's ethnic groups. See p.130

✳ **Xieng Men** The dusty paths and village life on the other side of the Mekong feel a world away from the tourist crowds of Sisavangvong Road. See p.132

✳ **Cookery courses** Learn how to cook fragrant Lao cuisine at one of the city's excellent cookery schools. See p.135

✳ **Boat trips on the Mekong** A slow boat trip down the Mekong from the Thai border to Luang Prabang remains the highlight of many a trip to Laos. See p.141

✳ **Kouang Si waterfall** This spectacular waterfall is the perfect place to cool off on a hot day. See p.143

▴ Taking a dip, Kouang Si waterfall

Luang Prabang

Nestling in a slim valley shaped by lofty, green mountains and cut by the swift Mekong and Khan rivers, **LUANG PRABANG** exudes tranquillity and casual grandeur. A tiny mountain kingdom for more than a thousand years and designated a UNESCO World Heritage Site in 1995, Luang Prabang is endowed with a legacy of ancient red-roofed temples and French-Indochinese architecture, not to mention some of the country's most refined cuisine, its richest culture and its most sacred Buddha image, the Pha Bang. For those familiar with Southeast Asia, the very name Luang Prabang conjures up the classic image of Laos – streets of ochre colonial houses and swaying palms, lines of saffron-robed monks gliding through the morning mist, the sonorous thump of the temple drums before dawn, and, of course, longtail boats racing down the Mekong before the river slips out of view through a seam in the mountains.

It is this heritage of Theravada Buddhist temples, French–Indochinese shophouses and **royal mystique** that lends Luang Prabang a pull unmatched by any other city in Laos. This is not only where the first proto-Lao nation took root, it's also the birthplace of countless Lao rituals and the origin of a line of rulers, including the rulers of Vientiane, Champasak and Lane Xang. Luang Prabang people are tremendously proud of their pivotal role in Lao history. Indeed, they're somewhat known for their cultured ways in the rest of the country; in Lao soap operas, the doctor or the intellectual invariably speaks with a Luang Prabang accent.

Luang Prabang's strict building code, drawn up by UNESCO, keeps it from becoming another modern architectural nightmare without turning it into a museum. Inevitably, the city has lost some of its sleepy charm and dreamy serenity as a result of the growing influx of tourists, but exploring the side streets and dusty lanes, its not hard to feel as though you've stepped into the city of yesteryear. Parts of the city do already feel over touristy – indeed, on stretches of Sisavangvong Road, were it not for the unmistakable architecture, you could be anywhere else on the well-trodden Southeast Asian tourist trail – especially when you've come from other parts of the country where tourism is still a novelty. Though the city remains surprisingly laidback, with none of the hassle associated with other parts of Asia, an airport expansion is due in 2013, which will allow larger planes to fly in and out of Luang Prabang, meaning the small-town charms of this beautiful city could be encroached on further.

Most travellers spend only a few days here on a whistle-stop tour of Laos, part of a wider Mekong trip, though the city really demands longer – this is a destination best savoured at a leisurely pace. If time is limited, top priority should go to the **old city**, dubbed by the UNESCO World Heritage team as a "historic preservation zone". In a day, you can easily tour the sights, beginning with the sunrise view from **Mount Phousi** and a wander around the lively **morning market**, before heading to the elegant **Royal Palace Museum** in the former Royal Palace, en route to Luang Prabang's most impressive temple, **Wat Xieng Thong**. If you're here for a second day, enjoy some of the sights around Luang Prabang by taking a boat up the Mekong River and contemplating the hundreds of Buddhas within the holy **Pak Ou Caves**, or travelling south through the surrounding hills to one of the area's two major **waterfalls**, Kouang Si and Tad Se. But whatever you do, be sure to soak up Luang Prabang's languid atmosphere by wandering the streets at dawn, when the town's legion of monks receives alms and life and the city seems to have little changed from a century ago, or at dusk, when the air fills with otherworldly chants wafting from the temples.

Luang Prabang's air of serenity is disturbed only at **festival** time. The most famous festivals last for days and inspire a carnival atmosphere that makes it easy to forget that these complex rituals held the very structure of the kingdom in place for centuries. **Lao New Year** in April is perhaps the town's biggest festival, but near the end of the monsoon, two holidays – the boat races and the Festival of Lights – also bring Luang Prabang to a festive standstill. A visit coinciding with one of these festivals would certainly enhance your stay, though the most popular time to visit remains the cooler months of December and January, when the weather is clear and dry.

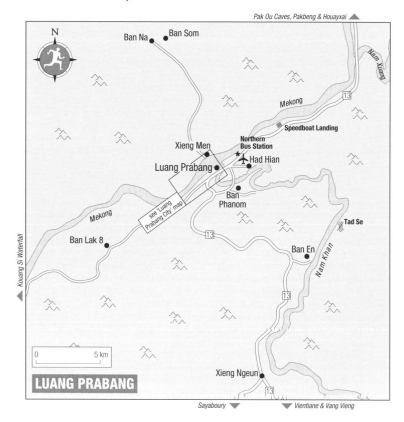

Smoke gets in your eyes

From March until the monsoon season, the city becomes markedly smoky – on some days it's impossible to tell that the sun has risen until a good few hours later. Combined with the intensifying heat, this can be quite an uncomfortable time to visit, so be prepared for stinging eyes and a dry throat during this period. However, it's impossible to deny the city's charms, even when seen through a smoke haze.

Some history

Knowledge of Luang Prabang's early history is sketchy, at best. The earliest Lao settlers made their way down the Nam Ou Valley sometime after the tenth century, absorbing the territory on which the city lies. At the time, the area was known as Muang Sawa, a settlement thought to have been peopled by the Austroasiatic ancestors of the Lao Theung. According to folklore, this migration of the Lao to Luang Prabang was led by Khoun Lo, who claimed the area for his people and called the settlement **Xieng Dong Xieng Thong**. By the end of the thirteenth century, Xieng Dong Xieng Thong had emerged as one of the chief centres of Lao life in the Upper Mekong region, a principality significant enough to be a vassal state of the great Siamese kingdom of Sukhothai.

However, it wasn't until the legendary Lao warrior **Fa Ngum** swept down the Nam Ou with a Khmer army in 1353 and captured Xieng Dong Xieng Thong that the town emerged as the heart of a thriving, independent kingdom in its own right. Claiming the throne of his grandfather, Fa Ngum founded the kingdom of **Lane Xang Hom Khao** – the Land of a Million Elephants and the White Parasol – and established the line of kings that was to rule Laos for six centuries.

With Fa Ngum came monks, artisans and learned men from the Khmer court and, according to histories written a century and a half later, a legal code and Theravada Buddhism. Yet Fa Ngum was still very much the fourteenth-century warrior. After his ministers grew weary of his military campaigns and his rather uncivilized habit of taking his subject's wives and daughters as concubines, he was exiled and replaced on the throne by his son, Oun Heuan, during whose peaceful reign the city flourished.

The sacking of the city in 1478 by the Vietnamese proved a catalyst for the ushering in of the city's **golden age**: striking temples, including the *sim* of Wat Xieng Thong, were built, epic poems composed and sacred texts were copied. In 1512, King Visoun brought the **Pha Bang**, a sacred Buddha image, to Xieng Dong Xieng Thong, a distinguishing event for the identity of the Lao people and the city itself, and a sign that Theravada Buddhism was flourishing.

Wary of encroaching Burmese, King Setthathilat, Visoun's grandson, moved the capital to Vientiane in 1563, leaving the Pha Bang behind and renaming the city after the revered image. The Pha Bang may have been known for its protective properties, but they were no match for the might of the Burmese, and Luang Prabang was engulfed by the chaos of successive **Burmese invasions**.

From then on, the city had a roller-coaster ride. With the disintegration of Lane Xang at the turn of the eighteenth century, **Kingkitsalat** became the first king of an independent Luang Prabang. When **French explorers** Doudart de Lagrée and Francis Garnier arrived in 1867, they found a busy market and port town of wooden homes, a town that Garnier called "the most eminent Laotian centre in Indochina". With Luang Prabang firmly in Siam's orbit, the explorers' suggestion that the kingdom would be better off French was scoffed at by King Oun Kham, but the explorers were proved right two decades later when the Siamese left the town virtually undefended and the city was set ablaze by a group of marauding

Haw. During the siege, French vice-consul Auguste Pavie plucked the ageing Lao king from his burning palace and brought him downriver to safety. From that moment, the king offered tribute to France.

Almost everything was lost during the sacking of the city, but the event provided Pavie with the ammunition he needed to "conquer the hearts" of the Lao and usher in Luang Prabang's **French period**. The town was quickly rebuilt, with the French counting ten thousand people and more than a thousand homes a year after the town's destruction. Within time, the French hired Vietnamese workers to build the homes that lend the city its classic French–Indochinese character, a trend quickly followed by Lao nobility. The city remained remote however: even in 1930 it took longer to travel by river from Saigon to Luang Prabang than it did to travel from Saigon to France.

During the two **Indochina wars**, Luang Prabang fared better than most towns in Laos, though while the city itself remained intact during the fighting that consumed the country over the next two decades, the Second Indochina War ultimately took its toll on Luang Prabang's ceremonial life, which lost its regal heart when the **Pathet Lao** ended the royal line by forcing King Sisavang Vatthana to abdicate in 1975. Two years later, Luang Prabang and Laos lost the king himself, as the new **communist government**, fearful that he might become a rallying point for a rebellion, allegedly exiled him to a Hoa Phan cave, a journey from which he and his family never returned.

In 1995, the city was designated an UNESCO World Heritage Site, in recognition of it's unique mix of traditional Lao architecture and old colonial buildings.

Arrival and information

If you're flying into the city, be sure to get a window seat on the plane in order to enjoy to the stunning bird's-eye views of Luang Prabang. The **airport** is situated just over 2km northeast of the city – visitors from most countries are issued with a thirty-day visa on arrival (see p.23). It's currently a very small airport, though there is a foreign exchange booth (limited hours), an ATM and a small information counter. A expansion is due in 2013, though, being Laos, it's likely this date could change. Minivans wait to shuttle tourists into the centre – on exiting the terminal, buy a ticket at the counter (60,000K for up to three people) and you'll be ushered to a vehicle and taken directly to your accommodation. Tuk-tuks are also available – anticipate paying around 20,000K to get to the city.

Buses from Vientiane, Vang Vieng, Phonsavan and other points south stop at the **Southern Bus Station**, 3km southwest of the centre; the minibus station is directly opposite. Buses from the north arrive at the **Northern Bus Station**, 2km northeast of town, near the airport. Share tuk-tuks meet all bus arrivals – expect to pay at least 10,000K per person to reach the old city.

Slow boats dock at the ferry landing directly behind the Palace Museum. From here it's a short walk to countless guesthouses in the old city, although tuk-tuks are always close at hand should you wish to head a little further out. The **speedboat pier** is in Ban Don, 7km out of the city; a tuk-tuk into the city should cost around 30,000K.

Information

The **tourist office** is on Sisavangvong Road (Mon–Fri 8–11.30am & 1.30–4pm; ☏071/212487), just before the post office, though they're not always open when they should be, and the large room feels rather understocked for such a popular tourist destination. The *Luang Prabang Indexed Map*, published by Hobo Maps, is the most useful city map available (20,000K) – most bookshops (see p.137) stock it.

Many streets in the city change their names numerous times (such as the main street, Sisavangvong, which becomes Sakkaline closer to the tip of the peninsula, and Chao Fa Ngum at the opposite end, once it's past the post office), which is made more confusing by the general lack of street signs. However, the city's generally grid-like layout and small size makes it easy to get around.

City transport

Although you can comfortably walk everywhere in the old city, **bicycles** are ideal for exploring the town at large. Most budget guesthouses and a number of shops along Sisavangvong Road (and the surrounding roads) hire out bikes for around 20,000K per day. **Motorbikes** – a great way to reach out-of-town attractions – are available to rent for $20 a day from rental shops in the old city, and near the Dara Market.

Tuk-tuks can be flagged down easily on most busy streets, and in the early morning there are always drivers hanging around guesthouse areas waiting for foreigners bound for the bus stations or airport. A tuk-tuk journey to most places within the city should cost 15,000–20,000K, but you'll probably be quoted a higher price and be expected to haggle.

Accommodation

Luang Prabang has a wide range of **accommodation**, from simple rooms in inexpensive guesthouses to five-star luxury resorts. Prices here are a lot higher than the rest of the country, so expect to pay out if you want to stay in an atmospheric old building with Mekong views. The high season is December and January (festivals, such as Lao New Year, are also very busy times), but regardless of the season, it's a good idea to book in advance if you have a particular establishment in mind or if you'll be arriving in the evening.

For most people, a location within the **old city**, occupying a finger of land created by the confluence of the Mekong and the Nam Khan, is the first choice. Here you'll find not only most of the city's best attractions but also many shops and restaurants; unsurprisingly, there's not a great deal of cheap accommodation. The streets between the post office and the river are a good place to head to if you're in search of **budget accommodation**, as are the little lanes that lead off Phomathat Road, south of Mount Phousi.

Building controls mean that if you want a hotel with a swimming pool, you'll have to stay outside of the old city – and be prepared to shell out a fair amount. If you're looking for upmarket accommodation, Luang Prabang has an almost overwhelming choice – but it's worth noting that a lot of the cheaper, mid-range places can be just as atmospheric (if not more so) than the fancy hotels.

A good booking site for accommodation, especially for the budget end where few guesthouses have websites or email addresses, is Ⓦ www.luang-prabang-hotels.com.

The old city

3 Nagas by Alila Sakkaline Rd ☎071/253888, Ⓦ www.alilahotels.com. Situated in two buildings on either side of the main road, this intimate boutique hotel is justifiably regarded as one of the city's best. The rooms, beautifully decorated with dark wood and Lao fabrics, are undeniably romantic. Check the website for internet specials. The company's newest hotel – the super luxurious *Alila Luang Prabang* (Ⓘ) – has recently opened in what was previously the city's prison. Ⓘ

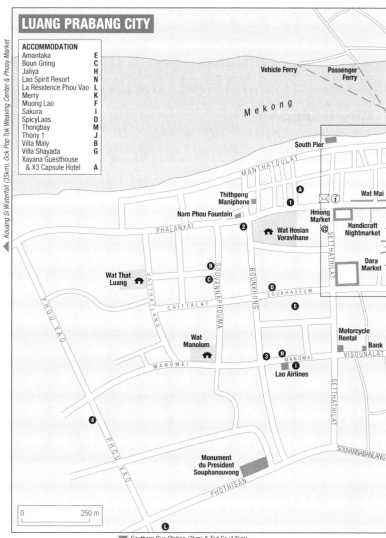

LUANG PRABANG CITY

ACCOMMODATION

Amantaka	E
Boun Gning	C
Jaliya	H
Lao Spirit Resort	N
La Résidence Phou Vao	L
Merry	K
Muong Lao	F
Sakura	I
SpicyLaos	D
Thongbay	M
Thony 1	J
Villa Maly	B
Villa Shayada	G
Xayana Guesthouse & X3 Capsule Hotel	A

Koung Si Waterfall (35km), Ock Pop Tok Weaving Center & Phosy Market

Vehicle Ferry   Passenger Ferry

Mekong

South Pier

MANTHATOULAT

Thithpeng Maniphone

Nam Phou Fountain

PHALANXAI

Wat Hosian Voravihane

Hmong Market

Wat Mai

Handicraft Nightmarket

Dara Market

Wat That Luang

VATTHATLANG

SOUVANNAPHOUMA

BOUNKHONG

SETTHATHILAT

CHITTALAT

SOUKHASEUM

PHOU VAO

Wat Manolom

MANOMAI

Motorcycle Rental   Bank

VISOUNALAT

Lao Airlines

SETTHATHILAT

PHOU VAO

SOUVANNABANLANG

Monument du President Souphanouvong

PHOTHISAN

0   250 m

▼ Southern Bus Station (3km) & Tad Se (17km)

Ammata Kounxoa Rd ☎071/212175, ✉pphilasouk@yahoo.com. This sweet guesthouse, spread across two buildings, is excellent value, with simple but nicely decorated rooms. Wi-fi is available in building 1, but the rooms in newer building 2 are brighter and a little larger. ⑤

🏃 **Belle Rive** Soulignavongsa Rd ☎071/260 733, ⒲www.thebellerive.com. An absolutely charming hotel situated opposite the Mekong. The rooms (all with river views) have been beautifully furnished with dark wood and Oriental touches,

such as decorated sinks and local fabrics. The suites in the main building are split level and have a slightly more contemporary feel than those in the 1920s annexe. ⑧

Heritage Near Wat Pa Phai ☎071/252537, ✉moradok2003@yahoo.com. Surprisingly smart rooms, all with TV, though let down by their large but shabby bathrooms. ⑤

🏃 **Lotus Villa** Kounxoa Rd ☎071/255050, ⒲lotusvillalaos.com. Lovely, light-filled rooms set around a shady courtyard filled with

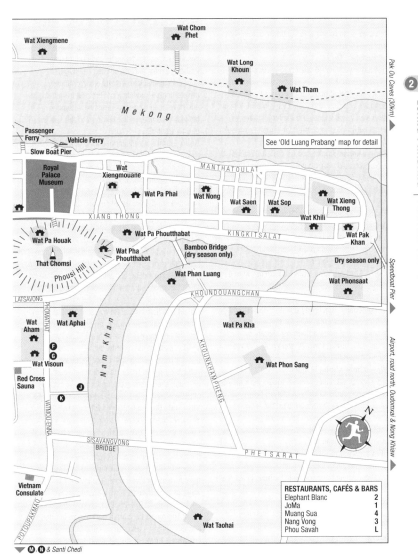

Map labels:
- Wat Chom Phet
- Wat Xiengmene
- Wat Long Khoun
- Wat Tham
- Mekong
- Passenger Ferry
- Vehicle Ferry
- Slow Boat Pier
- Royal Palace Museum
- Wat Xiengmouane
- MANTHATOULAT
- Wat Pa Phai
- Wat Nong
- Wat Saen
- Wat Sop
- Wat Khili
- Wat Xieng Thong
- XIANG THONG
- Wat Pa Houak
- Wat Pa Phoutthabat
- KINGKITSALAT
- Wat Pak Khan
- That Chomsi
- Wat Pha Phoutthabat
- Phousi Hill
- Bamboo Bridge (dry season only)
- Dry season only
- Wat Phan Luang
- Wat Phonsaat
- LATSAVONG
- KHOUNDOUANGCHAN
- Wat Aham
- PHOMATHAT
- Wat Aphai
- Nam Khan
- Wat Pa Kha
- KHOUNKHAMPHENG
- Wat Visoun
- Red Cross Sauna
- VATMOU-ENNA
- Wat Phon Sang
- SISAVANGVONG BRIDGE
- PHETSARAT
- Vietnam Consulate
- POTOUPAKMAO
- Wat Taohai
- See 'Old Luang Prabang' map for detail
- Pak Ou Caves (30km)
- Speedboat Pier
- Airport, road north, Oudomxai & Nong Khiaw

RESTAURANTS, CAFÉS & BARS
Elephant Blanc	2
JoMa	1
Muang Sua	4
Nang Vong	3
Phou Savah	L

▼ & Santi Chedi

banana trees. The charming staff make you feel instantly at home, and the breakfasts are among the best in the city. The luxurious two-room Orchid Suites (**8**) are worth the splurge for the extra space, and include a private balcony. **7**

Mekong Riverview Soulignavongsa Rd ☏071/254900, ⓦwww.mekongriverview .com. The excellent position at the head of the peninsula affords all rooms with a view of the river, which can be enjoyed from each room's private balcony. Rooms are large, with Lao bedspreads

adding a touch of colour, and staff provide guests with a map marked up with the best places to eat and drink, in addition to a very helpful (and regularly updated) information pack in every room. **8**

Nammavong Sisalearmsak Rd ☏071/252176, ⓔlainam45@yahoo.com. In an enviable position right opposite Wat Xieng Thong, this family-run guesthouse has basic but clean rooms and a real local atmosphere. **4**

Sackarinh Off Sisavangvong Rd ☏071/254512. Tucked down an alleyway off the main road, with

LUANG PRABANG | Accommodation

119

football-loving owners, this friendly guesthouse has basic en-suite rooms with windows, but no view, and beds with brightly coloured children's bedspreads. ❹

Sokxai Sakkaline Rd ℡071/254309 ✉sokxai @yahoo.com. The sweet owners will immediately make you feel at home at this new guesthouse opposite Wat Sop. The rooms vary in size, though all have TV and fridge, and the largest are excellent value; the communal veranda overlooks the wat. ❺

Sopha House Kingkitsalat Rd ℡020/5545825. In a gorgeous old building opposite the Nam Khan, the basic rooms here all have TV and fan but are a little musty. For the location, however, you can't beat the price. ❹

Thanaboun Sisavangvong St ℡071/260606, ✉thanaboum.gh@gmail.com. The plain but clean rooms at this popular guesthouse above an internet café are fairly spacious and light, though bathrooms are small. ❻

Thatsaphone Villa Ban Choum Khong ℡071/253577. Tucked down a little side street off Sisavangvong Rd, close to Wat Xiengmouane, this lovely guesthouse, set among palm trees, is a great deal for this part of town. Rooms on the ground floor are slightly on the small size, but all have TV and wi-fi, and are nicely decorated. ❺

View Khem Khong Manthatoulat Rd ℡071/213032. The cheapest rooms here may be rather cramped and without a view, but you'll struggle to find a better price on the Mekong road. If you want a river view, you'll pay considerably more (❻). The attached restaurant (see p.136) is good. ❸

Villa Saykham Sisavang Wattana Rd ℡071/254223, ✉villasaykham@laopdr.com. The traditional-style buildings and charming hosts really make this small hotel special. Rooms are spacious and light, with handicrafts adding a nice touch, and breakfast is served in the peaceful courtyard. ❻

Villa Xieng Mouane Facing Wat Xiengmouane ℡071/252152. This guesthouse in an attractive colonial-style villa takes its name from the nearby monastery, named for its old temple drum which produces a particularly sonorous thump (*xieng mouane* means "jolly sound"). The rooms in the annexe are set around a fragrant garden, while those in the main building are larger: all are plainly decorated, but nice enough. ❺

Xangkeo House Sakkaline Rd ℡071/254985, ✉xankeohouse@gmail.com. Set back from the main road, the simple but comfortable rooms here are set around a gorgeous courtyard with an ornamental pond. ❺

Southeast of the old city

Amantaka Kingkitsarath Rd ℡071/860333, ⓦwww.amanresorts.com/amantaka. The old hospital provides a fantastic setting for Luang Prabang's most exclusive hotel. The huge, high-ceilinged suites – many of which have private pools – provide a cool retreat from the city and have been elegantly furnished. Afternoon tea is served daily in the library, and the spa is a blissful treat. ❾

Boun Gning Souvannaphouma Rd ℡071/212274. A rustic two-storey wooden affair, on a quiet street just a short walk from the old city, with incredibly basic but clean rooms. ❷

Jaliya Manomai Rd ℡071/252154. Tucked away behind a shophouse travel agency, the rooms are all very clean and comfortable, and face onto a lovely private garden. Good value. ❷

Sakura Phamahapasaman Rd ℡071/213026, ✉sakura_lpb@yahoo.com. A friendly, welcoming place full of oversized wooden furniture. Rooms are small and quite dark, but with decent en suites and there's a great communal balcony. Discounts for longer stays. ❹

SpicyLaos Samsanthai Rd ℡020/6922829, ⓦwww.spicyhostels.com. In an atmospheric colonial building dating back to 1936 and just a short walk from the old city, this is a relaxed, popular hostel with ample space for guests to relax and mingle. There's a choice between en-suite, shared bathroom and single-sex dorms (all $6/person), plus a few basic double rooms. ❸

Villa Maly Souvannaphouma Rd ℡071/253902, ⓦwww.villa-maly.com. Just five minutes' walk from the old city, this luxurious property has a real colonial feel. The spacious rooms, decorated in dusky shades of pink and purple, make a nice change from the usual white interiors of hotels in the city, and the lovely pool area is a real bonus. ❾

Xayana Guesthouse & X3 Capsule Hotel Ban Choum Khong ℡071/260250, ⓦwww.mylaohome .com. The rooms here are a decent size but dull and uninspiring – and you can find better value elsewhere. However, the attached "capsule hotel" has bright, clean and spacious dorms with surprisingly large beds ($6). ❹

Pomathat Road and around

Chaophasith Phousi Rd ℡071/200420, ✉chaophasith@gmail.com. Spacious, light rooms with a modern touch and large bathrooms. Expect a fair amount of road noise from rooms at the front, though they boast nice balconies. ❹

Merry Chao Chomphou Rd ℡071/254445. Basic, rather cell-like rooms with walls that could do with a good scrubbing, though they're clean enough. Most rooms have shared bathroom, though it's only another 10,000K for a larger en-suite room. ❷

Muong Lao Pomathat Rd ☎071/25274, ✆www .heritagexplorer.com. The rooms at this popular guesthouse opposite Wat Visoun are simple but very pleasant, and some have a nice balcony overlooking the road. Book exchange, small restaurant and tour services on site. ❹

Thony 1 Chao Chomphou Rd ☎071/212805, ✆bangkeo@hotmail.com. The highlight of a stay here is the lovely communal area overlooking the river where you can enjoy a cold beer. The wood-panelled river-view rooms are the ones to go for (❹), though if you're on a budget, the smaller viewless rooms aren't a bad option. ❸

Villa Shayada Pomathat Rd ☎071/254872, ✆www.villa-shayada-laos.com.This gorgeous little guesthouse is a real find, with spacious rooms decorated with paper lanterns and access to a balcony or terrace. The friendly staff go out of their way to make you feel at home. ❹

Out of the centre

Lao Spirit Resort Xieng Lom, 15km out of Luang Prabang ☎030/5140111, ✆www .lao-spirit.com. A really special place, tucked among the jungle on the banks of the Nam Khan. The five gorgeous bungalows are incredibly

spacious, with large balconies perfect for soaking up the river views. Delicious meals are served throughout the day in the restaurant and various trips can be arranged, including to the nearby Elephant Village. ❽

La Residence Phou Vao On Kite Hill at the eastern end of Phou Vao Rd ☎071/212194, ✆www.residencephouvao.com. A beautiful, sophisticated hotel that lives up to its expensive price tag. All of the sumptuous rooms have private balconies, some with views of Phousi in the distance, and have been sumptuously decorated to provide the ideal surrounds to relax in. The spa, with pavilions set among the lush grounds, is a heavenly retreat, and the swimming pool is welcome respite after the heat of the city. A shuttle runs into town on demand (and hourly in the evenings), or it's just a fifteen-minute walk to the centre. ❾

Thongbay On the banks of the Nam Khan River, about 2km from the old city ☎071/253234, ✆www.thongbay-guesthouses.com. The eight Lao-style bungalows here are set in a beautiful garden, with the best looking over the river. Though a bit of a distance from the centre, the peaceful location more than makes up for it, and there's bikes and a regular shuttle to get you into town. It would be easy, however, to lose hours lounging on your balcony watching the villagers tend their vegetable gardens on the opposite bank. ❺

The City

The majority of Luang Prabang's architecture of merit – temple monasteries, Asian shophouses and French-influenced mansions – is found in the **old city**, along the main thoroughfare of **Sisavangvong/Sakkaline Road**. Kitsalat Road divides the old city from the commercial parts of Luang Prabang which, though newer, still contain plenty of colonial-era mansions scattered about, as well as a number of other important monasteries (most are open daily 8am–7pm), including **Wat Aham** and **Wat Visoun**. The most interesting areas outside the old city for tourists are the **riverbanks**, the old silversmithing district south of the GPO between **Wat Hosian Voravihane** and the Mekong, and **Visounalat Road**, with its numerous guesthouses. The boulevard of Phou Vao, which has many new hotels and restaurants but little character, forms the southern limit of town, while to the north and west, the opposite banks of the Mekong and Nam Khan have little in the way of tourist facilities but are extremely charming and provide a chance to get off the beaten track.

While other urban centres in the country are heavily populated by ethnic Vietnamese and Chinese, Luang Prabang is the only city in Laos where ethnic Lao are in the majority. The **Lao character** is particularly stamped on the backstreets and cobblestoned lanes, which have a distinctly village-like feel, in marked contrast to the shophouses and commercial scenes that you find on the streets of other Lao cities. One of the joys of a stay in Luang Prabang is simply strolling these lanes and absorbing the unhurried rhythms of traditional Lao culture.

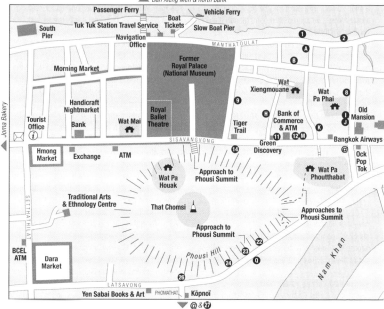

The old city

The **old city** is concentrated on a long finger of land, approximately 1km long by 300m wide. The thicker southern end of the peninsula is dominated by a steep, forested hill, **Phousi**, crowned by a Buddhist stupa that can be seen for miles around. As the city grew it expanded outwards from the peninsula to the south and east, and continues to do so to this day.

   Just four parallel streets run the length of the peninsula, but there are enough cross streets, lanes and dead ends to keep things interesting. Amazingly, each area seems to exude its own distinct personality. Although it is possible to knock off all the attractions in the old city in a couple of days, it's far more enjoyable to explore it a little at a time, and really soak up the atmosphere; the many temples and monasteries are certainly too charming be rushed through.

Phousi

Phousi (Sacred Hill; daily 8am–7pm; 20,000K) is the geographical as well as spiritual centre of the city. Believed to have once harboured a powerful naga who dwelt in its bowels, the hill is also seen as a miniature Mount Meru, the Mount Olympus of Hindu–Buddhist cosmology. Though there is nothing to see on the hill itself, save for an ancient-looking *sim* at its foot, Phousi is striking from a distance. Indeed, the golden spires of **That Chomsi** at its summit are the first glimpse of the city that visitors get if they are arriving by boat or plane. Likewise, the peak affords a stunning panorama of the city it crowns, and the shimmering rivers and jungle-clad mountains beyond are mesmerizing. Viewing the **setting sun** from the summit of Phousi has become a kind of tourist ritual, so don't expect to enjoy the moment alone – indeed, early morning is a better time to come, when the city and the hill are more peaceful. A quieter spot from which to watch the sunset is Sand Chedi (see p.133) on a hill due east of Phousi, which affords a marvellous view back towards Phousi, without the crowds.

M e k o n g

Ban Lao

Monument Books

Ock Pop Tok

SOULIGNAVONGSA

School of Fine Arts

Charter Boat Area

Wat Nong

Spa Garden

Wat Xieng Thong

School   School

Big Brother Mouse

Wat Saen

Wat Sop

Luang Say Cruise

SAKKALINE

KINGKITSALAT

Wat Khili

Wat Pak Khan

Bamboo Bridge (dry season only)

ACCOMMODATION			
3 Nagas by Alila	N	Sackarinh	K
Ammata	D	Sokxai	O
Belle Rive	C	Sopha House	P
Chaophasith	Q	Thanaboun	M
Heritage	J	Thatsaphone Villa	H
Lotus Villa	F	View Khem Khong	A
Mekong Riverview	G	Villa Saykham	I
Nammavong	E	Villa Xieng Mouane	B
		Xangkeo House	L

RESTAURANTS, CAFÉS & BARS		L'Elephant	5
3 Nagas	18	L'Etranger Books & Tea	26
Arisai	15	Lao Lao Garden	23
Au Jardins de l'Elephant	6	Luang Prabang Bakery Café	14
Big Tree Café	4	Morning Glory Café	19
Blue Lagoon	9	Nazim	12
Boungnasouk	2	Saffron	3
Café Toui	8	Sala Café	21
Coconut Garden	11	Tamarind	7
Dyen Sabai	25	Tamnak Lao	17
Hive	24	Tum Tum Cheng	10
The House	22	Un Petit Nid	13
La Banneton	20	Utopia	27
Le Café Ban Vat Sene	16	View Khem Khong	1

There are **three approaches** to the summit. The first and most straightforward is via the stairway directly opposite the main gate of the Royal Palace Museum. The second approach, on the other side of the hill, is up a zigzag stairway flanked by whitewashed naga, and can be used for descending to Phousi Road. The third and most rambling approach is via Wat Pha Phoutthabat near Phousi's northern foot (across from the *Saynamkhan Riverview Hotel*).

Most people choose the first ascent, which allows you to first stop at the adjacent **Wat Pa Houak** (free, donation recommended). This fine little temple, overlooking Sisavangvong Road and the Royal Palace Museum, has a charmingly weathered facade, but is mainly of interest for its **interior murals**. Though the French art historian Henri Parmentier once describing them as "ridiculous", they are in fact fascinating, and appear to depict Luang Prabang as a celestial city. Besides Lao characters in classical costumes, there are Chinese, Persians and Europeans in the city, but it is not clear whether they have come as visitors or invaders. After soaking up the murals it's a steep climb through a tunnel of shady plumeria trees to the peak.

Wat Pha Phoutthabat

Entering via **Wat Pha Phoutthabat** affords the most atmosphere. There are actually three monasteries in this compound, one of which is a school for novice monks. The most interesting structure in the compound is the *sim* of **Wat Pa Khe**, a tall, imposing building with an unusual inward-leaning facade. Most noteworthy here is a pair of carved shutters on the window to the left of the main entrance, said to depict seventeenth-century Dutch traders, and a similar if poorly preserved pair of shutters thought to depict Venetians. Why Dutch and Italians are part of the ornamentation on a Buddhist temple in Luang Prabang has been the subject of much conjecture. Perhaps it commemorates the visits of a travelling merchant of the Dutch East India Company who arrived in Vientiane in 1641, and an Italian

Alms-giving

The daily dawn procession of monks through the streets of the old city has become one of the quintessential images of Luang Prabang and is one of its biggest tourist "attractions". As a result, however, it can feel a little zoo-like, as tourists line up to watch the monks pass, cameras madly clicking to get the best shot.

There's no denying the serene beauty of the alms-giving ceremony (*Tak Bat*) as kneeled locals place sticky rice into the baskets of the passing saffron-robed monks. However, if you do wish to see it, it's important to behave properly – in particular, dress appropriately and modestly, don't make physical contact with the monks, and keep a respectful distance from them. It is possible to join the alms-giving, but locals request that you only do so if it would be meaningful to you. If you do so, buy sticky rice from the morning market beforehand rather than the street vendors that congregate along Sisavangvong Road as the rice can be of dubious quality.

missionary who arrived soon after, though the penned accounts of neither of these men ever mention reaching Luang Prabang. Perhaps more likely is the theory that these carvings were executed in the mid-nineteenth century and were meant to serve the same function as the images of demons commonly found carved on temple doors and windows: to keep evil spirits at bay.

Behind and to the left of the *sim* is a stairway leading to the "**Buddha's footprint**" after which Wat Pha Phoutthabat was named. The balustrade flanking this shady stairway is decorated with four pairs of curious sandstone carvings. The carvings resemble *somasutra*, found in ancient Khmer temple architecture, which were used to channel lustral water over a phallic stone sacred to the Hindu god Shiva. However, these carvings look distinctly Chinese, and fittings on the rear ends seem to indicate that the carvings were a decorative feature of a large structure before being incorporated into the balustrades of this stairway.

The larger-than-life stylized footprint (20,000K) is complete with the 108 auspicious marks said to be found on the historic Buddha's foot (for more on "Buddha's footprints", see the account of Wat Phabat Phonsan, p.93). On festival days, pilgrims make offerings by tossing banknotes into the footprint.

Continuing up the path, you come to a small concrete grotto with an image of Pha Kajai, the Mahayanist deity most Westerners associate with the Buddha. The path meanders rather steeply from here up to the summit, crowned by the stupa That Chomsi, which looks dented and dull up close.

The Royal Palace (Royal Palace Museum)

Occupying a fittingly central location in the old city, between Phousi Hill and the Mekong River, the former **Royal Palace** (daily except Tues 8.30–11.30am & 1.30–3.30pm; 30,000K) is now home to the Royal Palace Museum, preserving the trappings and paraphernalia of Laos's recently extinguished monarchy. The palace, at the end of a long drive lined with stately palms, was constructed in 1904 by the French and replaced an older, smaller palace of teak and rosewood. The new palace was supposed to be crowned by a European-style steeple, but King Sisavang Vong insisted on modifications, and the graceful stupa-like spire that you see today was substituted, resulting in a tasteful fusion of European and Lao design. Another striking feature is the pediment over the main entrance adorned with a gilt rendition of the symbol of the Lao monarchy: Airavata, the three-headed elephant, being sheltered by the sacred white parasol. This is surrounded by the intertwining bodies of the fifteen guardian naga (see p.244) of Luang Prabang.

The **king's reception room**, to the right of the entrance hall, is full of huge Gauguinesque canvases portraying what appears to be "a day in the life of old Luang Prabang", with scenes of the city as it appeared in the early twentieth century. The paintings, executed by Alex de Fautereau in 1930, are meant to be viewed at different hours of the day when the light from outside is supposed to illuminate the panels depicting the corresponding time of day.

More impressive is the **Throne Hall**, just beyond the entry hall. Its high walls spangled with mosaics of multicoloured mirrors set in a crimson background, the throne hall dazzles even in the dim light. These mosaics, along with others at Wat Xieng Thong, were created in the mid-Fifties to commemorate the 2500th anniversary of the historic Buddha's passing into Nirvana. On display in this room are rare articles of royal regalia: swords with hilts and scabbards of hammered silver and gold, an elaborately decorated fly-whisk and even the king's own howdah (elephant saddle). Also on show is a cache of small crystal, silver and bronze Buddha images taken from the inner chamber of the "Watermelon Stupa" at Wat Visoun. Somehow these treasures escaped the plundering gangs of "Black Flag" Chinese who, led by a White Tai warlord, sacked Luang Prabang in 1887. The stupa was destroyed, rebuilt in 1898, but collapsed in 1914. It was then that the Buddhas were discovered inside.

Leaving the Throne Hall via the door on the right, you come to the **royal library**, which is almost exclusively made up of official archives of the Ming and Ching dynasties, a gift from China during the Cultural Revolution. The corridors that surround the rooms at the rear are decorated with sixteen pictures that illustrate the legend of Prince Wetsantara, considered an important epic by Lao Buddhists.

King Sisavang Vong's bedchamber, located at the very back of the palace, is surprisingly modest. The only thing that looks especially regal is the massive

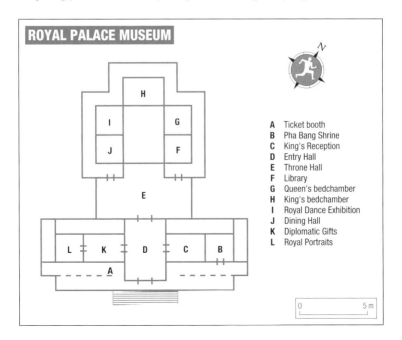

ROYAL PALACE MUSEUM

A Ticket booth
B Pha Bang Shrine
C King's Reception
D Entry Hall
E Throne Hall
F Library
G Queen's bedchamber
H King's bedchamber
I Royal Dance Exhibition
J Dining Hall
K Diplomatic Gifts
L Royal Portraits

0   5 m

The Pha Bang

Much more than an ancient image of the Buddha, the **Pha Bang** is the palladium of Laos. The pursuit and enshrining of palladial images has a long history in Southeast Asia, full of intrigue and Byzantine plotting. Like Thailand's "Phra Kaew" and Burma's "Mahamuni" Buddha images, the Pha Bang is believed to possess miraculous powers that safeguard the country in which it is enshrined. Formerly, palladial images were thought to legitimize the sovereignty of a king who had one in his possession. Only a pious king with sufficient religious merit could hope to hold onto such an image, and losing it was thought to be proof that a kingdom and its ruler did not deserve to possess it. Thus the histories of certain palladia read like the itinerary of some much coveted sacred sword or holy grail.

According to Lao legend, the Pha Bang image was cast of gold, silver, copper, iron and precious stones. Overseen by the god Indra, who donated gold for its creation, the image was crafted in the heavens above the Himalayas and then delivered to the capital of Sri Lanka. From there the image made its way to Cambodia and then to the city of Xieng Dong Xieng Thong, later renamed Luang Prabang (the Great Pha Bang) in honour of the image. In the early eighteenth century, the Pha Bang was moved to **Vientiane**, now the capital. Twice the Siamese invaded Vientiane, capturing the image, and twice they returned it to the Lao, believing that the Pha Bang was bad luck for Siam.

Since 1867, the Pha Bang has been kept in Luang Prabang, where to this day it is considered the most sacred Buddha image in Laos and centrepiece of the Lao New Year festival. At least, that's the official story. Persistent **rumours** have circulated since the revolution that the authentic Pha Bang was removed from its ornate pedestal and given to the Soviets in return for assistance to the Pathet Lao during the war. The image on display is said to be a copy, while the real Pha Bang is locked away in some vault in Moscow, its powers no longer serving as a talisman for Laos.

---

hardwood bed, the headboard of which sports the king's initials and a carved Buddha sheltered by a seven-headed naga. The footboard bears a rendition of the royal emblem of Laos, this time with a two-tiered parasol.

Of the two final rooms, the near room houses **diplomatic gifts** presented to the people of Laos by a handful of nations, as well as the rather tatty-looking flag of the Kingdom of Laos that was given a symbolic ride up into space and back on one of the Apollo missions. Not long afterwards, the Kingdom of Laos ceased to exist. In the far room hang larger-than-life **portraits** of King Sisavang Vattana, his wife Queen Kham Phoui and their son Prince Vong Savang. These are the only officially displayed portraits of the last members of the 600-year-old dynasty anywhere in Laos. Had they not been painted by a Soviet artist they almost certainly would not have survived the years following the revolution. The same goes for the bronze sculpture of King Sisavang Vong in the museum grounds near the front gate. This statue may look familiar if you have already passed through Vientiane, where a larger version stands in the park adjacent to Wat Simuang.

Turn left immediately upon exiting the museum to reach the small room that currently houses the **Pha Bang**, the most sacred Buddha image in Laos (see box, above). Flanking the Pha Bang are numerous other Buddha images, including ancient Khmer stone images and several pairs of mounted elephant tusks. One pair, deeply incised with rows of Buddhas, was noted by Francis Garnier on the altar of Wat Visoun in the 1860s. Displayed nearby in richly carved wooden frames are silk panels embroidered with gold and silver thread that depict yet more images of the Buddha.

Wat Mai

Just west of the Royal Palace on Sisavangvong Road, Wat Mai Suwannaphumaham, or **Wat Mai** for short (10,000K), has what must surely be Luang Prabang's most photographed *sim* after that of Wat Xieng Thong. The monastery dates from the late eighteenth or early nineteenth century (depending on whom you believe), but it is the *sim*'s relatively modern facade with its gilt stucco reliefs that forms the main focus of attention. Depicting the second-to-last incarnation of the Buddha set amid traditional Lao scenes, the facade was created in the 1960s and restored in the 1990s. Like most examples of modern Lao temple ornamentation, it looks interesting from a distance, but somewhat disappointing up close.

Ban Jek

The neighbourhood just north of the former Royal Palace is still known to locals as "**Ban Jek**" or Chinatown, as the rows of shophouses along Sisavangvong Road were once mostly owned by ethnic Chinese shopkeepers. Here you'll find some fine examples of Luang Prabang **shophouse architecture**, a hybrid of French and Lao features superimposed on the basic South China style that was once the standard throughout urban Southeast Asia. Downstairs was a shop or other place of business, while upstairs the residents lived under a roof of fired-clay shingles supported by brick and stucco walls. This combination kept interior temperatures cool during the hot season and warm during the chilly early morning hours of Luang Prabang's "winter". Shuttered windows, introduced by the French, were coupled with transoms of filigreed wood above doors and windows. This allows air to circulate even when doors and windows are bolted shut.

Many of the shops here are now rented out to entrepreneurs from Vientiane, but even with their inevitable conversion to souvenir and tourist outlets, the streets which they line retain much of the charm they exuded before the outbreak of World Heritage fever.

Wat Pa Phai to Wat Sop

In the area immediately northeast of the palace are three temples of note, **Wat Choum Khong**, **Wat Xiengmouane** and **Wat Pa Phai**, the Bamboo Forest Monastery. The principal attraction at Wat Pa Phai is the facade of the *sim*, painted and lavishly embellished with stylized naga (see box, p.244). Almost directly opposite from Wat Pa Phai sits a curious old **mansion** which is a fine example of a type of architecture that could be termed "French–Indochinese": the design of the house itself is unmistakably European, but the ornamentation is obviously Asian. The finely carved hardwood doors were almost certainly crafted by Chinese or Vietnamese, and hint at the origin of the curious "Buddha" on the facade posing in a very non-traditional *mudra*. Appropriately enough, it's now a centre for French language.

Situated a few blocks to the northeast, **Wat Saen** is the first of a row of monasteries that monopolize the west side of the street for nearly two blocks. Of interest at Wat Saen is an ornate boat shed housing the monastery's two **longboats**, used in the annual boat race festival. Held at the end of the rainy season, the boat races are believed to lure Luang Prabang's fifteen guardian naga (see box, p.244) back into the rivers after high waters and flooded rice paddies have allowed them to escape. Fittingly, the boathouse is decorated with the carved wooden images of these mythical serpentine creatures.

In 1888, the French counted nearly fifty monasteries in Luang Prabang and its environs. Today, there are just over thirty. Close inspection of the grounds of **Wat Sop**, just beyond Wat Saen, yields some clues as to the reason for the disappearance of many wats. The large Buddha image out in the open and the section of unmatched wall in front of it are evidence that this half of the grounds was once the site of a separate monastery. Sometime in the past the *sim* that once sheltered the Buddha was destroyed, and the monastery was absorbed by Wat Sop.

Wat Khili

On the opposite side of Sakkaline Road, **Wat Khili** is a rare example of a Xieng Khuang-style temple. Luang Prabang once boasted at least three temples in this low, squat design, which originated on the windy plains of the province and former kingdom after which the style is named. Legend has it that the Chinese "Black Flag" rebels who sacked and looted Luang Prabang in 1887 took special care to destroy Xieng Khuang-style temples because their shape resembled Chinese coffins. It's also said that the Buddha at Wat Khili broke into a cold sweat in 1958, a dark omen signalling the coming war. The province of Xieng Khuang was heavily bombed during the Second Indochina War, leaving no trace of Xieng Khuang-style architecture there and making the *sim* at Wat Khili possibly the last surviving example. The monastery is said to have been founded for the commemoration of the marriage of a Phuan prince from Xieng Khuang to a Luang Prabang princess in the early nineteenth century.

The Buddhist Archive operates a small **exhibition** (free) in one of the smaller temple buildings, displaying some fascinating photographs of monks from its collection which provide a historical insight not found elsewhere in the city.

Wat Xieng Thong

The most historic and enchanting Buddhist monastery in the entire country, **Wat Xieng Thong**, the Golden City Monastery (daily 6am–6pm; 20,000K), should not be missed. Near the northernmost tip of the peninsula, the temple compound alone is a delight to wander through, especially early in the morning before the tourist crowds descend on it. The main temple or *sim* was built in 1560 by King Setthathilat (who then promptly moved the capital of the Kingdom of a Million Elephants downriver to Vientiane) and it is this wonderfully graceful building that dominates the monastery. Unlike nearly every other temple in Luang Prabang, this *sim* was not razed by Chinese marauders in the nineteenth century or overenthusiastically restored in the twentieth. Indeed, an old photograph taken under Auguste Pavie's direction shows the temple to have changed little in the last century.

You'll need to stand at a distance to get a view of the **roof**, the temple's most outstanding feature. Elegant lines curve and overlap, sweeping nearly to the ground, and evoke a bird with outstretched wings or, as the locals say, a mother hen sheltering her brood. The **walls** of the *sim* are decorated inside and out with stencilled gold motifs on a black or maroon background. As you enter the dimly lit temple and your eyes adjust to the lack of light, the gold-leaf patterns seem to float on the blackened walls.

Besides stylized floral designs, the motifs depict a variety of tales, including the Lao version of the Ramayana, scenes from the Jataka and stories about the lives of the Buddha, as well as graphic scenes of punishments doled out in the many levels of Buddhist hell. In one of these punishment scenes, on the wall to the right of the main entrance, an adulterous couple is being forced to flee a pack of rabid dogs by climbing a tree studded with wicked thorns. Other unfortunate souls are being cooked in a copper cauldron of boiling oil (for committing murder) or are suspended by a hook through their tongues (guilty of telling lies).

In the rafters above and to the right of the main entrance runs a long wooden **aqueduct** or trough in the shape of a mythical serpent. During Lao New Year, lustral water is poured into a receptacle in the serpent's tail and spouts from its mouth, bathing a Buddha image housed in a wooden pagoda-like structure

Big Brother Mouse

Set up to promote literacy in Laos, **Big Brother Mouse** (Phayaluangmeungchan Rd; ☎071/254937, ⊛ www.bigbrothermouse.com) is an excellent scheme that publishes books in Lao and enables young people to gain new skills in reading, writing and computing. Books are still a rare commodity in Laos, so the work that Big Brother Mouse does is vital in helping young Lao people develop new skills and enhance their prospects.

The organization, which is non-profit and Lao-owned, encourages visitors to buy books to take on treks, rather than giving sweets or pens to village children. In addition, tourists can sponsor a book party ($300–400), help young adults practise their English (Mon–Sat 9am; 2hr) or volunteer in the office and shop (vacancies are regularly posted outside the shop). You are welcome to visit the shop and speak to the staff in more detail about their work and what you can do – look for the big cut-out of a mouse outside.

situated near the altar. A drain in the floor of the pagoda channels the water through pipes under the floor of the *sim* and the water then pours from the mouth of a mirror-spangled elephant's head located on the exterior wall.

Covering the exterior of the back wall of the *sim* is a **mosaic**, said to depict a legendary flame tree that stood on the site when the city was founded. This particular composition is especially beautiful during the Festival of Lights, when the *sim* is decked out with *khom fai dao*, star-shaped lanterns constructed of bamboo and mulberry paper. The flickering candlelight illuminates the tree and animals in the mosaic, making them twinkle magically.

To the left of the *sim*, as you face it, stands a small brick-and-stucco **shrine** containing a standing Buddha image. The purple and gold mirrored mosaics on the pediments of the structure are especially intricate and probably the country's finest example of this kind of ornamentation, which is thought to have originated in Thailand and spread to Burma as well. Directly behind the shrine is a larger structure known to French art historians as "La Chapelle Rouge", the **Red Chapel**. The **reclining Buddha** image enshrined within is one of Laos's greatest sculptures in bronze.

The Funerary Carriage Hall

On the other side of the monastery grounds is the **Funerary Carriage Hall** or *haw latsalot*, a rare example of a modern Lao religious structure that manages to impress. Built in 1962, it has wide teakwood panels deeply carved with depictions of Rama, Sita, Ravana and Hanuman, all characters from *Pha Lak Pha Lam*, the Lao version of the Ramayana. Check out the carved window shutters on the building's left side where Hanuman, the King of the Monkeys, is depicted in pursuit of the fair sex.

Inside, the principal article on display is the *latsalot*, the royal funerary carriage, used to transport the mortal remains of King Sisavang Vong to cremation. The vehicle is built in the form of several bodies of parallel naga, whose jagged fangs and dripping tongues heralded the king's final passage through Luang Prabang. Atop the carriage are three urns of gilded sandalwood, which were used to keep royal corpses in an upright foetal position until the cremation. The urns at the front and rear of the carriage held the remains of the king's father and mother respectively; the centre urn contained the remains of the king, which were cremated in April 1961.

Besides protecting these funerary paraphernalia from the elements, the building houses various **religious relics**. Among these are ornate wooden frames containing images of the Buddha that were given to the monastery as offerings. Most on

▲ Wat Xieng Thong

display here feature painted renditions of the Buddha, but more elaborate images, resembling a tapestry of silver or gold thread, are on display with the Pha Bang at the Royal Palace Museum.

The leafy **garden** beside the hall contains some grand bougainvillea, coconut trees and two grey-green fan palms. It was from this species of palm that traditional **palm-leaf manuscripts** were made. Using a stylus to scratch characters onto the palm leaves, monks wrote down Pali-language chants and recorded historical events that affected the kingdom. Before access to paper and cheap printing made palm-leaf manuscripts obsolete, two or three of these trees could be found growing at every wat.

Outside the old city

The old city may have the highest concentration of monasteries and old buildings, but there is plenty of interest on and beyond Setthathilat Road including an excellent museum, over twenty temples, several markets, and a choice of scenic walks. The most historically important of the temples are **Wat Hosian Voravihane**, **Wat Visoun** and **Wat Aham**, although a trip to the opposite banks of the Mekong and Nam Khan rivers will reward you with many other venerable riverside temples, as well as a relaxed rural ambience and good views back over the old city.

Traditional Arts and Ethonology Centre (TAEC)

Tucked up a steep unpaved road off Setthathilat Road, the **Traditional Arts and Ethnology Centre** (Tues–Sun 9am–6pm; 20,000K) provides an excellent introduction to Laos's ethnic groups. The small exhibition displays beautiful clothing, household objects and religious artefacts to illustrate the history and way of life for the Akha, Hmong and Khmu people, among others. All of the items are attributed to their makers, and the information that runs alongside the displays is insightful and interesting. Particularly fascinating is the short documentary on Taoist ordination ceremonies, complemented by some beautiful ceremonial masks made from tissue-thin mulberry paper, which are worn on the top of the head in order that they can be seen by the gods. A small shop attached to the museum sells reasonably priced handicrafts, and the charming café is a good place to stop for a cup of Lao coffee.

Wat Hosian Voravihane

Wat Hosian Voravihane is situated on a low hill to the west of Phousi Hill and is reached via a stairway flanked by some impressive and undulating seven-headed naga spewing from the mouths of snaggle-toothed *makara*. At the top of the stairs is the most photographed **window** in all of Luang Prabang, a blend of Lao, Chinese and Khmer design framed in ornately carved teak. Other elements of the wat suggest influence from northern Thailand, namely the gold-topped *that*. The graceful **stupa** is very similar to examples found in Chiang Mai, Thailand.

Wat Visoun and Wat Aham

Wat Visoun and **Wat Aham** (20,000K for both) share a parcel of land on the opposite side of Phousi from the Royal Palace Museum. The *sim* of the former, as seen in a wood-block print executed by French artist Louis Delaporte in 1873, was once a lavishly decorated example of the all-but-extinct Xieng Khuang style. The original *sim* was razed during the sack of Luang Prabang in 1887 by Chinese bandits, and the bulbous, finial-topped stupa, known as *that makmo* – the **watermelon stupa** – was destroyed as well. The looters made off with treasures

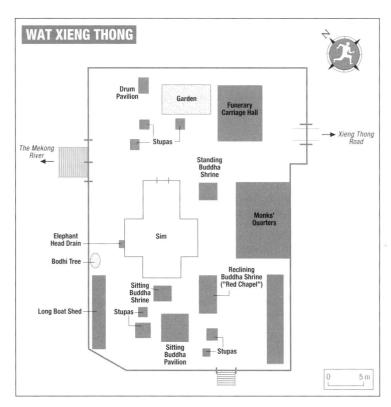

WAT XIENG THONG

Drum Pavilion

Garden

Funerary Carriage Hall

Stupas

The Mekong River

→ Xieng Thong Road

Standing Buddha Shrine

Sim

Monks' Quarters

Elephant Head Drain

Bodhi Tree

Reclining Buddha Shrine ("Red Chapel")

Sitting Buddha Shrine

Long Boat Shed

Stupas

Sitting Buddha Pavilion

Stupas

0   5 m

Along the banks of the Mekong and the Nam Khan

Surrounded by **rivers** on three sides, Luang Prabang not surprisingly feels almost waterborne, and the ship-like contour of the peninsula enhances this impression. Numerous stairways, flanked with whimsical guardian images, link palaces, monasteries and homes with nearby rivers, and are a statement of the importance of the **Mekong** and the **Nam Khan** in the lives of Luang Prabang's population. The banks along the Mekong side are the more lively, but the Nam Khan side is more evocative of old Luang Prabang, and on either side the show is a never-ending affair.

When the French arrived in Luang Prabang they noted a "floating suburb" anchored in the shallows on the Mekong's banks. Francis Garnier described how arriving boats and rafts would slowly poke among the houseboats looking for a place to land and discharge their passengers and cargo. With paved roads conveying much of the traffic into Luang Prabang, life along the river is less of a circus now, but sights and sounds of riparian commerce linger, and ferries between both sides of the Mekong usually groan under the weight of produce (and villagers) being taken to and from the city. On the Nam Khan side, groups of residents tend tidy riverside gardens and make their way down to the river to bathe during dusk's waning light. It is scenes like these, all but vanished and forgotten in more developed countries, that make Luang Prabang such a fascinating place.

stored within, but fortunately didn't take everything. What they left behind is now on display in the throne room of the Royal Palace Museum (see p.124). Wat Visoun's reconstructed *sim* is an unremarkable mix of Luang Prabang and Vientiane styles, but the watermelon stupa is still quite unique.

Neighbouring Wat Aham features a delightfully diminutive *sim* and a couple of mould-blackened *that*, one with a picturesque slant. This wat is associated with **Phu Nyoe** and **Nya Nyoe**, the shaggy, red-faced spirits that are believed to be the founders and protectors of Luang Prabang. Effigies of the two deities head the parade during the Lao New Year festivities in April, and they are believed to inhabit the two venerable banyan trees whose shade-giving canopies make this a pleasant place to linger.

Across the Mekong: Xieng Men and around

Surprisingly few tourists bother to cross the Mekong and explore the sleepy village of **XIENG MEN**, but it's a real delight to escape the crowds and experience village life so close to the city. A passenger ferry (5000K) operates regularly between Luang Prabang and Xieng Men, leaving from the landing near the northwest corner of the Royal Palace Museum compound (look for the steep steps down to the riverbank), while a vehicle ferry operates from the slow boat landing (5000K). Alternatively, you could charter a boat with one of the many boatmen that congregate by the landings – count on around 50,000–60,000K for a return trip, including waiting time.

Just up from the boat landing, a narrow path to the right leads through the village, full of traditional wooden houses and small noodle shops. After a few minutes, you'll reach **Wat Xiengmene** (5000K), on the left, which was built in 1592 and extensively rebuilt in modern times – though it still retains its beautifully carved doors. The bamboo forest behind the wat conceals a royal cemetery for those members of royalty who, for religious reasons, could not be cremated.

A little further on, a steep but short climb away from the path brings you to the *sim* and stupas of **Wat Chom Phet** (5000K). At dusk the views of the sunset from here are spectacular, further enhanced by the sounds of the city carrying across the water. Beyond here, the path is elevated and provides excellent views across the river to the city, before reaching the final temple, **Wat Long Khoun** (5000K). Set in peaceful grounds, it was once used by Luang Prabang's kings as a pre-coronation retreat involving ritual baths, meditation and reflection. The wat was restored in 1995 by the École Française d'Extrême Orient. Of note are the two Chinese door guardians painted either side of the main entrance to the *sim*, and the murals within.

Your ticket for the wat includes a guided visit to nearby **Wat Tham Sackkalin**, which is actually a **cave** repository for old and damaged Buddha images. As with Tham Ting upriver (see p.142), this cave is a focus of activity during Lao New Year, when the residents of Luang Prabang come here to gain merit by ritually bathing the Buddhas. There's not a great deal to see, but it's rather atmospheric and quite fun to scramble over rocks in the dark. Note that you will be expected to tip your guide at the end (1000–2000K should be fine).

Across the Nam Khan

Although a long walk along the Mekong foreshore and even around the point and back down Kingkitsalat Road is considered *de rigueur* on any walking tour of the old city, very few tourists make the short hop across the river to the **opposite shore of the Nam Khan**. Here, facing the old city and running for several kilometres alongside the Nam Khan and the Mekong to the village of Ban Don, is a string of old **wats** and **monasteries**, quiet neighbourhoods that see relatively few foreign faces, and boast a few crumbling old French mansions ready to tumble into the Mekong. To reach the far shore, simply cross the Sisavangvong Bridge, and turn left at the first big intersection. In the dry season, you can cross at the bamboo bridge (4000K from 8am–5pm) near Wat Pha Phoutthabat and turn left onto the path after *Dyen Sabai* restaurant (see p.136). The route, which can also be cycled, follows the banks of the Nam Khan all the way to the Mekong and then continues along the Mekong shore through several small villages all the way up to **Ban Don**, where the speedboat landing is located. Along the way you can visit many charming temples such as Wat Phan Luang, Wat Pa Kha or Wat Phonsaat, and take in superb views back across the Nam Khan towards the old city.

Santi Chedi

About 3km east of town stands Luang Prabang's largest religious monument. Constructed in 1988 and christened **Santi Chedi**, or "Peace Stupa", this modern, concrete pagoda is best known for its mural-splashed interior (open Mon–Fri 8–10am & 1.30–4.30pm), though its carved windows are great works of art in themselves. However, the main reason to come up here is for the impressive **views** of Phousi and the Nam Khan River, which needless to say are especially attractive at sunset, as is Santi Chedi itself when its golden surface catches the glow of the setting sun – most impressive from a distance. The best way to get here is by bike – though be prepared for a steep final slog up to the chedi.

Eating

Luang Prabang is a city that prides itself on its food. Some dishes are unique to the royal city, and others are simply done better here than elsewhere – all of which conspires to make this the town in which to dig into **Lao food** with a sense of mission, despite the wide availability of international cuisine. At the top of your list should be *or lam*, a bittersweet meat soup made with chilli wood, lemongrass, aubergine and dill. Another local speciality, *jaew bong*, a condiment of red chillies, shallots, garlic and dried buffalo skin, is an excellent accompaniment for *khai paen*, a highly nutritious **river moss** that's first sundried with sesame seeds, garlic and chilli, then fried in oil.

Phak nam, a type of **watercress** particular to the area, is a common sight in Luang Prabang's markets (see p.139), and is widely used in salads. The most common style appears on menus either as "watercress salad" or "Luang Prabang salad" and is in fact quite similar to a Western salad – a light alternative to the meat salads more commonly served in Lao restaurants. Locals even add a twist to the Lao staple, *tam màk hung* (**papaya salad**): the distinctive Luang Prabang flavour of this dish comes from the addition of crab juice.

Cafés

All the cafés reviewed below appear on the map on p.122 unless otherwise stated.

Aux Jardins de l'Elephant Kounxoa Rd. This café-cum-florist's, part of the *L'Elephant* family offers a cool reprieve on hot days with their refreshing rosella (hibiscus) iced tea (13,000K). The food is a mix of French and Lao, at more accessible prices than its sister restaurant, *L'Elephant*, next door and the Parisian baguette (ham, edam, gherkins, salad and olive oil; 35,000K) is exquisite. Daily 9am–6pm.

JoMa Chao Fa Ngum Rd, see map, p.118. Perenially popular, though you could really be anywhere in the world. A wide range of Western food and baked treats, with sandwiches from 16,000K, but there are undoubtedly more atmospheric and friendlier places in town to spend your kip.

Le Banneton Sakkaline Rd. Situated directly across from Wat Sop, this café-boulangerie feels decidedly French, with an excellent choice of patisseries, plus delicious baguettes. Daily 6.30am–5.45pm.

Le Cafe Ban Vat Sene Sakkaline Rd. This charming café, with it's artfully distressed exterior and cool, fan-spun interior, is a wonderful place to lose a few hours, especially for an afternoon coffee and one of their delicious cakes – including a heavenly banana tatin (20,000K).

L'Etranger Books & Tea Phousi Rd. The tables outside this great little bookshop (see p.139) are a great choice for a refreshing drink while you watch the world go by. Movies are shown nightly at 7pm (free but food or drink purchase necessary).

Morning Glory Café Sakkaline Rd. A great café with a lovely outside area facing Wat Saen, serving fruit shakes, fair-trade Lao coffee and great Thai food, including an incredibly coconutty *tom kha gai* (35,000K). Mon–Fri & Sun 7.30am–3.30pm.

Saffron Manthatoulat Rd. The airy interior of this little café is decorated with sepia photographs of coffee pickers, and there's more seating outside overlooking the Mekong. The coffee is excellent and strong (and grown in Luang Prabang province), and there's a good range of breakfast dishes including a delicious granola bowl (15,000K).

Restaurants

Thanks to the huge growth in tourism, Luang Prabang boasts more **restaurants** than anywhere else in the country outside of the capital. But the city is no centre for street food – there's nothing even remotely like the kind of food-stall scene you find in Thailand. That said, in the evenings you'll find stalls set up next to the post office selling grilled chicken and fish, and the narrow side street next to *Ancient Luang Prabang* is crammed with people selling noodle soup, grilled meat and papaya salad (with tables at which to eat), at very cheap prices. Baguettes and fresh fruit shakes are sold throughout the day in front of the Hmong Market, and during the evenings you'll also find someone selling delicious *kanom krok* (little coconut and rice pancakes) here.

The highest density of restaurants is along Sisavangvong Road, though it can seem at times like they all offer identikit menus. Cheaper and often tastier meals can be found at the delightful **riverside restaurants** along the western end of Manthatoulat Road; this is also the perfect spot to be at sunset and after dark for alfresco dining. Prices are a little higher in Luang Prabang than in the rest of the country, with mains generally starting at around 35,000K, but only in the poshest places will you be likely to spend over 120,000K per person.

Cookery Courses

Luang Prabang is a great place to learn more about Lao food, with a number of excellent cookery schools (all attached to acclaimed restaurants) offering a range of introductory classes.

Tamarind Opposite Wat Nong ☎020/7770484, ⓦwww.tamarindlaos.com. The excellent one-day class begins with a fascinating tour of Phosy Market (see p.139) before the group heads to the peaceful lakeside cooking school where you learn six Lao dishes – such as lemongrass stuffed with chicken, *môk pa* and *jaew*. $22.

Tamnak Lao Sakkaline Rd ☎020/5173154, ⓦwww.tamnaklao.net. This popular course offers the opportunity to learn how to cook five Lao dishes, plus the ubiquitous sticky rice and delicious *jaew bong*. $25.

Tum Tum Cheng Sakkaline Rd ☎020/242 5499, ⓔtumtumcheng@yahoo.com. A shorter course than most (running from 8.30am to 1.30pm), where you can learn how to prepare many of the more unusual Lao ingredients and more about the royal cuisine of Luang Prabang. $30.

The old city

3 Nagas Sakkaline Rd ☎071/253888. One of the best places in town for Lao food, with an atmospheric dining room that opens onto Sakkaline Rd. Try the exquisite *larp* ($7) and the lemongrass stuffed with pork ($4.50). The excellent wine list has bottles from $20.

Arisai Sakkaline Rd ☎071/255000. Smart yet unpretentious Mediterranean restaurant with a small but well-regarded menu. Dishes include country-style pâté (49,000K) and Provencal wild boar stew (94,000K), and the wine menu is among the best in town. Dinner only.

Blue Lagoon Ban Choum Khong ☎071/253698. Popular with expats, the best seats here are in the atmospheric garden courtyard. The mixed Western and Lao menu is a little overpriced for the quality (*larp* 78,000K) but the presentation and service is absolutely superb. Closed Mon.

Café Toui A small, intimate place with a couple of pavement tables. The menu is predominantly Lao, though the baguettes make this an excellent lunch stop; the highlight is the set Lao menu that offers a taster of local dishes including *mok pa* and *larp* for 70,000K.

Coconut Garden Sisavangvong Rd. The most atmospheric choice on this stretch of the main road, with a lantern-strung courtyard, coconut palms and ambient music. The Lao dishes are very tasty but a little on the small side – try the *kranab pa* (grilled river fish stuffed with pork and herbs and wrapped in a banana leaf; 38,000K).

L'Elephant Ban Wat Nong ☎071/252482. Situated in a beautiful colonial building, this acclaimed, upmarket restaurant is the kind of place where you almost expect to see Humphrey Bogart stroll in.

The menu is predominantly French, so expect the likes of frogs' legs and duck breast with potatoes dauphinois (150,000K).

Luang Prabang Bakery Café Sisavangvong Rd. This surprisingly smart little place has an extensive menu that encompasses pizza, sandwiches and a good choice of Lao dishes, plus a tempting selection of cakes.

Nazim Sisavangvong Rd. No frills but decent (and ever-popular) Indian restaurant serving the usual range of dishes including dhal (6000K) and various curries (from 26,000K).

Tamarind Opposite Wat Nong. ☎020/7770484. This small and very popular restaurant has a well-deserved reputation for some of the best Lao food in town. It's definitely worth splashing out on one of their "feast" menus, which allow you to experience a more authentically local side of Lao food (from 70,000K/person). They also run a very good cooking school (see above). Mon–Sat 11am–6pm.

Tamnak Lao Sakkaline Rd ☎071/252525. Popular with tour groups, though this shouldn't put you off as the Lao menu is more extensive than elsewhere in the city and the food full of flavour. The fried fish with Chinese mushrooms and ginger (50,000K) is highly recommended, though the service could be a little friendlier.

Tum-Tum Cheng Sisaleumsak Rd, near Wat Xieng Thong. The restaurant attached to the well-regarded cooking school of the same name (see above) provides a great introduction to Lao cuisine, with an atmospheric outdoor seating area among ferns and fairy lights. The papaya salad (40,000K) is perfectly spiced and the fried spring rolls (40,000K) are among the best in the city.

Un Petit Nid Sakkaline Rd. This relaxed "biblio-bistro" is set just off the main road and is a great place to try *kao pun* – a spicy soup made with galangal, coconut milk, spring onions, rice noodles and potatoes.

By the Mekong and Nam Khan rivers

Big Tree Café Manthatoulat Rd. One of many café-restaurants on this stretch with terraced seating overlooking the river, this cute gallery-cum-restaurant serves an interesting variety of Western, Japanese and Lao food, and has breakfast sets starting from 30,000K.

Boungnasouk Souvanbaniang Rd. The menu here features a wider selection of Lao and Asian food than most restaurants on this strip, including a delicious, herb-filled *larp ngua* (beef *larp*; 20,000K). Head for the seating on the lower terrace for good views of the river.

Dyen Sabai Ban Phan Luang, across the Nam Khan ☎ 020/5104817. Arguably the most atmospheric place in town, with bamboo "huts" scattered with cushions overlooking the river. The *sin dad* (Lao barbecue) is reason enough to cross the river, but the delicious cocktails (happy hour noon–7pm) and relaxed vibe will keep you here for much longer. During dry season, cross at the bamboo bridge (4000K from 8am–5pm) near Wat Pha Phoutthabat; in wet season a small boat ferries people across from the same point – look for the boat captain at the top of the steps. Dry season: daily 8am–11.30pm; wet season: Mon–Sat noon–11pm.

Sala Café Kingkitsalat Rd. Smart tables in an enviable position along the Nam Khan, with mulberry lanterns creating a romantic ambience at night, though you undoubtedly pay more for the location. The few French dishes, such as croque monsieur, are complemented by delicious Lao and Thai food, such as *nam thadeua* (crispy rice salad with pork, coconut and herbs; 55,000K).

View Kheamkhong Souvanbaniang Rd. A lovely outdoor restaurant right on the banks of the Mekong River, with candle-lit tables and big white umbrellas. The menu is quite extensive and the food inexpensive and delicious. Probably the best of the riverside options.

Outside the old city

Elephant Blanc *Maison Souvannaphoum* Chao Fa Ngum Rd ☎ 071/254609. The breezy restaurant at this lovely colonial hotel offers a range of Western and Lao dishes, including fresh spring rolls and fried riverfish, which start at a very reasonable $4. Daily noon–2.30pm & 7–10pm.

Nang Vong Visounalat Rd. This basic local noodle shop is a good choice for a quick, cheap bowl of food, offering various noodle soups as well as fried rice.

Phou Savanh La Residence Phou Vao ☎ 071/212094. Exquisite food inspired by both France and Asia, including delicious prawn tempura; make sure you save room for mango with sticky coconut rice. At night, it's impossibly romantic, with lanterns floating in the infinity pool and That Chomsi glowing in the distance. Mains from $16. Daily 11.30am–3pm & 6–10pm.

Drinking, nightlife and entertainment

In the evening, you might be content to sip a cool drink at one of the town's riverfront restaurants, but if you're looking for something with more of a local spin, head over to the popular nightclub, *Muang Sua* (nightly 9–11.30pm) on Phou Vao Road, situated at the back of the hotel of the same name. It's good fun, not least because it's frequented by a good mix of locals and tourists. The more popular choice at the time of writing was, surprisingly, the bowling alley south of town (30,000K) which has escaped the town curfew (11.30pm) and stays open until 3am. As can be expected, the bowling gets worse as the night progresses.

Bars

Hive Phousi Rd. This low-key bar remains one of the most popular places in town, with good music, a fantastically atmospheric outside area and a great happy hour with two-for-one cocktails (20,000K). An "Ethnik" fashion show at 7pm (Tues–Sun) displays clothes from Laos's various ethnic groups, in conjunction with nearby Kopnói (see p.139).

The House Phousi Rd. Relaxed Belgian place with a pleasant outdoor area and pub-like interior. Beers on offer include Chimay and Duval.

Lao Lao Garden Phousi Rd. This ambient garden bar is popular with backpackers who come for the *sin dad* and drinks deals (beer 9000K).

Luang Prabang Film Festival

This exciting new festival, which started in 2010, was set up to celebrate film-making in Southeast Asia, with the hope of encouraging a film industry in Laos. Running over eight days in December, the festival showcases films from all ten ASEAN countries, in outdoor locations such as the handicraft market, and is aimed at both locals and tourists. Following the festival, a smaller programme of films is toured around other major provinces in the country. Both events are supplemented by educational projects throughout the year in order to support film-making (still very much in its infancy) in Laos. For more information and future dates, see ⓦ www.lpfilmfest.org.

Utopia By the river, east of Wat Visoun – signposted from the main road. A chilled-out backpacker haven where the somewhat precarious bamboo structure overlooks the Nam Khan and provides a great place to hang out throughout the day. Life-sized Jenga, "beach" volleyball and DJs in the evening are just some of its attractions.

Entertainment

A building on the grounds of the Royal Palace Museum serves as the home of the **Royal Ballet Theatre**, which gives performances four nights a week (Mon, Wed, Fri & Sat 6.30pm; 75,000–170,000K). The shows include excerpts from the Lao version of the Ramayana, a mock Lao wedding ceremony, as well as some Lao interpretations of the dances of their tribal neighbours. The glittering costumes are stunning, and the traditional Lao music will be playing in your head long into the night.

L'Etranger (see p.139) shows nightly movies in English and French above the bookshop for free, though you are expected to buy a drink or food. Films are also shown most nights at *Xayana Guesthouse* (see p.120).

Shopping

As the royal capital of Laos, Luang Prabang was traditionally a centre for skilled **artisans** from around the former kingdom. Weavers, gold- and silversmiths, painters, sculptors of bronze, wood and ivory all held a place of importance in old Luang Prabang, and the most gifted artisans were awarded royal patronage. After the revolution these arts were seen as decadent and officially suppressed, while the artisans associated with the former royalty were shunned. Unable to practise their trade, many drifted to more acceptable occupations or fled the country. These days, with the boom in tourism, the traditional arts have been experiencing a revival, and there is a wide array of different crafts on sale – as well as the usual selection of tourist junk. **Silver** and **textiles**, in particular, can be good buys in Luang Prabang, but only if you buy from the right people and haggle.

The biggest tourist draw remains the **handicraft nightmarket** (daily 5–10pm), which sets up nightly on Sisavangvong Road between the post office and the Royal Palace Museum. From embroidered bedspreads and brightly coloured shoulder bags to *lào-láo*, lanterns and the obligatory Beer Lao T-shirts, you're bound to find something that appeals. A lot of what is sold is much of a muchness, and a high proportion is actually from Thailand and China, but nonetheless it's fun to browse and it's possible to get some good bargains. Be prepared to haggle (see p.56). During the day, a smaller number of stalls set up on the corner of Sisavangvong and Setthathilat roads at the **Hmong Market** – much of the produce is the same as at the nightmarket, though there's a little less pressure from sellers.

▲ Shoppers and sellers at the handicraft nightmarket

In addition, numerous shops along Sisavangvong and the surrounding roads sell textiles and other crafts. For antiques, one of the best places to head to is **Pathana Boupha Antique House** (daily 8.30am–7pm; ☎071/212262), in a lovely colonial building opposite Wat Visoun.

One of the nicest things to buy are mulberry-paper products – a number of little shops around Wat Xieng Thong sell colourful lanterns, books and photo-albums, as does SA Paper Handicrafts, tucked down a tiny lane opposite Wat Xiengmouane.

Silver

Although Thai antique dealers have made off with quite a bit of old Lao silver (and marketed it in Thailand as old Thai silver), there is still a fair amount of the stuff floating around. Items to look out for include paraphernalia for betel chewing, boxes or bowls and jewellery. With a few exceptions, the **hill-tribe jewellery** peddled in Luang Prabang is the handiwork of the Hmong. All of these articles are sold in the shops along Sisavangvong/Sakkaline Road.

New silver of superior quality can and should be bought directly from Luang Prabang's expert **silversmiths**. The best known of these is Thithpeng Maniphone, whose workshop is located just down the small lane opposite Wat Hosian Voravihane, and whose work is well respected – his customers include the Thai royal family. Other silversmiths are located near the Royal Palace, opposite Wat Aham and near the Dara Market. New silver for sale at souvenir shops and in the market is less expensive than that of the silversmiths, but the difference in workmanship is quite evident.

Textiles

Traditional **textiles** are practically Luang Prabang's signature product, and both antique and new textiles can be bought here. The city has many **boutiques** specializing in high-quality Lao textiles; the outlets themselves are often every bit as upscale as the best boutiques in Bangkok or Chiang Mai, from which they draw their inspiration.

Ban Lao Khemkong Rd. A fantastic range of silk scarves and other local handicrafts.

Kopnoi Phommathay Rd. This excellent shop sells a wide range of fair-trade Lao textiles from around the country, including beautiful table runners from Borkeo. Also sells Lao coffee, fruit teas and other household items. Upstairs you can find out more about the Stay Another Day project, which promotes sustainable tourism in Laos (ⓦwww.stay-another-day.org).

 Ock Pop Tok Ban Wat Nong & Sakkaline Rd. Though the textiles here are a little pricey, there's no denying the quality of the work, which surpasses most of what's on offer elsewhere in town. All of the produce has been made in Laos – either in the shop's Living Crafts Centre, 2km out of town, or through their Village Weaver Projects which support local communities. Excellent classes, in which you can try your hand at dyeing and weaving, are available – ask in store for details.

Mulberries Khemkong Rd. Beautiful fabric and clothing from this fair-trade company. Also has a silk farm and training centre in Phonsavan (see p.150).

Bookshops

Many guesthouses and cafés have small book exchanges.

L'Etranger Books & Tea Phousi Rd. The best second-hand bookshop in town (plus a number of new books), including some foreign fiction. Also lends books for a minimal fee, serves food and drinks (see p.134), and screens recent films nightly.

Monument Books Thou Gnai Thao Rd ⓣ071/254954. Great little bookshop stocking a good range of magazines, local and international fiction and non-fiction, travel guides and children's books.

Yensa Bai Books & Art Latsavong Rd. A small range of books (largely secondhand) to buy and borrow, plus maps, coffee and art.

Listings

Banks and exchange At the time of writing, there were three ATMs on Sisavanvong (see map, p.122 for locations), and a BCEL ATM near the Dara Market. There are a number of moneychangers on Sisavongvong Rd, including one at the eastern end of the Hmong Market, and most banks, including Lao Development Bank on Sisavangvong and Visounalat roads, will exchange the usual range of currencies.

Luang Prabang markets

The city's most famous market is the **handicraft nightmarket** that sets up along Sisavangvong Road (see p.137); during the day you'll find similar items at the **Hmong Market** (see p.137).

Dara Market, situated on the corner of Setthathilat and Latsavong roads, offers a varied range of products, from mobile phones and bike parts to Western clothing, Lao handicrafts and silversmiths. It's all rather sanitized and a little tacky, so don't expect any great finds.

The most interesting markets in the city are the produce markets, which give a taste of real Lao life. A **morning market** runs on the street parallel to Sisavangvong and the river, west of the Royal Palace Museum, and is the most convenient place to experience Luang Prabang at its most local. The crammed-in stalls sell a whole range of produce, from bug-eyed fish and scrawny chicken feet to piles of bright green veg and little round aubergines. Get there early to experience it at its best – by 10am, most of the stalls have started packing up.

For a real taste of daily life in Luang Prabang, head to **Phosy Market**, 2km out of town. This huge, largely covered market, sells almost everything you can think of, including dried buffalo skin, congealed blood (for soups) and highly pungent *pa dck*, as well as an endless variety of dry goods. Tuk-tuks should take you out there for about 20,000K.

Hospitals and clinics The main hospital is 2km west of town. There's an International Clinic (☎071/252049) opposite *Amantaka* on Soukhaseum Rd.

Internet access Most of the travel agents on Sisavangvong and Phomathat rds have internet connections for around 100K/min.

Laundry Most hotels and guesthouses will wash clothes for you – expect to pay around 12,000K/kilo.

Massage and herbal sauna The Red Cross on Visounalat Rd (☎071/252856; daily 9am–9pm) has traditional Lao massage at 40,000K per hour (reserve ahead) and an excellent sauna (from 5pm only) for 20,000K. Proceeds go to help poor villagers. For a wider choice of massages, Spa Garden, Ban Phonheuang (☎071/212325; daily 9.30am–10.30pm) is highly recommended – try

the "Mystic Lao Massage" (1hr; 60,000K) or an aromatherapy massage (150,000K).

Pharmacies There's a very helpful, well-stocked pharmacy in Dara Market.

Post office The GPO is on the corner of Sisavangvong and Setthathilat rds (Mon–Fri 8am– noon & 1–5pm, Sat 8am–noon).

Telephone services Most internet cafés have facilities for Skype.

Tour agencies All Lao Travel, Sisavangvong Rd ☎071/253522; Exotissimo, Khemkong Rd ☎071/252879, ⓦwww.exotissimo.com; Green Discovery, Sisavangvong Rd ☎071/212093, ⓦwww.greendiscoverylaos.com; Lao Discovery Tours, Sisavangvong Rd ☎071/212698; Luang Say, Sakkaline Rd ☎071/252553, ⓦwww .luangsay.com; Tiger Trail, Sisavangvong Rd ☎071/252655, ⓦwww.laos-adventures.com.

Around Luang Prabang

Once you've exhausted Luang Prabang's many monasteries and temples, you'll still find many more attractions in the surrounding countryside, all within easy reach of the city. The popular **Pak Ou caves** trip gets you out on the water, a wonderful day-trip, especially if you haven't had a chance to travel the Mekong by boat. There are also two picturesque **waterfalls** nearby, Tad Se and Kouang Si, both of which are good spots for a picnic and splashing around in turquoise waters. All the trips described here can be done in half a day – either by a tour through a travel agent (see p.143) or by chartering a tuk-tuk or boat for the trip.

The swift rivers, pretty rural areas and impressive mountains around Luang Prabang also offer many opportunities for **adventure sports**, including whitewater rafting, mountain biking, kayaking and trekking tours. Enquires for adventure tours can be made through your guesthouse or one of the tour agents listed above and on p.143.

Ban Phanom

A few hundred metres beyond the golden stupa of Santi Chedi, **BAN PHANOM** attracts its share of the tourist dollar through its pedigree as a former royal weaving village. If you take the time to wander Ban Phanom's quaint, red-dirt streets you'll find a few independent textile shops as well as women hard at work weaving in the relatively cool space beneath their raised, traditional wooden homes. Prices are generally lower here than in Luang Prabang, though the textiles are of a comparable quality.

Ban Phanom is easily reached by **bicycle** or **motorbike** by following Patoupakmao Road and turning left at the first major intersection beyond the *Wiang Mai* restaurant. After 500m, turn right onto a dirt road leading uphill; Ban Phanom is about 300m further on.

Henri Mouhot's tomb

Four kilometres up the Nam Khan from Ban Phanom is the final resting place of **Henri Mouhot**, the Anglophile French naturalist and explorer best known as the "discoverer" of Angkor Wat. A simple memorial, made from stone donated by the

Lao king Tiantha and erected by Doudart de Lagrée of the Mekong Commission in 1867, marks the spot, which is easily located by looking for the sign posted on the road above it. As you leave Ban Phanom, follow the right fork 3.7km until you reach a steep dirt path leading down to the bank of the river, a spot favoured by picnicking Lao from Luang Prabang on weekends. The whitewashed memorial lies 200m upriver from the path and about 20m from the river's edge, in a dried-up tributary of the Khan.

Moving on from Luang Prabang

Lao Airlines (Visounalat Rd; ☏071/212172) operates daily **flights** to Vientiane, and thrice-weekly flights to Pakse. Internationally, they fly daily to Bangkok, Chiang Mai and Hanoi, and regularly to Siem Reap. Alternatively, Bangkok Airways (Sisavangvong Rd; ☏071/253334) has flights twice-daily to Bangkok, while Vietnam Airlines (☏071/213/049) flies daily to Hanoi and four times a week to Siem Reap. A tuk-tuk to the airport should cost around 20,000K.

Buses

From the Southern Bus station, there are daily buses to Vang Vieng (8am) and Phonsavan (8.30am), and nine buses a day to Vientiane (last departure 7.30pm), including two VIP buses at 8am and 9am. **From the Northern Bus Station**, daily buses run to Nong Khiaw, Oudomxai, Luang Namtha, Houayxai (usually written as Bokeo, the name of the province), Phongsali and Sam Neua. A tuk-tuk to either bus station from the old city should cost around 20,000K. Bus tickets can be bought directly from the bus stations (get there at least 30min before departure), or in advance from travel agents and guesthouses in town, where the higher ticket price will include transport to the bus station and commission for the agent.

Buses to Vinh in **Vietnam** and Kunming in **China** also run daily from Luang Prabang's Southern Bus Station – it's advisable to get up-to-date information from a travel agent in advance for these.

Minibuses

Minibuses leave from the minibus station opposite the Southern Bus Station; though you can buy tickets here, most people choose to buy their tickets from a travel agent or guesthouse as this includes pick up and transportation to the terminal. Prices for minibuses are generally at least 20,000K more than for a local bus, but they are generally a much quicker way to travel (though only used by tourists). Destinations include Nong Khiaw, Oudomxai, Phonsavan, Vientiane and Vang Vieng. Prices can vary widely though so it's best to shop around before you buy your ticket – everyone from the various travel agents ends up on the same minibuses.

Boats

Slow boats leave from the landing behind the Royal Palace Museum in the old city. The ticket office is on your left on your way down – departures up the Mekong to Pakbeng/Houayxai, as well as up the Nam Ou River, are all posted on a chalkboard here. It's advisable to check times here the day before you plan to travel, and arrive at least half an hour before the stated departure time. Boats to Pakbeng (for Houayxai) leave at 8am, while boats to Nong Khiaw depart at 9am. Tickets can also be bought at most travel agents, and the increased fee should include transport to the boat landing. It's also possible to travel up the river on a luxury boat – the *Luang Say* – see p.201.

While they are not recommended due to safety issues (see p.201), eight-seater **speedboats** leave from a separate landing in the suburb of Ban Don, 7km north of the centre on the banks of the Mekong. Daily departures to Houayxai set off from here at 9am; a tuk-tuk to the pier will cost around 30,000K.

For further information on travelling on the Mekong, see the box on p.201.

While travelling in Laos, you'll probably come across many lowland Lao wearing one or more bracelets of white thread around their wrists. This is a sign that the wearer has recently taken part in a **basi**, the quintessential Lao ceremony of **animist** bent, which is performed throughout the year. Also known as *sukhuan*, the ceremony is supposed to reunite the body's multiple souls, which are thought to succumb to wanderlust and depart from the body every now and again. *Basi* ceremonies are held during Lao New Year as well as being an important part of weddings, births and farewell parties.

Before the ceremony can be performed, an auspicious time must be gleaned from an astrologer, and a *phakhuan* – made from rolled banana leaves and resembling a miniature Christmas tree – must be prepared. The *phakhuan* is decorated with marigolds and other flowers, and draped with white threads. This arrangement sits in a silver bowl filled with husked rice, which is placed in the centre of a mat laid out on the floor. Participants sit in a circle around the *phakhuan* and offerings of food and liquor are placed near it. These are used to entice the absent souls to return. An animist **priest**, known as a *maw phawn* or "wish-doctor", presides over the ceremony, inviting the souls to return with a mixture of Pali and Lao chants. The white threads that are draped over the *phakhuan* are then removed and tied around the wrists of the participants while blessings are invoked. During the *basi* ceremony performed at Lao New Year, each thread tied around the wrist may be accompanied by a shot of rice liquor, and this sometimes leads to an impromptu *lam wong*, or "circle dance", performed by euphoric participants.

A number of trips operating from Luang Prabang include the chance to experience a *basi* ceremony, though these have always been set up especially for the benefit of tourists; alteratively, you may find yourself invited to partake in one if you travel out to more remote towns and villages, where locals are often keen for foreigners to join the party.

The Pak Ou Buddha Caves and Whisky Village

A river excursion to the **Pak Ou Buddha Caves** (daily 8am–sunset; 20,000K), 25km north of Luang Prabang at the confluence of the Mekong and Nam Ou rivers, is one of the best quick trips you can make out of the city. Numerous caves punctuate the limestone cliffs on both sides of the Mekong in this vicinity, but the two "Buddha Caves" of **Tham Ting** and **Tham Phoum** are the best known. These caves have been used for centuries as a repository for old Buddha images that can no longer be venerated on an altar, either because they are damaged to the point of disfigurement – termite holes, burn marks and broken limbs being afflictions common to wooden Buddhas – or simply because newer images have crowded them out. In former times, before the caves became a tourist attraction, the inhabitants of Luang Prabang didn't give much thought to the caves or their contents except during **Lao New Year**, when boatloads of townsfolk would make the pilgrimage upriver and ritually bathe the semi-abandoned Buddhas to gain merit. The practice survives to this day and is worth seeing if you happen to be around. If not, the caves still deserve an hour or so, if only to gaze at the eerie scene of hundreds upon hundreds of serenely smiling images covered in dust and cobwebs. Tham Ting, the lower cave, just above the water's surface, is more of a large grotto and is light enough to explore without an artificial light source. The upper cave is unlit, so bring a torch (flashlight).

Opposite the Buddha Caves on the far side of the Mekong is the "mouth" of the "Ou" River – "Pak Ou" in Lao. The scenery here at the entrance of the Nam Ou is dramatic, with a huge limestone peak rising up over the junction of the two rivers. South of Pak Ou, on the banks of the Mekong, is a village that produced stoneware jars for thousands of years, but has now forsaken that activity, having found that distilling liquor is more lucrative. The inhabitants of **BAN XANG HAI**, referred to by local boatmen as the "**Whisky Village**", are quite used to thirsty visitors stopping by for a pull on the bamboo straw. The liquor is *lào-láo*, made from fermented sticky rice, and pots filled with the hooch are lined up on the beach awaiting transport up or down the river.

As it's logical to see the Pak Ou Caves and the Whisky Village on the same trip, most boatmen hired in Luang Prabang are happy to treat it as a package, assuming that after you've seen a cave-full of Buddhas you'll be ready for a good, stiff drink. **Boatmen** congregate throughout the day near the slow boat landing and at the tip of the peninsula near Wat Xieng Thong – expect to pay around 150,000K for a small boat, but be prepared to haggle. Alternatively, a tuk-tuk will cost around 60,000K for four people.

Kouang Si

One of the best day-trips from Luang Prabang is **Kouang Si** waterfall (20,000K), a picturesque, multi-level affair that tumbles 60m before spilling through a series of crystal-blue pools. The spray from the falls keeps the surrounding grounds cool even at midday. It's a great spot for a picnic and a refreshing swim – there are picnic tables and changing rooms at the site. The **upper pool** has a nice view of the falls, though swimming is only allowed at the **lower pool**, which lacks a direct view. If you didn't pack lunch, pay a visit to the vendors nearby selling *tam màk hung*, fruit and drinks.

If you're up for some exercise, the steep path on the opposite side of the falls leads to the top and a grassy **meadow** filled with brilliantly coloured butterflies.

Trips and Tours

Sisavangvong Road boasts a rather mind-boggling array of travel agents, many offering identical trips in and around Luang Prabang (and further afield); some will even arrange tours around the country. The following companies are particularly recommended, though it's best to shop around first – make sure you know exactly what you're paying for when you sign up for something.

Exotissimo Khemkong Rd ⓣ071/252879 ⓦwww.exotissimo.com. An excellent variety of mid-range and luxury tours around Laos are on offer from this well-regarded tour operator, as well as a number of interesting trips within the city, including one that focuses on textiles, in which you can try your hand at weaving.

Green Discovery Sisavangvong Rd ⓣ071/212093, ⓦwww.greendiscoverylaos.com. Adventure-travel specialist with offices throughout the country, Green Discovery has an excellent choice of programmes within Luang Prabang province, from kayaking on the Nam Khan and Nam Xuang rivers and cycling and motorbike tours to rock-climbing, caving and overnight treks.

Tiger Trail Sisavangvong Rd ⓣ071/252655, ⓦwww.laos-adventures.com. With a focus on sustainable tourism, Tiger Trail offers a superlative variety of tour options, including their excellent "Fair Trek" programme which strives to create positive opportunities for local people. Day-trips in Luang Prabang include hill-tribe trekking and mountain biking – or spend two days training to be a *mahout* at the nearby Elephant Village.

Tread carefully though, as the path can get quite slippery; more than a few barefoot trampers have slipped and broken a leg here.

There are several options for **getting to the waterfall**, which is situated 35km southwest of Luang Prabang. The most scenic approach is by boat down the Mekong River; the same boatmen who run the trips to the Pak Ou Caves will take you to the falls (around $30/boat for up to ten people), the final portion of the journey is by tuk-tuk, which is usually worked into the fee by the boatman – check when negotiating. Alternatively, it's possible to get there by road – tuk-tuk drivers in town will usually approach you about this, or head to the "Tuk-tuk Station Travel Service" in Luang Prabang which charges a flat fee of 200,000K for one to five people.

Tad Se

The wide **Tad Se** waterfall wanders down a gradual slope, serenely cascading through trees and easing through a dozen clear-blue pools, like some elaborate Zen meditation retreat, until it finally flows into the Nam Khan River. The pools here aren't good for swimming like those at Kouang Si, but are fine for a bit of splashing around. The excursion to the falls follows Route 13 south along the beginning of its most dramatically pretty stretch, winding around mountains and past hillside teak plantations, and culminates with a short trip by pirogue downstream to the waterfall. During the dry season, water levels can be rather low so check locally before travelling out there during this period. Tuk-tuks from the "Tuk-tuk Station" charge 150,000K for one to five people, or expect to pay at least 200,000k by boat.

Travel details

Buses

Luang Prabang Southern bus station to: Phonsavan (daily; 9hr); Sayaboury (2 daily; 3hr–3hr 30min); Vang Vieng (daily; 8hr 40min); Vientiane (9 daily; 10hr); Vinh (Vietnam; daily; 22hr). Northern bus station to: Houayxai (Borkeo; 3 daily; 15hr); Kunming (China; daily; 24hr); Luang Namtha (daily; 9hr); Nong Khiaw (2 daily; 4hr); Oudomxai (3 daily; 5hr); Phongsali (daily; 13hr); Sam Neua (daily; 14hr).

Slow boats

Luang Prabang to: Nong Khiaw (daily; 8hr); Pakbeng (daily; 10hr).

Speedboats

Luang Prabang to: Houayxai (2 daily; 6hr).

Domestic flights

Luang Prabang to: Pakse (3 weekly; 1hr 50min); Vientiane (3–4 daily; 40min).

The northeast

CHAPTER 3 # Highlights

✳ **Plain of Jars** Fields of ancient giant stone urns scattered across the Xieng Khuang Plateau stand as witnesses to a vanished civilization. See p.153

✳ **Muang Khoun** Travel back in time to the ancient kingdom of Xieng Khuang where temple ruins and a giant Buddha are all that remains of a once proud kingdom. See p.156

✳ **The Muang Kham hinterland** The village of Muang Kham is the launching point for trips to caves, hot springs and visits to Hmong, Khmu, Black Tai and Phuan villages. See p.157

✳ **Vieng Xai** The incredibly limestone karst scenery that surrounds this small town provided the perfect hiding place for the Pathet Lao during much of their Thirty Year Struggle. See p.164

✳ **Route 1** From Nam Neun junction to Nong Khiaw, ride across the rooftop of Indochina to one of the least-visited parts of the country. See p.167

▲ Giant Buddha, Muang Khoun

The northeast

T
he remote **northeast** of Laos was, until recently, difficult to reach, due to mountainous terrain and poor roads, which largely kept it isolated from tourism. Despite great improvements to the infrastructure – it's now possible to reach Sam Neua in less than a day from Luang Prabang, with no change of bus – the region remains one of the least-visited parts of the country due, partly, to being short on typical tourist sights, and because it doesn't fit too neatly with the typical north–south itinerary. However, there's a real frontier friendliness among the inhabitants, who come from more than two dozen ethnic groups, and it's a great area (especially north of Phonsavan) in which to feel as though you're getting off the beaten track. In addition, history, both ancient and modern, feels particularly tangible in the area.

Topographically diverse, the northeast region extends from the towering peaks that border the Vientiane Plain, across the Xieng Khuang Plateau, over the jagged backbone of the Annamite Mountains, and into the watershed of the Nam Xam River, which flows into Vietnam. The area encompasses **Hua Phan** and **Xieng Khuang provinces**, and part of **northern Luang Prabang province**. Historically, this swath of Laos was the domain of two independent principalities – the Tai federation of Sipsong Chao Tai in Hua Phan and the Phuan Kingdom of Xieng Khuang. Sandwiched between expansive empires to the west and east, both entities struggled to maintain their sovereignty until the late nineteenth century, when the French finally folded most of their territory into unified Laos.

The kings of the defunct royal house of **Xieng Khuang** came from the same family tree as those of Luang Prabang, both kingdoms claiming descent from Khoun Borom, the celebrated first ancestor of numerous Tai–Lao legends. Yet, unlike in Luang Prabang, few physical traces of Xieng Khuang's splendour survive. In the place of the distinctive Xieng Khuang-style temples are bomb craters doubling as fishing holes and houses erected on piles crafted from bomb casings – reminders that this was one of the most heavily bombed pieces of real estate in the world, and a testimony to the rugged perseverance of the Phuan, Black Tai, Hmong and Khmu peoples who inhabit the province. Much of the bombing was directed at the strategic **Plain of Jars**, which takes its name from the fields of ancient, giant funerary urns that are the northeast's main tourist draw. For most visitors a trip to the region means little more than a flying visit to Xieng Khuang's provincial capital **Phonsavan** to see the Jar sites, sometimes coupled with a quick side trip to nearby **Muang Khoun**, the former royal seat of Xieng Khuang, where a handful of ruins whisper of the kingdom's vanished glory.

It's remarkable that even with greatly improved roads, few travellers make the journey to **Hua Phan**, an impenetrable sea of rugged green mountaintops lost in mist and shallow valleys, far from the Mekong River and the traditional

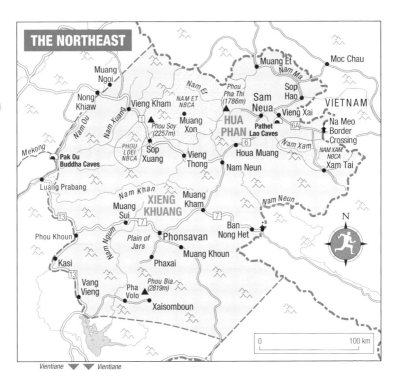

centres of lowland Lao life. The only provincial centre in Laos east of the Annamites is Hua Phan's capital **Sam Neua**, a frontier town closer to Hanoi than Vientiane, a proximity that lends it a distinctly Vietnamese flavour. This lightly populated region is home to more than twenty ethnic groups, most of them Tai, including the Black, Red and White Tai, all of whom share a distinctly Hua Phan character – a fortitude shaped by the remote mountainous terrain and by years spent living in the heart of the **Pathet Lao's liberated zone**. After the Pathet Lao rose to power in 1975, the communists further exploited Hua Phan's isolation by transforming their liberated zone into a massive prison camp. Thousands of former Royal Lao soldiers were interred in the province's notorious re-education camps. Hua Phan's wartime history has been etched into the land at **Vieng Xai**, a short ride from Sam Neua. Dozens of **caves** hidden in the sawtoothed limestone karsts of Vieng Xai served as the headquarters for the Pathet Lao during their Thirty Year Struggle.

Xieng Khuang and the Plain of Jars

Xieng Khuang province lies at the crossroads of important trade routes leading north to China, south to Thailand and east to Vietnam, and has been coveted throughout the centuries by rival Southeast Asian empires. Xieng Khuang, hemmed in by a ring of dramatic mountains, including the country's tallest peak, Phu Bia, is best known for the treeless flatlands and crater-ridden landscape of the **Plain of Jars**. A plateau of grassy meadows and low rolling hills situated at the centre of the province, the Plain takes its name from the clusters of chest-high funerary urns found there. For people with a very deep interest in archeology and Southeast Asian history the jars are worth the journey to Xieng Khuang, but for some tourists they are something of an anticlimax. However, their other-worldliness, against the flat barren landscape of the area, retains a certain mystique, and by choosing your guide wisely it's possible to get a lot more out of a visit here.

As the flattest area in northern Laos, the Plain of Jars is also a natural gathering point for **armies** – a fact not lost on military commanders of the early kingdoms of Lane Xang, Vietnam and Siam and later the Soviet Union, France and America, the Viet Minh, the Pathet Lao and the Lao Royalists. Fought over dearly in the Second Indochina War, the region was bombed extensively between 1964 and 1973, transforming the Plain into a wasteland, which leaves a lasting impression on those who fly over it into Phonsavan.

With much of the literature of the province's historical Phuan kingdom (see p.295) destroyed and many of the customs lost, **Hmong culture** and festivals have come to play an important role in Xieng Khuang life. Boun Phao Hmong, or the Festival of the Hmong, celebrated throughout the province in November, draws overseas Hmong back each year for an event featuring water buffalo and bull-fights. In December, Hmong New Year, a time for young Hmong to find a husband or wife, is celebrated, as is the lowland Lao festival of Boun Haw Khao, a two-day holiday in which food is offered to the dead. It has a distinctly Xieng Khuang flavour, however, with the addition of horse races, horses being especially prized by villagers who work Xieng Khuang's far-flung fields.

Some history

Even the **legends** surrounding the jars reveal how thoroughly life in Xieng Khuang has been overshadowed by **war**, with local lore telling of how the jars were created to hold rice wine by an army of giants to celebrate a military victory. Although the identity of the civilization that built the jars remains a mystery, local folk tales telling of the arrival of the Phuan people (see p.295), the lowland Lao group that still dominates the ethnic make-up of the area today, date back as far as the seventh century, when the divine Tai–Lao first ancestor Khoun Borom (see p.264) sent his seventh and youngest son, Chet Chuong, to rule over the Tai peoples of Xieng Khuang. Although the time frame for this version of events may be a bit premature, Xieng Khuang was nonetheless one of the earlier areas settled by Tai peoples in Laos, and by the fourteenth century, an independent **Phuan principality**, known as Xieng Khuang and centred on modern-day **Muang Khoun**, had already begun to flourish here.

Safety in Xieng Khuang

Occasional attacks by mountain **bandits or insurgents** have given Xieng Khuang province an uncertain reputation. In particular, tourists have long been discouraged from travelling along Route 7 between Phou Khoun and Phonsavan due to attacks on vehicles by armed bandits – these days, the threat appears to be less, and with limited flights into Phonsavan it's likely that you will travel this route in order to reach the area. In 2003, two foreign nationals were killed as a result of banditry on this stretch, but it's important to remember that hundreds of tourists visit the area each month without incident. Of more immediate danger are the **mines**, **bomblets** and **bombs** littering the province. The main Jar sites have been cleared of Unexploded Ordnance (UXO), but it's important to stick to the paths, and not to pick up or kick any object if you don't know what it is. See Basics, p.51, for more details.

While the **Kingdom of Xieng Khuang** had the wealth to build exquisite pagodas, it never amassed the might necessary to become a regional power. Sandwiched between the great empires lying to its east and west, Phuan kings maintained a semblance of independence over the years by offering tribute to Vietnam and Lane Xang and eventually Siam. Whatever price the royal house paid, however, it was not enough to keep Xieng Khuang from being repeatedly annexed, overrun and forcibly depopulated, beginning with the invading armies of the **Vietnamese** on their way back from sacking Luang Prabang in the late 1470s through to the Second Indochina War, when nearly every village in the province was obliterated.

In 1869, warrior horsemen from southern **China** raced across the plain, slaughtering villagers or carrying them off into captivity. These Black Flag bandits pillaged the riches of the kingdom and plundered the contents of the jars. Those that fled didn't get far: Lao and Thai soldiers on their way to Xieng Khuang to quell the invasion rounded up the refugees and frogmarched them through the jungle to the Chao Phraya River Valley in Siam, where they became slaves to Thai lords. The tortuous march lasted over a month, with many dying along the way, lost to sickness and starvation. In two generations, Siamese armies and Chinese bandits reduced the population by three-quarters through death and forced migration. The Phuan state never recovered.

Xieng Khuang enjoyed better protection from its neighbours with the arrival of the **French**, who considered the province's temperate climate – which can be downright cold by any measure for several months of the year – suitable for European settlement and plantation agriculture. The primary cash crop, however, was **opium**, a trade the French quickly moved to control (see box, p.196). Muang Khoun was chosen as the French provincial capital and the devastated former royal seat of the defunct kingdom was transformed into an architectural gem of French Indochinese villas and shophouses, which might have rivalled the charm of Luang Prabang and Savannakhet had Xieng Khuang not returned to its familiar role as battleground a few decades later.

One hundred years after the carnage of the Chinese bandits, American planes wreaked destruction that was equally indiscriminate, levelling towns and forcing villagers to take to the forest, as the two sides in the **Second Indochina War** waged a bitter battle for control of the Plain of Jars, which represented a back door to northern Vietnam. Throughout much of the 1960s, Xieng Khuang was the site of a seesaw war, with the Royalist side led by Hmong General Vang Pao gaining the upper hand in the rainy season and the communist side launching offensives in the dry months.

Today, villages have been rebuilt and fields replanted. Many of the valley-dwelling, wet-rice farmers, as well as a majority of the townsfolk in Phonsavan, are descendants of the Phuan kingdom. In addition to the Lao, the Phuan are joined by a third lowland group, the Black Tai, and also the Khmu – a Lao Theung group who ruled the lowlands until they were forced into the hills with the arrival of the Tai groups over a thousand years ago – and a significant population of Hmong, who arrived in Laos from China in the nineteenth century and now make up roughly a third of the provincial population.

Phonsavan

The capital of Xieng Khuang province, **PHONSAVAN** has gradually emerged as the most important town on the Plain of Jars since the total devastation of the region in the Second Indochina War. The bomb-casing collections in many guesthouse lobbies are grim galleries reflecting the area's tragic past when possession of the strategic plain was seen as the key to control of Laos. It was the new communist government that designated Phonsavan the new provincial capital, and parked Laos's fledgling collection of Soviet MiGs nearby, a smug reminder of who won the battle for this bitterly contested area.

Hastily rebuilt in the aftermath of decades of fighting, Phonsavan has only now, over 35 years after the end of conflict, begun to recover economically, thanks in a large part to international interest in the world-famous Jar sites scattered around the perimeter of the plain. Tourism has given the town new life: bombs at the Jar sites have been cleared away and Khoun Cheuam's jar – the largest of the scores of jars in the area – stares down from tourism posters across the country. Although most visitors come only to see the Jar sites, the Xieng Khuang Plateau is a place of great natural beauty and its backroads and villages are well worth exploring.

Arrival, transport and information

The **bus station** is 4km from the centre of Phonsavan; tuk-tuks (10,000–15,000K) will ferry you into town. The minibus station is situated just off Route 7, behind Sousath Travel (see p.155). Touts for guesthouses and tour operators will meet you here and ferry you to your accommodation. Landing at the **airport**, you'll need a tuk-tuk (20,000K) for the 5km ride into town, though you should be able to get a free lift with one of the hotel reps. Note that the airport is most commonly called "Xieng Khuang" rather than Phonsavan.

Phonsavan is small enough to explore on foot, though if you're staying out of town at the *Auberge*, note that tuk-tuks stop running by 8pm so you may have to hitch a lift back if you venture into town for dinner. The tourist office (daily 8–11.30am & 1.30–4pm), surrounded by UXO, is rather inconveniently situated in the southern part of town, a couple of kilometres away from most accommodation. Your best bet for information is to visit a couple of the many tour operators lining Route 7 (see p.155) to get a good idea of what's on offer.

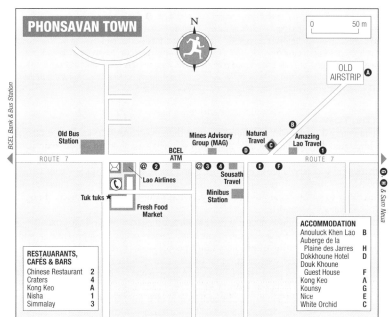

PHONSAVAN TOWN

Airport, Jar Sites & Tourist Office

At the time of writing, **Lao Airlines** (☏061/312027), next to the post office, was only operating flights to Vientiane (four weekly; $53). There's a BCEL **ATM** on Route 7, with the main branch, with **currency exchange** services, situated about 1km to the west on the same road. Most travel agents and some guesthouses will also change money and, occasionally, travellers' cheques. There's an **internet** café next to *Simmalay Restaurant*.

Accommodation

Phonsavan has many **guesthouses and hotels**, most of which line Route 7, east of the old bus station, though it's all much of a muchness. Most places offer tours to the Plain of Jars, though quality can vary.

Anouluck Khen Lao ☏061/213599. A smart, large hotel, tucked off the main road. The large, bright rooms are impressive for the price, and the attached bathrooms have arguably the best showers in town. ❹

Auberge de la Plaine des Jarres 1.5km from town ☏030/5170282, ✉info@plainedesjarres.com. Overlooking the town from a hill to the southeast, this rustic lodge is set in landscaped grounds surrounded by pine trees and bougainvillea, with wonderful sweeping views over the town and surrounding countryside. Accommodation is in wooden cabins that feel more alpine than Lao, with rather thin walls and hard beds, but this is definitely the most picturesque setting in Phonsavan, and there's a decent French–Lao restaurant on site. Very popular with tour groups, so book ahead. ❻

Dokkhoune Hotel ☏020/2342555. With a lobby full of decorative UXO and good views of the mountains from the hallways, the large but dull rooms here are a bit of a disappointment, but not bad value. ❸

Douk Khoune Guesthouse ☏061/312189. Attached to the back of a café that's a good choice for breakfast, the rooms here are large for the price, with fan, TV and en suite. They're clean enough, though the walls could do with a scrub, and it can be quite noisy. ❷

Kong Keo Guesthouse Situated 200m off Route 7 next to the old airstrip ☏061/211354, ✉kongkeojar@hotmail.com. The best, and most quirky, choice for budget travellers. Rooms are rather small and the bathrooms pretty poky, but the overall vibe of the place more than makes up for it, with a cool bar-restaurant and a garden littered with UXO. In addition to tours, they can also arrange visas for Cambodia, China and Vietnam. ❷

Kounsy ☏061/211170. This somewhat idiosyncratic hotel at the far eastern end of the main drag has a number of basic, rather dark rooms, though they're quieter than many others on Route 7. ❸

Nice ☏061/312454. Sweet little en-suite rooms off a lantern-strung hallway. There's a nice seating area downstairs where you can enjoy a cold drink. ❷

White Orchid ☏061/312403. This extremely friendly, family-run place, tucked off the main road, is an excellent choice. Rooms are a little dark, but good value and very clean. Travel and tour information (and bookings) can be provided by the very helpful staff. ❸

The Town

The original settlement of Phonsavan was, like every other town on the plain, obliterated during the war. The town you see today is a modern **reconstruction** that lacks any real character. There is really nothing of note to see, although the town grid is nicely laid out on a rather grand scale, extending quite a way south of Route 7. Indeed, if the length and width of Phonsavan's empty boulevards are anything to go by, local officials have very big plans for this little place, though they're yet to materialize.

The town's highlight is the great little **fresh food market** behind the post office, which is well worth a wander, the amount and variety of the fresh produce on sale giving a good indication of just how much people's lives here have improved since the government quietly swept communist economics under the rug. As with most markets in Laos, it's a great choice for a quick, cheap lunch, or to stock up on fruit and snacks before a long bus journey.

After a visit to the Plain of Jars, be sure to stop in at the **Mines Advisory Group** (MAG; Mon–Fri 8am–8pm, Sat & Sun 4–8pm; ⓦmaginternational.org; donations

Crossing into Vietnam from Phonsavan

It's possible to reach **Vietnam** from Phonsavan, crossing near Ban Nong Het. **Buses** to Vinh, from where connections to Hanoi are available, run on Tuesday, Thursday, Friday and Sunday at 6.30am (138,000K; 12hr), while one bus a week runs all the way to Hanoi (Mon 6.30am; 185,000K; 18hr). Check exact times with Phonsavan bus station or a travel agent in advance – Amazing Lao Travel is well regarded for booking onward travel (expect to pay at least 20,000K more to cover commission and pick-up).

welcome) which is carrying out vital work, not only in deactivating UXO, but in educating and informing local people, especially farmers and those involved in the scrap metal trade. An informative display provides an introduction to the work they are doing, with photographs making vividly clear the horrifying risks that UXO pose to local lives. Free films are shown every night; this is a great opportunity to find out more about the UXO situation and the work that MAG do.

Eating and drinking

There's a fair few places to eat along the main road, though you won't exactly be spoilt for choice. The fresh food market (see opposite) is a good choice for lunch. The most atmospheric place for a drink is the bar at *Kong Keo* (see opposite). All of the following are along Route 7.

Chinese Restaurant This basic place with no Western name is always crammed with locals. Service can be rather surly but the food (beef with oyster sauce, 20,000K) is good and tasty.

Craters A relaxed place with UXO lined up outside and weaponry decorating the interior. The menu offers everything you would expect from a travellers' café, including toasties, salads, pizza and a few Asian dishes. Breakfast is served all day.

Nisha Bare-bones Indian place serving great dosa, alongside the usual assortment of curries.

Simmalay This charming family-run Chinese restaurant is decorated with pictures of Beer Lao girls and always full of a good mix of locals and tourists. Portions are large and prices cheap, so it's easy to over-order – the fish with ginger (20,000K) is delicious.

The Plain of Jars

Many visitors mistake the Jar sites for the **PLAIN OF JARS** and vice versa. The latter is a broad rolling plain covering an area roughly 15km across at the centre of the Xieng Khuang Plateau, which sits high above the Mekong and the Vientiane Plain. The ancient **Jar sites** scattered around the perimeter of the plain led the French to name the region the Plain de Jars – the PDJ to the American pilots who flew over it. Topographically, the plain is something like the hole in a doughnut with concentric rings of increasingly high mountain peaks around it. Although the jars are the main tourist attraction of Xieng Khuang Province, there's much more to see here. The Plain itself offers beautiful scenery, which most visitors, obsessed with seeing the jars, completely overlook. Away from the main highway there are countless backroads to explore as well as friendly **Phuan and Hmong villages**, where it may feel like you're the first foreigner the children have seen.

The presence of the jars attests to the fact that Xieng Khuang, with its access to key regional trade routes, its wide, flat spaces and temperate climate, has been considered prime real estate in mainland Southeast Asia for centuries, but the story of the plain as a **transit route** for ancient man has yet to be told. As a natural corridor between the coasts of southern China and the vast plains of Korat beyond the Mekong, the Plain of Jars has certainly seen the passage of many tribes and races, perhaps even groups of *Homo erectus*, who ranged from northern China to Java between one million and 250,000 years ago.

The Jar sites

The **Jar sites** are among the most important prehistoric archeological sites in Southeast Asia. Clusters of stone jars thought to be 2000 years old, along with seemingly older stone pillars, are scattered across the Plain and also in other parts of Xieng Khuang and Hua Phan province. The largest urns measure 2m in height and weigh as much as ten tonnes. Little is known about the **Iron Age megalithic civilization** that created these artefacts; war and revolution kept archeologists from working on the sites for decades. By the time French archeologist Madeleine Colani began excavating at the Jar sites in the 1930s, most of the urns had been looted, although she did find bronze and iron tools as well as coloured glass beads, bronze bracelets and cowrie shells. Colani theorized that the jars were **funerary urns**, originally holding cremated remains. More recent discoveries have revealed underground burial chambers, further supporting Colani's theory.

Of the dozens of Jar sites, twelve are currently open to tourists, though the **three main sites** are those most commonly visited on tours. The closest one, known as Site 1, just 2km southwest of town, has over two hundred jars. Sites 2 and 3 are much more scenic and are located about 10km southwest of the market village of **Lat Houang**, which is 10km south of Phonsavan, on the road to Muang Khoun. See opposite for details on visiting the sites.

Site 1

Site 1 or **Thong Hai Hin** ("Stone Jar Plain") is the most visited of the sites. Following the path from the car park to the jars, you'll quickly come to **Hai Cheaum** ("Cheaum Jar"), a massive jar 2m high that was named after the Tai–Lao hero of lore, who is celebrated in one version of the jar myth as the liberator of the

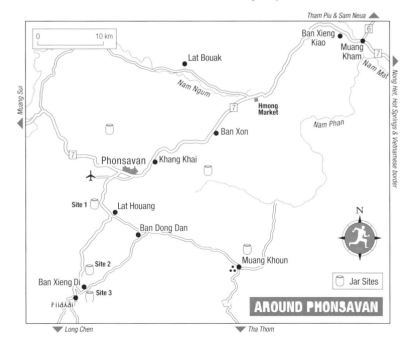

people of the Plain of Jars from a cruel overlord named Chao Angka. Legend has it that the jars were made to ferment rice wine to celebrate the victory; as the jars bear a passing resemblance to *lào hái* jars used today, the liquor-loving locals didn't have to stretch their imaginations too far to come up with this theory. Walk downhill a little way and you'll find yourself amid another group of jars, one of which has a crude human shape carved onto it. In the hill off to the left is a large **cave** that the Pathet Lao used during the war, and which, according to local legend, was used as a kiln to cast the jars. Erosion has carved two holes in the roof of the cave – natural chimneys that make the cavern a worthy kiln of sorts. Colani suggests that the cave was used as a crematorium: in and around the cave she found the remains of what she believed to be commoners not lucky enough to be interred in the stone funeral urns, which were reserved, she argued, for the ashes of the nobility.

Sites 2 and 3

Back on the Phonsavan–Muang Khoun road, the turn-off for **sites 2 and 3** is 3km further on at Lat Houang. Zipping across the flats surrounding Lat Sen, the town that played host to the old French airstrip, towards Phaxai and the Jar sites, you'll pass narrow dirt runways on the grassy meadows and hillsides. These clearings are used by hunters to trap swallows in nets that they trigger from camouflaged huts at one end of the strip; smoky fires bring bugs to the surface of the clearing, attracting the swallows. The most skilful hunters can catch several hundred birds on a good day, netting a tidy sum.

Ten kilometres on from the turn-off, you turn left along a dirt track – a road in slightly worse condition than the Phaxai road – and follow it for 2km through a village just large enough to support a tiny monastery, until you wind up at two adjacent hills, one on either side of the road. Nearly a hundred jars are scattered across the twin hills here, lending the site the name **Hai Hin Phou Salato** ("Salato Hill Stone Jar Site").

The gateway to Site 3, the most atmospheric of the three, lies in the village of Ban Xieng Di, 4km up the Phaxai road on the left. Large Lao Phuan houses line the way to Wat Xieng Di, a simple wooden monastery 1km from the turn-off, where you'll find the path leading to **Hai Hin Lat Khai**, also known as Hai Hin Xieng Di. There's a depressing, bomb-damaged Buddha here that the guides like to point out. Pick up the path at the back corner of the monastery compound, which hops a stream and cuts uphill through several fields before arriving at a clearing with more than a hundred jars and sweeping views of the surrounding countryside.

Practicalities

It's now possible to visit the Jar sites independently by chartering a tuk-tuk (expect to pay around 90,000K) or hiring a motorbike or bicycle. However, it's highly recommended to go with a guide in order to gain a better understanding of the history and myths surrounding the sites, in addition to finding out more about the UXO situation in the area. That said, as many places offer the same tour, it can be hard to know just how well informed your guide will be.

The most popular **tour**, and one that's offered by every travel agent and guesthouse in Phonsavan, is one that takes in sites 1, 2 and 3 (around 150,000K/person) though in all honesty you'll probably find that just visiting one site is more than enough. For something a little different, speak to the very knowledgeable and friendly Mr Nouds at **Sousath Travel** (☎020/2967213, ✉rasapet_lao@yahoo.com), whose father was involved with opening up the Jar sites to tourists. Highly recommended is his unique tour that takes in Jar Site 1, local Hmong villages (with the chance to see weavers at work) and a visit to his "bomb garden", where you might even get the rather thrilling experience of seeing him attempt to blow up some UXO; expect to pay between

▲ The Plain of Jars

$20–35 dollars, depending on the number of people. Tours to Muang Khoun (see below) and further afield are also available. Other travel agents offering well-regarded tours are Natural Travel at the *White Orchid Guesthouse*, and Amazing Lao Travel, just west of *Nisha Restaurant* on Route 7.

Muang Khoun (Old Xieng Khuang)

A ghost of its former self, **MUANG KHOUN**, old Xieng Khuang, 35km southeast of Phonsavan, was once the royal seat of the minor kingdom Xieng Khuang, renowned in the sixteenth century for its 62 opulent stupas, whose sides were said to be covered in treasure. Years of bloody invasions by Thai and Vietnamese soldiers, pillaging by Chinese bandits in the nineteenth century and a monsoon of bombs that lasted nearly a decade during the Second Indochina War taxed this town so heavily that, by the time the air raids stopped, next to nothing was left of the kingdom's exquisite temples. The town was all but abandoned, and centuries of history were drawn to a close. All that remains of the kingdom's former glory is an elegant Buddha image towering over ruined columns of brick at Wat Phia Wat, and That Dam, both of which bear the scars of the events that ended Xieng Khuang's centuries of rich history. Although the town has been rebuilt and renamed, it has taken a back seat to Phonsavan, and, with little in the way of amenities for travellers – there are a few *föe* shops around the market, but no hotel – it's most convenient to visit Muang Khoun as a day-trip.

A long row of low-slung wooden shophouses springs up along the road from Phonsavan in the shadow of towering **That Dam**, signalling your arrival in Muang Khoun. A path alongside the market leads up to the blackened hilltop stupa, the base of which has been tunnelled straight through to the other side by treasure seekers hoping to find more than a simple bone of the Enlightened One inside. A British surveyor who travelled through the area in the service of the Siamese king in 1884 – shortly after the invasions by Chinese Haw – surmised that the bandits pillaged the stupa, making off with 7000 rupees' weight of gold. Continuing on the main road beyond the market, you'll pass the ruins of a villa, the only reminder that this town was once a temperate French outpost of ochre colonial villas and shophouses, and arrive at the ruins of sixteenth-century **Wat Phia**. Brick columns reach skywards around a seated Buddha of impressive size, a mere hint at the temple architecture for which the city was renowned. The more recent temple of **Wat Siphoum**, the uninspiring structure nearest the market, bears little trace of the old designs for which the city's monasteries were known and serves notice of how much of Xieng Khuang's culture has been lost.

Phonsavan to Muang Kham

Many of the ethnic groups that populate Xieng Khuang are well represented in the area between Phonsavan and Muang Kham to the northeast, and a trip out to the village of **Muang Kham** and its nearby hot springs makes an interesting excursion. Route 7 winds through valleys hemmed by hills bursting with *dok bua khom* – yellow flowers that are crushed into a natural fertilizer for vegetable gardens – passing dusty Khmu, Black Tai, Phuan and Hmong villages, with their wooden huts.

Leaving Phonsavan, you first pass through **Khang Khai**, the town that became the seat of Prince Souvannaphouma's neutralist government after the Battle of Vientiane in December 1960, before arriving in **Ban Xon Tai**, 12km north of Phonsavan, where two village women etched the name of their hometown into Pathet Lao lore when they shot down an American plane during the war. Apparently armed with little more than rifles, the heroines inspired the addition of the adjectives "patriotic" and "brave" to generations-old songs praising the beauty of Xieng Khuang women.

Fourteen kilometres further on, you'll pass through the Hmong village of Tha Cho before arriving in **Daen Thong**, 12km further on, a village peopled by Khmu, a midland tribe that makes up around seven percent of Xieng Khuang's population. Widely considered to be among the original inhabitants of Laos, the ancestors of the Khmu are thought by some to have built the funerary urns scattered across the Plain of Jars. The next village, **Ban Lao**, was settled by Black Tai (Tai Dam), who fled to Laos several decades ago from Dien Bien Phu, the Vietnamese valley where the final battle of the First Indochina War was fought. After a further 7km, a dirt track forks off to the east leading to another Black Tai village, **Ban Xieng Kiao**, while the main road continues over a bridge spanning the Nam Mat stream and winds it way into **Muang Kham**, a large village formerly known as Chomthong.

Around Muang Kham

There are several sights around Muang Kham on the itineraries of day-tours out of Phonsavan. None is worth a special journey all the way from Phonsavan in its own right, but collectively they're a good excuse to see more of rural Xieng Khuang province. A number of tours now include a sombre pilgrimage to **Tham Piu**, a cave in which hundreds seeking refuge from the wartime bombing were killed when a fighter plane fired a rocket into the grotto; the turn-off for the cave lies on the left-hand side of Route 6, 4km north of Muang Kham. Follow the road 1500m to the foot of the hill and you'll find a steep set of stairs climbing up to the wide mouth of the cave. Only blackened rock testifies to the tragic incident.

From Muang Kham, Route 7 east towards the Vietnamese border leads you to two **hot springs**, Baw Nam Hon Lek and Baw Nam Hon Nyai – "Little Hot Spring" and "Big Hot Spring". The smaller of the two isn't worth a visit, while the larger spring has been converted into a resort of sorts, further east along Route 7. After passing through the tiny Na Ba market and crossing a bridge, turn right at Ban Nam Dien – 16km from Muang Kham – and head for the cliffs to find the spring. The road ends at the resort's gate, 3.5km away from Route 7, where you'll need to pay an entrance fee (5000K). The hot spring fills a swampy green pond of no remarkable beauty, but blooming flowers in the rainy season attract Phonsavan couples, who make the trip out on weekends to picnic and canoodle. A crude piping system draws the spring's steamy water to the site's main attraction: the **hot baths**, which are situated in a long shed among a small cluster of rustic bungalows. A warm bath (5000K) – there are two large tubs per private room – is certainly worth the trip during Xieng Khuang's chilly winters.

Many travel agents in Phonsavan will be able to add a visit to the hot springs onto a morning at the Jar sites – expect to pay around $35.

Muang Sui

From Phonsavan, Route 7 winds west towards the mountainous edge of the Plain of Jars and then begins working its way through the mountains to the outpost of Muang Phoukhoun on Route 13. This section of the French-built highway – a favourite target of Hmong insurgents as recently as the 1990s – grinds through pine-topped hills and steep-banked stream beds for 48km to **MUANG SUI**. Roughly at the halfway mark, the road fords the Nam Ngum as the river builds up steam en route to the Nam Ngum Dam, and then passes a pair of villages populated by Hmong, who were forcibly resettled here in the late 1990s.

Once a significant village known for its temples, Muang Sui was yet another casualty of the intense fighting in Xieng Khuang province. Now rebuilt alongside **Nong Tang**, a pretty lake hemmed in by stubby limestone karsts and praised for its serenity in local folk songs, it's a sleepy town of wooden shophouses and a small market. Nearby is **Tham Pha**, a forest cave that shelters a Buddha image and a *that*. One kilometre from town, an old 1500m-long landing strip, in a state of disuse, cuts across Route 7 as it begins its 90km journey towards Muang Phoukhoun.

Basic accommodation is available in the town, though most people who make the trip out here do so in conjunction with a tour of the Plain of Jars.

Hua Phan province

Sparsely populated **Hua Phan province** is a sea of misty mountains, dotted with isolated bowl-like valleys. The country's northeasternmost province, it's also one of the most spectacularly beautiful provinces in all of Laos, with some of the north's highest mountains, a large number of diverse ethnic groups, extensive forest cover and one of Laos's largest NBCAs. There are also enough caves, waterfalls and limestone karst scenery to give Vang Vieng hoteliers sleepless nights: you only need to drive the road in from Nam Neun to realize what amazing tourist potential Hua Phan has. The problem of course is infrastructure – though roads are now greatly improved, there are still very few of them, and unless they're travelling through to or from Vietnam, very few travellers make the effort to see the area.

The difficult terrain and the province's proximity to Vietnam made Hua Phan the perfect headquarters for the Pathet Lao, who operated out of the caves that honeycomb the karst formations in Vieng Xai for the better part of their Thirty Year Struggle. Along with Phongsali (see p.180), Hua Phan was set aside as a regroupment area for the communist forces under the Geneva Agreements of 1954. While the province formed the backbone of the Pathet Lao's liberated zone, not all of Hua Phan was under communist control: for years, the 1786m mountain peak of **Phou Pha Thi** was crowned by a "blind bombing" device to guide air raids on Hanoi (see box, p.163).

The real muscle behind the Pathet Lao during the war, **Vietnam**, retains much political and economic control over Hua Phan, and a steady flow of Vietnamese goods, electricity, merchants and construction workers arrives in the Lao province via three border points – one of which is open to foreign travellers. Travelling beyond Sam Neua town is a more attractive option than it used to be now that the **Na Meo border crossing** gives overland access to Thanh Hoa province in Vietnam. Regular buses from Sam Neua travel up to the border, though you'll need to already have a Vietnamese visa in order to make the crossing.

Hua Phan is predominantly populated by various Tai groups – Red, Black, Neua and White – and, in the towns, migrants from Vietnam and China. With more than twenty **ethnic groups** in the mix, it's perhaps not surprising that even residents from neighbouring Xieng Khuang complain about the difficulty of understanding Hua Phan dialect. During the centuries before French rule, the area was part of a Black Tai principality, known as the Sipsong Chao Tai, which spanned the present-day Lao–Vietnamese border. The principality fell under the sway of the lowland Lao kingdoms of Luang Prabang, Xieng Khuang and Vientiane and under the control of the greater powers that in turn controlled them – Siam and Vietnam. Stone pillars (known as Suan Hin), located several kilometres off Route 6 near Houa Muang, suggest that the area was a hub of some forgotten culture long before Tai–Lao and Vietnamese rulers squabbled over this region.

Sam Neua

You could be forgiven for thinking that you'd crossed into Vietnam on descending into **SAM NEUA**, the provincial capital and the only sizeable Lao town east of the Annamite Mountains. Unlike the rest of Laos, which drains west into the Mekong, all of Hua Phan province's rivers flow southeast into the Gulf of Tonkin – Sam Neua itself sits in the narrow Nam Xam River valley. If you want to feel like you're in the middle of nowhere, Sam Neua fits the bill, sitting in a bowl surrounded by low, pleasant hills with the narrow river rushing through its centre.

Although there's little to see in the town itself, it serves as a comfortable base for the Pathet Lao Caves in Vieng Xai, or a stopover on the push to northern Vietnam. Though there's a number of guesthouses and an excellent tourist office, tourist infrastructure in Sam Neua is otherwise quite limited, and you're likely to find that you're regarded as something of a novelty, even in the centre of town. Be warned that Sam Neua can be a lot colder than the rest of the country, so a sweater and long trousers come in very handy if you're planning on stopping here.

Arrival and information

There are two **bus stations** – destinations within the province arrive at Nathong bus station to the east of town, while destinations further afield arrive at the main bus station to the south of town; a tuk-tuk from either should cost 20,000K. At the time of writing, no flights were running to or from Sam Neua airport, 2km east of the centre. The excellent **tourist office** (Mon–Fri 8–11.30am & 1–4.30pm)

Crossing into Vietnam from Sam Neua

Most people who stop in Sam Neua are on their way to or from Vietnam, via the border crossing at **Na Meo**. Sawngthaews run from Nathong bus station to Na Meo at 7.10am every morning, taking three hours to make the 84km journey (25,000K). In addition, a coach service departs on Tuesday, Thursday and Saturday at 8am, travelling to Thanh Hoa (contact the tourist office or the bus company on ☏020/4629939 for further information).

is situated on Phathy Road, the main boulevard in town; the very helpful staff can advise on visiting the area, including Vieng Xai, nearby waterfalls and hot springs, and have the most up-to-date information on bus and sawngthaew times. In addition, minibus charters to Vieng Xai (450,000K) are also available.

Also on Phathy Road, the **Lao Development Bank** changes US dollars (cash and travellers' cheques), Thai bhat and sterling, and can also do cash advances – though note that this can be temperamental so it's best not to rely on it. There are two internet cafés in town (150K/min) – one across the river, past *Samneau Hotel*, the other on Phathy Road near *Khongmany* restaurant – connections are fairly pedestrian.

Accommodation

Despite the lack of tourists in Sam Neua, there's certainly no shortage of **accommodation** available. The greatest concentration of guesthouses is in the streets around the dry market.

Bounhome ☎064/312223. Housed in a modern building, with smallish but clean rooms. The more expensive rooms, with en-suite bathrooms, are on the ground floor, while guests on the top floor use a (somewhat inconvenient) shared bathroom and toilet downstairs. ❶

Khaemxam ☎064/312111. Facing the river, this family-run hotel is hands down the best value in town and is the most popular place to stay. Rooms are a decent size and pleasant, if basic, with a choice between en-suite and shared bath. The most expensive rooms (❷) have televisions. ❶

Phetphousay ☎064/312943. On a small lane, this modern concrete building has three floors of rooms. Rooms are clean and large but spartan, and noise tends to echo around in the building. Each floor has shared hot water, bath and toilet facilities. ❶

Samneua ☎020/5094444. This grand peach-coloured building, just across the river from the centre of town, is probably the classiest place to stay. All rooms are en suite and have TVs, though can feel rather cramped due to the large, decorative wooden beds. Minivan service available. ❹

The Town

There's little to occupy the traveller in Sam Neua, save absorbing the rugged frontier atmosphere of this most un-Lao outpost. The main street is the 2km-long, four-lane **Phathy Road** – a huge central boulevard lined with institutional-looking government buildings and bearing the unmistakable mark of the Vietnamese, who rebuilt the town after the war. It does seem remarkably empty, however, as though the city was destined for great things that never quite materialized.

There are almost no cultural sites, but you can walk up Phathy Road to the **victory monument**, an easy climb that affords a good view of the valley, and a bit further on, near the main street's end, to **Wat Phoxaysanalam**. Construction of the wat began in 1958 and took nearly a decade to complete, whereupon it was almost immediately destroyed by the bombing. The modest structure that now stands here was completed in the 1980s. It was until very recently the only wat in town and there are only a handful of resident monks. As journalist Christopher Kremmer (see p.307) wrote in *Stalking the Elephant Kings*: "if you're tired of seeing monks in Laos, come to Sam Neua." The town's three other prewar wats, including the 200-year-old Xieng Khuang-style Wat Inpeng, were never rebuilt. The sad little spires along Phathy Road leading up to the wat indicate where these holy sites once were.

Much more cheerful is the vibrant food **market**, on the eastern side of the river, which is a good place to get a feel for the province's character. Vietnamese goods,

Sam Neua textiles

Experts on **Lao textiles** all seem to agree that the most sophisticated pieces, in terms of both design and colour scheme, are produced in the region around **Sam Neua**. A fashion revolution followed the political revolution in 1975, when the victorious communists abandoned their headquarters near Sam Neua and moved into Vientiane. The wives of the new leaders enthusiastically sported the Tai Daeng styles of Sam Neua, and it wasn't long before the look caught on. Today the bold, spidery patterns of Sam Neua textiles are a favourite all over Laos.

Among Lao textiles, the work of the Tai Daeng and Tai Nua stand out. Classified by ethnologists as "tribal Tai", these ethnic groups are related culturally and linguistically to the lowland Lao. However, unlike the lowland Lao, they are animists for the most part, though Mahayana Buddhist influence can be seen in their textile motifs. These groups believe that death is the most important rite of passage in a person's life, and the funeral ceremony is correspondingly elaborate. To prepare for it, a woman will weave a special skirt to wear to the grave. A geometric design woven into the waistband of the skirt will serve to ward off spirits that might attempt to block her passage into the "Garden of Golden Mangoes". Another significant textile used by the Sam Neua cultures is a "shaman's shawl", worn by spirit mediums while performing healing ceremonies. Symbols on these shawls are remarkably similar to those found on bronze frog-drums of the sixth-century BC Dong-son culture which was centred in northern Vietnam. Other motifs found on Sam Neua textiles include the swastika, a Hindu symbol that was adopted by Mahayana Buddhism, and the stylized "third eye". Perhaps the most striking and the most "Lao" of the Sam Neua motifs are realistic naga imprinted in the textiles by tie-dyeing.

many of which are bought by merchants at weekend border markets in Xieng Khoun and Na Maew, flood the stalls in a display of vegetables, meats and the occasional severed dog head. The market buzzes throughout the day, its vendors bundled against the cold with their heads wrapped in colourful scarves, a sartorial twist that most likely lent the province its name – "Hua Phan" means "wrapped head". It's a great place to head to for a cheap bowl of *fǒe*, or to try some local snacks.

On the opposite side of the river is the **dry market**. Here you'll find all manner of individual wooden stalls selling various goods, including a minor smattering of Lao **textiles**, although much of the best stuff gets sent directly to Luang Prabang or Vientiane. Although a lot of cloth is produced in Hua Phan, it's all made in people's homes, not factories. The alley behind the dry market houses all kinds of electrical shops bulging with refrigerators, televisions, rice-cookers, bicycles and home karaoke systems.

Eating and drinking

Sam Neua has a few decent restaurants, but nothing out of the ordinary. Expect to wait a while for your food – most places are just a two-person operation. In addition to the restaurants listed below, the food market is a good option for *fǒe* or for snacks during the day.

Chittavanh The restaurant below the guesthouse of the same name is a popular choice with locals at lunchtime, offering a menu that includes beef noodle soup, fried rice and fried sour fish.
Dannaomuangxam This family-run place, decorated with antlers and pictures of Beer Lao girls, is a good choice throughout the day, serving cornflakes and fried eggs for breakfast, and tasty fried rice and noodle dishes for dinner. The free hot tea is especially welcome on cold days.
Khongmany A sweet little "restaurant", if you can call it that, with a few tables in a bare-bones garage-like room, dishing up decent Indian food, including *channa masala* (14,000K) and chicken fry (25,000K).

Around Sam Neua

The best reason to visit Sam Neua is to explore the surrounding countryside – the tourist office (see p.159) can provide up-to-date information about transport options. To really explore, rent a motorbike – a shop just south of the tourist office offers them for 60,000K per day, though the staff speak little English.

Phou Pha Thi

Some 35km northwest of Sam Neua, **Phou Pha Thi**, a 1786m-high limestone mountain, is the tallest peak in northern Hua Phan and the most distinctive mountain in the province: a broad-based massif, with a near-vertical summit. The Nam Xam River, which flows through the centre of Sam Neua and all the way to the Gulf of Tonkin, runs directly down from the peak's southern flanks.

Phou Pha Thi is famous for being an important Lima Site during the **Second Indochina War** when the CIA and Special Forces set up a navigation radar tower on the summit. As this secret mountain base, run by the CIA and guarded by three hundred Thai mercenaries, was in the very heart of Pathet Lao territory, the story of its eventual capture and destruction is the stuff of local legend (see box, opposite). Contact the tourist office for information about reaching the mountain, though hiring a motorbike may be your best bet; note that you can't actually climb the mountain at present.

Hintang Archeological Park

Located just off Route 6, 50–60km southwest of the town of Houa Muang, **Hintang Archeological Park** is home to the **Suan Hin** or "Stone Garden". Surrounded by forest, the megalithic stone gardens consist of large slabs of rock that

The fall of Phou Pha Thi

In a decision that would prove to be the turning point of the war in Laos, US President Lyndon Johnson ordered the installation of a navigational beacon to guide air strikes against the North Vietnamese atop **Phou Pha Thi**. Here, US air force cargo helicopters dropped off the components of the device, code-named Commando Club, which was assembled a few hundred metres from fields growing some of the best opium in Laos. Hmong soliders, not known for their ability to defend fixed positions, were assigned to protect the latest in military wizardry.

A few weeks before Commando Club became operational in late 1967, a couple of monks were caught on the summit of Phou Pha Thi carrying cameras and sketch-books; they were Vietnamese spies, and soon after Commando Club began directing its all-weather, high-altitude air strikes on the Hanoi valley, two Soviet-built biplanes, dark-green museum pieces with cloth-covered wings and wooden propellers jury-rigged to fire mortar shells, buzzed the site – the only time during the war that the North Vietnamese attacked a target with biplanes. The planes were shot down, but the Vietnamese, provoked by this high-profile site that threatened their security, moved more troops into Laos. By the time North Vietnamese commandos scaled the summit with grappling hooks and ropes to take the position on March 10, 1968, the nineteen Americans operating Commando Club knew the end was near.

The **fall of Phou Pha Thi** was typical of the lack of unified command that plagued the United States' war in Laos. As historian Roger Warner wrote in *Shooting at the Moon*: "The radar installation belonged to the air force, but the CIA was supposed to defend it. The CIA couldn't defend it as it chose, because the ambassador didn't want unauthorized weapons on the mountaintop. Kept from direct accountability for its own men, the air force lost interest, even though it had proposed the installation in the first place, and, on the mountain itself, nothing held the villagers from wandering where they pleased, including to the little opium patch near the summit, which they harvested just as they always had."

Phou Pha Thi also signalled a shift in the demands the US placed on its Hmong allies: they were no longer being armed to defend their own mountaintops, but were now pawns of the war in Vietnam. Eight Americans were pulled off Phou Pha Thi, leaving eleven dead or missing – the beginning of prolonged confusion, as Warner indicates, over the fate of Americans missing in action in Laos, and for whom the search actively continues today.

have been stood upright and arranged in circles. The age and origin of the sites as well as the culture that created them remain a mystery, though the pillars have been linked by archeologists to the stone funerary urns of the Plain of Jars (see p.153) and it's thought that they're approximately 2000 years old. To get there, take the bus toward Phonsavan and let the driver know where you want to get off.

Nam Nua waterfall and the road to Vieng Xai

The road heading east out of Sam Neua passes through the Striped Hmong village of **Ban Houa Khang** before descending into a valley of rice fields surrounded by shaggy karsts – the first glimpse of the heart of Pathet Lao territory. Passing through the lowland Lao town of **Ban Muang Liat** and the Hmong village of **Houai Na**, you'll arrive at a fork, 21km from Sam Neua. Bearing left leads to Sop Hao and Xieng Khoun on the old French road to Hanoi, right to **Vieng Xai**, 8km away, and eventually the Vietnamese border town of Na Meo. Three kilometres down the Vieng Xai road you'll come to a bridge over a swift-flowing stream, and from here a track leads off left to the top of a 70m waterfall, **Tad Nam Nua**, most stunning during the wet season. Cutting away from the path, it's possible to scramble along the rocks and riverbank to a viewpoint at the crest of the falls. The classic frontal view is harder to attain: back at the junction, take the Sop Hao road for roughly 2km where you'll find a track leading for over 1km through paddies and eventually across a stream and a sticky thicket of bamboo.

Nam Xam NBCA

Located to the south of Route 6A, the **Nam Xam NBCA** is the smallest individual NBCA in Laos at just 580 square kilometres. The conservation area basically encompasses a broad bend in the **Nam Xam River** where it makes a lengthy detour around two large mountains within the NBCA, before extending over to the Vietnamese border to the east that comprises the park's eastern boundary. The tallest peak is located in the centre of the park and is 1741m. The eastern area of the park is said to provide a habitat for elephants, bears, tigers and gibbons. The park can only be reached by a four-wheel-drive vehicles; ask about trips at the tourist office in Sam Neua.

Vieng Xai

Arriving in **VIENG XAI** ("City of Victory"), you wouldn't know the Pathet Lao and their communist allies in Vietnam had won the Second Indochina War. Sprawled across a valley surrounded by the cave-riddled karst formations used by the Pathet Lao as their wartime headquarters, Vieng Xai was cobbled together by comrades from Russia, North Korea and Vietnam as well as labourers from Hua Phan's notorious re-education camps (see box, pp.166–167). In 1973, at the end of the war, there were plans to make Vieng Xai the heart of the newly socialist nation, but in the end Laos's socialist friends could not be convinced to foot the bill to turn a backwater into a gleaming new capital, and so the Pathet Lao leadership decamped to Vientiane. With time, Vieng Xai couldn't even compete with nearby Sam Neua as a provincial hub. People moved out and many buildings fell into a state of crumbling decay. These days, the town has a slow, dusty charm, complemented by its stunning backdrop of limestone karsts.

Very few travellers stay in Vieng Xai, most preferring to do the caves (see below) as a **day-trip** from Sam Neua, which has much better food and accommodation. However, for those who can afford the time, the scenic countryside and ambience around Vieng Xai reward further exploration, evoking Guilin in China. In fact, if you want to know what Vang Vieng was like before it was overrun with trippy backpackers, Vieng Xai is the place for you.

The Pathet Lao caves

When American air force Chief of Staff General Curtis LeMay jested that the United States would bomb the enemy "back to the Stone Age", what he hadn't realized was that living like cavemen would prove to be the key to the survival of the North Vietnamese Army and Pathet Lao during the heaviest aerial bombardment in history. Like Vang Vieng in central Laos and Mahaxai in the south, the limestone karst formations in the valleys east of Sam Neua are pockmarked with **caves** and crevices – which proved a perfect hideout for the Pathet Lao's parallel government. **Viet Minh** army units began using the caves and enlarging them in the early 1950s while fighting the French in the days before Dien Bien Phu. Soon, the Lao leftists had joined the Vietnamese underground, and by the middle of the 1960s, Vieng Xai and the surrounding area had become a troglodyte city of thousands living in the more than one hundred caves. The caves – some at the foot of hills, others high up, hidden by surrounding escarpments and accessible only by scaling steps cut into sheer rock faces – were an impregnable fortress, but even poking your head outside could prove deadly as craters near the caves attest.

The inhabitants of the caves followed a routine of sleeping by day and working at night in the fields outside (animals had to be dark-coloured in order to remain

▲ Outside the Pathet Lao caves

undetected by the enemy) or in the caves themselves: caverns held weaving mills, printing presses and workshops where American bombs and worn-out trucks were upgraded into farming tools and appliances. On Saturdays, adults would take a break and attend **classes** consisting of professional, cultural and political courses as well as lessons in algebra, geometry and geography.

The conclusion of the war didn't bring the hardships experienced in the caves to an end: what changed were the inhabitants. After 1975, the caves became a **"re-education camp"** for functionaries of the Royal Lao government – from the lowliest foot soldier to the former king (see box, pp.166–167).

Seven caves are now open to the public, and the guided tour takes about two hours. Each of these caves, most named after the Pathet Lao leaders who lived there, had multiple exits, an office and sleeping quarters, as well as an emergency chamber for use in case of chemical-weapons attacks (these chambers were kitted out with a Soviet oxygen machine and a metal door of the sort you'd find on an old submarine). Tours often begin with the large cave of **Kaysone Phomvihane** (see p.220), who became leader of the Lao communist movement at its formation in 1955, and remained unchallenged in his post as head of the Lao People's Democratic Republic from its inception in 1975 until his death in 1992. Born in Savannakhet of a Lao mother and a Vietnamese father, Kaysone spent far more time in Vieng Xai than the Pathet Lao's face man, Prince Souphanouvong. While the Red Prince was off playing Vientiane's game of cat-and-mouse politics, Kaysone stayed in Hua Phan, attending frequent meetings in Hanoi – a risky two-day journey from Vieng Xai – with North Vietnamese leaders Ho Chi Minh and General Vo Nguyen Giap, the legendary military strategist behind the French defeat at Dien Bien Phu.

One of the most fascinating caves is **Xanglot Cave**, a huge natural cave which housed a large concert hall where rallies and meetings were held, alongside festivals and musical and dance performances. It's fascinating to imagine the residents attempting to maintain some semblance of normal life while living in these extraordinary conditions.

Re-education camps

The first group of prisoners to be transported to **re-education camps** – the Pathet Lao's means of neutralizing its wartime enemies – arrived by invitation in full military dress months before the communist takeover in December 1975. After receiving letters signed by Prince Souvannaphouma, seventy high-ranking Royal Lao Army officers and provincial governors came to what they thought would be an important meeting and were whisked off to the Plain of Jars, where they were fêted with a banquet and a movie. Any hope of a uniquely Lao solution to the Second Indochina War ended there, as these officials were shortly thereafter flown off to Hua Phan, where they were stripped of their rank and separated into small work parties. In the following months, thousands of civil servants and army officers voluntarily entered the re-education centres in Hua Phan, Attapeu and Phongsali after being assured the "seminars" would last only a few weeks. With their opponents safely out of the way in the most remote corners of the country, or having opted already to flee to Thailand, the Pathet Lao moved ahead with the final stage of their bloodless takeover virtually unopposed.

Joined later by thousands more who arrived somewhat less willingly, the internees were turned loose in the fenceless camps, which were heavily guarded and hemmed in by the extreme geographical features of the Lao wilderness, and left to forage for food and build their own shelters out of bamboo. Each morning, a bell was rung at 5am and the prisoners were assigned a job for the day – cutting wood in the jungles, building roads, working in the fields. In the evenings, self-criticism and political indoctrination sessions were held. Although there was no physical torture, mindless rules were established in order to control the captives, who were never allowed to settle into one place. The cumulative effect of the "re-education", according to a former Royal Lao Army officer, who spent thirteen years in a Hua Phan camp, was a sort of "brainwashing". Life in the camps was hard – the officer is certain that he only made it because of a Green Beret survival course he attended in the United States – and many ran off or died of malaria.

Practicalities

Sawngthaews from Sam Neua to Vieng Xai (10,000K; 45min) leave almost every hour until mid-afternoon from Nathong bus station, stopping in front of Vieng Xai's market. Coming back, the last sawngthaew is at 3pm, though occasionally it won't run if there are not enough passengers – if you're not planning on staying overnight, the best option is to catch the 7.15am sawngthaew to Vieng Xai and return at 1pm.

To get to the **tourist office** (daily 8–11.30am & 1–4.30pm), turn right out of the market and follow the main road for about five minutes until you reach a stupa, where the road splits in two. Bear left – the tourist office is on the right a few minutes later. The only way to visit the caves is on one of the tourist office's **guided tours**, which run at 9am and 1pm (2hr; 60,000K) – the guides can be a little hit and miss, but the excellent audio tour (included) now takes centre stage, with accounts from people who lived in the caves really bringing them to life. In order to get the most out of the tour, it's recommended to hire a bike (15,000K from the tourist office) – this will allow you to see more caves as some of them are quite spread out, but it does depend on everyone in your group hiring one. Outside of these times, it's possible to arrange for a private tour, which will incur an additional 50,000K per group.

There're a number of places to stay in Vieng Xai, the choice of which are the small huts at *Naxai Guesthouse* (T064/314336; ❶), right opposite the tourist office, with a lovely garden area in which to relax. A more modern option is the *Thavisay Hotel* (T020/5712392; ❷), which has decent rooms with television a few streets back from the tourist office. Aside from the bowls of *fŏe* rustled up during the daytime by the **noodle stalls** in the bare-bones market, satisfying meals can be hard to come by in Vieng Xai. If you're planning to stay for more than one night

Drug addicts, prostitutes and other "anti-social" elements were also rounded up and shuttled off to **Ang Nam Ngum** near Vang Vieng (see p.94), where an estimated three thousand people were placed on "Boy Island" and "Girl Island". In 1977, the **royal family** too was arrested and banished to Camp 01 at Sop Hao, in Hua Phan, where the king and crown prince reportedly died of starvation two weeks apart in May 1978. The queen is said to have died in 1981, and, like her husband and son before her, was buried in an unmarked grave outside the camp. The only government acknowledgement of their deaths came a decade later, when Party Secretary General Kaysone mentioned in an aside during a visit to Paris that the king had died of old age.

There are **no official figures** for the number of people who were interned in the camps, but estimates based on reports by former inmates and their families suggest that at the height of the camps, in 1978–79, the number of internees may have been as high as fifty thousand. Whatever willingness supporters of the Royalist regime had to work with the new government quickly evaporated when it became clear that those interned in the camps weren't coming home anytime soon. Confronted with the prospect of being sent off for re-education, more than three hundred thousand people, nearly a tenth of Laos's population, fled the country.

The first group of prisoners, low-ranking members of the former regime, was **released** in 1980, and despite finally being deemed fit to live in socialist Laos, many took the first chance they got to cross the Mekong. As the 1980s wore on, more and more prisoners were gradually released under pressure from Western nations and Amnesty, which reported that in 1985 seven thousand people remained in the camps, a number which had dwindled to 33 by March 1991. The camps may now be empty, but the current number of political prisoners in Laos is not known, and Amnesty International has described Laos as "a country which has a zero-tolerance policy towards dissent in any form".

you may want to bring supplies from Sam Neua's market; alternatively the restaurant attached to the *Thavisay Hotel* serves a range of Lao and Western dishes.

Nam Neun to Nong Khiaw

The journey from **Nam Neun** to **Nong Khiaw** along Route 1 is one of northern Laos's great road journeys, crossing numerous mountain ranges and valleys. These days, you're most likely to travel directly from Sam Neua to Nong Khiaw or Luang Prabang (twelve and fourteen hours, respectively), but if you want to experience local Lao life then it's worth considering stopping en route, though don't expect much more than basic accommodation and noodle shops.

Nam Neun

Until relatively recently, travelling through the region meant stopping at the village of **NAM NEUN** for a change of vehicles, usually overnight. Now, the longest you're likely to stop is for an extended break – a small selection of grilled meats on bamboo skewers and bags of sticky rice can usually be bought in the pint-sized market, and two or three restaurants cater to travellers in transit with bowls of instant noodles and warm drinks. The town is set in a steep valley perched above the swift-flowing **Nam Neun River** – spanned here by a sturdy Russian-built bridge – which flows out of the Nam Et NBCA and eventually empties into the Gulf of Tonkin at Vinh in Vietnam. From here, Route 1 winds through the mountains towards Vieng Thong.

Vieng Thong

VIENG THONG, more popularly known by its old name **Muang Hiam**, lies in the upper valley of the Nam Khan River, which sweeps across the wide swath of rice fields on the town's western flank. The town itself winds along the bottom of the narrow river valley and its main street begs for a high-noon shoot-out. These days, it's unlikely that you'll stop here for anything more than a food and toilet break on the long journey from Sam Neua to Nong Khiaw, but if you do find yourself hanging around here for a bus, the 1km walk to the nearby **hot springs** is a pleasant diversion. While the pools are large enough for a good soak, they're far too hot; a tiny pool near the main road is cooler and a popular spot for villagers to bring their infants for a warm bath. There are a number of cheap guesthouses near the dry market, plus the usual noodle shops – to get here, turn left down Route 1 from the bus stop until you come to a T-junction; the centre of town lies just to the right.

After the long overland loop to reach Vieng Thong, it's strange to think that the swift-flowing river through town ends its journey in distant Luang Prabang. Starting from the Nam Et NBCA north of Vieng Thong, the Nam Khan River heads southwest between two ranges of high mountains, over difficult rapids and through dense jungles. The entire area is a big blank on most maps and no passenger boats travel this length of the river. If you are interested in potentially exploring the area by boat, the best people to talk to are Green Discovery in Luang Prabang or Nong Khiaw (see p.143 & p.174, respectively), though it's not currently something featured on any of their organized trips.

Southeast through Phou Loei NBCA

West of Vieng Thong, Route 1 labours up forested hills and through ethnic minority villages, with their rough huts precariously perched along the ridges above a sea of mountains. The **scenery** is simply spectacular, with row upon row of mountain ranges extending into the distance.

Route 1 passes through **Phou Loei NBCA** (National Protected Area), covering an area of 1465 square kilometres. In the high, mountainous divide separating Luang Prabang, Hua Phan and Xieng Khuang provinces, the park consists of north–south ranges, with its highest peak, **Phou Soy** at 2257m, at the northern end. Almost bordering Phou Loei is stunning **Nam Et NBCA**, an area of 1915 square kilometres that runs right up to the Vietnamese border in the north. At the time of writing, there was talk of eco-tourism opportunities being set up in the region – for up-to-date information, check with the helpful tourist office in Sam Neua (see p.159), or with Tiger Trail (see p.143) in Luang Prabang. None of the ridge-top Hmong villages along Route 1 has any formal accommodation.

Travel details

Buses

Phonsavan to: Hanoi (weekly; 18hr); Luang Prabang (daily; 8hr); Sam Neua (daily; 8hr); Vang Vieng (daily; 4hr); Vientiane (5 daily; 10hr); Vinh (4 weekly; 12hr).
Sam Neua to: Luang Prabang (daily; 14hr); Nong Khiaw (daily; 12hr); Phonsavan (2 daily; 8hr); Vientiane via Luang Prabang (daily; 27hr); Vientiane via Phonsavan (2 daily; 25hr)

Flights

Phonsavan to: Vientiane (4 weekly; 40min).

The far north

CHAPTER 4 # Highlights

✳ **Nam Ou River** The spectacularly scenic Nam Ou, flanked by jagged karst and rustic riverside villages, can be explored by local river boats. See p.172

✳ **Nong Khiaw** Surrounded by stunning limestone peaks and straddling the Nam Ou, idyllic Nong Khiaw is the perfect place to lose a few days. See p.174

✳ **Phongsali** This remote town has a quiet charm and is the perfect base for exploring the vast tropical forests and diverse traditional cultures of the region. See p.180

✳ **Hill-tribe trekking** Trekking in northern Laos offers the fascinating opportunity to experience life in a local village. See p.182, p.186 & p.194

✳ **Nam Ha NBCA** Hike, kayak or raft, but don't miss this stunning national park near the trekking centre of Luang Namtha. See p.190

✳ **Slow boats on the Mekong** Enjoy the leisurely journey along the Mekong through the vast mountain wilderness of northern Laos. See p.201

▲ Slow boating on the Mekong

The far north

While history has seen the rise and fall of a Lao dynasty enthroned at Luang Prabang, little has changed on the elevated **northern fringes** of the former kingdom. Decades of war and neglect have done their part to keep this isolated region of Southeast Asia from developing and have unwittingly preserved a way of life that has virtually vanished in neighbouring countries. While the fertile valleys of the Upper Mekong and its tributaries have for centuries been the domain of the **Buddhist lowland Lao**, the hills and mountains to the north have been the preserve of a scattering of animist tribal peoples, including the **Hmong**, **Mien** and **Akha**. Anthropologists, gleaning evidence largely from oral tradition, speculate that some of these tribal peoples, such as the **Khmu**, were actually here before the lowland Lao migrated onto the scene; others, such as the Akha, are relative newcomers. The highlanders make their living by painstakingly clearing and cultivating the steep slopes while bartering with the lowland Lao for anything that they themselves cannot harvest, hunt or fashion with their own hands. It is largely the chance to experience first-hand these near-pristine cultures that draws visitors to the region today.

The far north still has an air of being untamed – and nowhere is this more evident than in **Phongsali**, a remote, mountainous district where the provincial capital feels as though it hasn't changed for decades. Improved transport means that it's now easier to explore the region than ever before, though you can still expect long journeys on endlessly windy roads. The trekking scene in Phongsali is relatively new, which makes it a great opportunity to visit hill tribes that retain a very traditional way of life. Many people come this far north in order to do the amazing boat trip down the **Nam Ou**, which can take you as far south as Luang Prabang, and allows you to visit otherwise inaccessible **Muang Ngoi**, long a favourite with visitors to the region wanting to kick back for a few days. An hour south of Muang Ngoi, **Nong Khiaw** straddles the river, nestling among some of the region's most dramatic scenery, with limestone mountains all around, and excellent opportunities for exploration.

Striking east from here takes you to **Oudomxai** – a town with little to recommend it other than as an important transport hub; from here it's possible to connect to most other places in northern Laos, as well as Vientiane. The most popular northern town is undoubtedly the tourist centre of **Luang Namtha**, a good place to relax for a few days if you're after some home comforts. More laidback is nearby **Muang Sing**, reached by a stunning road journey through Nam Ha NPCA, a pristine and beautiful protected area of the country. Both towns have become popular bases for trekking, due to their comfortable accommodation and easy access to nearby Akha, Mien and Tai Dam villages.

While boat traffic on the rivers isn't quite what it used to be, the border town of **Houayxai** is the popular starting point for the memorable slow boat down the

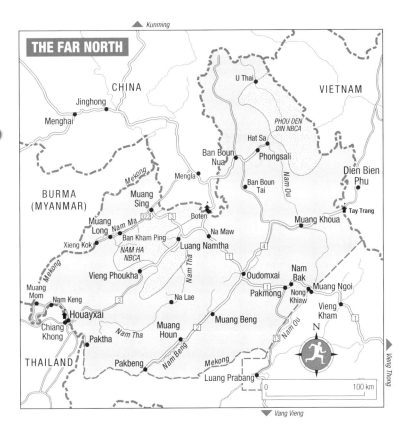

Mekong, via the port town of **Pakbeng**, to gracious Luang Prabang. It's now also the starting point for the fantastic **Gibbon Experience**, which provides a great opportunity to explore the jungle, on foot and by zip line.

Many visitors see comparatively little of the region, travelling from the Thai border down to Luang Prabang on the Mekong, perhaps swinging first up to Luang Namtha for a couple of days' trekking, and then maybe travelling up to Nong Khiaw and Muang Ngoi from Luang Prabang. But if you've got time, the area deserves further exploration, and can easily be covered in a **broad loop** that covers both river and road, beginning with the wonderful journey up the Nam Ou from Luang Prabang to Phongsali (via Nong Khiaw, Muang Ngoi and Muang Khoua), then dropping down to Oudomxai to reach Luang Namtha and Muang Sing before heading to Hoayxai to pick up the slow boat back to Luang Prabang.

The Nam Ou River Valley

Starting on the China border, the **Nam Ou** drains all of Phongsali province and flows down through western Luang Prabang province to meet the Mekong above Luang Prabang. Much of the Phongsali province watershed is devoid of roads and still well covered with old growth forest, and the river and its many tributaries remain in many ways as they were when nineteenth-century French explorers passed through. That said, the advent of improved roads has meant that river traffic has somewhat diminished; while this can mean that you may have to wait a few days (or charter a boat) to travel up (or down) it, it does retain an unhurried, very local charm, without the uncomfortable crowds of the more famous Mekong journey.

An important Mekong tributary, the Nam Ou holds a cherished place in Lao lore as the original route followed by Luang Prabang's founding father, Khun Lo, and later by Fa Ngum, the warrior-king, as he headed towards Luang Prabang to claim the throne and found the Kingdom of a Million Elephants. The river begins its journey in the southern flanks of the mountains separating Laos and Yunnan in China. This northernmost part of Laos, Phongsali province, is hemmed in by high mountains on three sides, and the Nam Ou is joined by no less than eight major tributaries before entering Luang Prabang province and beginning its final run down to the Mekong. Two of these tributaries, the Nam Khang and the Nam Houn, pass within the huge **Phou Den Din NBCA**, along the border with Vietnam.

The main city of the upper Nam Ou is **Phongsali**, the provincial capital. To the east, **Hat Sa** effectively acts as Phongsali's river port on the Nam Ou. The other two important towns on the Nam Ou are Muang Khoua and Nong Khiaw: **Muang Khoua** sits astride the river where **Route 4** continues from Oudomxai to Dien Bien Phu, Vietnam, while **Nong Khiaw** is located where **Route 1** crosses the river on its way from Oudomxai to Hua Phan province in the extreme northeast. Aside from tiny **Muang Ngoi**, all of the towns listed in this section can be reached by both road and river, though undoubtedly the latter is the more enjoyable option.

Slow boats on the Nam Ou

The southern leg of the journey up the Nam Ou is the six-hour ride between Luang Prabang and **Nong Khiaw** which is wildly scenic, especially the karst forests around Nong Khiaw and Muang Ngoi. Closer to Luang Prabang, where the river follows Route 13, extensive logging and slash-and-burn agriculture have stripped the surrounding mountains: only where the slopes are too rocky or too steep for cultivation have stands of forest been left intact. In an effort at reforestation, however, rows of young teak trees, recognizable by their enormous leaves, have been planted. After the road leaves the river, the scenery takes a turn for the spectacular, with vertical limestone peaks and pristine little white-sand beaches.

Upriver from Nong Khiaw the scenery continues to impress, possibly even surpassing that of the stretch below Nong Khiaw, the river snaking through impenetrable jungle. Because many of the surrounding mountains are simply too steep for slash-and-burn agriculture, the forests have been left virtually untouched. When the river is not too high and fast, this leg is also blessed with shelves of squeaky-clean beach, perfect for taking a lazy swim and admiring the dramatic scenery. However, this primeval landscape lasts only a third of the distance to **Muang Khoua** and is then replaced by arable hills with a beaten, domesticated air about them. The journey between Nong Khiaw and Muang Khoua takes approximately five hours.

Beyond Muang Khoua, it's another 100km to **Hat Sa**, the last town of any size on the Nam Ou until U Thai, far to the northeast. The mountainous scenery on the Muang Khoua–Hat Sa leg may be a little less dramatic than around Nong Khiaw, but the journey is nonetheless impressive and peaceful.

Passenger boats continuing up the Nam Ou River beyond Hat Sa are few and far between, but it is possible to charter a boat to explore Laos's northernmost corner. Anticipate paying upwards of $60 for a day-trip. North of Hat Sa there's no formal accommodation but it should be possible to find lodging in villages.

Pakmong

The road route from Luang Prabang to Nong Khiaw takes about two and a half hours. Well-maintained Route 13 takes you north out of Luang Prabang, hugging the Nam Ou for much of the way. Over halfway along, the road veers away from the river and into a wide valley, passing through **Hmong villages** whose inhabitants were resettled here from the highlands by the Lao government in an ongoing programme to control and assimilate them. The majority of villages along this stretch are located far from the road, but periodic glimpses of the people who inhabit them reveal something about the labour-intensive lives they lead. When not engaged in cultivating their teetering hilltop gardens, the highlanders spend daylight hours hunting and gathering in the forest.

Straddling the junction of Route 1 and Route 13, **PAKMONG** roughly separates the northeast from the northwest. There's no reason to stay in Pakmong, but it's a key spot for bus transfers – with increased direct buses you're unlikely to need to change here, though you will find that taking a bus to Pakmong from Nong Khiaw increases your choice of onward destinations. Be sure to travel as early as possible as most buses leave before noon.

Nong Khiaw

Resting at the foot of a striking red-faced cliff, amid towering blue-green limestone escarpments, the dusty town of **NONG KHIAW** on the banks of the Nam Ou River lies smack in the middle of some of the most dramatic scenery in Indochina. The relatively slow advent of tourism here has allowed it to retain its village-like charm; it's a great place to lose a few days, preferably watching the river from your own private balcony.

Arrival and information

Nong Khiaw is spread over either side of the long bridge that stretches over the Nam Ou – the old town heads southeast of Route 1, while the vast majority of tourist facilities are clustered at the northern end of the bridge. Boats arrive at the pier on the south side of the river, from where it's a five-to ten-minute walk to most accommodation. Buses stop at the small T-junction just south of the bridge (if you're heading here on a local bus, your driver will announce it); some buses from Luang Prabang will make a final stop at the boat landing, which is handy if you want (and are early enough) to head straight to Muang Ngoi. The bridge isn't terribly well-lit at night, so it's worth having a torch to hand if your bus gets in after dusk.

There are two excellent **tour operators** in Nong Khiaw. Green Discovery (Ⓦwww .greendiscoverylaos.com), situated close to *Nong Kiau Riverside*, offers a particularly good range of cycling and kayaking trips. Across the river, ⚑ Tiger Trail (Ⓦwww .laos-adventures.com; daily 8–11am, 12.30–4.30pm & 6.30–9pm), enthusiastically run by Hom, offers an impressive range of day and overnight treks, including the highly recommended "100 Waterfalls" one-day trek, which begins with a beautiful journey on the Nam Ou before hiking up the eponymous waterfalls (170,000K). At the time of writing, **internet** access was limited to the connection at *Nong Kiau Riverside* (wi-fi 300K/min, hotel computer 500K/min, free for guests; see opposite).

Accommodation

Most of Nong Khiaw's accommodation is in bungalows with river views.

Bamboo Paradise ☏020/55545286. The basic rooms here are cheered up by brightly coloured bedspreads and are set around a rather rubble-filled compound – though this will hopefully change once their new rooms have been completed. Balconies are at a right angle to the river, but you can still enjoy a bit of a view. ❷

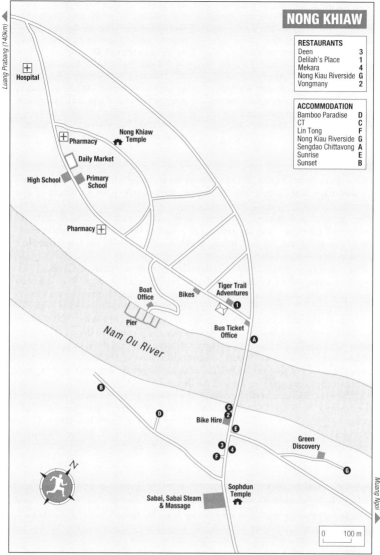

NONG KHIAW

RESTAURANTS
Deen	3
Delilah's Place	1
Mekara	4
Nong Kiau Riverside	G
Vongmany	2

ACCOMMODATION
Bamboo Paradise	D
CT	C
Lin Tong	F
Nong Kiau Riverside	G
Sengdao Chittavong	A
Sunrise	E
Sunset	B

Hospital

Luang Prabang (140km)

Pharmacy

Nong Khiaw Temple

Daily Market

High School

Primary School

Pharmacy

Boat Office

Bikes

Tiger Trail Adventures

Pier

Bus Ticket Office

Nam Ou River

Bike Hire

Green Discovery

Muang Ngoi

N

Sophdun Temple

Sabai, Sabai Steam & Massage

0   100 m

Pha Tok Caves (2.5km) & Sam Neua (320km)

CT ☏071/253919. Simple bungalows that feel somewhat cobbled together with rather cell-like attached bathrooms. Still, the views are lovely, and the breezy restaurant is a good place to relax over a drink. ②

Lin Tong A cluster of basic bungalows, set just off the main road. Those with shared bathroom are just big enough for a double bed, but the en-suite rooms (②) are more spacious and nicely decorated with local handicrafts. The staff speak better French than English. ①

Nong Kiau Riverside ☏020/2137187, ⓦwww.nongkiau.com. Incredibly spacious bungalows with arguably the best views in town from their wonderful private balconies. Decorated with dark wood, large four-poster beds, writing desks, and with showers with hot water, you'll find it hard to drag yourself away. Amazing value, and the restaurant (see opposite) is also worth a visit. Free wi-fi for guests. ❺

Sengdao Chittavong ☏071/600001. Conveniently located on the south side of the bridge, directly opposite where the buses stop, this friendly place has small rooms with Asian toilets and a nice restaurant that looks over the river. The riverside bungalows have the best views, though there are newer (and better) rooms set further back. ❶

Sunrise North side of the river, on the left ☏020/2478799. The bamboo bungalows here are basic but sweet, with nice balconies, en suites (Asian toilets) and good views of the river, though the beds are a little hard. ❸

🏃 Sunset ☏071/810033. These cute bungalows on the northern side of the river are justifiably popular, with lovely hammock-strung balconies from which to soak up the beautiful river views. The restaurant (daily till 10pm) is a good spot throughout the day, especially for breakfast (muesli with fresh fruit 15,000K). ❹

The Town

Though there's not a great deal to the town itself, Nong Khiaw makes a good base for **day-trips** in the scenic surrounding countryside (see p.174 for details of tour operators), though it's also a lovely place to just do nothing for a few days. The old town is worth a wander – heading left at the T-junction immediately after the bridge will take you along the rather dusty road to the **morning market** (Mon–Fri & Sun 6–7.30am, Sat 6–8.30am), which is worth a look; the town **temple** is situated on the street behind.

One day-trip that can be done independently is to the **Pathok Caves**, 2.5km north of town, where villagers hid during the Second Indochina War. The easy walk takes you along quiet Route 1 past wooden village houses as the scenery becomes gradually more dramatic, with limestone karsts rising around you. The caves are indicated by a small blue sign on the right; buy your ticket (5000K) from the little wooden hut before the bamboo bridge and you're then free to explore the caves by yourself. They are surprisingly extensive and very dark, so bring a torch or hire one from the hut (5000K). **Mountain bikes** (40,000K/day) can be hired from the northern side of the bridge, next to *Vongmany Restaurant*, and are well recommended for exploring the area further.

There's an excellent **herbal sauna and massage** place in town, just north of the turning to *Sunset Guesthouse*. Sabai Sabai (massage 9am–9pm, 40,000K; sauna 4–9pm, 15,000K), run by the family of Hom at Tiger Trail (see p.174) is the ideal place to unwind, with the fragrant steam bath (using cinnamon, lemongrass, eucalyptus and basil, among other things) leaving you utterly relaxed.

Moving on from Nong Khiaw

Buses run from the small lot at the southern end of the bridge – there's a small ticket office here, with departure times posted up outside. Local buses run to Luang Prabang at 9am and 11am, alternatively there's a minibus service at 2pm. You could also potentially pick up a bus around 7pm to Luang Prabang when the bus from Sam Neua arrives, but it's often full. Buses also run to Oudomxai (11am) and Sam Neua (11.30am); occasionally minibuses run as far as Luang Namtha, so it's worth asking around if you want to go that far.

If you're travelling to Luang Prabang, it's much more scenic to go by **boat** (11am, 5hr); head down to the boat ticket office the day before you plan to travel to sign up (if there's not enough people you'll either have to charter or go by bus). At 11am there's also a departure to Muang Ngoi (sometimes also at 2pm; 1hr), and, if there's enough people, to Muang Khoua (6hr). Tickets should be bought at least half an hour beforehand. A chartered boat to Muang Ngoi should cost around 100,000K.

Eating

There's a fair few decent restaurants in Nong Khiaw, and many of the guesthouses have restaurants attached.

Deen This relaxed place, with colourful table-cloths, paper lanterns and Indian music on the stereo, serves up decent Indian dishes such as *channa masala*, plus some Lao and Malay options like *mee goreng*.

Delilah's Place A lovely little travellers' café with a chef who trained in Germany, turning out *falang* food like lasagne, deep-fried chicken and a good choice of sandwiches. The fruit shakes are delicious. Basic rooms with shared bathroom () are also available.

Mekara The widest selection of Lao food in Nong Khiaw. The thatched roof, fairy lights and ambient music make this the most atmospheric choice for

dinner, though it's a shame that the service can be surly and that the owner has an unfortunate habit of slinging cats across the road.

Nong Kiau Riverside A breezy, casual restaurant with superlative views, serving excellent Lao food, including a delicious vegetable noodle soup, *mok pa* and Lao sausages. Unfortunately, service can be painfully slow, even on nights when it's near-empty. Daily 6am–10am, noon–2pm & 6–10pm.

Vongmany This open-sided restaurant has a good breakfast selection, with an American set for 30,000K and a choice of local dishes.

Muang Ngoi

Tiny **MUANG NGOI**, idyllically set among beautiful scenery on the banks of the Nam Ou, has long been an attractive spot for tourists, many of whom end up whiling their days away here. Just an hour's boat ride north of Nong Khiaw, the fact that the village can only be reached by river gives it an edge-of-the-world feel. Although it's easy enough to just hang out here sipping coffee and swinging in a hammock (as, indeed, most people do), there are a lot of **activities** on offer, including trekking to nearby hill-tribe villages, canoeing on the river, organized fishing trips, and outings to the caves and waterfall. However, wandering the main street, especially during high season, you can't help but feel this sleepy little place has been somewhat ambushed by tourism, with every second property seeming to be a guesthouse or a travellers' café.

Arrival and information

Boats from Nong Khiaw and Muang Khoua arrive at the northern end of the village; the ticket office is situated just uphill from the boat landing, on the first path to the left. If you head straight on, you will meet the village's main street. Leaving Muang Ngoi, boats depart at 9.30am to both Nong

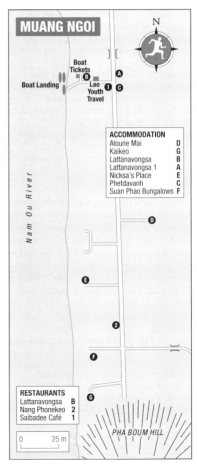

MUANG NGOI

N

Boat Tickets

Boat Landing

Lao Youth Travel

ACCOMMODATION
Aloune Mai	D
Kaikeo	G
Lattanavongsa	B
Lattanavongsa 1	A
Nicksa's Place	E
Phetdavanh	C
Suan Phao Bungalows	F

Nam Ou River

RESTAURANTS
Lattanavongsa	B
Nang Phonekeo	2
Saibadee Café	1

0   25 m

PHA BOUM HILL

Khiaw (1hr) and Muang Khoua (4–5hr); for the latter, you'll need to sign up in advance – be prepared to wait a day or two if there's not enough people travelling. There's no tourist office in the village, but Mr Kong Keo, the local English teacher, can provide information about trekking in the area; his house is signposted through the village.

Accommodation

All of Muang Ngoi's accommodation is in wooden bungalows, many of which have wonderful river views that make up for their basic interiors. As you head up from the boat landing you'll be approached by a number of guesthouse owners – it's worth having a look at what they have to offer as new places are springing up all the time, and accommodation gets snapped up very quickly in high season. Electricity only runs from 6.30 to 9.30pm, though there are rumours of this changing over the next few years.

Aloune Mai Though it may not overlook the river, this is the most atmospheric accommodation in Muang Ngoi, tucked down a dusty side street with the mountains towering overhead. The bungalows are set around a lush, green garden that's perfect for a relaxing afternoon; rooms are large and very pleasant, and there's a lovely bar on site. ❷

Kaikeo Right at the end of the village are these very simple bungalows which appear to have been cobbled together rather quickly. The shared facilities could be cleaner, but their hammocks are ideal for soaking up the views. ❶

Lattanavongsa Just up from the boat landing, on the left, this is a justifiably popular guesthouse, with four very clean, large rooms in a low wooden bungalow. They also have a number of newer bungalows at *Lattanavongsa 1* just up the road, set around a palm-and flower-filled compound, with proper hot-water showers. ❷

Nicksa's Place Quite small, basic bungalows, though the setting, among beautiful flowers and with gorgeous views of the river, makes it feel a little special. ❷

Phetdavanh Just opposite the road leading down to the boat landing. A cute wooden guesthouse with a book exchange, and a lovely communal veranda strung with hammocks. Serves a popular evening buffet for 10,000K. ❶

Suan Phao Bungalows Light-filled and pleasant bungalows, though they feel a little flimsy and the welcome could be warmer. ❷

The village

Muang Ngoi is pretty much a one street village, with dusty pathways striking off it in both directions. One excursion that you can take without a tour guide is to the nearby caves, where villagers' hid during the war; to get there, turn left near *Kaikeo* and follow the path for a few kilometres. Take a torch.

Most guesthouses now offer **trips and activities** around Muang Ngoi, as do a few cafés along the main street. Situated on the path up from the boat landing, just beyond *Lattanavongsa*, **Lao Youth Travel** offer perhaps the most extensive range of options, from a half-day kayaking trip that includes a stop at a beach and time for a swim (150,000/person) to a one-day trek that visits three local villages (180,000/person).

Eating

Virtually all of the town's bungalow operations serve **food**, though with limited electricity you can expect service to be rather slow.

Lattanavongsa The restaurant attached to this guesthouse is one of the nicest in town, with a breezy balcony overlooking the boat landing. A good place to spend the evening over a cold Beer Lao.

Nang Phonekeo This little wooden restaurant has a good range of baguettes, such as one with fried aubergine and omelette, plus the usual fried noodles and papaya salad.

Saibadee Café Cute corner café with low wooden tables and chairs overlooking the street – a pleasant spot to spend an afternoon. The sandwiches are made with lovely hot French baguettes (from 10,000K) and the staff (and their gorgeous children) are very friendly. They can also arrange tubing for 75,000K/person.

Muang Khoua

Located on the left bank of the Nam Ou where Route 4 crosses the river on its way to Vietnam, **MUANG KHOUA** is an important crossroads and outpost in southern Phongsali province. The town itself is built on a steep hillside where the Nam Phak river enters the Nam Ou, and is named for an ancient rust-clad suspension bridge which connects Muang Khoua with the village of Natun. A stroll out onto the high, swaying structure is worth it for the view, but is a stomach-fluttering experience and not for the vertigo-prone. The area around Muang Khoua is rugged and hilly, but the surrounding hills have been clear-cut and are covered in bamboo and secondary growth.

If you follow the road uphill from the boat landing, it leads to the main road – both are crammed with old shophouses. A left turn off the main road will take you to the daily market – though small compared to many others, there's decent *fõe*, fruit and cold drinks available.

Though there's not a great deal to see in Muang Khoua, it does have a certain charm, and some travellers end up staying for a couple of days to explore the area further. If you're interested in doing so, contact Bounma (☏020/4264232), an informal tour guide. For most visitors, however, it's just a stopover en route to Hat Sa (for Phonsali) on the river, or to or from Vietnam via the border crossing at Dien Bien Phu.

Practicalities

Muang Khoua can be reached by road or river. At one time Route 4 continued across a pontoon bridge over the Nam Ou at Muang Khoua, but it has been destroyed. Off the main road, a long curving road leads down to the boat landing on the pebble beach along the Nam Ou. The dirt road on the opposite bank is the other half of Route 4; a basic vehicle ferry makes the regular crossing.

The **tourist office** is situated on the main road, close to the road down to the boat landing. The Agricultural Promotion **Bank** is situated on the main road, just down from the Tourist Office, and can exchange currency.

Accommodation

Muang Khoua has a number of **guesthouses**; your best option on arrival is to follow the road uphill from the boat landing. Electricity is only available from 6 to 10.30pm – and don't be surprised if it doesn't quite run when it should.

Chaleusouk On the road up from the boat landing ☏088/210847. Arguably the nicest choice in town, with clean, cool rooms with oversized beds and attached bathrooms with Western toilets – ask to see a few as they vary in size. The reception area also sells handicrafts, and there's a nice communal veranda. ❷

Keophila Just up from *Chaleunsouk* ☏088/21087. Very bare rooms, some with just a thin mattress on a solid base. Quality varies so look around – most are rather overpriced, and some bathrooms are decorated with naked ladies. ❷

Nam Ou Right above the boat landing – look for steps to the left leading up to it ☏088/210844. Muang Khoua's most popular backpacker choice, with rather cell-like rooms that feel a little flimsy. The shared bathrooms are pretty dingy, but those with private bath are a bit better. ❶

Sernnaly Hotel On the main road, opposite the tourist information office ☏021/414214. The surprisingly grand entranceway, full of wood furniture and marble floors, gives way to pretty basic rooms, though bathrooms are bigger than those available elsewhere in town. ❹

Eating

There are a few **restaurants** in town, including the travellers' favourite at the *Nam Ou Guesthouse*, which has a pretty standard menu with dishes for about 12,000K. *Saylon Restaurant* has great views of the river – come for a beer at sunset, but the food is pretty grotty. The best choice for something to eat is the Vietnamese restaurant (no Romanized name) next to *Chaleunsouk Guesthouse*. A small, bare-bones place, it's got a great local feel, and serves up deliciously spiced fried rice (10,000K) and a gorgeous Lao-style yellow curry (25,000K).

Hat Sa

The village of **HAT SA** consists of barely sixty homes, most of which are constructed from the ubiquitous bamboo and palm thatch, although concrete construction has reached even this remote outpost. Most travellers bypass Hat Sa since they're either in a hurry to start downriver or to press on to Phongsali, but Hat Sa and the villages further up the Nam Ou are about as far off the beaten track as you can get and are worth exploring, especially if you find Nong Khiaw and Muang Ngoi too touristy and are looking for something a little bit different.

Hat Sa is reached in five hours by passenger boat from Muang Khoua (100,000K) – though boats will only run if there are enough passengers. Regular passenger boats only really go this far, though if you're interested in exploring the Nam Ou further north it's worth enquiring here.

Sawngthaews to Phongsali (25,000K; 1hr) meet the boat – though you might have to hang around a while before it departs.

Phongsali

Perched just below the peak of Phou Fa ("Sky Mountain"), **PHONGSALI** looks and feels every bit the capital of Laos's northernmost province. The altitude gained becomes apparent once the sun drops below the horizon and the chill sets in; on clear nights, as soon as the lights go out, the view of the heavens is unparalleled. The crisp air seems to amplify the stellar glow and the Milky Way is splashed across the sky like a giant, luminescent cloud. Despite being a large town, it lacks any real tourist infrastructure, and wandering around you will most likely find yourself the object of curious (but not bad natured) stares. Though at first you may wonder where you've ended up, soon enough the lack of other tourists, cool mountain air and stunning surrounding countryside will work their charm on you. With the trekking scene still fairly low-key here, the town is a great place to do an overnight trip to the province's fascinating **hill-tribe** villages.

A wide slice of terrain wedged between China's Yunnan and Vietnam's Lai Chau provinces, Phongsali province would surely be a part of China today were it not for the covetous nineteenth-century French. During the Second Indochina War, Phongsali came under heavy Chinese influence, a fact evident in the fortress-like former Chinese consulate, now the *Phou Fa Hotel*. It was during this time also that much of the province was stripped of its hardwood forests, compensation for China's support for the Pathet Lao. The town's inhabitants are made up of the Theravada Buddhist, Tibeto-Burman-speaking Phu Noi people and the Chinese Haw, descendants of Yunnanese traders who annually drove caravans of pack-ponies south into old Siam.

Arrival and information

Sawngtheaws from Hat Sa stop at the small Hat Sa bus stop just under 1km east of town, from where it's an easy downhill walk to the centre. **Buses** from Oudomxai leave from the bus station 3km west of town, from where you can get a shared tuk-tuk to the centre (5000K).

The helpful **tourist office** (Mon–Fri 8–11.45am & 1.30–4.45pm; ☏088/210098) is situated just south of the main road; they can provide good information about the town and transport options, and offer a range of tours (see p.182). There are two **banks** in town: the Agricultural Promotion Bank, just east of the Tribes Musuem, exchanges US dollars and Thai baht only; Lao Development Bank, further down the main road from the *Phonsaly Hotel*, changes a wider range of currencies, as well as US travellers' cheques. Both are open 8am to 3.30pm. There's a Lao Airlines office in the *Viphaphone Guesthouse*.

Accommodation

The standard of accommodation in Phongsali is surprisingly low considering the high prices. Electricity is available from 7 to 11am and 6 to 9am; be warned that you're most likely to be woken up by the government announcements broadcast on loudspeakers around town as soon as the electricity comes back on.

Phongsaly Hotel ☏088/210043. A rather soulless hotel, but well situated in the centre of town, with large rooms with decent bathrooms. ❷

Phou Fa Hotel ☏088/21031. Situated on a hill with great views over the town, this is undoubtedly the best, most interesting place to stay in Phongsali. The initial impression of its institutional exterior isn't great, but the rooms to the far right, which are set around a sweet garden, are the nicest, with gold bedspreads, decorated headboards, TV and good bathrooms. ❸

Viphaphone ☏088/21099. Musty, overpriced rooms with very hard beds; the best are those at the back which have views of the mountains. ❸

Yeehua ☏088/210186. The basic rooms attached to this restaurant have shared baths and are the cheapest option in town, with singles for 30,000K. ❶

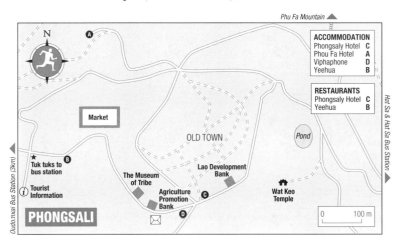

Phu Fa Mountain ▲

ACCOMMODATION
Phongsaly Hotel   C
Phou Fa Hotel   A
Viphaphone   D
Yeehua   B

RESTAURANTS
Phongsaly Hotel   C
Yeehua   B

Market

OLD TOWN

Pond

★ Tuk tuks to bus station B

ⓘ Tourist Information

The Museum of Tribe

Lao Development Bank

Agriculture Promotion Bank C

Wat Keo Temple

0   100 m

PHONGSALI

The Town

On a slope directly behind the *Phongsaly Hotel* is the town's **old quarter**. A wander through these friendly but medieval-looking lanes is like stepping back in time. Interspersed among the squat houses of mud bricks and rough-hewn planks are a few architectural standouts, including one distinctly Chinese building with a beautifully carved wooden facade that looks like it belongs on the backstreets of old Kunming. The quarter's three main streets run parallel for a stretch and then converge at a large basketball court, from which leads Phongsali's main commercial thoroughfare, a tidy street of low shophouses, some with roofs constructed of oil drums hammered flat and laid out like shingles. Situated on the opposite bank of the town's green bathing pond is **Wat Kaeo**, the local monastery.

Anyone interested in seeing what Phongsali's ethnic groups dressed like before the influx of cheap Western-style clothing from China should pay a visit to the **Museum of Tribes** (Mon–Fri 7.30–11am & 1.30–4pm; 5000K) on the main road. Unfortunately, the rather small display of costumes and traditional wooden utensils isn't done any favours by its lack of English explanations.

The nearby **market** is fairly small, considering this is a provincial capital, but as usual is a good bet for a cheap bowl of noodles. It's worth making the stiff but not unpleasant walk up the forested hillside of **Phou Fa** hill, the top of which (4000K entrance) offers excellent views over the town and surrounding countryside on a clear day.

The main attraction of a visit to Phongsali is the opportunity to **trek** in this beautiful region. At the time of writing, the only treks available were offered by the tourist office (see p.181), which clearly outlines where your money will go. Tours range from one- to multi-day treks, taking in local hill-tribe villages, with prices ranging according to the size of the group (one person 30,000K/day, two people 400,000K/day).

▲ Trekking in Phongsali

Moving on from Phongsali

Sawngthaews depart from the Hat Sa bus stop at 8am (get there 7.30am) for the 10am boat departure from Hat Sa. Note that if there aren't enough passengers, your only option will be to charter a boat or try again the next day. Tuk-tuks run to the main **bus** station from the turning to the tourist office at 7am for the 7.30am departures to Vientiane and Oudomxai.

Eating

Most of the **restaurants** in Phongsali are Chinese – expect chicken dishes to be full of feet and lots of bones. As usual, you can get bowls of *fŏe* in the market, tucked away off the main street.

Phongsaly Hotel The large impersonal restaurant on the ground floor of this hotel has a rather interesting Chinese menu that includes mysterious dishes such as "the palace protects the meat cubelets" and "prevail large intestines". For the less adventurous, there's plenty of other options, including fried rice and sautéed chicken with chilli and peanuts (30,000K).

Yeehua This no-frills but very friendly restaurant may be the only place in town serving Lao dishes – the pork *larp* (20,000K) is very tasty, but watch out for the chillies.

Phongsali to Oudomxai

Regardless of which direction you travel this route, it's long, hard journey requiring a eight to twelve gruelling hours, often in a bus that looks as though it was discarded by the Chinese in the 1980s. If you can grab a window seat, however, it'll be a little more bearable as you can take in the stunning scenery. This road passes through some prime **Akha territory**, and the tribal women use the thoroughfare to hike between villages and conduct trade. It's very common in fact to see groups of Akha women parading their wonderful apparel along the roadsides. A few of the villages actually straddle the road and afford fleeting snapshots of Akha life: women displaying glittering headdresses and betel-stained smiles, men shouldering long-barrelled muskets, and gaggles of gaping kids clad only in a layer of ochre-coloured dust. You may find that your bus driver stops regularly to buy (or for his passengers to buy) various furry mammals (such as civet cats and porcupines), which are hung up like prizes at the side of the road, and

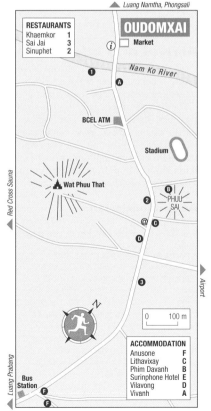

Luang Namtha, Phongsali

RESTAURANTS
Khaemkor	1
Sai Jai	3
Sinuphet	2

Market

BCEL ATM

Stadium

Wat Phuu That

PHUU SAI

Nam Ko River

Red Cross Sauna

Luang Prabang

Bus Station

Airport

0   100 m

ACCOMMODATION
Anusone	F
Lithavixay	C
Phim Davanh	B
Surinphone Hotel	E
Vilavong	D
Vivanh	A

Phou Den Din NBCA

Phou Den Din is Laos's northernmost NBCA and runs along the Vietnamese border for over 100km. The scenery here is rugged and mountainous, rising up to the peaks in the Phou Den Din range which reach heights of over 1800m and form the border with Vietnam. The 2220-square-kilometre park is said to contain Asian elephants and Asiatic black bears as well as leopards and tigers. This is one of Laos's most inaccessible NBCAs, though it can be reached by boat up the Nam Ou, or on foot. Your best option is to speak to the tourist office in Phongsali for up-to-date information.

generally bought to be eaten. It may not be particularly appetizing to the Western eye, or, indeed, a very environmentally friendly practice, but it's a fascinating glimpse of rural life that you don't necessarily experience elsewhere in the country.

Oudomxai

Any prolonged travel in the north will eventually involve a stop at the rather charmless town of **OUDOMXAI**, sitting at the junction of routes 1 and 4. However, with good facilities, a few decent places to stay and excellent transport connections, it's not a bad place to spend the night.

Arrival and information

Oudomxai's **bus station** is situated fifteen minutes' walk southwest of the town centre. There are three flights a week from Vientiane; Oudomxai's **airport** is just under 2km southeast of town, from where tuk-tuks run into the centre.

The **tourist office** (daily 7.30am–5.30pm) is situated on the northern side of the river, opposite the dry goods office. As well as having maps and information on the town and transport connections, they offer a range of tours and treks (see opposite). Just south of the river, on the main road, is the BCEL **bank** (Mon–Fri 8.30am–5.30pm), which exchanges currency and travellers' cheques, with an ATM in front. **Internet** access is available across the road from *Lithavixay Guesthouse* (12,000K/hr).

Accommodation

Coming from the bus station, the easiest thing is to walk north up Route 1, where you'll find a number of hotels and guesthouses lining the road into town.

Anusone Down a small side street just across from the bus station. ☎030/5130777. The rooms here are in concrete bungalows, set around a pleasant family compound. Though quite dark and a little worn around the edges, it's not a bad choice if you're making an early start in the morning. ❷
Lithavixay ☎081/212175. Excellent, well-sized rooms with small en suites, TVs, desks and safety cupboards, and nicely decorated with wall hangings. Internet and breakfast are available in the large reception area. ❷
Phim Davanh ☎081/211141. Overlooking the football field, the basic rooms here are all en suite (squat toilets) and clean enough, though the

walls are in need of a scrub and the welcome could be a little friendlier. ❶
Surinphone Hotel ☎081/212789. The posh option in town, just a few minutes up Route 1 from the bus station, on the right-hand side. Rooms are smart and bright, and the staff very helpful. ❸
Vilavong ☎081/212303. Cool, dark rooms with large en suites, though the whole place smells a bit too strongly of air freshener. ❷
Vivanh ☎081/212219. A really sweet little guesthouse offering sparkling rooms with TV and brightly coloured bedspreads; the predominantly female staff are very welcoming and friendly. ❷

Moving on from Oudomxai

Oudomxai's excellent transport links mean that **buses** can often get very busy – aim to arrive at the bus station (see opposite) around an hour before departure as they do occasionally leave ahead of schedule if they're full. Most departures take place between 8 and 10am, though for some destinations, like Luang Namtha, Luang Prabang and Vientiane, there are also afternoon departures around 2.30/3pm. Buses to the **Chinese border** at Boten depart daily at 8am, taking four hours to reach the border. Note that Hoayxai usually appears on schedules as Bokeo (the name of the province).

The Town

The best way to spend your time in Oudomxai is with a visit to the Red Cross **Herbal Sauna and Massage** (⊕081/212022; massage: daily 9am–7.30pm; 30,000K; sauna: daily 3–7.30pm; 10,000K) – the perfect way to relax after a bone-numbing bus journey. The money goes towards supporting the Red Cross's work in helping and educating local people. To get here, bear left off the main road (if coming from the bus station) and follow the signs.

Head up **Phou Sai Hill**, just southeast of the centre, for a good view over the town; the hill is crowned by a white stupa with a golden spire. The tourist office (see opposite) runs a number of interesting tours and treks in the area, including a walking tour of the town, a one-day visit to beautiful **Muang La**, stopping at hot springs along the way, and a three-day trek to Khmu villages.

Eating

There are lots of places to eat along the main road, including a number of Chinese restaurants and the usual *föe* places around the bus station. For **breakfast**, the bus station is the best option, with women selling baguettes, sticky rice and bags of fruit for 2000K each. Alternatively, *Sai Jai* serves breakfasts, sandwiches and coffee. For dinner, *Sinuphet*, has a reliable menu of Chinese–Lao dishes including fried fish with chilli (20,000K) and a tasty veg curry (10,000K), served in pleasantly homely surroundings. A good spot for a drink is *Khaemkor*, with a scattering of tables in a nice position by the river.

Luang Namtha and around

Surrounded by forested hills that remain lush even when the rest of the country-side is a dusty brown in the hot season, **LUANG NAMTHA** is the north's most touristy town, though it still has a quiet local charm, away from the travellers' cafés and tour operators. The town is a popular base from which to access beautiful **Nam Ha NBCA**, with a whole range of activities available, from rafting and kayaking on the Nam Tha, to exploring the surrounding area by bike and trekking to hill-tribe villages. Most of the tourist services are situated in the new town, 6km north of the old town – exploring the latter gives an idea of what Luang Namtha was like before the advent of tourism. It's a great place in which to hire a bicycle or motorbike – just a few kilometres' ride will take you into small traditional dusty-street villages, surrounded by rice paddies and grazing buffalo.

Luang Namtha was heavily contested during Laos's civil war and was razed to the ground. Once the fighting stopped, the surrounding hills were stripped of their trees and the mammoth logs were trucked away to China. Today, the once devastated and depopulated valley is thriving again, and from the lush surroundings you'd be hard-pressed to believe how recently it had taken place.

Arrival, transport and information

The **bus station** is situated 11km southeast of the new town; a shared tuk-tuk to the centre should cost 10,000K. **Buses** from Muang Sing and Muang Long pull into the local bus station, just south of the centre – tuk-tuks are on hand to make the short trip to the guesthouses, though it's an easy enough walk (5min) up the street. The **airport** and **boat landing** are both about 6km south of the main town close to the old town; again, expect to pay around 10,000K for a shared tuk-tuk.

Most tourists stick to the new town, where most of the tourist accommodation is. Should you want to go further afield, there're always a number of tuk-tuks hanging around on the main road, or you could hire a bicycle or motorbike from your guesthouse or the rental shop on the main road, near *Manychan* (bike 10,000K; motorbike 60,000K).

The **tourist office** (Mon–Fri 8am–noon & 1.30–8pm, Sat & Sun 8.15–11.30am, 2–4pm & 5.30–8pm) is situated two streets west of the main road; they mainly operate as the Nam Ha Eco-Guide Service (see box below), but can also provide information on the surrounding area, plus bus and air timetables. A useful local **map** ("Bike, Area Map") is available from most guesthouses, and is automatically provided if you rent a bike.

The most central **bank** is BCEL, just south of the nightmarket, which can exchange currency and travellers' cheques; there's an **ATM** adjacent to it. Further south, diagonally opposite Green Discovery, Lao Development Bank also exchanges foreign currency and travellers' cheques, and does credit card advances. There are various **internet cafés** on the main road, including Smile Internet which has Skype facilities (12,000K).

Accommodation

Luang Namtha has the best selection of **accommodation** north of Luang Prabang, and standards are generally very high. Apart from a couple of places, all

---

Trekking and boat trips

At times it can seem as though every other business in Luang Namtha is offering some kind of trek, so it can be difficult to know which company to choose. The best thing is to talk to other travellers who have returned from trips to find out what their experience was like, and to visit a number of operators to gauge what's on offer. In low season, you'll probably find that your choice of treks is limited by those that have already been signed up for by other travellers – most companies have whiteboards outside detailing which trips are in need of people joining them.

Green Discovery (☎086/211484; ⊛www.greendiscoverylaos.com) are undoubtedly one of the best set up and well-regarded operations in town, offering an excellent range of trips and treks, from a two-day kayaking adventure on the Nam Tha (from $43), to overnight treks into beautiful Nam Ha NBCA, staying at hill-tribe villages (from $51). They are committed to low-impact, eco-conscious tourism, using local staff, and the office staff will help you choose the right trip for you.

Another well-established option is the **Nam Ha Eco Guide Service** at the tourist office (see above), whose options include a one-day biking tour taking in local villages and waterfalls (from 160,000K) and an intensive four-day trek to near Sam Yord Mountain (from 680,000K).

Note that for all treks and activities, the price you pay is dependent on the number of people on it, and you should make sure that if you're visiting a local village, a percentage of the money you pay goes towards supporting the community.

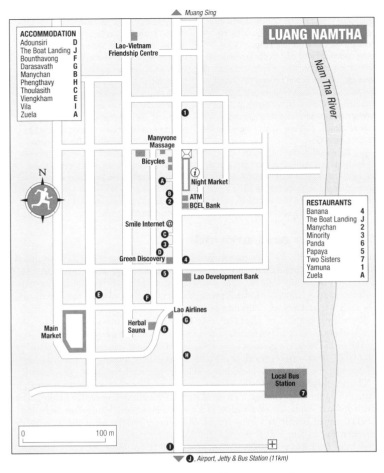

LUANG NAMTHA

ACCOMMODATION
Adounsiri	D
The Boat Landing	J
Bounthavong	F
Darasavath	G
Manychan	B
Phengthavy	H
Thoulasith	C
Viengkham	E
Vila	I
Zuela	A

Lao-Vietnam
Friendship Centre

Nam Tha River

Manyvone
Massage

Bicycles

Night Market

ATM

BCEL Bank

Smile Internet @

Green Discovery

Lao Development Bank

RESTAURANTS
Banana	4
The Boat Landing	J
Manychan	2
Minority	3
Panda	6
Papaya	5
Two Sisters	7
Yamuna	1
Zuela	A

Lao Airlines

Herbal
Sauna

Main
Market

Local Bus
Station

0   100 m

of the following are situated north of the local bus station in the new town. Note that many guesthouses get full by early evening, so it's worth booking ahead if you know you'll be arriving later in the day.

Adounsiri ☎020/2991898. Tucked down a side street parallel to the main road, this popular guesthouse has simple but very pleasant rooms, some of which are off a sweet communal veranda. The friendly owners can book bus tickets and hire out bikes. ❷

The Boat Landing 6km south of the centre on the banks of the Nam Tha River ☎086/312398, ⓦ www.theboatlanding.laopdr.com. This justifiably well-regarded eco-resort is excellent value, with spacious, utterly charming bungalows scattered among a flower- and butterfly-filled garden overlooking the river. The beautiful, peaceful location is the perfect base for exploring the area

(Green Discovery tours can be booked here), though some may find it a bit too far from town. The on-site restaurant offers superlative local cuisine (see p.189). ❻

Bounthavong ☎086/312256. In a quiet location on a side street, with rooms set off a small compound. Pretty basic accommodation, with low hard beds and squat toilets in the en suites. ❷

Darasavath Just north of the local bus station ☎086/211299. A selection of rooms and bamboo bungalows, set a little back from the main road. Ask to see a few as their condition varies. There's a popular, relaxed restaurant on site. ❶

187

Manychan ☎086/312209. Situated above the restaurant of the same name (see opposite), the basic en-suite rooms here are a popular choice, being right on the main drag, though in comparison to other options in town they're rather overpriced. ❷
Phengthavy Just north of the local bus station ☎020/5557768. A sweet wooden building with just nine rooms. Those with shared bathroom (Asian toilets) are on the small side but brightened up with local handicrafts; the larger en-suite rooms are just 10,000K more. ❷
🏃 **Thoulasith** A graceful building set just off the main street with a sweet garden area out front. The rooms upstairs, set off a veranda, are brighter and bigger than those below them; all are nicely decorated with surprisingly modern bathrooms that are arguably the best in town. ❷

Viengkham Just north of the market ☎086/211090. The musty but decent-sized rooms here all have TV, though the walls and hallways could do with a bit of a scrub. The communal veranda has good views of the surrounding mountains.
Vila A pleasant blue mid-range place housing cool, nicely decorated rooms, set in a leafy green compound. Staff are charming and there's a good restaurant on site. Popular with tour groups. ❻
🏃 **Zuela** ☎020/5886694. The best, most atmospheric, rooms in town, in a gorgeous wooden building tucked just off the main street. The friendly staff will make you feel at home, there's free internet access, and a sweet restaurant across the courtyard (see p.190). Families can be accommodated. ❸

The Town and around

In the town itself, the only formal attraction is the **Luang Namtha Provincial Museum** (Mon–Fri 8.30am–noon & 1–3.30pm; 5000K), now housed in Lao–Vietnam Friendship Centre, where you'll find displays of traditional hill-tribe costumes and artefacts, a model depicting battles that took place in the area during the civil war and a rusty collection of weaponry.

There are a number of places offering **Lao sauna and massage** in town – the perfect way to relax after a few days' trekking. Opposite *Panda Restaurant*, just west of the main street, is a good but basic place offering both (sauna 10,000K; massage 30,000K), while further north Manyvone Massage (☎020/9661112) offers a range of massages from 30,000K, including a welcome post-trek foot massage (40,000K).

The new **nightmarket** (daily 5–10pm), opposite *Manychan* on the main street, is rather disappointing, though it's a good choice for a cheap dinner (see below). The main bulk is made up of a rather tacky mix of clothes, houseware and pirate DVDS, aimed largely at a local crowd. Much more interesting is the daily **fresh market**, five minutes' walk west of the main street, where stalls groan under the weight of fruit and vegetables.

The best way to spend a day in Luang Namtha is to hire a bike and explore the local area – the map provided with all hire bikes details some good routes. The best takes you south through the old town to *The Boat Landing* (a good stop for lunch), from where you head east into the Black Thai villages of Ban Pasak, Ban Pong and Ban Tongkwa, following dusty streets through paddyfields with children shouting *sabai di* (hello) as you pass. The last stretch is on a generally very quiet main road, which loops past a few more villages before taking you back to the town.

Eating

The main road is lined with a number of travellers' cafes, most of which offer near-identical menus of Lao and Western dishes. During the day, the **fresh market** is a great place for a cheap bowl of *foe* and you can also buy small portions of *larp* and other dishes here. At night, the main street fills with the scent of grilled meat from the nightmarket – there's a number of tables in the central compound where you can enjoy the food over a cold beer, and be sure to try the delicious sweet sticky rice with grated coconut for dessert.

Banana A popular choice for a pre-trek breakfast, conveniently situated right opposite Green Discovery. The illustrated menu ranges from American and European set breakfasts (from 15,000K) to a substantial amount of lunch and dinner dishes, such as steamed fish with lemon, ginger, garlic and parsley (25,000K).

Boat Landing *Boat Landing Guesthouse*. It might be the priciest place in town to eat but the location doesn't get better than this, overlooking the river and surrounded by a peaceful garden. This is a great place to sample quality Lao food, with plenty of *jeows* (dips) on offer, including an Akha one made with lemongrass (8000K). Try the tongue-tingling Akha ginger chicken soup with chilli, garlic, mint and shallots (32,000K), accompanied by one of their speciality fresh juices. During high season Green Discovery run a nightly tuk-tuk to the restaurant from the centre of town – pop into the office for more details.

Manychan Main street. A relaxed place, popular throughout the day, offering a good range of Lao food and some interesting French-influenced Western dishes such as steak with blue cheese sauce. The fruit shakes are particularly delicious (5000K), and there's free wi-fi for customers.

Minority A cute wooden restaurant tucked down a small path off the main street, which prides itself on offering a range of dishes attributed to the area's various ethnic groups (though there's a surprising amount of Western options on the menu). The stew made with sticky rice powder, parsley, garlic, lemongrass, chillis and spring onion (20,000K) is very tasty. There's also a branch of Big Brother Mouse (see p.129) here.

Papaya Tucked away on a side street with just a few wooden tables, the menu here focuses on local food (though it's remarkably similar, though cheaper, to that at *The Boat Landing*) such as Luang Namtha fried noodles (12,000K) and *kao soi* noodle soup (10,000). Local handicrafts are on sale.

Panda West of the main street. No longer the small shack it once was, *Panda* remains a popular choice with a good, cheap range of tasty dishes starting at around 10,000K.

Two Sisters Local bus station. It may not be the most obvious location for a restaurant

Moving on from Luang Namtha

Buses to Muang Sing and Muang Long run from the local bus station just south of the main tourist centre; buses to Boten (on the border with China) also depart daily from here. All other destinations, including Oudomxai, Houayxai, Vientiane and Luang Prabang, are served by the main bus station, some 11km out of town; a daily bus runs to Jinghong in China at 8am. A tuk-tuk out here will cost around 10,000K. Tickets for all buses can be bought directly at the bus station or, for an increase of around 20,000K, from travel agents and guesthouses; the price includes transfer to the bus station.

The Nam Tha is navigable from about June until November, during which time travellers heading for **Houayxai** have the option of going by passenger boat. The most convenient option is to speak to the very helpful Green Discovery office in Luang Namtha (see p.186), who offer packages starting at $96 per person (based on six or more people travelling), though you may also be able to charter a boat outright directly with a boatman (expect to pay around $220 for a boat); passenger boats are a rarity these days. The journey takes two days, usually overnighting in Ban Khonkham at the boatman's house. If you're hiring a boat independently, it's very important to strike a clear deal with your boatman, as they have been known to renegotiate the fare en route if they run into adverse conditions, and some may not be prepared to take you all the way to Houayxai. Note that the boats travelling on this route have no roof, so be prepared to get a little wet. From December to January, it is possible to travel between Luang Namtha and Nalae by road (2hr), and then pick up a boat to Houayxai from Nalae; again, your best bet is to speak to Green Discovery for more information.

recommendation, but this sweet place, decorated with birds' nests, antlers and local basketry, is a good lunch stop, especially if you're hanging around for a bus. The beef noodle soup (6000K) is lovely, and there's a good variety of other dishes including *larp* and catfish salad.

Yamuna On the main street. If you fancy a change from the usual breakfasts on offer, head to this no-frills Indian restaurant for tasty *dosai* (12,000K). A decent range of curries,

including keema (26,000K), are served up for lunch and dinner.

Zuela The courtyard restaurant attached to the guesthouse of the same name is a good choice for breakfast, serving a delicious muesli with loads of fresh fruit and yoghurt for 20,000K, including tea or coffee. There's the usual range of Western and local dishes on offer for lunch and dinner, and the courtyard is a lovely place to relax over a Beer Lao.

Nam Ha NBCA

Established in 1993, the **Nam Ha NBCA** is one of Laos's most convenient and easily accessible conservation areas. Covering 1470 square kilometres contiguous with the Xieng Yong Protected Area in Yunnan, China, the park straddles two high mountain chains and boasts two peaks in excess of 2000m. The NBCA is an important biological habitat for many forest creatures, including 37 species of large mammals and 288 species of birds. However, it's unlikely you'll see much in the way of wildlife on a trek into the park – though the forest teems with birdsong. The best known of the park's rivers are the **Nam Ha** and the **Nam Tha**, both of which are developed for **kayaking** and **rafting** trips.

The park is accessible by car, with Route 3 crossing the NBCA in two separate places. Within the NBCA itself are some 25 **hill-tribe villages**, the most populous ethnic groups being Akha, Hmong, Khmu and Lantaen, and multi-day trekking tours between these settlements are also possible. More **information**, as well as bookings for organized tours within the NBCA, can be obtained through the Luang Namtha Guide Services Office, Green Discovery or the *Boat Landing Guesthouse* (see p.187).

Muang Sing and around

MUANG SING, located some 60km northwest of Luang Namtha, has developed a small, low-key tourist scene based around the trekking opportunities in the beautiful surrounding valley. The town makes a nice alternative to Luang Namtha, retaining a much more local feel, and with the market drawing people from the local tribes, you're likely to encounter a number of women in traditional dress. Though the opportunities for trekking are not quite as developed as in Luang Namtha, for many this remains the premier hill-trekking destination in Northern Laos.

Lying within the boundaries of the region known as the Golden Triangle, Muang Sing has a long connection with **opium**. During the late French colonial era, Muang Sing became an important collection point and way-station for the French colonial government's opium monopoly. In the post-colonial period and before the communist takeover, quantities of local opium found their way to RLA-controlled refineries near Houayxai. There was a brief tourist rush to Muang Sing during the 1990s, which saw opium dens reappear for a brief period, but the town now, though increasingly well set up for tourists, is a quieter choice than Luang Namtha, and has retained a definite local feel.

Arrival and information

The **bus station** is in the northwest of town opposite the morning market, though you should be able to ask your bus driver to let you off on the main road. From the bus station, it's just a five-minute walk to the main road – turn left out of the compound, then left again at the first major intersection; this will eventually bring you onto the main road, next to the tribal museum. Alternatively, tuk-tuks meet all buses.

There are a couple of **banks** in town, the most convenient of which is the Agricultural Promotion Bank (Mon–Fri 8am–3.30pm) which exchanges dollars and baht; it's situated on the road that runs down the side of the tribal museum. A little further on, on a side street, the Lao Development Bank (same hours) additionally exchanges sterling, euros and travellers' cheques (US dollars only). The **post office** is situated adjacent to the police station, opposite the old market on the main road. The **tourist office**, Muang Sing Tourism Information and Trekking Guide Service Centre (☎086/400015; Mon–Fri 8–11.30am & 1.30–5pm, Sat & Sun 8–10am & 3–5pm) can issue you with a map of the town, but is largely concerned with booking people on tours and treks (see box, p.194). **Internet** access is available at the tourist office (300K/min) and at *Taï Lu Guesthouse* (10,000K/hr).

Accommodation

Muang Sing is surprisingly well stocked with guesthouses, though standards are a little lower than in Luang Namtha.

Adima ☎030/5110860 8km north of town on the road to the Chinese frontier. Muang Sing's first eco-resort, featuring bamboo architecture in a rural setting. There is a choice of rooms in big bungalows with grass roofs or in A-frame cabins. The bamboo restaurant with a deck overlooking the fields is worth visiting even if you stay in town. *Vieng Xai Guesthouse* (see p.193) can arrange a tuk-tuk out here (expect to pay around 5000K/person). ➋

A & Chinese Border

MUANG SING Hospital

N

ACCOMMODATION
Adima — A
Chanthimmeng — H
Pouiu 2 — F
Seng Deaun — B
Sing Cha Lern — G
Taï Lu — C
Viengsing — D
Vieng Xai — E

Creek

Market, Banks & Bus Station

Tribal Museum

Wat Sing Jai

Nam Ha Eco Trek Service

Muang Sing Tourism Information & Trekking Guide Service Centre (i)

Old Market

Police

Sauna

0   20 m

RESTAURANTS
Muang Sing View — 2
Taï Lu — C
Viengphone — 1
Viengxai — E

Xieng Kok

Luang Namtha

While it is possible to organize trekking entirely on your own, if you arrange to be accompanied on your trek by a local who will act as a **guide** and **interpreter**, your experience will be greatly enhanced. Do-it-yourself trekkers often find that their visit to a hill-tribe village degenerates into an exercise of mutual gawking. A good guide will be able to explain customs and activities that you might otherwise find incomprehensible and can help you to interact with the hill folk, who may be unaccustomed to or apprehensive of outsiders. If you do decide to do a trek independently, using a bit of common sense and following a few rules should make for a smooth, memorable visit.

(1) Never trek alone. While Laos is a relatively safe country in terms of violent crime, there have been **robberies** of Western tourists in remote areas. Owing to the government's total control of the Lao media, word of these incidents is suppressed, making it impossible to ascertain just how much risk is involved in solo trekking. Encountering armed men while hiking through the woods does not necessarily mean you are going to be robbed, but it is best to treat all such encounters with caution. If you are approached by armed men and robbery is clearly their intent, do NOT resist.

(2) Most hill-tribe peoples are animists. **Offerings** to the spirits, often bits of food, left in what may seem like an odd place, should never be touched or tampered with.

(3) The Akha are known for the elaborate **gates** which they construct at the entrances to their villages. Far from being merely decorative, the gates are designed to demarcate the boundaries between the human and spirit worlds. If you come across a spirit gate at the entrance to a village, you should find another way to walk, skirting the village to avoid disrupting it while it is being "cleansed" of bad spirits. It goes without saying that climbing onto such a gate to pose for a photograph is poor form.

(4) Many hill folk are willing to be **photographed**, but, just like everyone else, do not appreciate snap-and-run tactics. Old women, particularly of the Hmong and Mien tribes, are not always keen on having their picture taken. It's best to make it clear to a potential subject that you wish to photograph them and to gauge their response before taking a photo.

(5) Don't give out sweets or pens to village children, which often leads to them begging the same things off future tourists, and insults the self-sufficient nature of these tribal peoples. Likewise, the indiscriminate handing out of **medicine**, particularly antibiotics, does more harm than good. Unless you are a trained doctor, you should never attempt to administer medical care to hill people.

Chanthimmeng East of the main road ☎020/212351. Smart modern guesthouse, with gleaming floors, cool rooms and hot showers that are actually hot. Ask for a room that looks out over the paddy fields at the back. ❷

Pouiu 2 West off the main road ☎030/5110326, ⓦwww.muang-sing.com. Arguably Muang Sing's most stylish accommodation, with lovely bungalows set around a delightful garden compound, each decorated with local handicrafts. The larger bungalows are incredibly overpriced (❹) but a lot newer and more pleasant. Treks can be booked here, and there's a restaurant and herbal sauna and massage on site. ❸

Seng Deaun ☎020/5086611. This well-constructed, two-storey building has eight rooms and a *sin dad* (Lao barbeque) restaurant downstairs. But the real draw here are the bungalows behind the main building, set in a nice compound, though the bathrooms are a little grubby looking. ❷

Sing Cha Lern West of the main road ☎020/9663913. The largest hotel in town, with modern, if rather institutional, rooms, though they're a lot less flimsy than many others in Muang Sing. ❷

Taï Lu Main road. A rather picturesque wooden building built in the Tai Leu style, which was the town's first and only hotel until the mid-1990s. The basic rooms above the restaurant feel rather rickety, but all have en-suite bathrooms with Asian toilets. It's definitely got a rustic charm, but it's looking rather worn these days and feels rather like a flophouse. ❶

Viengsing Main road. Neat little rooms, some with shared bath, run by a friendly family. Those at the back have views over the nearby wat. ❶
Vieng Xai Main road. The few rooms here are small and clean; though they're beginning to look a bit old they're still pleasant enough. Those at the back are shielded from the noise on the main road, with lovely views over the rice paddies. ❶

The Town and around

Muang Sing, though small, is fairly spread out; that said, most tourist facilities lie on the main road, though it's worth exploring the quieter roads behind for a glimpse of local life. On the main road, the **tribal museum** (daily 8–11am & 1–4.30pm; 5000K), a simple but elegant wooden building, houses local textiles, tribal costumes and some Buddha images. Unfortunately, it's rarely open during its advertised hours – though you might be able to find someone who can let you in if you walk around the building. Tucked behind the museum is the town's principal **temple**, the ancient-looking Wat Sing Jai, which has a wonderfully rustic *sim* painted in festive hues. If you come in the morning there's usually a lot of activity, mostly the village ladies coming to pray and make offerings.

The principal sight in Muang Sing is its large **morning market**, situated opposite the bus station in the northwest of town. Clustered around the gates you'll often find women selling mounds of bright green watermelons, beyond which is the covered food market, a good spot to pick up snacks, such as melt-in-the-mouth fried bananas. A few tribal ladies sell textiles at the far end of the food market, though expect some hard selling, even if you're just looking. If you want to take a photo of a vendor, it's only polite to buy something first and ask permission. The market kicks off very early, just after sunrise, and though goods are on sale throughout the day, it's best to get there before 10am in order to see the best of it. Many wandering street **vendors** in hill-tribe costume hang around the main street; they aren't rude but they are extremely persistent. Practise your Lao with them until they get bored and go away.

One of the nicest things in town is the **herbal sauna** attached to the *Puoiu 2 Guesthouse*; massages are also available here.

▲ Tribal women shop at Muang Sing's market

Villages and treks around Muang Sing

Muang Sing is located in the centre of a flat, triangular plain surrounded on all sides by high mountains. The Nam Youan River flows down to the plain from China, and numerous other streams water the valley. Scores of **hill-tribe settlements** are located both in the valley basin and all through the surrounding mountains; ethnic groups in the region include Tai Leu, Tai Dam, Akha, Mien, Hmong and others.

A number of places along the main road now offer a range of treks in the area – it pays to shop around before putting your name down for anything, and make sure you know exactly what you're signing up for (and paying for) in advance. At quieter times of year, you will probably find that what trek you do is dependent on what other people are signed up for – prices reduce according to the number of people on a trip – though if you can get a group of four or more people together in advance you're options will be a lot more open.

Muang Sing Tourism Information and Trekking Guide Service Centre (see p.191) offers a range of trips, with a two-day trek, including a night in an Akha village, ranging from 340,000–500,000K. They also offer well-regarded longer treks, plus one-day trips to Xieng Kok (180,000–400,000K). A little further down the road, Nam Ha Eco-Trek Service (℡063/05111044; daily 8am–5pm) offers full-day hill-tribe treks (170,000–500,000K) and a one-day jungle trek and waterfall excursion (200,000–500,00K), plus a decent range of overnight trekking opportunities.

You can explore the surrounding **countryside** and traditional villages on foot or by motorbike or bicycle. However, to get the most out of the area, join a one- to three-day trek through the surrounding mountains to remote and unspoilt villages where life has barely changed in centuries. A number of tour operators now offer treks in Muang Sing – see box above for more details.

Eating

The choice of places to eat in Muang Sing is far from overwhelming – most guesthouses have an attached restaurant, offering the standard mix of Lao and Western dishes. During the day, your best bet is at the morning market, where you can get decent bowls of *fŏe* and stock up on snacks for bus journeys.

Muang Sing View East off the main road. The best choice in town is this rustic bamboo structure looking out over the paddy fields – the perfect place to relax with a cold Beer Lao at the end of the day. Service is rather leisurely, though you're unlikely to be in any rush, and the menu includes a very spicy *larp* (25,000K) and quite a few Chinese-inspired dishes.

Taï Lu The friendly restaurant below this popular guesthouse offers a decent menu, including banana flower soup (25,000K).

Viengphone Main road. This large restaurant offers a range of Western breakfasts, from rather dry baguettes (3000K) to banana pancakes (5000K), plus a mix of Lao and Thai food for lunch and dinner.

Vieng Xai Main road. The menu at this guesthouse restaurant is much the same as at *Viengphone* next door, serving up decent noodle dishes from around 10,000K.

The Akha Road (Route 322)

The road that links **Muang Sing** and **Xieng Kok** passes through one of Laos's most remote regions. While the peaceful scenery of forest-covered hills belies it, the history of this region is tied to the production of illicit drugs: opium, heroin and, more recently, methamphetamine. It is believed that most meth is produced in labs in neighbouring Burma, but smugglers use routes through Laos on their way south to Bangkok, a principal market and distribution point for the drug, which finds its way to discos and dance clubs all over Southeast Asia. Travellers are unlikely, however, to see any indication of this activity from the road.

While the Lao government has mundanely designated this 75-km stretch of road **Route 322**, a more apt designation might be the **Akha Road**, given the high density of Akha villages through which it passes. The Akha of this isolated region have had little contact with the lowland Lao, and this is reflected in their dress. Indeed, the area is one of the few in Laos where you will see Akha men still wearing their traditional headgear: disc-shaped red turbans or tall hats festooned with seed-beads. The road is paved all the way and buses run in both directions in the mornings. The main stop between Muang Sing and Xieng Kok is **Muang Long**, long known as an excellent base for self-organized **trekking**.

Muang Long

MUANG LONG is an up-and-coming Tai Leu town surrounded by Akha and Hmong villages. If you're looking for good trekking in unspoilt areas and don't mind basic food and facilities, then this is the place for you.

In town itself there are a few "sights". At dawn a parade of tribal peoples comes down from the hills to trade at the makeshift **market**. Besides the usual basketloads of peppers, tubers and gourds, villagers bring pieces of rare eaglewood which they gather from the dense forest. This resinous wood, used in Middle Eastern countries in the manufacture of perfumes and incense, is warehoused here before being shipped off to Bangkok, where it fetches astonishingly high prices at shops in the small Arab quarter off Bangkok's Sukhumvit Road. There's also a diminutive Tai Leu **stupa** resembling those found in China's Xishuangbanna region, which stands a few metres off Muang Long's main road. If you look closely at concrete tablets built into the stupa, you'll see examples of the Tai Leu script, which differs greatly from written Lao.

Buses going in both directions stop on the main road in the morning before noon. There are a few decent guesthouses in Muang Long, including *Ouseng* (❶), near the market, and *Jony* (❶); both have basic rooms, and the latter is attached to a decent restaurant.

Around Muang Long

Muang Long lies in a flat narrow valley bottom, with the Nam Ma River flowing right down the valley to enter the Mekong at Xieng Kok. Two tributaries intersect the Nam Ma right at the junction of Muang Long: the Nam Dok Long flows down from the north while the larger Nam Luang River enters from deep in the mountains to the south. Together, the two **river valleys**, heavily populated with ethnic tribes, form corridors into the mountains north and south of Muang Long.

There are several easy areas to explore around Long, which can be done as **day-trips**. To the south of town, you can follow the main road up into the mountains to a scenic waterfall and tribal villages. To the north of town is another road leading to Ban Jamai, which will eventually go all the way to Ban Chak Keun. Another option is to take Route 322 south towards Xieng Kok to the village of Somphammai where you then take a dirt road south into the mountains which leads to a number of **Akha villages**.

Another good location near Long is up Route 322 to the village of **Ban Cha Kham Ping** near Kilometre 35. This is the narrowest section of the Ma River valley and the steep mountains come right to the edge of the road. At Ban Cha Kham Ping there's some amazing pristine subtropical **rainforest** which, with a guide, is well worth the effort of reaching. Regardless of what routes you take, if

A brief history of opium

Opium was introduced to Laos from two directions. Opium cultivation and use was known among **tribal peoples** such as the Hmong and Mien, who brought the poppy's seeds with them as they migrated south into Laos during the nineteenth century. Because the best parcels of arable land in Laos were already occupied by the lowland Lao and Tai Leu, the tribal immigrants were forced to live at high elevations. But the newly arrived minorities soon made an important discovery: opium poppies used up less of the soil's nutrients than other crops, reducing the frequency with which farmers had to perform the labour-intensive slash-and-burn technique. Growing opium and trading it for rice made their lives easier. By the early twentieth century, the **government of French Indochina** began encouraging the migration of Vietnamese and Chinese to Vientiane and the cities of southern Laos, primarily to stimulate trade, and opium addicts among these immigrants created a demand for the drug. Despite these subsequent developments, it is doubtful that the small amounts of opium grown in the hills of northern Laos ever reached the opium dens of the south. Indeed, the French opium monopoly, Opium Régie, suppressed cultivation of the poppy among the tribes of northern Laos in order to tax and control the supply of opium to the licensed dens of Indochina.

By the beginning of World War II, **taxes** on the sale of opium throughout French Indochina made up fifteen percent of the colonial government's revenues. When global war disrupted the traditional maritime route of opium into Indochina, Opium Régie turned to the **Hmong** farmers. Past French attempts to deal with the Hmong on the issue of opium had been disastrous, leading to Hmong uprisings in the provinces of Hoa Phan and Xieng Khuang. Their fear of provoking the obstinate Hmong led the French to select tribal leaders to act as brokers. The result was an eight hundred percent increase in Hmong opium production within four years. By the close of World War II, a weakened France had lost control of much of Laos to the Viet Minh and their protégés, the fledgling Pathet Lao. A rivalry formed between two powerful Hmong opium brokers and they took opposing sides, one supporting the colonialist French, the other the communists. The defeat of the French at Dien Bien Phu in 1954 put them out of the picture for good, but the Americans were soon to fill the vacuum.

America's efforts at combating the spread of communism in Southeast Asia created what has been termed a "Cold War opium boom". US involvement in the civil war in Vietnam escalated during the 1950s, leading to all-out intervention and the commitment of American troops in the 1960s. In Laos, a similar situation was occurring, but with a crucial difference. Instead of sending troops into "neutral" Laos, the US sought by unconventional means to preserve the illusion of non-intervention; CIA operatives trained the Hmong guerrillas who had previously sided with the French, using their cash crop to fund their operations. A Byzantine alliance between the Royal Lao Government, opium warlords and the CIA was formed. Utilizing its own fleet of "Air America" aircraft, the CIA coordinated the collection of opium, which was transported to refineries in the **Golden Triangle**, the resulting heroin eventually finding its way to markets all over the globe. By the war's end, the production of opium in the Golden Triangle, which overlaps into Myanmar and Thailand, had reached epic proportions.

Opium **eradication programmes** in Thailand have had much success in curtailing cultivation of the opium poppy there, and although Myanmar and Laos continue to grow opium, most experts agree that the once lucrative poppy crop has been largely replaced by the production of methamphetamine, which is in high demand in Bangkok and other urban centres in the region.

you do go for a do-it-yourself trek in this region, keep in mind that wandering around on remote trails in these mountains without a **guide** is foolhardy – ask around town.

Many people travel to Muang Long from Luang Namtha and Muang Sing by motorbike, which is probably the best option if you want flexibility and independence.

Xieng Kok and around

A rowdy frontier town on a remote stretch of the Mekong, **XIENG KOK** is the last river-town stop before China. The Upper Mekong scenery here is fantastic, the river narrow, fast and studded with islets of craggy stone, and the region's remoteness gives it a real wilderness feel. Xieng Kok is right on the border with Myanmar, though the crossing isn't open to foreigners. The town itself has a ramshackle charm, not least because few tourists make the trip out here.

Buses to and from Muang Long and Muang Sing depart around 7/8am, though it can be much later if there aren't enough passengers. From Xieng Kok it is possible to travel **downriver**, but note that the boatmen, who know well that many travellers need to get down to Houayxai and exit into Thailand before their visas expire, have a reputation for extorting money from tourists. Expect to pay upwards of $90 for a boat. Unless you can get onto a cargo boat making its way downriver, the only other option is by speedboat, which is not recommended due to their appalling safety record (see p.201).

Some boats will only agree to travel as far as Muang Mom, about an hour's trip north of Houayxai by speedboat, from which it should be easy enough to arrange a boat for the final stretch. There's basic guesthouse accommodation available here (❶), and the usual noodle stalls.

There's a handful of places to stay in Xieng Kok, the best of which is the *Xieng Kok Resort* (❷), on the embankment overlooking the river and landing. The self-contained wooden bungalows all have en-suite bathrooms (with squat toilet) and charming balconies overlooking the Mekong. Another popular choice is *Khemkong Guesthouse & Restaurant* (❷), above the boat landing and close to where buses normally drop off. The double rooms here are passable; some have en suites with squat toilets and bucket showers. All guesthouses have attached restaurants, though don't expect any culinary marvels. Electricity in Xieng Kok is from private generators and generally available from dusk until 9pm.

Houayxai and around

HOUAYXAI, sandwiched between the Mekong and a range of hills, is for many visitors their first introduction to Laos, lying across the river from Thailand. It was long an important crossroads for Chinese merchants from Yunnan, who, driving caravans of pack-ponies laden with tea, silk and opium, would pass through Houayxai on their way south to Chiang Mai, and again on the return north with their loads of gold, silver and ivory. Today, Chinese goods are still much in evidence, but exotic cargoes of silks and opium have been replaced by dirt-cheap hand tools and brittle plastic wares that are floated down the Mekong by the barge-load.

Most tourists hurry through Houayxai, either rushing through to Thailand at the end of their visas or entering from Chiang Khong and immediately heading downriver by slow boat. Despite being a border town, it's not completely

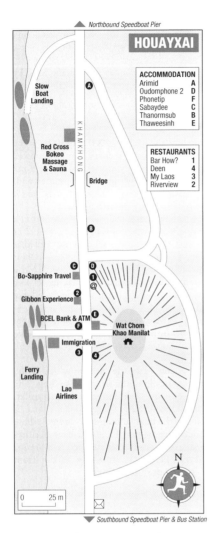

Northbound Speedboat Pier

HOUAYXAI

ACCOMMODATION
Arimid | A
Oudomphone 2 | D
Phonetip | F
Sabaydee | C
Thanormsub | B
Thaweesinh | E

RESTAURANTS
Bar How? | 1
Deen | 4
My Laos | 3
Riverview | 2

Slow Boat Landing

K H A M K H O N G

Red Cross Bokeo Massage & Sauna

Bridge

Bo-Sapphire Travel

Gibbon Experience

BCEL Bank & ATM

Wat Chom Khao Manilat

Immigration

Ferry Landing

Lao Airlines

N

0   25 m

Southbound Speedboat Pier & Bus Station

devoid of charm, though the main reason to stop here now is to take part in the acclaimed Gibbon Experience (see p.200).

Arrival and information

Houayxai's immigration station and **ferry pier** are directly across the river from Chiang Khong's pier, which also has an immigration post. Arriving in Houayxai from Thailand, make absolutely sure that you go through Lao immigration formalities and have your passport **stamped**. The **slow boat** pier (for boats to and from Luang Prabang/Pakbeng) is 500m north of here. There are also two **speedboat piers** – those coming from the north (Xieng Kok and Muang Mom) arrive at Ten Pheung, 27km out of town (tuk-tuk 30,000K), while those from the south arrive 2km downriver (tuk-tuk 10,000K). **Buses** from Luang Namtha, Luang Prabang and Oudomxai arrive at the bus station, 8km south of town; a shared tuk-tuk to the centre will cost 10,000K. Note that on many timetables, Houayxai is marked as Bokeo, the name of the province.

There's a BCEL **bank** (Mon–Fri 8.30am–3.30pm) on the main road, opposite the road down to the ferry landing, which can exchange currency and travellers' cheques, and has an **ATM** outside. **Internet** access is available from a handful of places along the main road (200K/min).

Accommodation

There's a lot of accommodation on offer in Huayxai – if possible, arrive before noon as a lot of the better places fill up early.

Arimid On its own small lane running between the main road and bank, north of the slow boat landing and opposite the petrol station ☏084/211040. A collection of a dozen thatched bungalows, quite pleasant if a bit squeezed together, with en-suite bathrooms and hot water. The restaurant is one of the nicest in town. If you're looking for something with Lao flavour, or are planning on staying in Houayxai a few days, this is a good choice. ❷

Oudomphone 2 Tucked down an alleyway just off the main road, the simple rooms here are pleasant enough, though nothing special. There's a decent restaurant attached. ❷

Phonetip Just north of the ferry landing. The cheapest rooms here are rather cramped, with shared bathrooms, but an extra 20,000K will buy you a bit more space and an en suite. Some rooms have views down to the ferry landing. ❷
Sabaydee ☎084/211503. North of the ferry landing. This modern hotel boasts spotlessly clean rooms featuring tiled en-suite bathrooms. The four back corner units offer terrific views of the Mekong. The best deal in town. ❷
Thanormsub North of the ferry landing ☎084/211095. This blue-roofed house has fourteen very clean, tiled rooms with en-suite bathrooms and hot water. No views, but the staff are friendly and it's fairly quiet. ❷
Thaweesinh Main road north of the ferry ☎021/211502. This four-storey, concrete building may not have much Lao ambience but it's clean and modern, with a nice rooftop patio, and is popular with group tours coming across from Thailand. There's a wide selection of rooms, ranging from windowless singles (55,000K) to a/c doubles with TV (❸). ❷

The Town

Houayxai's only real sight is **Wat Chom Khao Manilat**, situated atop a hill, and reached by stairs across the road from the ferry landing. The gaudy modern *sim* is barely worth doing a lap around, but the adjacent, tall, Shan-style building, which was originally a *sim* but is now being used as a classroom for novice monks, is made of picturesquely weathered teak. Behind the modern *sim* is a collection of *heuan pha*, literally "cloth houses", built to store belongings of the dead. Originally, these homes for the spirits were fashioned from cloth or mulberry paper, but nowadays many are constructed from plywood – a practice unique to parts of northern Laos and northern Thailand. The top of the stairway leading up to the monastery from the main road is a perfect place to watch the sun set.

There's a traditional Lao **herbal sauna** run by the Red Cross (daily 4–9pm; sauna 10,000K, massage 35,000K), located just past the wooden bridge as you go north up the main road.

Eating

Houayxai is unsurprisingly well set up with eating options. In the evenings, a number of places along the main road sell freshly barbequed fish and chicken.

Moving on from Houayxai

Those exiting Laos here can obtain a thirty-day visa on arrival from Thai immigration in Chiang Khong on the Thai side; boats make the five-minute journey across the river from Houayxai's ferry terminal from 8am to 6pm. From Chiang Khong, there are direct buses to Chiang Rai or Chiang Mai.

Slow boats to Luang Prabang (via Pakbeng; 200,000K) depart at 11am from the slow boat pier, 1km upriver from the ferry landing. Speedboats also make the journey to Luang Prabang (375,000K) and Pakbeng (225,000K), departing from Ban Tin That, 2km downriver. They aren't recommended, however, due to their appalling safety record. If you're in a hurry, consider taking the bus to Luang Prabang instead (see below). Speedboats going upriver to Xieng Kok leave from the northbound speedboat pier at Ten Pheung, a ridiculous 27km north of town (30,000K by tuk-tuk). Note that there is no regular service for Xieng Kok so you'll have to hire a boat (expect at least $90).

Buses run from the bus station, 8km out of town (tuk-tuk 10,000K), to Luang Namtha, Oudomxai, Luang Prabang, Vientiane and Muang La in China. Note that there's an overnight VIP bus every afternoon to Luang Prabang, which is a little more comfortable than the local daytime options.

Tickets for buses and boats can be bought directly from the ticket offices at the bus station and pier, or from travel agents on the main road; the price for the latter will include commission and a tuk-tuk ride to the bus/boat, so anticipate paying around 20,000K more.

Bar How? This relaxed place is a favourite with backpackers (especially those just back from the Gibbon Experience), not least for its cold Beer Lao. Serves a range of reasonably priced Lao, Thai and *falang* food, and also has a book exchange.

Deen A small Indian restaurant serving a decent, if predictable, range of curries, such as korma for 22,000K.

My Laos Looking rather out of place in Houayxai with its very smart, modern interior, the tasty

Lao and Thai food here, combined with live music, makes it a good place to unwind in the evening.

Riverview A nice little place that feels like it's been tacked onto someone's home. The largely Western menu includes pizzas (from 45,000K), but tasty fried rice and noodle dishes (15,000K) are also available. It's also a good place to pick up a sandwich before a long boat or bus journey south.

Around Houayxai: the Bokeo gem mines

While not as well known as Mogok in Burma or Pailin in Cambodia, the **gem mines** of Bokeo province are said by some to be just as rich. Indeed, the name of the province – "baw kaew" – actually means "gem mine", and locals claim that when it rains hard, the sapphires wash right out of the hills.

Deposits of corundum (the crystalline form of aluminium oxide, the substance which rubies and sapphires are made of) are plentiful around Houayxai and, when not working their rice fields, farmers take to the gem fields, digging shallow pits into the red earth until the yearly monsoon fills their excavations with rainwater. In 1996, a Danish firm won a contract from the Lao government to mine a 72-square-kilometre tract of land near Houayxai for twenty years. Once the operation was up and running a few years later, the Lao government took over the mine and deported or jailed the foreigners. The mine is fenced off and closed to casual visitors, but watching the antics of part-time prospectors, who have turned the land surrounding the mine into a cratered moonscape, is an interesting half-day diversion.

Bo-Sapphire Travel, next to *BAP Guesthouse* on the main road, offers tours out to the mines.

The Gibbon Experience

One of the country's pioneering eco-tourism projects takes place just outside of Houayxai in **Bokeo Nature Reserve**, a pristine area of jungle that had previously been unexplored by tourists. The acclaimed **Gibbon Experience** (T 084/212021, W www.gibbonexperience.org; $250) is unlike anything else on offer in Laos, and has quickly become a must-do among backpackers (and others), despite its rather high price tag. Groups of no more than eight spend two nights in the reserve, on one of two trips – "Waterfall", which involves two to three hours of trekking a day and thus gets you further into the reserve, and "Classic" which is a little more relaxed, with only an hour of walking. Each tour runs on alternate days.

Regardless of which tour you do, days are spent zip-lining through the forest canopy (an exhilarating experience) and exploring the reserve (with guides), while nights are spent in the specially crafted tree houses. Guides can be a little hit and miss, but most people say that the overall experience makes up for this. Don't expect to see the eponymous gibbons, however, though you may hear them calling in the early morning.

Bookings should be made by telephone or in person at the Houayxai office (on the main street); the price includes all meals, accommodation, local guides and transportation to and from Houayxai.

Down the Mekong

Originally, the Mekong's **slow boats** (*heua sa*) were primarily for cargo and the occasional Lao passengers who relied on them for trade and transport in a part of Laos where roads are sometimes impassable. Since the Lao government eased travel restrictions allowing foreigners to ride these antiquated diesel-powered boats, thousands of tourists have made the two-day journey between Houayxai and **Luang Prabang** (and vice versa), stopping overnight at the village of **Pakbeng**.

Many travellers agree that the journey is one of those definitive Southeast Asian experiences. The riverbanks along the Mekong are sparsely populated, though the forest is not as pristine as one might imagine. Logging and decades of slash-and-burn agriculture have left their mark, and, on the more accessible slopes and summits, trees have been supplanted by rows of corn stalks and banana plants. Of as much interest are the glimpses into local **village life**. Fisher-folk utilizing bamboo fish-traps and prospectors panning for gold can be seen among the sandbars and jagged rocks that make this stretch of the Mekong a treacherous obstacle course. Along the way, boats often call briefly at tiny villages situated at confluences, and the villagers take the opportunity to hawk fish, game and other local products to passengers and crew.

The boats usually carry far more passengers than there are seats – take a cushion with you if possible, which will really make a difference on the long journey, as well as plenty of drinks and snacks. Turn up at the boat landing as early as you can – you may need to sign up in advance so check locally what the situation is.

A couple of luxury tourist boats also make the journey up the Mekong, the pick of which is *Luang Say* (Ⓦ www.luangsay.com), run by the same company as *Luang Say Lodge* in Pakbeng (see p.202). The price ($403/person) includes overnight accommodation in Pakbeng, meals and drinks, plus stops at Pak Ou Buddha Cave (see p.142) and minority villages along the way. If you can afford the splurge, its definitely worth it to do this wonderful journey in more comfortable surroundings.

You'd be foolish to risk your life travelling the river in one of the **speedboats** (*heua wai*) which also make the journey from Houayxai to Pakbeng (4hr) and Luang Prabang (6hr); crash helmets and life-vests are supposed to be provided, and don't forget to bring earplugs.

Note that in February 2010, water levels in the Mekong were so low that boats were suspended for a few weeks – those that did run often ended up with tourists having to camp on riverbanks and in nearby villages when the boat couldn't make it as far as Pakbeng for the night. There seems to be no clear answer about whether it was due to low rainfall or Chinese dams further up the river limiting the flow, so it could certainly happen again. If it does, your best option is to take the bus back to Luang Prabang (see p.199), rather than risk a very slow, uncomfortable and potentially dangerous journey.

Pakbeng and around

The bustling, river port of **PAKBENG** is the halfway point between Houayxai and Luang Prabang, and the only sizeable town or roadhead along the 300km stretch of river between them. As slow boats don't travel the Mekong after dark, a night here is unavoidable if you're travelling this way – a taste of backcountry Laos complete with hill tribes and rustic accommodation. As you stumble off the slow boat at the end of a long day, the ramshackle settlement of wood-scrap, corrugated tin and hand-painted signs that constitutes the port area can be a bit of a culture shock. Since Pakbeng is many travellers' first night in Laos, the expression on a lot of faces is one of "What have I got myself into?" Don't worry: Pakbeng is typical of the northern backwoods only, and provided you don't miss

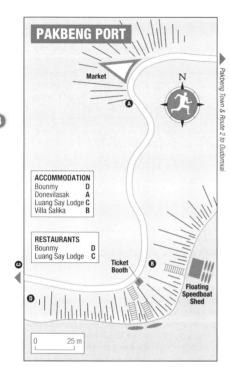

PAKBENG PORT

Market

N

Pakbeng Town & Route 2 to Oudomxai

ACCOMMODATION
Bounmy	D
Donevilasak	A
Luang Say Lodge	C
Villa Salika	B

RESTAURANTS
Bounmy	D
Luang Say Lodge	C

Ticket Booth

Floating Speedboat Shed

0   25 m

your morning boat you'll be sipping lattes in Luang Prabang in no time.

Arrival and information

Slow boats stop at the landing at the bottom of the port road. **Speedboats** pull up to the floating speedboat landing. Both are a short walk from the guesthouses. You may find that young boys offer to help you lug your bag uphill – negotiate a fee for this beforehand. **Buses** from Oudomxai stop first in Pakbeng town and then down at the port area. **Moving on** from Pakbeng by boat, you should be down at the landing by 8.30am. Boats to Luang Prabang will sometimes stop at Pak Ou (see p.142) before reaching the city, charging a couple of thousand kip per passenger for the privilege. Two buses run daily to Oudomxai, leaving from the foot of the hill in the morning.

The town has a lot of small **shops** selling imported foods and household products, since it's an important distribution centre for the interior. There are also several pharmacies. Electricity in Pakbeng is currently by generator from 6 until 10pm, though this is likely to change soon.

Accommodation

Once the boat pulls in, don't waste any time securing a **room**. From the landing, the majority of guesthouses are just up the hill well before the town itself. You may find yourself approached by touts on arrival – you're best off searching for accommodation yourself to avoid being overcharged.

Bounmy Turn left from the boat landing and walk about 200m ☎081/212294. Set just a short way from most other guesthouses in Pakbeng, the main appeal of *Bounmy* is its lovely open restaurant with a two-tier deck over the Mekong. Rooms are a little grotty, though those in the newer building are better and have hot showers. **②**

Donevilasak ☎081/212315. The last place at the top of the hill, with rooms across two buildings. Those in the new building are much more pleasant (and cleaner) than the scruffy rooms in the old building; singles are available (30,000K). **②**

Luang Say Lodge ⊛www.luangsay.com. About 800m down the road running west from the landing. The most luxurious place in

these parts, with eighteen luxury Lao-style bungalows by the river, featuring all mod cons including hot water. On stilts, the bungalows are connected by a beautifully built covered walkway which leads to the reception. The resort even has its own boat pier and fancy restaurant with uniformed staff. And you thought this was the middle of nowhere. Note that unless you're booked on the Luang Say cruise, bookings are only taken for Sunday nights or last-minute. **③**

Villa Salika Right above the landing ☎081/212306. One of the smarter places to stay in town, with prices to match. Rooms are large and clean, though the en-suite bathrooms have cold-water showers. **③**

The Town

Although first impressions of the town are generally unfavourable, Pakbeng is actually a very interesting place. Once extremely poor, it is now growing rapidly, with even a few big mansions going up. The town's change of fortune is due to its role as an important **trading post**; goods from Thailand come down the river from Houayxai and then make their way up into the interior from here. Tourism has also been a big boon for the town, with the slow boats alone disgorging up hundreds of hungry backpackers a day.

Since most tourists to Pakbeng come by slow boat, arriving late and leaving early, many people think the port area around the landing is Pakbeng. In fact, the real town lies past the top of the hill and stretches for a good kilometre along the main road that follows the Mekong before turning north to Muang Beng and Oudomxai. The town is well worth a wander and has a couple of pleasant **wats** overlooking the Mekong. There's no accommodation or restaurants in the old town, although you will find a few noodle shops and some stalls selling sausages and sticky rice.

The small **market** is located right at the top of the landing road past the *Donevilasak* where the road turns sharply right towards the town proper. There's not a lot happening here but it's worth visiting and there are some *föe* stalls. The market convenes every morning and goes most of the day, and is frequented by Hmong women and children, although it appears that traditional dress has gone out of fashion among the Hmong in this vicinity. Heading out of town in either direction will quickly take you to very poor, traditional villages where you'll soon be the centre of attention.

Eating

Because of the fierce competition, Pakbeng's restaurants aren't too shoddy. A lot of the guesthouses have restaurants, serving a fairly predictable mix of Western and Lao/Thai dishes; one of the nicest is that at *Bounmy Guesthouse*, where you can enjoy the reasonably priced food while soaking up the river views. The best option is out at *Luang Say Lodge*, which features an outdoor patio bar with a view of the Mekong, a great place for a sundowner. In the morning, makers of takeaway submarine sandwiches line the road down to the boat landing; alternatively, get up a bit earlier to head up to the morning market, where you can pick from a whole range of Lao treats.

Travel details

Buses and sawngthaews

Hat Sa to: Phongsali (1hr).
Luang Namtha to: Boten, China (4–6 daily; 2hr); Houayxai (Bokeo; 2 daily; 4–5hr); Jinghong, China (daily; 11hr); Luang Prabang (daily; 9hr); Muang Long (daily; 4hr); Muang Sing (5–6 daily; 2hr); Oudomxai (3 daily; 4–5hr); Vientiane (2 daily; 19hr).
Muang Sing to: Luang Namtha (4–6 daily; 2hr); Muang Long (4 daily; 2hr).
Nong Khiaw to: Luang Prabang (2 daily; 2hr); Oudomxai (daily; 3hr 30min–4hr); Sam Neua (daily; 12hr).
Oudomxai to: Boten (daily; 3hr); Houayxai (Bokeo; 2 daily; 8hr); Luang Namtha (3 daily; 3hr 30min–4hr); Luang Prabang (3 daily; 4hr 30min); Muang Khoua (3 daily; 3hr); Pakbeng (2 daily; 3hr 30min); Phongsali (daily; 12hr); Vientiane (4 daily; 15hr).
Phongsali to: Hat Sa (1hr); Oudomxai (daily; 12hr), Vientiane (daily; 27hr).

Boats

The following all depart daily, dependent on passenger numbers.
Houayxai to: Luang Namtha (2 days); Luang Prabang (slow boat 2 days; speedboat 6hr); Pakbeng (slow boat 1 day; speedboat 3hr); Xieng Kok (speedboat 4hr).
Luang Namtha to: Houayxai (2 days); Paktha (2 days).
Luang Prabang to: Houayxai (slow boat 2–3 days; speedboat 6hr); Nong Khiaw (slow boat; 8hr); Pakbeng (slow boat 1 day; speedboat 3hr).
Muang Khoua to: Hat Sa (slow boat 6hr); Muang Ngoi (slow boat 4–5hr); Nong Khiaw (slow boat 6hr).
Muang Ngoi to: Hat Sat (slow boat 4–5hr).
Nong Khiaw to: Luang Prabang (slow boat 8hr); Muang Khoua (slow boat 6hr); Muang Ngoi (slow boat 1hr).

Domestic flights

Houayxai to: Vientiane (3 weekly; 55min).
Luang Namtha to: Vientiane (3 weekly; 50min).
Oudomxai to: Vientiane (3 weekly; 50min).

South central Laos

CHAPTER 5 # Highlights

✳ **Mahaxai Caves** Excellent hiking, cycling and cave-exploring near Thakhek. See p.213

✳ **Tham Lot Kong Lo Cave** This seven-kilometre stretch of underground river is one of Asia's most unusual kayaking sites. See p.215

✳ **Trekking near Savannakhet** Splendid trekking just a short drive from the French–Indochinese shophouses of the south's colonial gem. See p.219

✳ **That Ing Hang** This revered sixteenth-century Buddhist stupa next to the Mekong provides a great excuse for a bicycle ride out of Savannakhet. See p.219

✳ **Ho Chi Minh Trail** Numerous relics – rusting tanks, downed helicopters and the like – of the famous clandestine highway can still be visited. See p.223

▲ Worshippers at That Ing Hang

South central Laos

M any travellers see very little of **south central Laos**, spending just a night or two in the principal towns of **Thakhek** or **Savannakhet** before pressing on to the far south or crossing the border into Vietnam. However, those willing to take time out from the more popular north and south of the country will find that there is much more to the region than the main Mekong towns, not least the otherworldly beauty of the **Mahaxai** stone formations at the edge of the **Khammouane Limestone NBCA** near Thakhek, and the largest of all Laos's conservation areas, the massive **Nakai–Nam Theun NBCA** to the northeast.

The three narrow provinces that dominate this part of Laos, namely **Bolikhamxai**, **Khammouane** and **Savannakhet**, are squeezed between mainland Southeast Asia's two most formidable geographical barriers: the Mekong River and the Annamite Mountains. The mighty **Mekong** has long served as a lifeline for the inhabitants of this stretch of the interior, providing food and a thoroughfare for trade and transport. In the late nineteenth century, European colonialism turned the life-giving "Mother of Waters" into a political boundary, and the Lao on its west bank were incorporated into Siam. During the 1970s and 1980s, the river became a further political and economic divide, when short-lived but draconian post-revolutionary policies forced large numbers of the inhabitants of the towns along this stretch of the Mekong, primarily ethnic Vietnamese and Chinese, to flee across the river into Thailand.

East of the river, the elevation gradually increases, culminating in the rugged **Annamite Mountains**, which, throughout much of recorded history, have divided Indochina culturally into two camps, Indian influence prevailing west of the chain and that of China dominating the east. Until very recently these mountains made up one of the region's least inhabited areas and were teeming with wildlife, including some of Asia's rarest and most endangered species, such as the tiger, Javan rhinoceros and Indian elephant. In recent years, however, this area has been the target of heavy logging, and some observers claim that the damage done to the forest since the start of the new millennium is irreversible.

As might be expected, the three principal settlements and provincial capitals of south central Laos – Paksan, Thakhek and Savannakhet – are all on the Mekong. **Paksan**, the smallest of these, lies at the mouth of the Xan River, which flows down from the 2620-metre Phou Xaxum on the Xieng Khuang Plateau. **Thakhek** now sees few foreign visitors, though it was once a casino town that drew gamblers from Thailand. East of Thakhek is a dramatic landscape of imposing and impossibly vertical mountains of the kind often depicted in old Chinese scroll paintings, which forms the southern boundary of the **Khammouane Limestone NBCA**. Easily visited on a day-trip from Thakhek, these awesome limestone formations

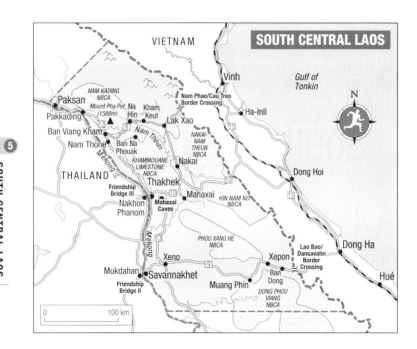

are riddled with labyrinthine tunnels and caverns. **Savannakhet** has been described as southern Laos's equivalent of Luang Prabang, its inhabitants living comfortably among architectural heirlooms handed down by the French. Situated at the junction of two ancient trade routes, the town also displays evidence of other cultures – Vietnamese, Thai and Chinese – that have left their mark while passing through.

Aside from the main north–south artery of **Route 13**, central Laos has three important highways – Routes 8, 12 and 9 – which cross the region from west to east, connecting the Mekong River Valley with the provincial interior, and extending beyond into Vietnam. The northernmost highway, **Route 8** – paved and served by daily buses from Vientiane – snakes up through mountains, rainforests and the Phu Pha Maan "stone forest" before winding down to the city of Vinh on the Gulf of Tonkin. The middle route, **Route 12**, begins at Thakhek and crosses the Annamites, connecting with Vietnam's Highway 15 and the coastal city of **Dong Hoi**. Southernmost of the three is **Route 9**, served by daily buses connecting Savannakhet with **Dong Ha**, **Da Nang** and **Hué** in Vietnam.

Near **Xepon**, Route 9 bisects another route of more recent vintage: the **Ho Chi Minh Trail**. Actually a network of parallel roads and paths, the trail was used by the North Vietnamese Army to infiltrate and finally subdue its southern neighbour. The area is still littered with lots of war junk, some of it dangerous. The best way to view these rusting relics is to use Xepon as a base, making trips to nearby Muang Phin and Ban Dong.

Paksan and Pakkading

Route 13 passes through **PAKSAN**, capital of Bolikhamxai province and the northernmost major settlement on the narrow neck of Laos, but few travellers actually stop over in this small and sleepy Mekong town, and the ferry crossing to and from **Beung Kan** in Thailand is still little used, despite being open to foreigners. After years of planning, workers have finally moved in to fix the terrible road between Paksan and Phonsavan, which would make it possible for northbound travellers from Savannakhet to head straight to the Plain of Jars without having to make a detour through Vientiane. Reports say the project, which could knock five hours off the current eight-hour slog, will be finished in 2012. By that time, the increased through-traffic and ensuing facilities should make spending a night in Paksan a more tempting option than it is at present.

Practicalities

The town's **bus station** is on Route 13 next to the Lao Development **bank**, which changes money. **Accommodation** is decidedly downmarket here. The long-running *BK Guesthouse*, on the road leading down to the river (T054/212638; ❶), has clean rooms, and is a good budget standby. Much better, if you can afford the upgrade, is the relatively modern *Paksan Hotel* (T054/791333; ❸), which has air-conditioned rooms, some with TV.

A handful of **restaurants** with river views can be found where Route 13 crosses the Xan. Of these, *Tavendeng* is the most geared towards non-Lao, with a smattering of English-speaking staff. Located just beyond it, the *Paknamxan Restaurant* is more of a local favourite; just across the bridge, the *Saynamxan Restaurant* is the oldest in town and does good fish dishes.

Pakkading

Forty kilometres southeast of Paksan, **Nam Kading NBCA** is Bolikhamxai province's largest conservation area and a place of dramatic scenic beauty. Running parallel to the Mekong and encompassing 1740 square kilometres, the park has a chain of mountains down its length, the highest peak being the 1588-metre **Mount Pha Pet**, which can clearly be viewed as you travel Route 13. Unfortunately, this is likely to be as intimate a glimpse as you'll get, as there are no roads into the reserve, and no facilities for visitors whatsoever.

Behind the ridge on the eastern boundary of the NBCA, the **Nam Mouan** and **Nam Theun** rivers converge to form the **Nam Kading**, so named because the waterfalls where the Nam Theun spills off the plateau are said to make a "kading" sound – the sound of a water buffalo's bell. The Nam Kading flows out through a gap in the mountains to join the Mekong at the village of **PAKKADING**. There are a number of good fish **restaurants** along the highway here, making it a favourite lunch spot for truckers and travellers plying Route 13.

To the east of Pakkading, the highway crosses a Russian-built bridge and heads south out of town. Drivers often pause to light a cigarette before crossing the bridge, and then respectfully toss the lit cigarette into the swift waters below, an offering to appease the feisty water serpent believed to live at the river's mouth. Every year a buffalo is sacrificed to the water serpent, though the offerings weren't enough to spare the lives of a Russian engineer and several Lao workers who died during construction of the bridge.

Route 8 via Lak Xao

At the tiny junction town of **Ban Vieng Kham**, 47km south of Pakkading, **Route 8** begins its journey over the Annamite Mountains to Vietnam. These days the majority of travellers pass through here on direct, air-conditioned buses running the Vientiane–Vinh route, but it's worth pausing at the frontier town of **Lak Xao**, a base for trips to both the **Ho Chi Minh Trail** and the **Nakai-Nam Theun NBCA**.

Tracing a centuries-old trading route to Vietnam, Route 8 zigzags through hilly countryside, dotted with woods and tiny stream valleys, the southern horizon punctuated by black-topped limestone pillars draped in lush vegetation. An hour's drive along this route takes you to the village of **NA HIN**, which sprang up during the construction of the **Theun-Hin Boun Dam**, completed in 1998. The hydroelectric potential of the area is vigorously demonstrated during the monsoon season, when the rains recharge a medley of waterfalls on the surrounding hillsides. The densely forested hill guarding the valley's southeastern side alone supports as many as six sizeable falls, all visible from the highway.

Today Na Hin has found a new lease of life as a gateway into the Phou Hin Poun NBCA, more popularly known as the **Khammouane Limestone NBCA** (see p.215), and from the bus station there are direct daily connections to both Vientiane and Thakhek. The village itself has a couple of cheap **guesthouses** but if it's serenity you're after check out *Sainamhai Resort*, (Ⓦ www.sainamhairesort .com; ❹), 3.5km south of town, which has gorgeous riverside bungalows and good trekking right on its doorstep.

Continuing east on Route 8, you pass **Ban Phonhong** and cross a toll bridge spanning the Nam Theun, the river that powers the Theun-Hin Boun Dam. The road then reaches **KAM KEUT**, a quaint, shady village of traditional homes, set in an expansive valley of rice fields hemmed in by a low wall of hills.

The Nam Phao/Cau Treo border crossing

If you want to travel from Lak Xao to the **Nam Phao/Cau Treo** border crossing into Vietnam, your best option is to hop into a shared tuk-tuk (20,000K) at the main market. For those crossing into Laos from Vietnam, there's usually a tuk-tuk on hand, but you may well have to charter it outright (expect to pay 100,000K to Lak Xao).

Crossing the border (daily, roughly 8am–5pm) can be a hassle, so it's best to start your journey early to ensure you don't end up stuck at the border. On the Vietnamese side there's usually a small army of touts ready to pull you into a van headed for Vinh. Neither immigration post is near a town of any size; the settlement on the Vietnamese side of the border is **Cau Treo**, 105km west of Vinh on Highway 8. A small exchange kiosk sits in the Lao terminal, but don't expect to get a decent rate. Lao visas on arrival are available at the border, but you'll need to arrange Vietnamese visas in advance. For details of the Vietnamese embassy in Vientiane, see p.90.

Thakhek and around

Less visited than Savannakhet to the south, **THAKHEK**, capital of Khammouane province, is gradually gaining popularity as the best base to explore the nearby **Mahaxai Caves** and karst formations, and the massive **Khammouane Limestone NBCA**. It is also an entry point into Laos from Nakhon Phanom in Thailand, as well as being a good place to break the long journey down Route 13 to Savannakhet.

5

Thakhek's roots date back to the Chenla and Funan empires. The name Thakhek, which means "Visitor's Landing", is relatively new, but is a reference to the town's importance as far back as the eighth century. As Sikhotabong, and later Lakhon, Thakhek was a principality spanning both banks of the Mekong, and a hub for trade routes connecting civilizations in Vietnam, Thailand and Cambodia. Its former spiritual centre, the shrine of That Phanom, is now in present-day Thailand and is still the holiest site in ethnically Lao northeastern Thailand. When the kingdom of Lane Xang was formed under the leadership of Fa Ngum in the fourteenth century, Sikhotabong's governor oversaw the southern extent of the Lao empire. Under the French, the town became an administrative outpost with a bustling Vietnamese community: the colonial administration thought that an influx of Vietnamese workers was the key to finally turning a profit on their sparsely populated Lao territory. By the 1940s, the town was 85 percent Vietnamese. After the revolution, large numbers of these Vietnamese families fled across the Mekong to Nakhon Phanom on the opposite bank, with the result that Thakhek has slipped into being the sleepy Lao town it is today.

Arrival, information and transport

Bus passengers disembark either at the Kilometre 2 Market (2km from the riverbank), or at the inter-provincial **bus station**, around 4km northeast of town on Route 13. There are plenty of **tuk-tuks** on hand at both markets,

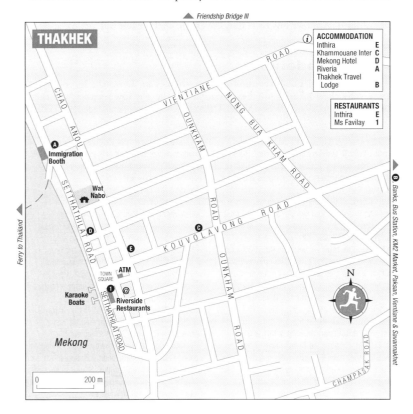

handy, as the town is sprawling. Rogue drivers have been known to agree one price for the journey, only to pull over after a kilometre or so, demanding more cash. Hold firm, keep calm and you should get there for the price you agreed.

The new **tourist office** on Vientiane Road (Mon–Fri 8am–4pm ☎051/212512) is by far the best place for information on the local area, and Mr Somkiad is on hand to help organize eco-tours and treks with English-speaking guides. To change **travellers' cheques**, head for BCEL on Vientiane Road, or the Lao Development Bank opposite the Kilometre 2 Market. There's also a kiosk run by the same bank at the ferry pier, but it only exchanges cash. On the town square there are two IDD telephone booths, an ATM and a Kodak Express film shop. **Internet** access is available just across the road from the ATM.

Motorbikes for exploring the Mahaxai caves and karst formations can be rented at most guesthouses for about $10 a day; the *Travel Lodge* has vans for rent. **Bicycles** are available from various guesthouses ($2/day) for getting around town.

Work has begun on the third Thai–Lao **friendship bridge**, which will eventually create direct road and rail links between Thakhek and Nakhon Phanom; even if things go to plan, it's unlikely to open until the end of 2011. Until then, the only option is the daily **ferry**, which leaves Thakhek during daylight hours from the ramp near the Immigration Office, making crossings every half-hour or so (15,000K). From Nakhon Phanom bus terminal, buses leave for Ubon Ratchathani, Mukdahan, Khon Kaen and Nong Khai. A direct bus to Hanoi leaves Thakhek's main bus station at 8pm every Thursday.

Accommodation

There are several good **accommodation** choices in Thakhek. If you want to stay by the Mekong, just head straight for the old town square and then walk north up riverside Setthathilat Road, where there's a decent selection of hotels.

Inthira Chao Anou Rd, just off the town square ☎051/251237 ⓦwww.inthirahotels.com. Thakhek's first proper boutique hotel is actually comprised of two restored colonial-era trading houses in the heart of town. Each room has a modern, studio feel, with red-brick walls and minimalist bathrooms, plus a minibar, TV and a/c. The two big rooms at the front of the building have balconies with views of the square. Excellent value. ❹

Khamouanne Inter Kouvolavong Rd, 300m east of the river ☎051/ 212171. If you can put up with kitsch 3D floor tiles and a spot of rising damp, this government-run guesthouse is probably the best budget option near the river. Ask to see a few rooms before checking in, as quality and cleanliness varies. ❶

Mekong Hotel Setthathilat Rd ☎051/250777 ⑤250778. Formerly the *Khammouane Hotel*. The free toiletries have five gold stars printed on them, but this huge riverfront block is far from luxurious. The rooms are big and reasonably clean though, and most have balconies with excellent views over the Mekong. Ground-floor lodgings are best avoided as they smell bad and are a little too close for comfort to the late-night massage joint out front. wi-fi in lobby. ❸

Riveria Setthathilat Rd, opposite the Immigration Office ☎051/250000 ⓦwww .hotelriveriathakhek.com. Undoubtedly the swankiest place in town, the shiny-new *Riveria* has a range of double and twin rooms – some with million-dollar views of the Mekong – and a glut of modern facilities, including a business centre and banquet hall. Helpful staff, free in-room internet access and big buffet breakfast included with the room rate. ❺

Thakhek Travel Lodge ☎020/515137, ⓔtravel @luotcl.com. Located up a slde road halfway between the Kilometre 2 and 3 markets, this three-storey guesthouse is the most popular budget option in town. It features basic dormitories ($3) and fan rooms with shared facilities, as well as a/c en-suite rooms, all reasonably priced. They also rent bicycles, motorbikes and vans. ❸

The Town

Take a short walk out from Thakhek's tiny **town square** and you'll find crumbling French villas, overgrown gardens, and an almost haunted atmosphere pervading the too-wide streets. It's hard to believe that during the Second Indochina War, Thakhek was a sort of Havana on the Mekong, with visiting Thais flocking to its riverbank casino; these days, it's Nakhon Phanom on the opposite bank that's the big metropolis. Separated only by the Mekong River, the two Lao peoples living on each bank couldn't have a more different way of life.

For most visitors this lost-in-time atmosphere is the main draw. There are a few nice colonial-era buildings around the town square, and on **Chao Anou Road**, north of the square, is a fine row of 1920s shophouses featuring interlocking swastika designs of moulded stucco (although this Hindu motif appears in Lao weaving, it is rare in Lao architecture). Between Chao Anou and Setthathilat is a large temple, Wat Nabo.

Thakhek's main attraction is 6km to the south and easily reached by tuk-tuk. Known locally as Muang Kao, **Wat Pha That Sikhotabong** is one of the country's holiest pilgrimage sites and a great scenic spot, especially at sunset. The third lunar month, which usually falls in July, is the best time to visit, when the temple celebrates its annual *bun* and a carnival-like atmosphere prevails.

Eating and drinking

Thakhek is no centre of culinary excellence, but eating options have diversified in recent years, and there are now a few decent restaurants on and around the town square. The *Inthira* on Chao Anou Road serves consistently good Asian and Western dishes from a clean, shop-front kitchen. Cheaper but equally tasty is the food at *Ms Favilay*, a popular noodle and soup joint at the southwest corner of the square – just look out for the tables that appear near the river road first thing in the morning. Around the corner on Setthathilat Road you'll find four riverfront restaurants in a row; the first three serve duck but, mercifully for our feathered friends, the last one grills goat.

Mahaxai Caves

East of Thakhek, potholed Route 12 is swallowed up by a surreal landscape of karst formations. Hidden among the sea of jagged limestone hills are the **Mahaxai Caves**, many of which lie within the Khammouane Limestone NBCA. A number of the more easily accessible caves are popular both with Lao families on a weekend picnic and with foreign tourists. These more visited caves line the Thakhek–Mahaxai road, the furthest one only about 20km from Thakhek. The best caves here are spectacular and a day-trip out to explore them is a must if you're staying in Thakhek.

The easiest way to reach the caves is by renting a motorbike ($10/day) or chartering a tuk-tuk from Thakhek, but some visitors prefer to cycle out or catch a Mahaxai-bound bus to the caves and then explore on foot. Public transport can be tricky, however: pick-ups and buses travel the road frequently enough in the morning but aren't so reliable late in the afternoon. To get back, you'll have to flag down one of the buses or pick-ups coming from Mahaxai – of which there are several a day – although again, you can't count on catching one late in the afternoon. If you want to do a **walking tour** of the caves, a good starting point is **Tham Ban Tham**, on the road to Mahaxai 7km from Thakhek; from here you can walk to **Tham En** (see p.214), taking in other caves en route, a 12km walk in all.

Visiting the caves

To find the first cave, turn south down the dirt road that leads off Route 12 towards **Ban Tham**, a small village nestling at the base of the first limestone escarpment. The gaping mouth of the tautologically named **Tham Ban Tham** ("tham" meaning "cave") should be visible from the highway. Cut through the village to find the concrete stairs leading up to the cave, which contains a shrine, centred around a sizeable Buddha image. Perched partway up the side of the hill, Tham Ban Tham offers a commanding view of the surroundings, and is particularly pretty at sunset. If you've come with a local, ask to see the shrine to Ganesh, an elephantine rock hidden in a tunnel within the main cavern. From Ban Tham, follow the road cutting north to get back on the main road.

Just before the second wooden bridge along this road, roughly 17km from Thakhek, a dirt path on the right leads to **Tham Xieng Liap**. After 300m the trail reaches a stream, which flows into the entrance of the cave on the opposite bank (during the monsoon, the water level may be too high to enter the cave). While not the most inspiring cave, Tham Xieng Liap is a pleasant stop chiefly for its seclusion and the novelty of scrambling across a stream full of rocks into the half-submerged cave mouth. Further east along the main road is the disappointing **Tha Falang**, reputedly a favourite spot during colonial times with Thakhek's French residents, who would come here to picnic by a stream among the hills.

Drink vendors set up shop in the recesses of two cliffs 100m beyond the turn-off for Tha Falang, signposting the path leading to **Tham Sa Pha In**, which is without question the best of the caves. A small sign on the left points towards the path leading to the cave, a short walk from the main road. Look for the bamboo gate to find the cave entrance. The cave was renamed for the Hindu god Indra after the Second Indochina War, when villagers claimed to see the Hindu deity's image reflected in the pool. Illuminated by an inaccessible opening in the ceiling of the cave, the pool glows emerald green, the colour of Indra's skin. You can pause to light a candle by the shrine in the back of the cave before clambering down to sit by the pool, where swifts dive-bombing the surface and the drone of insects conspire to give the deep cavern an otherworldly atmosphere. A sign at the mouth of the cave asks visitors not to touch the water, which is considered sacred.

The most visited of Mahaxai's caves, **Tham En**, named for the large number of sparrows that are said to inhabit the cave and popular for what the Lao call its natural air conditioning, lies another 4km up the road; it's easily located by the gate, where an official collects 5000K per visitor, plus a vehicle fee. A concrete stairway takes you deep into the tunnel mouth, but there is still plenty of room to clamber around on the rocks and climb up to one of the several cave mouths that offer great views of the forest outside. On weekends, the cave is packed with day-tripping locals picnicking and playing cards.

Mahaxai

Fifty kilometres east of the Mahaxai Caves lies the beautifully situated town of **MAHAXAI**, engulfed in limestone karst formations, on the banks of the Xe Bang Fai River. A bumpy 50km drive from Thakhek, this lively little town lacks sights of its own but is nevertheless a charming place offering visitors enchanted by the strange beauty of Khammouane's karst formations a chance to soak up the surroundings at a more measured pace.

Buses and pick-ups grind to a halt at the central market, next to an old tin-roofed temple. There's just one **hotel**, with huge rooms (❷), as well as several noodle shops and *tam màk hung* vendors, all just steps away. Hiring a boat to cruise the river, which stretches from the mountainous Vietnamese border to the Mekong, can be a bit of a chore – ask by the river or around town – but if you can swing it, a two-hour round-trip by motorized pirogue is scenic in either direction, with the upstream route taking in stunning cliffs and the downstream option skimming through gentle rapids, past submerged water buffalo and villagers catching fish. Most cave touring originates in Thakhek, but the area surrounding Mahaxai is also honeycombed with caves – ask the villagers.

Khammouane Limestone NBCA

The most accessible of Khammouane province's three NBCAs is the Phou Hin Poun NBCA, more popularly known as the **Khammouane Limestone NBCA** and home to a dizzying array of wildlife, including elephants, tigers and macaques. Unlike the neighbouring Nakai-Nam Theun and Hin Nam No NBCAs to the east, the Khammouane Limestone NBCA can be accessed by road or river from a number of approaches, making it the most practical and affordable of the three to visit.

The best way to experience the park is on one of the organized tours that operate out of Thakhek or Vientiane, and that generally include kayaking, hiking and **village stays**. Although it will not allow you to penetrate the interior of the park to the degree a professionally organized expedition can, a do-it-yourself tour from Thakhek is also easily arranged and affordable.

The chief highlight of many of the tours is the journey by kayak through the wonderfully dramatic **Tham Lot Kong Lo Cave**, a natural 7km river tunnel through a limestone karst mountain into a hidden valley. Bring a torch (flashlight) and some rubber flip-flops as it can be necessary to wade through the more shallow stretches of the river. Green Discovery (℡021/264680, ℗www.greendiscoverylaos .com), which may have opened a new Thakhek office on the town square by the time you read this offers a three-day kayaking, cycling and trekking tour to the cave.

There's an **eco-resort** within the park, the *L'Auberge Sala Hine Boun* (℡020/755220, ℗www.salalao.com; ❹), on the banks of the Nam Hin Poun River; it's reached by taking a tuk-tuk from **Na Hin** (on Route 8) to Ban Na Phouak on the northern boundary of the NBCA, and then a boat up the Nam Hin Poun ($15; 2hr). The resort has comfortable bungalows and is within easy day-hiking distance of a number of hill-tribe villages, Tham Thieng cave and Tham Lot Kong Lo. Kayak excursions through the underground river can be arranged here but a cheaper option, especially if you're travelling solo, is to arrive at the cave with your own transport and wait until you can split the cost of a boat and driver (around $10) with other sightseers.

Savannakhet and around

SAVANNAKHET (known locally as "Savan") is Laos's third-largest city after Vientiane and Luang Prabang, and the surrounding area that makes up Savannakhet province, stretching from the Mekong River to the Annamite Mountains, is Laos's most populous region; for centuries the inhabitants fought off designs on their territory from both Vietnam and Thailand. The city is also southern Laos's most visited provincial capital, its popularity with travellers due in part to its central location on the overland route between Vientiane and Pakse and between Thailand and Vietnam, the two countries linked to each other by a 240km-long road carved by the French. Aside from being an important junction, Savannakhet also possesses very impressive **architecture**, and is a major staging post for **jungle treks** and cycling tours.

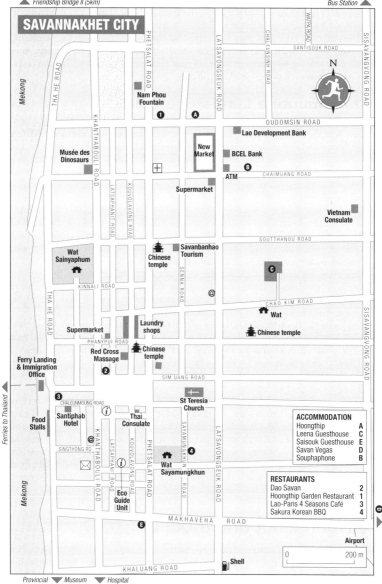

Savannakhet's inhabitants, as travellers who have recently arrived from Vietnam are quick to note, are much mellower than their neighbours east of the Annamite Mountains, despite the fact that a large percentage of the town's population is ethnic Vietnamese, descendants of entrepreneurs who migrated to Laos during French rule. Most have been living here for generations and consider themselves to be more Lao than Vietnamese in habit and temperament.

Arrival, information and city transport

Most **buses** offload at the station on the north side of the town, with **tuk-tuks** on hand to make the 2km run into the city centre (15,000K). **Ferries** still run between Savannakhet and Mukdahan in Thailand, using the landing at the Immigration Office in the town centre, but most tourists now use the 1600m-long **Friendship Bridge II**, which has connected the two cities since 2007. The **airport** is on the southeastern side of the town, off Makhaveha Road a few blocks from the centre, with regular Lao Airlines flights connecting Savannakhet with Vientiane and Pakse.

As Savannakhet is incredibly spread out, you may find **tuk-tuks** easier than trying to walk the long blocks outside the old quarter, especially in summer. Tuk-tuks can be flagged down around town and cost 5000K for short distances within the centre. **Bicycles** are another excellent way of seeing the town and can be rented at *Santiphab Hotel* near the square and at some guesthouses. *Savanbanhao Tourism* on Senna Road (☏041/212944), three blocks north of the church, has vans with drivers for hire.

The **Tourism Administration office** south of the main square (Mon–Fri 8–11.30am & 1.30–4pm ☏041/212755) can help with general enquiries but if you want to go **trekking** in Savannakhet province, make a beeline for the **Eco Guide Unit** (☏041/214203 ⓦwww.savannakhet-trekking.com), around the corner on Latsaphanit Road. The exceptionally helpful team here (led by English-speaking Mr Oudomsay, ☏020/2605046) can organize a range of one- to five-day community-based treks.

Accommodation

Savannakhet has a very good range of **accommodation**, including family-run guesthouses, business hotels and even a Vegas-style casino. Generally, the most atmospheric and convenient area to stay is in the old city, but don't expect to find charming guesthouses in colonial buildings as in Luang Prabang. Most of the best modern options are scattered on the wide streets outside the immediate vicinity of the old city, but these places can be inconvenient for those without their own car.

Hoongthip Between Phetsalat Rd and Latsavong-seuk Rd ☏041/212262. It lacks the atmosphere of Savannakhet's central guesthouses, and you may need a bike to get to and from the old town, but this modern business hotel is still a good mid-range option, especially if you want to recuperate after a

few days' trekking. Rooms in the newer part of the hotel are the best value, with plenty of space and nice clean bathrooms. Free wi-fi. ⑤

Leena Guesthouse Head 200m east along Chao Kim Rd, off Latsavongseuk Rd, and follow the signs ☏041/212404. Two spotless buildings in a quiet

Moving on to Vietnam and Thailand

A daily bus to **Vietnam** leaves Savannakhet at 10pm. Different cities are served, including Dong Ha, Hué and Da Nang ($8–12), depending on the day of the week you travel. A VIP bus bound for Dong Ha (seven hours) leaves the Savanbanhao Tourism office each morning at 8am. Note that even "direct" buses usually require a vehicle change at the border. Local buses leave Savannakhet's main bus station for the Lao Bao border (six hours) at 7am, 9am and 12pm.

If you're heading for Thailand, you can now cross using Friendship Bridge II, 5km north of Savannakhet. Twelve daily buses bound for Mukdahan leave Savannakhet's main bus terminal (8.15am–7pm; 13,000K), stopping at Thai immigration, where visas on arrival are available. The forty-minute bus ride ends at Mukdahan's main bus station, a short ride from the town centre.

residential area with en-suite rooms, some with a/c, hot water and TV, and all (bizarrely) with free condoms. It is a bit out of the old town, but there's a huge wat and a Chinese temple nearby, plus a pleasant restaurant serving Western breakfasts downstairs in the next building. Great value; reservations advised. ❸

Saisouk Guesthouse Phetsalat Rd, at the corner of Makhaveha Rd, two blocks south of Wat Sayamungkhun on the opposite side of the road ☏041/212207. Facilities are shared, but if you're looking for a relaxed atmosphere this lovely wooden house, in a quiet area, is the place for you. The rooms, some with a/c, are spacious and well lit, and the toilets are immaculately clean. ❷

Savan Vegas Nongdeune Village, just south of the airport ☏041/252200 ⓦwww.savanvegas.com. If Savannakhet is really to become the new "Lao Vegas", this vast resort is the first place on The Strip. The spanking-new five-star hotel features a range of rooms, suites and apartments, all with top-end fixtures and fittings. Non-guests are welcome to try their luck at the tables (Thai baht only), which makes for a fun, if slightly surreal, night out. ❽–❾

Souphaphone Chaimuang Rd ☏041/214150. Clean, spartan rooms with fan or a/c. An excellent budget option, but quite a trek into the centre of town. Little English spoken. ❷

The Old City

Savannakhet's **town square** was the heart of the French settlement, the surrounding neat grid streets reserved for the villas of French officials and the shophouses of Vietnamese merchants. One of the best areas for a stroll or spin on a bike to see old buildings is the district of tree-lined streets and former French administrative offices south of the post office. The old town also has several pleasant wats and a few Chinese temples worth a wander.

The **Old French Quarter** boasts some fine examples of European-inspired architecture, though most of this looks much more ancient than it really is – it's doubtful that any of these crumbling structures predate the early twentieth century. The main square is dominated by the octagonal spire of **St Teresia Catholic Church**, built in 1930, its thick masonry walls keeping the interior blessedly cool even on the hottest of days. Just west of here, the **Thai Consulate**, housed in a 1926 mansion on Kouvolavong Road, is a fine example of how beautiful French-era buildings can be when properly restored.

▲ Savannakhet architecture

Vietnamese and Chinese joss houses and schools in the area attest to the wealth and influence of Savannakhet's merchant class, who came to the town in search of business opportunities. They left after the revolution, taking their money and entrepreneurial skills with them, and only recently have foreign investors begun to return.

Wat Sainyaphum

Just north of the ferry landing, on the road running along the Mekong, sits **Wat Sainyaphum**, Savannakhet's largest Buddhist monastery. Nearly all the structures at the wat, save for the school building in the northwest corner of the compound, have been restored in garish, circus-like hues. It is worth a visit, however, especially if you are looking for a serene, shady spot to while away the afternoon.

Musée des Dinosaurs

Set up with some help from French paleontologists, the **Musée des Dinosaurs** on Khanthabouli Road (daily 8am–noon & 1–4pm; 5000K), north of Wat Sainyaphum, showcases finds from the five digs going on in the countryside around Savannakhet – little of interest aside from a few old bones and photos of the digs.

Provincial Museum

Housed in a peeling colonial-era mansion, 1km south of the ferry landing, the unkempt **Provincial Museum** (daily 8–11.30am & 1–4pm; 5000K) is mostly given over to old photographs of Kaysone, Savannakhet's most revered native son (see box, p.220), and the events leading up to the communist takeover in 1975. There's a giant bust of the great leader, and pictures of him bear-hugging a variety of dictators including Ho Chi Minh, Fidel Castro, Hun Sen and Jiang Zemin.

Around Savannakhet

Savannakhet province is packed with options for environmentally sensitive trekking, cycling and wildlife tours – many of them still in their infancy. Staff at the Eco Guide Unit (see p.217) can offer advice on what's available and, if you're interested, find you an English-speaking guide.

If you'd rather stay closer to town, a **bike ride** out in any direction from the centre gives an opportunity to view the difference in lifestyles between the ethnic Vietnamese of the town and the ethnic Lao in the countryside. As you head out, brick and stucco give way to teak and bamboo, while rows of shade trees come to an abrupt halt and fruit trees – mango, guava and papaya – begin to appear in every yard.

That Ing Hang

A much revered Buddhist stupa dating from the sixteenth century (although some locals claim it's over a thousand years old), **That Ing Hang** (admission 5000K) is located just outside Savannakhet and can be reached by bike or motorcycle: follow Route 13 north for 13km until you see a sign on the right and follow this road for a further 3km. The stupa is covered in crude yet appealing stucco work, and the well-manicured courtyard that surrounds it offers a pleasant opportunity for a stroll and photographs.

The stupa is best visited during its annual festival in February when thousands make the pilgrimage, camping in its grounds. During the celebrations, the door to a small chamber at the base of the stupa is opened, and male devotees queue up to make offerings to the Buddha images inside. By custom, women are prohibited from entering this inner sanctum.

Kaysone: the man behind the bamboo curtain

When Lao prime minister and communist leader **Kaysone Phomvihane** died in 1992, party leaders commissioned 150 bronze statues of him, which have since been erected in pavilions across the country. Whether these busts are a faithful portrayal of Kaysone remains irrelevant to most Lao, since from 1958 until 1975, the leader of the People's Revolutionary Party was rarely seen in public. Only now that the state has begun remaking itself in his image is the cloud of secrecy surrounding him dissipating, but the lack of biographical details about his life makes it difficult to discern the private Kaysone from the state-cultivated one.

What is known is that Kaysone was born in Savannakhet in 1920, the only son of a Vietnamese civil servant father and a Lao mother. As a teenager he left for Hanoi, where he studied at a law school under the name of Nguyen Tri Quoc before dropping out to devote himself to the life of a revolutionary. By 1945, he had attracted the attention of North Vietnamese leader Ho Chi Minh, who instructed him to return home and infiltrate a Lao nationalist movement supported by the American Office of Strategic Services, a forerunner of the CIA.

Later that year, Kaysone and his followers deferred to the leadership of **Prince Souphanouvong**, whom he followed to Bangkok after the French returned to power in 1946. Soon after, Kaysone joined the newly formed Committee for Resistance in the East, coordinating anti-French guerrilla raids along the Lao–Vietnamese border and responsible for liaisons with the Viet Minh, a tie that was to earn him the trust of the North Vietnamese, who eventually recruited him into the Indochinese Communist Party (ICP). After training at the Viet Minh's military academy, Kaysone became commander of the Latsavong brigade, the guerrilla unit in southeastern Laos that marked the beginnings of the Lao People's Liberation Army. By 1950, Kaysone had been named defence minister in the Pathet Lao resistance government, where he spent four years recruiting and training members for the Pathet Lao's fighting force, of which he formally became commander in 1954. When the Lao People's Revolutionary Party formed in 1955, Kaysone became secretary general – a post he would hold for the next 37 years. His control of the revolutionary movement was further solidified in 1959 when Souphanouvong and other Pathet Lao leaders were jailed in Vientiane. Though Kaysone relinquished his post as commander of the army in 1962, he continued to direct military strategy until the end of the Thirty Year Struggle in 1975.

It was only fitting that Kaysone – a man who disdained the perquisites of military rank, indeed who was never even referred to by rank – should emerge as the first prime minister of the Lao People's Democratic Republic in December 1975. For the next seventeen years, Kaysone firmly held the reins of power in Laos and, among diplomats, earned a reputation as a clever man, eager to learn and willing to acknowledge his mistakes. He earned praise for ditching botched policies and initiating economic reforms, and by the time of his death at the age of 72, Kaysone's Laos hardly fitted the mould of a typical socialist country at all.

Since his **death**, the image of Kaysone's greying hair and full face has been employed by a party reaching out for symbols of nationalism. But more striking than the party's decision to transform Kaysone into a "man of the people", who relished simple food, are the pedestals upon which his bust has been placed. Shaded by red and gold pavilions topped by tiered parasols, Kaysone's monuments exude something of the regal splendour once reserved for the Theravada Buddhist monarchs who ruled over the kingdom of Lane Xang.

Eating

The food and service at Savannakhet's **travellers' cafés** are passable, but the town does have some good local **restaurants**. One famous local noodle dish worth seeking out is *baw bun* (Vietnamese rice noodles served with chopped-up spring rolls and beef). Vietnamese spring rolls are also quite good here. Other local delights include bamboo shoots and watermelon and *sin Savannakhet* – sweet, dried, roasted beef.

Dao Savan Northern edge of the town square ☎041/260888. French cuisine *par excellence* at this beautifully restored colonial house right in the heart of town. Try the delicious set menu featuring green garden salad, rib-eye steak with pepper sauce and ice cream for dessert. Internet access available.

Hoongthip Garden Restaurant Phetsalat Rd, just west of the *Hoongthip Hotel* ☎041/212262. The nicest restaurant in town, housed in a big wooden building with open sala-style seating under a green

roof. If you're after a good meal in pleasant surrounds with some atmosphere, look no further.

Lao-Paris 4 Seasons Café 30 Chaleunmoung Rd, near the river. Many travellers seem to end up at this Vietnamese shophouse near the river. The food isn't the greatest, but it's a pleasant enough place for a beer or an iced coffee.

Sakura Korean BBQ Sayamungkhun Rd. Very good Korean barbecue with a choice of beef or fish and lots of fresh veggies and glass noodles. Cheap, delicious and highly recommended.

Listings

Airlines Lao Airlines, at the airport, southeast of the city centre ☎041/212140.
Banks and exchange The Lao Development Bank and the BCEL are near the intersection of Latsavongseuk and Oudomsin rds, the former facing Oudomsin Rd and the latter facing Latsavongseuk Rd.
Consulates Thailand, Kouvalavong Rd, one block south of the square (Mon–Fri 8am–noon & 1–4pm; ☎041/212373); Vietnam: on Sisavangvong Rd (Mon–Fri 7.30–11am & 1.30–4pm; ☎041/212418).
Hospitals and clinics The biggest hospital is located on Khanthabouli Rd, near the provincial

museum; a 24hr clinic operates on Phetsalat Rd, a block south of the *Hoongthip Hotel*.
Internet access A handful of internet places can be found in town, charging around 4000K/hr.
Laundry Fast and cheap at the laundry shops along Kouvalavong Rd, north of the town square.
Post and telephone The GPO is on Khanthabouli Rd, a few blocks south of the town square (Mon–Fri 7.30am–5pm, Sat & Sun 8am–5pm). The Lao Telecom building, with overseas phone and fax services, (daily 8am–10pm) is just behind it.

East to Xepon and the Vietnam border

From Savannakhet, **Route 9** heads east through a series of drab and dusty towns, passing Muang Phin and then Xepon, where it begins its climb up into the Annamite Mountains. The road ends its Lao journey at the **Lao Bao pass**, before crossing into Vietnam and continuing down to **Dong Ha**, where it joins Highway 1. The French completed the road in 1930, as part of an Indochinese road network intended to link Mekong towns with the Vietnamese coast, bringing in Vietnamese migrants and trucking out Lao produce. Today, the Thais, too, have an interest in Route 9 as a trade corridor, linking their relatively poor northeastern provinces with the port of Da Nang in Vietnam.

While most travellers barrel through here on direct buses to and from Vietnam, the frontier is not without sites of interest. As you approach **Muang Phin**, Route 9 begins to cross the north–south arteries of the **Ho Chi Minh Trail**, a network of dirt paths and roads that spread throughout southeastern Laos, running from the Mu Gia Pass in Bolikhamxai province south through Attapeu and into Cambodia. While much of the debris from the war lies off the beaten track, some of these war relics are easily accessible. Another place worth stopping in to explore the surrounding area is the recently rebuilt market town of **Xepon** which, along with neighbouring towns, is populated predominantly by Phu Tai people, a lowland Lao group.

Xeno and Muang Phin

Route 9 heads past teak plantations until, 35km from Savannakhet, it reaches **XENO**, where it intersects the country's north–south axis, Route 13. Once a French military outpost and later a Royal Lao airfield, Xeno these days is known mostly for its gypsum quarries.

You'll know you've reached **MUANG PHIN**, roughly 100km east of Xeno, when your bus halts right in front of the massive Vietnamese–Lao friendship monument. The golden rendering of a Pathet Lao and North Vietnamese soldier dwarfs the town, whose run-down appearance attests to Muang Phin's unfortunate position on one of the fronts during the war.

Xepon

A picturesque village in the foothills of the Annamite Mountains, 40km from the Vietnamese border, **XEPON** is a pleasant rural stopover for those in transit on the route to Vietnam or Savannakhet. The original town of Xepon was destroyed during the war – along with every house of the district's two hundred villages – and was later rebuilt here 6km west of its original location, on the opposite bank of the Xe Banghiang River. The old city (written as "Tchepone" on some old maps) had been captured by communist forces in 1960 and became an important outpost on the Ho Chi Minh Trail. As such, it was the target of a joint South Vietnamese and American invasion in 1971 (see opposite), aimed at disrupting the flow of troops and supplies headed for communist forces in South Vietnam.

Practicalities

Xepon is such a small town that even the **market**, where the bus drops passengers, fails to generate much of a buzz. If you're looking for **accommodation**, the most central option is *Vieng Xai*, near the market (❶), which has cheap rooms and a

---

Vietnamese influence

Ties between Muang Phin and **Vietnam** go back a long way. During much of the eighteenth and nineteenth centuries, the area's Phu Tai inhabitants paid tribute to the court in Hué. In the middle of the nineteenth century, the Vietnamese rulers, having just wrapped up a war with Siam, were content to exact a light tribute of wax and elephant tusks from the Phu Tai, preferring to leave the Tai minority's territory as a loose buffer zone between regional powers. By this point, Vietnamese merchants, following the traditional trading route across the Lao Bao pass, were already arriving in Muang Phin with cooking pans, iron, salt and fish sauce, and returning east with cows and water buffaloes in tow. A story told by an early French visitor to the town attests to the business acumen of one of these merchants. Upon arriving in town, the merchant found prices too high, but was reluctant to return home without making a good profit. With a quick conversion to Buddhism the merchant's problem was solved: he shaved his head and shacked up in the local temple where he could defray his expenses until prices dropped, at which point the merchant donned a wig, bought up a few buffalo and hightailed it back to Hué.

Operation Lam Son 719

On the outskirts of the village of Ban Dong on Route 9 sit two rusting American tanks, all that remains of a massive invasion and series of battles that have become a mere footnote in the history of the decade-long American military debacle in Indochina. In 1971 President Nixon, anticipating a massive campaign by North Vietnamese troops against South Vietnam the following year (which happened to be an election year in the US), ordered an attack on the Ho Chi Minh Trail to cut off supplies to communist forces. Although a congressional amendment had been passed the previous year prohibiting US ground troops from crossing the border from Vietnam into Laos and Cambodia, the US command saw it as an opportunity to test the strengths of Vietnamization, the policy of turning the ground war over to the South Vietnamese. For the operation, code-named **Lam Son 719**, it was decided that ARVN (Army of the Republic of Vietnam) troops were to invade Laos and block the trail with the backing of US air support. The objective was Xepon, a town straddled by the Trail, which was some 30–40km wide at this point. Nixon's national security adviser, Henry Kissinger, was later to lament that "the operation, conceived in doubt and assailed by scepticism, proceeded in confusion". In early February 1971, ARVN troops and tanks pushed across the border at Lao Bao and followed Route 9 into Laos. Like a caterpillar trying to ford a column of red ants, the South Vietnamese troops were soon engulfed by North Vietnamese (NVA) regulars, who were superior in number. Ordered by President Thieu of South Vietnam to halt if there were more than 3000 casualties, ARVN officers stopped halfway to Xepon and engaged the NVA in a series of battles that lasted over a month. US air support proved ineffectual, and by mid-March scenes of frightened ARVN troops drastically retreating were being broadcast around the world. In an official Lao account of the battle, a list of "units of Saigon puppet troops wiped out on Highway 9" included four regiments of armoured cavalry destroyed between the Vietnam border and Ban Dong.

shared bathroom. *Nangtoon Guesthouse* (❷), 1500m east of the market, has decent doubles with hot-water showers. There's an excellent **noodle shop** on the western side of the market. Although there aren't any official forex services in Xepon, **cash** can usually be exchanged at the market. From Xepon, frequent sawngthaews leave for Ban Dong (10,000K) and the Lao Bao border post (20,000K).

The Ho Chi Minh Trail at Ban Dong

As you head east out of Xepon, the highway gradually climbs through the foothills of the Annamite chain, passing bomb craters – often obscured by brush – and unexploded ordnance, dragged to the roadside by villagers clearing their land. Women squat by the road with their intricately woven baskets, selling bamboo shoots – a local speciality. The area's abundant bamboo crop is in fact partially a by-product of the spraying of defoliants by American forces who hoped to expose the arteries of the Ho Chi Minh Trail: hardy bamboo is quick to take root in areas of deforestation.

Rows of drink shops, competing to quench the thirst of Vietnamese truckers, signal your arrival in **BAN DONG**, a popular stop on any tour of the **Ho Chi Minh Trail.** Villagers are slowly growing accustomed to tourists poking around for a glimpse of the Republic of Vietnam's American-made tanks left over from one of America's most ignominious defeats during the war, at the battle known as **Lam Son 719**.

The tank that's easiest to find lies five minutes' walk off the road that cuts south out of town towards Taoy, which was once a crucial artery of the Ho Chi Minh Trail. Shaded by a grove of jackfruit trees, it rests atop a small hill east of the road, and has been partially dismantled for its valuable steel. Ban Dong was cleared of unexploded war debris in 1998, but it's still a good idea to ask a villager to show you the way, as you should always take extra care when leaving a well-worn path, and vegetation in the rainy season can obscure the tank's location. If you're travelling by public transport, the best time to visit Ban Dong is in the morning, as there are no late-afternoon buses plying this stretch of highway. Guesthouses in Xepon may be able to help you organize a round-trip.

Dansavanh and the border

Pushing east, tiny ethnic minority villages hug the roadside until you come to **DANSAVANH**, the last town on the Lao side of the pass.

For a relatively remote border town, Dansavanh is actually quite tourist-friendly. There are several buses a day from here to Savannakhet (all leaving in the morning) and there's also an early-afternoon bus to Xepon.

Crossing the **Dansavanh/Lao Bao border** (7am–6pm) can take time, so it pays to head for the Lao immigration post early in the morning. You can walk here from the centre of Dansavanh (about 1km) but motorbike taxis are on hand if you're feeling sluggish.

Travellers **to Vietnam** must arrange a visa before travelling and ensure their passport is stamped for "Lao Bao". On the Vietnamese side, there are motorcycle taxis to take you down the hill to **LAO BAO** town where buses leave for Khe Sanh and Dong Ha, where bus or train connections can be made to Hanoi and Hué.

Travel details

Buses

Dansavanh/Lao Bao to: Muang Phin (3 daily; 2hr); Savannakhet (3 daily; 5hr); Xepon (4 daily; 1hr).
Lak Xao to: Thakhek (1 daily; 5hr); Vientiane (3 daily; 7hr).
Muang Phin to: Dansavanh/Lao Bao (3 daily; 2hr); Savannakhet (3 daily; 3hr); Xepon (3 daily; 1hr).
Savannakhet to: Attapeu (2 daily; 10hr); Dansavanh/Lao Bao (4 daily; 4hr); Da Nang (daily; 13hr); Hanoi (2 weekly; 24hr); Hué (daily; 13hr); Muang Phin (3 daily; 3hr); Pakse (9 daily; 5hr); Salavan (1 daily; 8hr); Thakhek (9 daily; 2hr); Vientiane (8 daily; 8–9hr); Xepon (3 daily; 4hr).

Thakhek to: Hanoi (weekly; 24hr); Dong Hoi (4 weekly; 7hr); Mahaxai (5 daily; 2hr 30min); Pakse (2 daily; 9hr); Savannakhet (5 daily; 4hr); Vientiane (6 daily; 8hr).
Xepon to: Dansavanh/Lao Bao (4 daily; 1hr); Muang Phin (3 daily; 1hr); Savannakhet (3 daily; 4hr).

Ferries

Thakhek to: Nakhon Phanom (hourly during daylight; 10min).

The far south

CHAPTER 6

Highlights

✷ **Champasak** Unwind in this chilled-out backpacker town, among temples, sacred mountains and Khmer ruins. See p.234

✷ **Wat Phou** The most harmonious Khmer ruin outside of Cambodia, this fifteen-century-old hillside landmark exudes a serenity lost in overrun Siem Reap. See p.236

✷ **Si Phan Don – the "4000 Islands"** Discover crashing waterfalls and crumbling colonial buildings on these beautiful tropical islands, or spend your days stretched out in a riverside hammock. See p.243

✷ **Dolphin-watching off Khon Island** Try to spot endangered Irrawaddy freshwater dolphins in one of their last surviving habitats. See p.250

✷ **Explore the Bolaven** Ascend the Bolaven Plateau for cool breezes, towering hundred-metre falls and the freshest coffee around. See p.251

✷ **Boat down the Xe Kong** Would-be Huck Finns shouldn't resist the chance to slip down this river in one of Laos's most remote provinces. See p.256

▲ Island family, Si Phan Don

6

The far south

T he tail end of Laos is anchored by the provinces of **Champasak**, **Xekong**, **Attapeu** and **Salavan**, a region that lay at the crossroads of the great empires that ruled Southeast Asia centuries ago – Champa, Chenla and Angkor. Bordered by Thailand, Cambodia and Vietnam, the **far south** conveniently divides into two sections, dictated primarily by topography, with **Pakse**, the region's most important market town, as the hub. In the west, the **Mekong River** cuts Champasak province roughly in half, while further east, the fertile highlands of the **Bolaven Plateau** separate the Mekong corridor from the rugged Annamite Mountains that form Laos's border with Vietnam.

There are dozens of ancient Khmer temples scattered throughout the lush tropical forests that skirt the Mekong, the most famous of which, **Wat Phou**, is the spiritual centre of the region and the main tourist attraction in southern Laos. An imposing reminder of the Angkorian empire that once dominated much of Southeast Asia, Wat Phou is one of the most impressive Khmer ruins outside Cambodia, and lies a few kilometres from the town of **Champasak**, the former royal seat of the defunct Lao kingdom of the same name.

From here it makes sense to follow the river south until you reach **Si Phan Don** – or "Four Thousand Islands" – where the Mekong's 1993km journey through Laos rushes to a thundering conclusion in a series of picturesque **waterfalls**. As the region's name suggests, there are thousands of sandy islands cluttering the river, many of them home to long-established ethnic Lao villages, but just three – **Don Khong**, **Don Det** and **Don Khon** – have been properly developed for tourists.

Much of the area east of the Mekong lies off the beaten track, with travel here often involving long, bumpy journeys to spots of raw natural beauty. Easier to explore is the **Bolaven Plateau**, just east of Pakse, with its rich agricultural bounty and crashing waterfalls. Historically, the isolation of this region made it an ideal place for insurgents to hide out – from anti-French rebels to the North Vietnamese in the Second Indochina War. The latter transformed trails and roads along Laos's eastern edge into the Ho Chi Minh Trail, which American forces and their allies later subjected to some of the most intensive bombing in history. By braving the primitive transport links between the far-flung villages of Salavan, Xekong and Attapeu, you'll witness the resilience of the land, still home to a diverse variety of wildlife.

Pakse, the region's commercial and transport hub, provides the most convenient **gateway** to the far south, with travellers arriving either from Savannakhet or from Thailand via the Chong Mek border crossing. It's also possible to arrive from Stung Treng in Cambodia by road (see p.251), or from Vientiane by air.

The most pleasant **time of year** to visit the region is during the cool season (Nov–Feb), when the rivers and waterfalls are in full spate and the scenery is at its greenest.

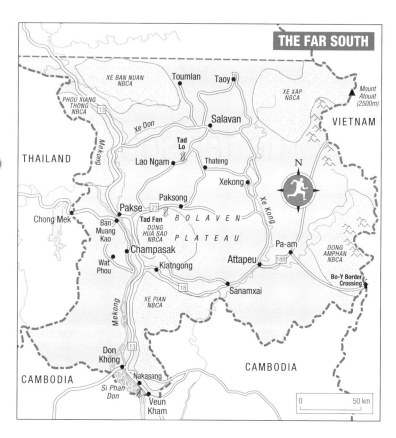

Some history

The **early history** of the far south remains a hot topic of debate among archeologists. Although the ruins of an ancient city buried near Champasak (and not far from Wat Phou) indicate that the area was the centre of a thriving civilization as early as the fifth century, no one seems sure if the town was part of **Champa**, a Hinduized kingdom that ruled parts of central Vietnam for more than fourteen centuries, or the **Chenla** kingdom, which is thought to have been located near the Mekong River in present-day northern Cambodia, extending through what is now southern Laos. The **Khmer** were the first people to leave a clear imprint on the area, and the temple ruins that survive throughout the far south along the Mekong River suggest the region was an important part of the Khmer empire from the eighth to the twelfth century, when the Angkor empire was at its height. It is also thought that the better part of southern Laos was dominated by ethnic Khmer, in particular the **Mon-Khmer ethnic groups** that still inhabit the Bolaven Plateau region and the Annamite Mountains.

The **ethnic Lao** are relative newcomers to the region, having made their way slowly south along the Mekong as Angkor's power, and its hold over present-day southern Laos, waned. By the early sixteenth century, King Phothisalat was spending much of his time in Vientiane and eventually, in 1563, the capital of Lane Xang was shifted from Luang Prabang to Vientiane. While the origins of the first ethnic Lao principality in the Champasak region are unclear, legends trace the roots of the **Lao kingdom of Champasak** back to Nang Pao, a queen said to have ruled during the mid-seventeenth century. The story goes that **Nang Pao** was seduced by a prince from a nearby kingdom and gave birth out of wedlock, initiating a sex scandal for which she has been remembered ever since. The queen supposedly acknowledged her mistake by decreeing that every unwed mother must pay for her sin by sacrificing a buffalo to appease the spirits, a tradition continued into the late 1980s by unwed mothers, known as "Nang Pao's daughters", from some of the ethnic groups in the area. Legend has it that Nang Pao's actual daughter, Nang Peng, ceded rule over the kingdom to a holy man, who in turn sought out **Soi Sisamouth**, a descendant of Souligna Vongsa, the last great king of Lane Xang, and made him king in 1713.

Soi Sisamouth ascended the throne of an independent southern kingdom centred on present-day Champasak, near Wat Phou, and extended its influence to include part of present-day Thailand, as well as Salavan and Attapeu. But the king and his successor only managed to maintain a tenuous independence and, after its capital was captured by Siamese forces in 1778, Champasak was reduced to being a **vassal of Siam**, and so it remained until the French arrived more than one hundred years later, claiming all territory east of the Mekong River.

Caught between French ambition and a still-powerful Siam, Champasak was split in half – a situation which lasted until 1904, when a Franco–Siamese treaty reunited its territories. Following this, Champasak's king, Kam Souk, had to travel to Pakse to swear his allegiance to France.

In 1946, Kam Souk's son, **Prince Boun Oum na Champasak**, renounced his claim to the throne of a sovereign Champasak (in exchange for the title of Inspector General for life) and recognized the king of Luang Prabang as the royal head of a unified Laos, effectively ending the Champasak royal line. When he fled Laos after the communist takeover in the mid-70s, the Prince said the kingdom was doomed from the start because of Nang Pao's misdemeanour: "With an unmarried mother as queen, everything started so badly that the game was lost before it began."

Pakse

Capitalizing on its location at the confluence of the Xe Don and the Mekong rivers, roughly halfway between the Thai border and the fertile Bolaven Plateau, **PAKSE** is the far south's biggest city. For travellers, the place is mostly a convenient stopover en route to Si Phan Don and Wat Phou, though it's also a more comfortable base than Paksong for exploration of the Bolaven Plateau and nearby NBCAs, and the border crossing to Thailand just west at Chong Mek makes Pakse a logical entry or exit point for travellers doing a north–south tour of Laos.

Unlike other major Mekong towns, Pakse is not an old city. Rather it has risen in prominence, from relatively recent beginnings a hundred years ago as a French administrative centre, to being the region's most important market town, attracting traders from Salavan, Attapeu, Xekong and Si Phan Don, as well as from Thailand. The diverse population of Vietnamese, Lao and Chinese today numbers some 70,000.

Arrival and city transport

Pakse is served by an airport, three bus stations, a sawngthaew station, and an all-but-defunct passenger boat landing. **Buses** to and from the north use the **Northern Bus Station**, 7km north of the city on Route 13. Buses to and from

Southern Bus Station (6.5km) ▲

PAKSE

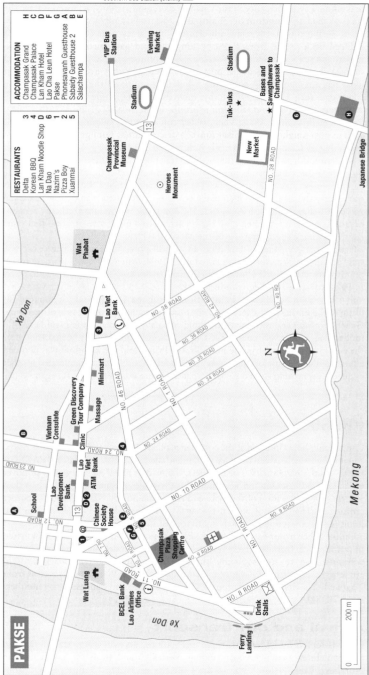

ACCOMMODATION	
Champasak Grand	H
Champasak Palace	C
Lan Kham Hotel	D
Lao Cha Leun Hotel	F
Pakse	G
Phonesavanh Guesthouse	A
Sabaidy Guesthouse 2	B
Salachampa	E

RESTAURANTS	
Delta	3
Korean BBQ	4
Lan Kham Noodle Shop	D
Na Dao	6
Nazim's	1
Pizza Boy	2
Xuanmai	5

Evening Market

'VIP' Bus Station

Stadium

Stadium

Tuk-Tuks ★

★ Buses and Sawngthaews to Champasak

New Market

NO. 38 ROAD

Champasak Provincial Museum

Heroes Monument

Wat Phabat

Xe Don

Lao Viet Bank

NO. 38 ROAD

NO. 42 ROAD

NO. 36 ROAD

NO. 35 ROAD

NO. 34 ROAD

NO. 40 ROAD

Green Discovery Tour Company

Minimart

Massage

NO. 46 ROAD

NO. 1 ROAD

Vietnam Consulate

Clinic

Lao Viet ATM Bank

NO. 24 ROAD

NO. 24 ROAD

NO. 23 ROAD

School

Lao Development Bank

Chinese Society House

NO. 12 ROAD

NO. 10 ROAD

N

Mekong

NO. 9 ROAD

Wat Luang

BCEL Bank

Lao Airlines Office

Champasak Plaza Shopping Centre

NO. 8 ROAD

NO. 9 ROAD

NO. 1 ROAD

NO. 11 ROAD

Drink Stalls

Xe Don

Ferry Landing

Japanese Bridge

200 m

0

points south and east use the **Southern Bus Station**, 8km southeast of town on Route 13 at the big T-junction. Tuk-tuks from either bus station into town cost around 20,000K. The VIP **Bus Station**, just off Route 13 near the stadium, is for buses to Vientiane and Thailand. The **airport** lies 2km northwest of the city on Route 13, and is served by tuk-tuks on hand to greet flights.

Pakse is compact enough to get around on foot, but for getting out to the bus stations or the museum, **tuk-tuks** can be flagged down just about anywhere, especially on **Route 13**, which serves as the town's main boulevard. Expect to pay 5000K for short inner-city journeys.

For **tourist information**, head to the Provincial Tourism Office (Mon–Fri 8am–noon & 1.30–4pm; ☏031/212021) on No. 11 Rd, near the Xe Don River.

Accommodation

Pakse isn't chock-full of cheap hotels, but there's something to choose from in nearly every price bracket, although the **budget hotels** are not particularly good value compared with the north of the country.

Champasak Grand South of the New Market, next to the Japanese Bridge ☏031/255111 ⓦwww.champasakgrand.com. More luxurious than the *Champasak Palace*, with much better amenities and (somehow) cheaper room rates. It's a way out of town, and pretty soulless, but it's hard to argue when you're paying so little for a modern room with spectacular river views, a quality buffet breakfast, and access to the blissfully cool pool. Minibar, a/c & TV. ❺

Champasak Palace Route 13, opposite the Lao Viet Bank ☏031/212263, ☏212781. Though he didn't actually live here, this ninety-room hotel was once a palace built for Prince Boun Oum, who fled to France after the 1975 revolution. Royal-sized rooms lead onto wide terraces with sweeping views of the Xe Don River. Evening meals at the downstairs restaurant are far better than the lousy buffet breakfast. No longer the fanciest place in town, but still the most atmospheric. ❺

Lan Kham Hotel Route 13, 150m east of No. 12 Rd ☏031/213314 ✉lankhamhotel@yahoo.com. A popular hotel above an equally popular noodle bar, offering a range of decent a/c and fan rooms with hot water and TVs. Ask to see the "new" rooms, which are $1 more expensive but well worth the extra, with cosier beds and flat-screen sets. ❷

Lao Cha Leun Hotel No.10 Rd, directly opposite the *Salachampa* ☏031/251333, ☏251138. Boxy but above-average rooms, with kooky

clocks and paintings adorning the walls. Centrally located and reasonable value, if you're not claustrophobic. ❸

Pakse No. 5 Rd, near the shopping centre ☏031/212131 ⓦwww.paksehotel.com. Still the city's best-value hotel, offering spotlessly clean rooms in a central location. This former cinema is expertly managed by Jérôme, a Frenchman, and food served in the panoramic rooftop restaurant is sublime, if a little pricey. "Eco" rooms are cheapest, but you'll have to forgo a view of the city. Bookings advised. ❹

Phonesavanh Guesthouse No. 12 Rd, a block north of Route 13 ☏031/212842. The long-running but uninviting *Phonesavanh Hotel* has a relatively modern annexe which has seven newer rooms at the same low prices. All rooms have en-suite bathrooms, some also have a/c. ❷

Sabaidy Guesthouse 2 No. 24 Rd ☏031/212992. All budget travellers seem to head straight to this guesthouse, sited in an old residential area and hence quieter than the middle of town just across Route 13. Rooms are clean if spartan, and the dorm is the best in town. Dorm 25,000K. ❷

Salachampa No. 10 Rd, near Champasak Plaza ☏031/212273. An elegant restored French villa, with teak floors, breezy verandas and a sitting room filled with antique furniture. All rooms have bathrooms and a/c, but spurn the cheaper modern cottages on offer; rooms in the old building are spacious, with high ceilings. ❹

The Town

Nestling between the Mekong and a bend of the Xe Don, Pakse's centre, where you'll find the market and most of the hotels and restaurants, is surrounded by water on three sides. For some reason the streets in the centre of the city have all been laid out diagonally, but it's such a small place that finding your way around isn't a problem.

Along No. 11 Road, the street that follows the Xe Don, are a few remaining examples of crumbling Franco–Chinese **shophouses** and the town's main temple, **Wat Luang**. Turning away from the river here, you'll soon find yourself by the big new **Champasak Plaza Shopping Centre**, built on the site of the old market that was razed by fire in 1998. In the interim, the market vendors all moved out to a new venue located east along No. 38 Road, known in English as the **New Market**, and there seem to be few takers willing to occupy the overpriced spaces in Champasak Plaza; indeed, the top floors are completely vacant.

For one of the few surviving examples of colonial architecture in the far south, be sure to check out the **Chinese Society House**, on No. 5 Road near *Salachampa*, yet another French-era building. With many of the town's French-influenced buildings in disrepair or already replaced by modern shophouses, the Society House, beautifully renovated in 1998, is an elegant example of a style on the way out in rapidly modernizing Pakse.

Along Route 13

On a low hill just west of Wat Phabat stands the **Champasak Palace Hotel**, a majestic eyesore resembling a giant cement wedding cake, and one of the few prominent reminders of the late Prince Boun Oum na Champasak, a colourful character who was the heir to the Champasak kingdom and one of the most influential southerners of the last century. Legend has it that Boun Oum needed a palace this size so that he could accommodate his many concubines. The palace, left incomplete after the one-time prime minister wound up on the wrong side of history and left for France in the 1970s, was converted into a hotel by Thai investors, who retained its original wooden fittings, tiled pillars and high ceilings. The stucco motifs on the gables depicting the country's post-revolutionary zeal were not in the prince's original plans. **Wat Pha Baht**, just east of the bridge that crosses north over the Xe Don, features a stylized Buddha's footprint, but like the rest of Pakse's monasteries, the architecture doesn't reflect much divine inspiration.

The **Champasak Provincial Museum** (Mon–Fri 8–11.30am & 1.30–4pm; 10,000K), 1500m east of the town centre on Route 13, houses some fine examples of ornately carved pre-Angkorian sandstone **lintels** taken from sites around the province.

The New Market

The huge **New Market** (Talat Dao Heuang) on No. 38 Road is well worth a visit. Along with the usual array of mounds of tobacco, plastic ware and live chickens, specialities available at the market include tea, coffee and a variety of fruit and vegetables, much of this from the bountiful Bolaven Plateau, as well as fish from the islands of Si Phan Don, including gigantic golden carp featherbacks, and the fermented fish paste known as *pa dàek*, sold out of ceramic jars.

Eating and drinking

Pakse has the best range of **restaurants** south of Vientiane, not just because of its size but because of the number of foreigners working here and its mix of ethnic Vietnamese, Chinese and Lao communities. Most of the town's better restaurants are found either on Route 13 between No. 12 and No. 24 roads, or on No. 46 Road just east of No. 24 Road.

Aside from restaurants, there are also a handful of **karaoke lounges** in the town proper, though more peaceful spots for a cold beer are the cheap drink stalls under the shady trees directly above the ferry landing, where you can look out over the Mekong and Xe Don rivers.

Delta Route 13, near the Lane Xang Bank ☎031/5345895. Two separate menus for Asian and Western dishes, and an unusual ordering system where you tot up your own bill before eating. Good pasta and decent Western breakfasts.
Korean BBQ No. 46 Rd, just east of No. 24 Rd. Serving very tasty, inexpensive, barbecued meat fantastic with cold beer.
Lan Kham Noodle Shop Route 13, below the hotel of the same name. This very clean noodle shop is only open at lunchtime, when it's packed.
Na Dao No. 38 Rd, across from the New Market ☎031/255558. The classiest act in town, *Na Dao* serves a delicious range of Viet–French dishes (like Mekong fish with gravy, caramel and ginger) in stylish modern surroundings. Good wine list.

Nazim's Route 13, beneath the *Royal Pakse Hotel* ☎031/254059. Another branch of Laos's most popular Indian restaurant chain, serving affordable meat and veggie curries to roadside tables. Wash down the chillies with an ice-cold mango lassi.
Pizza Boy Route 13, opposite the Lao Development Bank ☎031/255255. Small but ever-popular *falang*-food outlet dishing up excellent yet expensive pizzas that are big enough for two. The shop next door hires motorbikes, bicycles and cars.
Xuanmai Corner of No. 5 and No. 10 Rds ☎031/213245. Hearty fried rice and noodle dishes served up on a wide roadside patio. Popular with booze-swilling Thai and Chinese businessmen, which means it's open later than most places – perfect if you've just stepped off one of the late-night buses.

Listings

Airlines Lao Airlines, No. 11 Rd, near BCEL Bank (Mon–Fri 8–11.30am & 1.30–4.30pm; ☎212140).
Banks and exchange BCEL, No. 11 Rd; Lao Development Bank, Route 13 opposite the *Lan Kham Hotel*; Lao Viet Bank, Route 13, opposite the *Champasak Palace Hotel*.

Consulates Vietnam, on No. 24 Rd (Mon–Fri 8–11am & 2–4.30pm; ☎031/212058).
Hospital South of the shopping centre on No. 9 Rd.
Internet access These come and go; your best bet is to look around the Champasak Plaza Shopping Centre or on Route 13.

Moving on from Pakse

Most towns in the far south are served by daily sawngthaews, which tend to leave Pakse early in the morning – schedules change every few months, so check at the tourist office before setting off. Express vans depart the Southern Bus Station for Attapeu (2–3hr; 65,000K) every afternoon. **Daily sawngthaews** to the three main islands of Si Phan Don (3hr; 30,000K) also leave here between 7am–2.30pm. The trip includes a boat transfer to the island of your choice.

Buses for Savannakhet, Thakhek and Paksan leave the Northern Bus Station each morning. The huge **sawngthaew lot** on the eastern side of the New Market serves local destinations, including Champasak (2hr including a ferry crossing; 20,000K), while the new VIP Bus Station deals with nightly sleeper buses to Vientiane.

Route 13 is now such an easy drive that public boats have stopped running south from Pakse. It may still be possible to get a seat on a private boat heading downstream – ask at the tourist office. The **Lao Airlines** office, next door, is on No. 11 Road (☎031/212252), near BCEL bank.

Crossing the border at Chong Mek

The easiest way to cross the border at Chong Mek (daily 5am–8pm) is to board one of the **VIP buses** bound for Udon Ratchathani (55,000K), which leave Pakse four times a day. A cheaper, slower and more complex option is to take a **sawngthaew** from the New Market to the border (10,000K). After you've crossed into Thailand, local sawngthaews will be waiting to shuttle you to the town of Phibun Mangsahan, where you can transfer to buses to Ubon Ratchathani, which has an airport and plentiful road and rail links. Whichever way you're crossing, Lao and Thai visas are available on arrival at the border.

Post office At the corner of No. 8 and No. 1 rds (daily 8am–4pm).
Telephones International calls and faxes at Lao Telecom, on the corner of No. 1 and No. 38 rds (Mon–Fri 8.30–11.30am & 2–4pm).

Tour agencies Diethelm Travel, No. 21 Rd, north of Route 13 ☎031/212596; Green Discovery, Route 13 ☎031/252908; Pakse Travel Co, Route 13, opposite *Nazim's* ☎031/212842.
Tourist information Provincial Tourism Office, No. 11 Rd, next door to Lao Airlines ☎031/212021.

Around Pakse

As more and more tourists make their way south to Pakse, the number of **day-trip options** has begun to grow. **Ban Saphai**, a silk-weaving village north of the city, offers the chance to see villagers weaving *sin* according to age-old practices, and experience life in a traditional town on the island of **Don Kho** in the middle of the Mekong. In the hills south of the city, the villagers of **Kiatngong** raise elephants, which can be hired for trekking, while nearby **Ban Phapho** presents the opportunity to observe elephants being trained for work in the forest.

From Pakse, daily **sawngthaews** head south to the charming riverside town of **Champasak**, past misty green mountains and riverbanks loaded with palm trees. An up-and-coming backpacker town, Champasak serves as a gateway to **Wat Phou** and other **Khmer ruins**. Although it is easily possible to visit Wat Phou as a day-trip from Pakse, there is plenty of cheap accommodation available in Champasak, and basing yourself here allows you to take in the sights at a leisurely pace. With its old wooden houses, three temples, Khmer ruins, mountains and river-boat trips, plus guesthouses and good food, it's easy to imagine Champasak becoming another Muang Ngoi in no time.

Other sights, such as the coffee plantations and waterfalls of **Bolaven Plateau** (see p.251), can also be taken in on day-trips from Pakse.

Ban Saphai and Don Kho

Sawngthaews leave regularly from the sawngthaew lot near Pakse's New Market to make the 15km trip north to the cluster of villages known locally for their **silk weaving**. Of these, **BAN SAPHAI**, a sizeable village on the left bank of the Mekong River, a few kilometres west of Route 13, has become increasingly popular with tourists keen on seeing women weaving on traditional hand looms, set up in the shade under the family house. Their textiles are sold in one or two shops in the village market, or, if you prefer, you can negotiate with one of the weavers directly, although there's nothing here that you won't find in Pakse. Sawngthaews stop at the market in the centre of town; check to see when they return to Pakse, as transport along the route is rather limited.

The villagers of **DON KHO**, a shady island located directly across the river from Ban Saphai, are also known for their talent at the loom. In fact, you might well opt to head straight here, as the friendliness of the villagers and the meandering dirt paths along the Mekong make for a pleasant visit. You should be able to hire a boat from the riverbank to ferry you across and back (10,000K).

Champasak

Meandering for 4km along the right bank of the Mekong, **CHAMPASAK** is an unassuming town of wooden shophouses and recently paved roads, with a pace so decidedly leisurely that it's difficult to imagine it as the capital of a once bustling kingdom, whose territory stretched from the Annamite Mountains into present-day Thailand. However, when France's Mekong expedition, led by

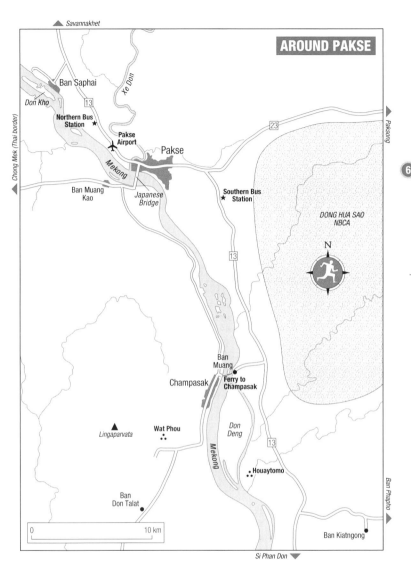

Savannakhet

Ban Saphai

Ye Don

Don Kho

13

Northern Bus
Station

Pakse
Airport

Pakse

Paksong

23

Chong Mek (Thai border)

Mekong

Ban Muang
Kao

Japanese
Bridge

Southern Bus
Station

DONG HUA SAO
NBCA

N

13

Ban
Muang

Ferry to
Champasak

Champasak

Lingaparvata

Wat Phou

Don
Deng

Mekong

13

Houaytomo

Ban
Don Talat

Ban Phapho

0   10 km

Ban Kiatngong

Si Phan Don

Doudart de Lagrée and Francis Garnier, arrived in 1866, they found it to be the most important city in the south, a status later usurped by Pakse when it became a French administrative centre.

These days, the quiet cluster of ten villages that constitutes Champasak makes Pakse seem like a pulsing metropolis. On the main road, downstream from what is probably the least-used roundabout in Laos, two elegant **French mansions**, tanned a pale yellow by the tropical sun, stand out from the traditional wooden shophouses. The first mansion belonged to the former **palace of Prince Boun Oum na Champasak**. Although in 1946 he renounced claims to sovereignty over the former kingdom of Champasak, Boun Oum retained his royal title and continued to perform his ritual duties as a Buddhist monarch until he fled the country prior to the Pathet Lao takeover; he died in France in 1980. During Lao New Year, Boun Oum performed purification rites at the town's temples to expel evil spirits, and on the final day of celebrations he would preside over ceremonies at this palace, in which a *maw thiam*, or medium, called the spirits of Champasak's past rulers, and a *basi* ceremony was held. Since the advent of the new government, however, the pageantry has been abandoned and New Year ceremonies in this former royal seat have become a strictly family affair.

As is the case with the nagas in front of Boun Oum's house, which were taken from Wat Phou, the area's most exquisite **pre-Angkorian relics** wound up in the late prince's private collection, some of which is now on display at Wat Phou's small museum.

Practicalities

Buses and **sawngthaews** (20,000K from Pakse) should let you off at Champasak's tiny roundabout, where you'll find almost everything you need, including a **post office** (open until 9pm weekdays for phone calls), and a tiny **bank**, which can exchange cash and travellers' cheques. The wooden **tourist office** ☏020/2206215 has a few useful maps and handouts. The **ferry dock** is about 2km north of here; **tuk-tuks** wait at the boat landing. Sawngthaews may drop you at the *Anouxa Hotel*, 1km north of the roundabout, claiming you're in the centre of town. It's a peaceful enough location, but the bungalows here are overpriced.

There are two proper hotels in town: *Siamphone* (④), a huge apricot-coloured eyesore near the roundabout featuring basic, air-conditioned rooms with hot water and TV; and the boutique-style *Inthira* (⑤), which has luxurious Lao-style rooms and suites. The most popular **guesthouse** is *Vongpasit* (②), 2km south of the roundabout, which has en-suite bungalows and a restaurant with a nice deck overlooking the Mekong. Just south of the roundabout, *Kham Phou* (①) has roomy doubles and triples and wooden en-suite bungalows in the garden. Fifty metres south, the *Souchittra Guesthouse* (①) has above-average rooms in another old wooden house with a shared bathroom, plus self-contained bungalows on the lawn overlooking the Mekong. *Dok Champa Guesthouse*, on the roundabout, offers the best selection of **Lao dishes** in town and also rents bicycles, as do most of the guesthouses.

Moving on, three Pakse-bound buses pass by Champasak each morning on Route 13; (2hr; 20,000K); to catch one you'll need to board a ferry to Ban Muang (7000K) and then take a tuk-tuk to the main road. For **bus connections** to Si Phan Don, cross the river to Ban Muang (ferries leave when full), get a lift up to Route 13 and wait for a bus heading south.

Wat Phou

One of the most evocative Khmer ruins outside Cambodia's borders, **Wat Phou** (daily 8.30am–4.30pm; 30,000K), 8km southwest of Champasak, should be at the top of your southern Laos must-see list. It's not hard to see why the lush river valley here, dominated by an imposing 1500m-tall mountain, has been considered prime real estate for nearly two thousand years by a variety of peoples, in particular the Khmer. The surrounding forests are rich with wildlife, including the rare Asiatic black bear. The pristine state of the environment – it is without question one of the most scenic landscapes chosen by the Khmer for any of their temples – was a major factor in UNESCO's decision to name the area a World Heritage site.

The legacy of the Angkorian empire

In the mid-nineteenth century, French explorers began stumbling across the **monumental ruins** of a centuries-dead empire that had once blanketed mainland Southeast Asia. When word of these jungle-clad "lost cities" reached Europe, the intrigued populace assumed they must have been the work of expatriate Romans or perhaps some far-wandering tribe of Israelites. But as French exploration and colonization of Indochina expanded, scholars began to acknowledge they were the work of a highly sophisticated Southeast Asian culture.

The Khmer, whose descendants inhabit **Cambodia** today, controlled a vast empire that stretched north to Vientiane in Laos and as far west as the present-day border of Thailand and Burma. From its capital, located at Angkor in what is now northwestern Cambodia, a long line of kings reigned with absolute authority, each striving to build a monument to his own greatness which would outdo all previous monarchs. With cultural trappings inherited from earlier Khmer kingdoms, which in turn had borrowed heavily from Indian merchants that once dominated trade throughout Southeast Asia, the Khmer rulers at Angkor venerated deities from the **Hindu** and **Buddhist** pantheons. Eventually, a new and uniquely Khmer cult was born, the *devaraja* or god-king, which propagated the belief that a Khmer king was actually an incarnation of a certain Hindu deity on earth. Most of the Khmer kings of Angkor identified with the god Shiva, although Suryavarman II, builder of **Angkor Wat**, the most magnificent of all Khmer monuments, fancied himself an earthly incarnation of Vishnu.

In 1177, around 27 years after the death of Suryavarman II, armies from the rival kingdom of Champa took advantage of political instability and sacked Angkor, leaving the empire in disarray. After some years of chaos, **Jayavarman VII** took control of the leaderless Khmer people, embracing Mahayana Buddhism and expanding his empire to include much of present-day Thailand, Vietnam and Laos. But the days of Khmer glory were numbered. Soon after the death of Jayavarman VII the empire began to decline and by 1432 was so weak that the **Siamese**, who had previously served as mercenaries for the Khmer in their campaigns against Champa, were also able to give Angkor a thorough sacking. The Siamese pillaged the great stone temples of the Angkorian god-kings and force-marched members of the royal Khmer court, including the king's personal retinue of classical dancers, musicians, artisans and astrologers, back to Ayutthaya, then the capital of Siam. To this day, much of what Thais perceive as Thai culture, from the sinuous moves of classical dancers to the flowery language of the royal Thai court, was actually acquired from the Khmer. When the Angkorian empire collapsed, Siam moved in to fill the power vacuum and much of the Khmer culture absorbed by the Siamese was passed on to the Lao.

Wat Phou ("Mountain Monastery" in Lao) is actually a series of ruined temples and shrines dating from the sixth to the twelfth centuries. Although the site is now associated with Theravada Buddhism, sandstone reliefs indicate that the ruins were once a **Hindu place of worship**. When viewed from the Mekong, it's clear why the site was chosen. A phallic stone outcropping, easily seen among the range's line of forested peaks, would have made the site especially auspicious to worshippers of Shiva, a Hindu god that is often symbolized by a phallus.

Archeologists tend to disagree on who the original founders of the site were and when it was first consecrated. The oldest parts of the ruins are thought to date back to the sixth century and were most likely built by the **ancient Khmer**, although some experts claim to see a connection to Champa. Whatever the case, the site is still considered highly sacred to the ethnic Lao who inhabit the region today, and is the focus of a **festival** in February, attracting thousands of Lao and Thai pilgrims annually.

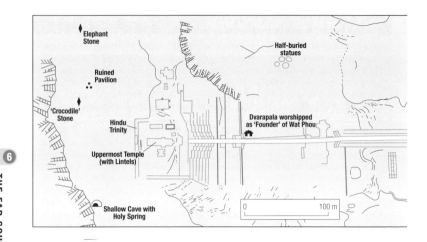

Tuk-tuks can be hired in Champasak for the 8km journey to Wat Phou. Drivers charge 10,000K per passenger, or 80,000K for the vehicle, and wait for you while you visit the ruins. If you're on your own and can't find anyone to share a ride with, hire a bike from town (10,000K) – it's a flat, pleasant ride.

The site

At the entrance to the site, a small **museum** houses pieces of sculpture found among the ruins as well as some said to have belonged to Prince Boun Oum. The **stone causeway** leading up to the first set of ruins was once lined with low stone pillars, the tips of which were formed into a stylized lotus bud. On either side of the causeway there would have been reservoirs known in Khmer as *baray*. As ancient Khmer architecture is rich in symbols, it is surmised that these pools represented the oceans that surrounded the mythical Mount Meru, home of the gods of the Hindu pantheon.

Just beyond the causeway, on either side of the path, two megalithic structures of sandstone and laterite mirror each other. According to local lore, they are segregated **palaces**, one for men and the other for women. Archeologists are sceptical though, pointing out that stone was reserved for constructing places of worship, and, even if this hadn't been the case, the vast interiors of both buildings were roofless and would have afforded little shelter. The structure on the right as you approach is the best preserved. Its carved relief of Shiva and his consort Uma riding the sacred bull Nandi is the best to be found on either building.

As the path begins to climb, you come upon jagged stairways of sandstone blocks. Plumeria (frangipani) trees line the way, giving welcome shade and littering the worn stones with delicate blooms known in Lao as *dok champa*, the national flower of Laos. At the foot of the second stairway is a shrine to the legendary founder of Wat Phou. The statue is much venerated and, during the annual pilgrimage, is bedecked with offerings of flowers, incense and candles. When and why this one statue has come to be venerated in such a fashion is unknown, and once again, local folklore and archeological record diverge.

Continuing up the stairs, you come upon the final set of ruins, surrounded by mammoth mango trees. This uppermost temple contains the finest examples of **decorative stone lintels** (see box, p.241) in Laos. Although much has been damaged or is missing, sketches done by Georges Traipont, a French surveyor who visited the temple complex in the waning years of the nineteenth century, show

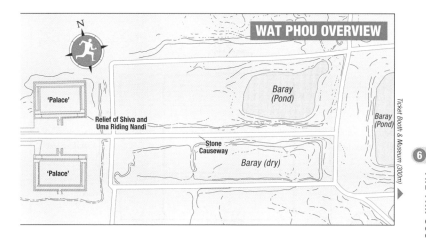

WAT PHOU OVERVIEW

N

'Palace'

Relief of Shiva and
Uma Riding Nandi

'Palace'

Baray
(Pond)

Stone
Causeway

Baray (dry)

Baray
(Pond)

the temple to have changed little since then. On the exterior walls flanking the east entrance are the images of *dvarapalas* and *devatas*, or female divinities, in high relief. On the altar, inside the sanctuary, stand **four Buddha images**, looking like a congress of benevolent space aliens. Doorways on each side of them lead to an empty room with walls of brick; it is thought that these walls constitute the oldest structure on the site, dating back to the sixth century.

To the right of the temple is a Lao Buddha of comparatively modern vintage, and just behind the temple is a relief carved into a half-buried slab of stone, depicting the Hindu trinity – a multi-armed, multi-headed Shiva (standing) is flanked by Brahma (left) and Vishnu (right). Continuing up the hill behind the temple, you'll come to a **shallow cave**, the floor of which is muddy from the constant drip of water that collects on its ceiling. This water is considered highly sacred, as it has trickled down from the peak of Lingaparvata. In former times, a

▲ Wat Phou

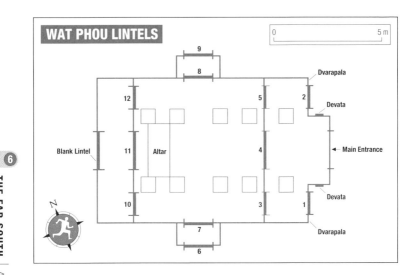

WAT PHOU LINTELS

0   5 m

9
8
Dvarapala
12   5   2
Devata
Blank Lintel   11   Altar   4   ← Main Entrance
Devata
10   3   1
Dvarapala
7
6

N

system of stone pipes directed the run-off to the temple, where it bathed the enshrined Shivalinga. By tradition, this water was utilized in ceremonies for the coronation of Khmer kings and later the kings of Siam. Even today, Lao pilgrims will dip their fingers into a cistern located in the cave and ritually anoint themselves, although this is something foreign visitors should respectfully avoid.

If you follow the base of the cliff in a northerly direction, a bit of sleuthing will lead you to the enigmatic **crocodile stone**, which may have been used as an altar for pre-Angkor-period human sacrifices, though there is no hard evidence that ritual sacrifice was a part of the ceremonies that took place here. Nearby is a pile of sandstone rubble that once formed a pavilion and is thought by archeologists to be one of the oldest structures on the site. A few metres away to the north is the **elephant stone**, a huge, moss-covered boulder carved with the face of an elephant. This carving is relatively recent, probably dating from the nineteenth century.

If you were to hike straight up the mountain to the **summit of Lingaparvata**, it would take two days of rigorous climbing over vertical cliff faces and dense forest. In 1997, an Italian team of archeologists did just that. On the very tip of the natural phallic outcropping that is the peak of the mountain, they discovered a small Shivalinga of carved stone. Sadly, the archeologists found it necessary to remove this artefact that had crowned the sacred mountain for untold centuries, catching raindrops that would eventually filter down to the cave of lustral waters at the foot of the mountain. The trophy now rests in the small museum at the entrance to Wat Phou.

Hong Nang Sida Temple

Situated about 1km south of Wat Phou, **Hong Nang Sida** is a small twelfth-century Khmer temple, built on an ancient thoroughfare that once stretched from Wat Phou to Angkor Wat. The trail leading south to the temple from Wat Phou through the rice paddies is easy to locate during the dry season, but you may have to ask the guards at the entrance to Wat Phou for directions once the rains have started and the trail becomes obscured by weeds. This little-visited ruin can be taken in in just a few minutes: the dimensions of Hong Nang Sida are modest compared to those of Wat Phou, and very few of the sandstone blocks from which

The importance of the **decorative lintel** in Khmer art cannot be overstated. Here, more than anywhere else, Khmer artisans were free to display their superb stone-carving skills. Their imaginative depictions of deities, divinities, characters and events from Hindu and Buddhist mythology are recognized as some of the most exquisite art ever created. Early examples date from the seventh century, and as the styles and motifs have evolved over the centuries, experts are able to date lintels by comparing them to known works. The lintels at Wat Phou are listed below; the numbers correspond to those on the map below.

1 The god Krishna defeats the naga Kaliya In this story from the Bhagavad Purana, Krishna defeats Kaliya, a menacing water serpent that has been terrorizing villagers.

2 The god Vishnu riding the bird-man Garuda Although Vishnu on Garuda was a common theme in Khmer art, images of the two were rarely depicted on lintels.

3 Indra riding Airavata Despite being a Hindu god, Indra holds a significant place in Theravada Buddhist mythology. Until the Lao revolution Airavata, **the three-headed elephant,** was the official symbol of the Lao monarchy.

4 Indra on Airavata A larger and more detailed depiction of #3.

5 Deity atop Kala Although this deity is very commonly depicted on lintels, it is uncertain just who it is supposed to be. As the deity is holding a mace and sitting in the "royal ease" pose, perhaps it depicts a generic king or ruler.

6 Deity atop Kala (see #5) On the portico above the lintel is what is left of a scene from the Churning of the Sea of Milk myth, a contest between gods and demons for possession of the elixir of immortality. This scene is depicted most spectacularly on the bas-reliefs at Angkor Wat in Cambodia.

7 Krishna killing Kamsa From the Bhagavad Purana, a gruesome depiction of Krishna tearing his uncle in half. According to this myth, it was foretold that King Kamsa's death would come at the hands of one of his own family members. This prophecy launched the king on an orgy of killing which was only halted when his nephew put him to death.

8 Deity atop Kala (see #5)

9 Deity atop Kala (see #5) On the ruined portico above this lintel are the remains of a depiction of the god Vishnu in his incarnation as Narayana, reclining in cosmic slumber as he floats atop a naga on the waters of a vast primordial ocean.

10 Shiva as a rishi atop Kala Shiva is depicted as a wandering ascetic, perched above Kala.

11 Deity atop Kala (see #5) This lintel has been badly damaged, possibly by looters trying to remove part of the sculpture for the thriving stolen-antiquities trade in Thailand.

12 Deity atop Kala (see #5)

it was constructed are adorned with carvings. Still, as with Wat Phou, the warm light on the venerable stone walls is particularly magical during sunrise and sunset.

Houaytomo Temple

If your thirst for Khmer temples has yet to be quenched, a visit to **Houaytomo**, a tenth-century temple, is an option. Best visited as a day-trip from Champasak, the ruin is set in the midst of a lush forest on the banks of a stream, for which it is named. Also known by various other names, including Oum Muang, the temple is thought to have been dedicated to the consort of Shiva in her form as Rudani, and was "discovered" by Frenchman Etienne Edmond Lunet de Lajonquière early in the twentieth century.

The best way to reach Houaytomo is to hire a **pirogue** in Champasak (2hr; around $10) to zip you south along the river.

Kiatngong, Phou Asa and Ban Phapho

Located approximately 50km southeast of Pakse, **KIATNGONG** is one of several villages in the area whose inhabitants keep **elephants**. In recent years, it's become possible for tourists to hire out elephants for treks up nearby **Phou Asa**, a jungle-clad hill with some mysterious ruins atop its summit. Phou Asa is thought to date back to the nineteenth century, and the site's layout suggests it was possibly used as a fort, though archeologists admit that the crudely stacked stone walls and pillars are an enigma. Local villagers, believing the ruins to be the remains of an ancient Buddhist monastery, periodically make pilgrimages to the site to leave offerings at a "Buddha's footprint" carved into a low cliff below the ruins. From the summit, commanding views of the surrounding dense jungle, rice fields and villages lend credence to the fort hypothesis.

Elephants have been traditionally used by the people of Kiatngong to haul timber and rice. Villages located far in the interior used to hire Kiatngong's elephants and mahouts to carry their rice harvest to main roads, where it could be transferred to trucks. Recently, though, new roads have made this mode of transport obsolete and mahouts have begun selling off their elephants. The last time villagers organized a hunt to round up wild elephants was in 1988, and many are turning to water buffalo as a more practical beast of burden. A steady stream of potential elephant trekkers, however, will ensure that at least for the time being, villagers here will continue to keep elephants as their ancestors did for centuries.

The **best way to get here** is by your own transport: travel agents in Pakse (see p.234) rent out vans and pick-ups, charging around $50 for the round trip, but it's much cheaper to hire a sawngthaew from the New Market to Kiatngong. Once in Kiatngong, you'll find elephant hire costs about $10 for a trek that takes in Phou Asa and the ruins on its summit. The best time to come is at dusk, when spectacular sunsets can be enjoyed from the top of the hill. It's also possible to get here by bus from Pakse in less than two hours, but you may have to flag down a passing bus or sawngthaew to return to Pakse at the end of the day. Some wooden cottages have been built for tour groups that sometimes overnight in the village, and it is usually possible to stay here – just contact the village headman.

Another elephant village, **Ban Phapho**, is involved in the training of elephants for the timber trade. As in Kiatngong, elephant trekking can be arranged at the village, located some 20km from Kiatngong, although Ban Phapho lacks the picturesque ruins and views that make Kiatngong the more popular destination, though it does have a very basic **guesthouse** here with shared facilities. Both villages can be visited in one day if you charter a vehicle from Pakse.

Xe Pian NBCA

Just southeast of Houaytomo and running the entire length of Route 13 all the way to Si Phan Don is the **Xe Pian NBCA**, roughly triangular in shape and bounded by Route 18 to the north. Although many tourists travel right alongside it for almost 150km en route to Don Khong, few are aware they are right next to Laos's southernmost NBCA and one of the country's largest (2665 square kilometres) nature reserves. The terrain here is mostly plains, although there are mixed deciduous forests and several peaks between 300m and 800m. In the east, the **Xe Kong** flows into Cambodia through the park, and tigers, elephants, leopards and **rhinoceros** may survive here. The best way to visit the NBCA is from Pakse, where tour companies can organize four-wheel-drive trips through the north of the park.

Si Phan Don

In Laos's deepest south, just above the border with Cambodia, the muddy stream of the Mekong is shattered into a 14km-wide web of rivulets, creating a landlocked archipelago. Known as **Si Phan Don**, or Four Thousand Islands, this labyrinth of islets, rocks and sandbars has acted as a kind of bell jar, preserving traditional southern lowland Lao culture from outside influences. Island villages were largely unaffected by the French or American wars, and the islanders' customs and folk ways have been passed down uninterrupted since ancient times. As might be expected, the Mekong River plays a vital role in the lives of local inhabitants, with

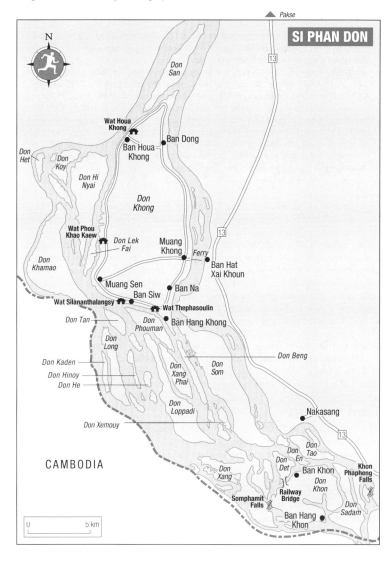

6

Naga and ngeuak: water serpents of Lao legend

The origins of the **naga** are debated. Snake cults are thought to have existed in Southeast Asia long before the arrival of Buddhism in the region, particularly in Cambodia, so it is possible that this snake-like icon is indigenous. Another possibility is that the naga is a cultural migrant from Hindu India. In Hindu mythology, the naga, Sanskrit for serpent, is sometimes associated with the god Vishnu in his incarnation as Narayana, a cosmic dreamer reclining on the body of a giant naga and floating on an endless sea. Buddhism adopted the icon, and a story relates how, while meditating, the historic Buddha was sheltered by a seven-headed naga during a violent rainstorm. In Laos, it is probable that the present-day form of the naga, called nak or phayanak in Lao, is a fusion of both indigenous and imported beliefs.

The naga is both a symbol of water and its life-giving properties, and a protector of the Lao people. An old legend is still related of how a naga residing in a hole below Vientiane's That Dam stupa was known to rise up at critical moments and unleash itself upon foreign invaders. While the naga is mainly a benign figure, a similar water serpent, the **ngeuak**, is especially feared by Lao fishermen. Believed to devour the flesh of drowning victims, ngeuak are said to infest the waters around Si Phan Don. As for the existence of naga in modern-day Laos, the Lao point to "proof" that can be seen in a photograph displayed in some homes, eateries and places of business. The photo shows a line of American soldiers displaying a freshly caught deep-sea fish that is several metres long; some copies of the photograph have the Lao words nang phayanak (Lady Naga) printed below. Where and when the photo was taken is a mystery, but many Lao believe that the photo depicts a naga captured in the Mekong by American soldiers during the Second Indochina War.

95 percent of island families fishing for a living. Ecological awareness among locals is high, with nearly half of the villages in the district participating in voluntary fisheries conservation programmes.

The archipelago is also home to rare wetland flora and fauna, including an endangered species of freshwater **dolphin**, which it's sometimes possible to glimpse during the dry season. Southeast Asia's largest – and what many consider to be most spectacular – waterfalls are also located here. The area's biggest sightseeing attractions, the **Khon Phapheng** and **Somphamit** waterfalls, dashed nineteenth-century French hopes of using the Mekong as a trade artery into China. The remnants of a French-built railroad, constructed to carry passengers and cargo past these roaring obstacles, can still be seen on the islands of **Don Khon** and **Don Det**, along with a rusting locomotive and other ghosts of the French presence. The most developed place to base yourself is the popular island of **Don Khong**, with its collection of quaint villages and ancient temples, but there's also plenty of accommodation on Don Khon and Don Det.

Don Khong

The largest of the Four Thousand Islands group, **DON KHONG** draws a steady stream of visitors, most of whom use it as a base to explore other attractions in Si Phan Don. That said, it's nowhere near as popular as Don Det and Don Khon, further south, which means it's far easier to find a peaceful place to watch the sunset.

Don Khong is surprisingly wide for a river island, and is known locally for its venerable collection of **Buddhist temples**, some with visible signs of a history stretching back to the sixth or seventh century. These, together with the island's good-value accommodation and interesting cuisine, based on fresh fish from the

Mekong, make Don Khong the perfect place for indulging both adventurous and lazy moods.

Don Khong has only three settlements of any size, the port town of **Muang Sen** on the island's west coast, the east-coast town of **MUANG KHONG**, where most of the accommodation and cafés are situated (see the map below), and the smaller town of **Ban Houa Khong**, where slow boats from Pakse moor. Like all Si Phan Don settlements, both Muang Sen's and Muang Khong's homes and shops cling to the bank of the Mekong for kilometres, but barely penetrate the interior, which is primarily reserved for rice fields. The best way to explore Don Khong and experience the traditional sights and sounds of riverside living is to rent a **bicycle** from one of the guesthouses and set off along the road that circles the island. Don Khong's flat terrain and almost complete absence of motor vehicles make for ideal cycling conditions. For touring, the island can be neatly divided into **two loops**, southern and northern, each beginning at Muang Khong, or done all in one big loop that takes about three hours without stops.

Arrival and information

A total of six public **buses to Don Khong** (30,000K) leave from Pakse's Southern Bus Station daily, stopping at Ban Hat Xai Khoun to cross the Mekong by boat. Much faster are the **minibuses** operated by tour companies in Pakse (60,000K) and Champasak (50,000K), but look out for the pirogue drivers who meet buses at the riverbank; plenty of travellers have handed them all-inclusive bus and boat tickets, only to be told they have to pay an extra 10,000K for the crossing once they reach Muang Khong.

In Muang Khong you'll find the island's only **post office**, just south of the bridge across the creek, and further south, near the colonial mansion, a small Agricultural Promotion Bank where you can exchange money. **Internet** and **telephone services** are offered by a handful of guesthouses along the main drag. Several of the guesthouses and shops here offer **bicycles** for rent; *Pon's River Guesthouse* also rents out **motorbikes**.

ACCOMMODATION
Auberge Sala Done Khong	E
Done Khong Guesthouse	D
Mali Guesthouse	F
Pon Arena Hotel	B
Pon's River Guesthouse	C
Souksan	A

MUANG KHONG TOWN

Accommodation

Most of the island's accommodation is concentrated in Muang Khong. Over in Muang Sen there are only a few guesthouses, including *Say Khong* (❷), directly above the ferry landing, with spacious doubles and triples with fans and a balcony; and *Muong Sene Guest House* (❶), situated a little further east, on the road to Muang Khong – but Muang Khong has much better eating options. All the below are in Muang Khong.

Auberge Sala Done Khong 100m south of the ferry landing ☎031/212077 ⊛www.salalao.com. A nicely restored French-era villa with a/c and hot water, catering largely to package-tour clientele. Atmospheric, but the warped floors and lack of natural light conspire to make it feel like the crooked house at a theme park. ❺

Done Khong Guesthouse Adjacent to the ferry landing ☎031/214010. This long-established place has basic but rather grubby rooms with shared facilities, a popular restaurant and very friendly staff who speak both English and French. ❷

Mali Guesthouse 250m south of the ferry landing ☎030/5346621 ⓔathalo@netzero.com. Quaint double and twin rooms in a colonial-style house that's separated from the riverfront by a well-kept garden. TV, a/c and a tiny shared plunge pool, which may or may not be finished by the time you read this. ❹

Pon Arena Hotel 50m north of *Pon's River Guesthouse*, around the corner ☎031/253065 ⓔpon_arena@hotmail.com. Muang Khong's most comfortable hotel by a country mile, featuring a range of luxurious, modern rooms. Bathrooms have big tubs, free toiletries and stylishly tiled walls. Breakfast, served on a lofty terrace overlooking the river, is included in the rate. Visa accepted. wi-fi available. ❻

Pon's River Guesthouse 150m north of the ferry landing. A great place to stay, offering a range of tidy rooms in a wooden house with private or shared facilities, hot water and a very popular restaurant downstairs. TV and a/c are available as extras. The English-speaking owner, Mr Pon, is more than happy to answer questions about Si Phan Don and can arrange a variety of tours. ❷

Souksan 300m north of the ferry landing ☎031/212071. The best rooms in this Lao Chinese-owned establishment offer unmatched value. The fan rooms furthest from the river, in a garden full of birdsong, have spotlessly clean private bathrooms. Ask to see a few bedrooms before settling in for the night. ❷

Southern loop

The chain of picturesque villages that line the south coast makes the **southern loop**, roughly 20km long, the more popular of the two itineraries. Follow the river road south from Muang Khong (taking care to stick to the narrow path along the river, not the road that parallels it slightly inland) until, a couple of kilometres south, you reach the village of **Ban Na**, where the real scenery begins. Navigating the trail as it snakes between thickets of bamboo, you'll pass traditional southern Lao wooden houses trimmed with painted highlights of white and royal blue.

Near the tail of the island the path forks. A veer to the left will lead you to the tiny village of **Ban Hang Khong** and a dead end; keeping to the right will put you at the gates of **Wat Thephasoulin**, parts of which were constructed in 1883. The *sala* and monks' quarters, composed of teak-plank walls and terracotta tile roofs, arc particularly pleasing to the eye, making this a good place for a breather and a swig on the water bottle. From here the path soon skirts the edge of a high riverbank, at intervals opening up views of the muddy Mekong flowing sluggishly southwards. The dense canopy of foliage overhead provides welcome shade as you pass through **Ban Siw** – the bamboo-and-thatch drink shops that line this section of the path are a good place to linger while enjoying a rejuvenating sip of coconut juice. Worth a look is the village monastery, **Wat Silananthalangsy**; the recently restored *sim* lacks charm, but a school building at the back of the compound has been left in a wonderfully decrepit state. This is often the case in Laos, as Buddhist laymen believe that much more merit is acquired by donating money towards the restoration of a structure that shelters Buddha images than by rebuilding a mere school for novice monks.

As you continue on from here, the path widens at the approach to Muang Sen, Don Khong's sleepy port. While there is nothing to see, it's a recommended stop for rest and refreshment before heading east via the shade-stingy 8km stretch of road that leads back to Muang Khong.

Northern loop

The long, sometimes shadeless, route of the **northern loop** rewards handsomely with access to what is certainly one of southern Laos's most idyllic spots. The total distance of approximately 35km is probably best covered by **motorbike**; in the hot season, industrial-strength sunblock and a wide-brimmed hat are a must.

Starting from Muang Khong, you begin by heading due west on the road that bisects the island. During the hot season the plain of fallow rice paddies that makes up much of the island's interior looks and feels like a stretch of the Kalahari. After the rains break and rice paddies are planted, the scenery is actually quite beautiful.

Just before **Muang Sen**, turn right at the crossroads and head north; follow this road up and over a low gradient and after about 4km you'll cross a bridge. Keep going another 1500m and you'll notice large black boulders beginning to appear off to the left. Keeping your eyes left, you'll see a narrow trail that leads up to a ridge of the same black stone. Park your bike at the foot of the ridge, and, following the trail up another 200m to the right, you'll spot a cluster of monks' quarters constructed of weathered teak. These structures belong to **Wat Phou Khao Kaew**, an evocative little forest monastery situated atop a river-sculpted stone bluff overlooking the Mekong. The centrepiece is a crumbling **brick stupa** crowned with a clump of grass; a fractured pre-Angkorian stone lintel sits at the base of the stupa and, assuming it was once fixed to it, would date the structure to the middle of the seventh century.

Nearby sits a charming miniature *sim*, flanked by plumeria trees. A curious collection of carved wooden deities, which somehow found their way downriver from Burma, decorates the ledges running around the building. If you want to have a look at the inside of the *sim*, ask one of the resident monks to unlock the door for you, or you can peer through the windows on either side of the main entrance, which faces the river.

If, after a look round Wat Phou Khao Kaew, you're still feeling energetic, continue another 6km north to **Ban Houa Khong**, on the outskirts of which stands the modest **residence of Khamtay Siphandone**, former revolutionary and ex-prime minister. Not far away is a **monastery** that has been restored to reflect the status of the village's most important part-time inhabitant. The wat is not all that remarkable, except perhaps for the collection of artefacts in the main temple. Sharing the altar with rows of Buddha images is a gargoyle-like object, actually a *somasutra* from an ancient Khmer temple, used to channel lustral water onto an enshrined Shivalinga. Next to the altar is a display case filled with small Buddha images and other dusty relics.

Pushing on from Ban Houa Khong, follow the road east to Ban Dong and then south to Muang Khong, a journey totalling 13km. On arriving at the northern outskirts of Muang Khong, just before reaching the high school, you pass a trail bordered with white stones, which leads to **Tham Phou Khiaw**, or Green Mountain Cave. Although it has gained quite a reputation among travellers, based no doubt on the obscurity of its location, the cave is no Lost City of Gold: in reality, it's a shallow grotto sheltering one termite-riddled Buddha and a number of clay pots containing crude votive tablets, each with an image of the Buddha pressed into it. Unless you're here during the Lao New Year celebrations, when islanders visit the site to make offerings and ritually bathe the images, or the Bun Bang Fai festival, a month later, when bamboo skyrockets are launched in a rain-making ritual, it's not really worth the effort.

Eating

All of Don Khong's guesthouses serve food, and, as you might expect, **fish** is the island's staple. The islanders have dozens of recipes, all worthy of a place on your plate – from the traditional **làp pa** (a Lao-style salad of minced fish mixed with garlic, chillies, shallots and fish sauce) to fish steamed in coconut milk – but whatever you do, be sure to try the island speciality, **mók pa**. Steamed in banana leaves, this sublime fish dish has the consistency of custard and takes an hour to prepare.

For this and just about anything else, *Pon's River Guesthouse* stands out as having the best **restaurant** in Muang Khong. If it's Chinese food and a perfect river view you're after, head for the restaurant at the *Souksan*, which stands on stilts above the Mekong. *Done Khong Guesthouse*, once the only place to eat in town, remains popular and its banana crepes are divine. Most restaurants and guesthouses rustle up tasty Western breakfasts.

The people of Si Phan Don are very proud of their *lào-láo*, which has gained a reputation nationally as one of the best **rice whiskies** in Laos. For those who haven't taken a liking to Lao white lightning, you're in luck: Muang Khong has devised a gentler blend known as the "Lao cocktail", a mix of wild honey and *lào-láo* served over ice with a dash of lime.

Moving on

The chances of getting on a **public bus to Pakse** are pretty slim, but if you want to chance your arm, cross the river by pirogue and wait for one to pass by on Route 13. An easier and more reliable option is to arrange a ride through *Mr Pon's Restaurant* (2hr 30min; 70,000K) – boats leave the ferry landing near the restaurant at 11.30am each morning and the subsequent bus ride includes a drop-off at your hotel.

Don Khon and Don Det

Tropical islands in the classic sense, **DON KHON** and **DON DET** are fringed with swaying coconut palms and inhabited by easy-going, sarong-clad villagers. Located south of Don Khong, the islands are especially stunning during the rainy season when rice paddies in the interior have been ploughed and planted in soothing hues of jade and emerald. Besides being a picturesque little haven to while away a few days, the islands, linked by a bridge, provide opportunities for some leisurely trekking, cycling and tubing. As yet, there only a handful of motor vehicles on the islands, making them one of the precious few places in Southeast Asia not harried by the growl and whine of motorbikes. There is, however, a fee of 20,000K (payable at the bridge) to cross between the islands, but this includes access to the waterfalls.

Arrival and getting around

It is possible to do both Don Khon and Don Det plus the waterfall at Khon Phapheng as a **day-trip** from Don Khong, although Don Khon alone is worth a few days' visit. Muang Khong's guesthouses and restaurants offer boat trips (60,000K\person) that take you to see the waterfalls and the defunct railroad. The boat can't go directly to Khon Phapheng Falls, so the boatman will take you to the right bank and wait there while a sawngthaew collects you and takes you on the 30km round-trip to the falls (admission 10,000K).

The cheapest option for **getting to the islands** independently from Muang Khong is to take the ferry (10,000K) across the river to Ban Hat Xai Khoun and then get a bus to **Nakasang**, where you can get a boat to Don Khon or Don Det (15,000K). The boats depart from the landing, a short walk from the market. It's possible to join a Don Khon day-trip and negotiate a one-way, discounted price – expect to pay about 40,000K.

Accommodation and eating

Although Don Khon was the first island to take off with backpackers, Don Det has now surpassed its larger neighbour in popularity, and is already beginning to take on a distinctly Vang Vieng feel. There's not a huge difference in **accommodation** on the two islands, and where you stay is largely a matter of shopping around for a bungalow or room to suit your taste and budget. On **Don Khon**, most of the bungalows are located near Ban Khon on the north end of the island. Bungalow places are scattered all the way around **Don Det**, but the north side of the island has by far the highest concentration. In fact, this part of the island can get so busy in high season that it's difficult to cycle down its winding dirt streets. **Food**, not accommodation, is the real money-earner here, and every bungalow place has a **restaurant** serving Lao food and the usual traveller's fare, so you may want to take some of your meals at the bungalow you're staying at.

Don Khon

Mr Bounh's East of the railway bridge near the Don Khon landing. Offers simple bungalows with shared facilities in a quiet compound close to the river. **1**
Sala Don Khone Next door to *Mr Bounh's*,☎035/256390 ⓦwww.salalao.com. The rooms in this converted French-era bungalow, which was once a hospital, feature a/c and hot-water showers. Further down the road there are stylish floating rooms with vaulted ceilings, separate daybeds and balconies just inches above the water. The fanciest place in town. **6**
Sompamit Opposite *Mr Bounh's*, on the riverbank. Very basic bungalows. **1**

Don Dhet

Don Det Bungalows Roughly halfway between the boat landing and the northern tip of the island. For something a bit classier, this place has ornately decorated bungalows. **4**
Little Eden Right by the northernmost beach. Refined brick bungalows, but let down by its stand-offish staff. **4**
Paradise Bungalows 20m north of the boat landing. Popular place with basic waterfront bungalows and a sociable restaurant. **1**
Santiphab Right next to the railroad bridge. Friendly Lao-owned (but German-managed) bungalows with majestic views of the river. **1**

The islands

A delightfully sleepy place with a timeless feel about it, **BAN KHON**, located on Don Khon at the eastern end of the bridge, is the largest settlement on either island and has the most upmarket accommodation (see above). Quaintly decrepit French-era buildings with terracotta tile roofs add some colonial colour to the village's collection of rustic homes of wood, bamboo and thatch. A short walk west of the old railroad bridge, past the ticket booth, stands the village monastery, **Wat Khon Tai**. Hidden behind the newly built *sim* is the laterite foundation of what was once a Khmer temple dedicated to the god Shiva. As with several Buddhist temples in southern Laos, this one was built upon the ruins of an ancient Hindu holy site, suggesting that the otherwise humble Ban Khon is around 1000 years old. On a pedestal nearby stands a Shivalinga, which was probably enshrined in the original Khmer temple. Because Khmer Shivalinga are usually simple and lack the intricate carving for which Khmer art is famous, they are rarely the target of art thieves and so stand a better chance of remaining on or near their original place of enshrinement.

Taking the southwestern path behind the wat, you'll soon be aware of a low, almost inaudible purr that gradually becomes a roar the further you proceed. After following the path for 1500m, you'll come to a low cliff overlooking **Somphamit Falls**, a series of high rapids that crashes through a jagged gorge. Fishermen can sometimes be seen carefully negotiating rickety bamboo catwalks suspended above the violently churning waters.

To see the remnants of Laos's **old French railroad**, head south from the old railroad bridge. A short distance back from the bridge lies the rusting locomotive that once hauled French goods and passengers between piers on Don Khon and Don Det, bypassing the falls and rapids that block this stretch of the river. Nearby, behind thick brush bordering rice fields, is an overgrown **Christian cemetery** that includes the neglected tomb of a long-forgotten French family that died on the same day in 1922 – some say murdered by their Vietnamese domestics. It is actually possible to follow the former railroad all the way across both islands; however, with the exception of two alarmingly precarious bridges constructed from railroad scrap and lengths of rail recycled as fences, there are few signs that a railway ever existed.

A similar but shorter walk is from Don Khon to Don Det across the bridge and along the 3km elevated trail to the now bustling village at the northern end of the island. Here, dozens of backpacker-friendly **guesthouses and restaurants** have opened just a stone's throw from an incongruous industrial structure once used for hoisting cargo from the train onto awaiting boats; it's all that remains of the railroad's northern terminus.

Dolphin-spotting and tubing

One of Don Khon's most popular activities is a boat trip in search of the **Irrawaddy dolphins** that can occasionally be spotted off the southern side of the island. Take the railroad trail for 4km through rice paddies and thick forest to the village of **Ban Hang Khon**, the jumping-off point for dolphin-spotting excursions. The April–May dry season, when the Mekong is at its lowest, is the best time of year to catch a glimpse of this highly endangered species. The dolphins tend to congregate in a deep-water pool, and boats can be chartered from the village to see them ($10). During the rest of the year, chances of seeing the dolphins decrease, as deeper water allows them more range. Recent efforts to protect the dolphins have seen the number in this region increase from thirty in 1993 to around sixty today, but their future here is still uncertain (see box below).

The Irrawaddy dolphin

If there's one creature that's exempted from a Lao diet famous for consuming every-thing that hops, flies, swims or crawls, it's the rare **Irrawaddy dolphin**, which has been known to make its way upstream from Cambodia to frolic in the waters of Si Phan Don. Bluish-grey and up to 2.5m long, the freshwater dolphins are looked upon by islanders as reincarnated humans with a human spirit – an idea that's been etched into local lore by folk songs and stories of dolphins rescuing people from the jaws of crocodiles. But sadly, the dolphins themselves may soon be no more than legend.

Over the past one hundred years their population in the Mekong has dwindled from thousands to little more than sixty, and as few as ten now inhabit the area near Don Khon. Gill-net fishing and, across the border in Cambodia, the use of poison, electricity and explosives have caused dolphin **numbers to plummet**. In the past, fishermen were reluctant to cut costly nets to free entangled dolphins, causing them to drown, but this no longer happens, as Lao villagers are now compensated for their nets – part of an initiative begun by the Lao Community Fisheries and Dolphin Protection Project.

However, with the Lao government looking to dam more Mekong tributaries, (which could permanently alter the dolphins' fragile habitat) plus the continued use of harmful pesticides in farming, conservationists are warning that the outlook for the species remains extremely bleak.

Following the success of **tubing** in Vang Vieng, enterprising islanders on the northern side of Don Det have started renting out tubes (5000K/day). The sandy beach at the island's northern tip is the favoured jumping off point, but you should be aware of the strong currents – and parasites – found in these waters.

Khon Phapheng Falls

Despite technically being the largest waterfall in Southeast Asia, **Khon Phapheng**, to the east of Don Khon, is not all that spectacular. Indeed, it's best described as a low but wide rock shelf that just happens to have a huge volume of water running over it. The drop is highest during the March–May dry season and becomes much less spectacular when the river level rises during the rainy season. Still, the sight of all that water crashing down on its way to Cambodia is quite mesmerizing, and a well-built tourist pavilion above the falls provides an ideal place to sit and enjoy the view. There's also no shortage of food shacks serving snacks. Most tourists do the falls as a package from Don Khong (see below) but it is also possible to get there by sawngthaew from Ban Hat Xai Khoun (opposite Muang Khong) or Nakasang (5000K). There is a 10,000K admission fee for foreigners and 1000K extra for a motorcycle.

Moving on

From the southern end of Don Khon, it's possible to charter a boat down the river to **Veun Kham** ($5 for up to three passengers), where there is a Lao immigration office and a **border crossing** into Cambodia. Because there's rarely any public transport on the Cambodian side of the border, most travellers cross the border on a VIP bus bound for Stung Treng ($12).

The Bolaven Plateau

As gradual as Route 23's eastwardly climb out of Pakse is, there's no mistaking when you've reached the **Bolaven Plateau**, roughly 30km from Pakse. The suffocating heat of the Mekong Valley yields to a refreshingly cool breeze, and coffee and tea plantations, exulting in the rich soil, begin cropping up along either side of the highway. Hilly, roughly circular in shape, and with an average altitude of 600m, the high plateau has rivers running off in all directions and then plunging out of lush forests along the Bolaven's edges in a series of spectacular **waterfalls**, some more than 100m high, before eventually finding their way to the Mekong. Four provincial capitals – Pakse, Salavan, Xekong and Attapeu – surround the Bolaven, while the main settlement on the plateau itself is the town of **Paksong**.

The French, recognizing the fertility of the terrain, cleared wide swathes of forests and planted strawberries, coffee, tea and cardamom. Although it was cardamom that provided the south's chief export during colonial times, coffee is the crop that dominates the plateau these days, earning the well-paved highway that links Pakse with Paksong the moniker the **Coffee Road**.

Long before the French planted their first coffee crop, midland **hill tribes** were practising swidden agriculture on the plateau. Today, twelve ethnic groups, including lowland Lao, Laven, Alak, Suay and Taoy, live in the area. Given that ethnic minorities are in the majority here, it's only fitting that the plateau takes its name from one of these groups, the **Laven**.

One of the easiest waterfalls to access here is **Tad Lo** on the forested northern edge of the plateau, a popular spot with travellers looking for somewhere pleasant to relax for a few days and enjoy the plateau's cool climate. You can lounge in the pools of the Xe Set River below the waterfall and do some elephant trekking to nearby tribal villages. South of Route 23 between Pakse and Paksong is the **Dong Hua Sao NBCA**, containing the **Tad Fan Waterfall**. **Paksong** was levelled in bombing raids during the war and has not been able to rekindle the charm it once possessed.

Lak Sao-et, the tiny village 21km from Pakse along Route 23, is an important junction for **bus transfers** – there are connections here for Tad Lo and Salavan in the northeast, and for Paksong and beyond.

Dong Hua Sao NBCA

Located in the southwest quarter of the Bolaven Plateau, **Dong Hua Sao** is the only NBCA up on the plateau itself.

Falling water enthusiasts will get a kick out of **Tad Fan** (admission 5000K), a cascade some 100m high, set amid primeval jungle that stretches as far as the eye can see. Travelling east on Route 23 from Pakse to Paksong, turn right at the Kilometre 38 marker onto a dirt road that leads through a coffee plantation and then forks; take the branch to the left and you will end up at the edge of a cliff overlooking the falls. A trail leads down to a better vantage point, but it's not advisable to attempt this slippery path during the rainy season, as it's a long drop down into the abyss. If you're travelling by **bus**, ask to be let off at Tad Fan, and you'll be able to walk the dirt road in.

At the falls, you'll also find the *Tad Fane Resort* (☎020/5531400, ⓦwww.tadfane .com; ⓞ) which has a restaurant and fourteen nicely built Lao-style rooms near the falls.

Head east from Tad Fan for 1km along the main road and you'll see signs for **Tad Yuang**, a spectacular dual cascade that's popular with picnicking locals and tourists. The actual falls are 800m from the main road up a very bumpy dirt track (so take care if you're riding a motorbike) and you'll need to climb down some steep steps to reach the swimming hole below them. At the top of the falls there's *Pusawan Resort* (☎020/2677784 ⓦwww.pusawan.co.cc; ④), which has beautiful wooden bungalows built into the hillside on stilts. Facilities are quite basic but the setting, with tiny rapids flowing by, is wonderfully sedate.

Paksong

Laos's famed coffee capital, **PAKSONG**, some 60km east of Pakse, was rebuilt after the war and has finally to find a market for its traditional cash crop. Those searching for some epicentre of coffee culture will be disappointed, but arriving on the plateau from the baking lowlands, especially during the torrid March–May hot season, will make you wonder how a bit of altitude can turn the cruel midday sun into a shoulder-warming friend.

The temperate weather and amiable locals notwithstanding, Paksong's sights are almost nil. The **town** itself is a small collection of mould-blackened concrete shophouses lining wide, dust-scoured streets, which wouldn't look out of place on the set of a spaghetti Western. A gatepost at the entrance of the market is possibly the only structure in town to have survived the war. Beyond it is a depressing block of ramshackle shops and noodle stands. Despite the bleakness of the town, the surrounding countryside and **coffee plantations** provide some diverting scenery, especially during March and April when the coffee trees are covered with intoxicatingly fragrant white blossoms.

Practicalities

Paksong is still starved of good **accommodation** and, for as long as tour operators in Pakse continue to run cheap day-trips to the Plateau, that situation looks unlikely to change. *Paksong* (❷), 500m beyond the market, is friendly enough but quite bad value, especially if you end up in the grotty older building. About 2km north of the market there's *Borlaven Guesthouse* (❶), with clean rooms but rock-hard mattresses. **Moving on**, buses headed for Xekong and Attapeu pass the town, and sawngthaews leave from the market for Pakse (20,000K). Your best chance of catching one is to get to the market first thing, as connections tend to tail off by early afternoon.

Tad Lo

The 10m-high **Tad Lo**, a waterfall on the banks of the Xe Set 90km northeast of Pakse and about 30km southwest of Salavan, draws a steady stream of foreign visitors, providing the perfect setting for a few days' relaxation and the opportunity to ride an elephant along the breezy western flank of the plateau. In the hot season, the pools surrounding **Tad Hang**, the lower falls, are a refreshing escape from the heat; large boulders in the river shade a few surprisingly deep swimming holes and are perfect spots for lounging in the sun. Just be sure to clear the water before darkness, however, when the floodgates of a dam upstream sometimes unleash a torrent of water without warning.

Elephant treks ($10 for 90min) through the forested hills around Tad Lo are easy to arrange through any of the guesthouses here. A ride typically involves a round-trip from the *Tad Lo Resort*, and includes a short stop at Tad Lo, 500m upstream, before pulling through a nearby village inhabited by midlanders of Alak ethnicity, who have a long history of settlement on the plateau.

▲ Tad Lo falls

Practicalities

The road between Pakse and Salavan is now mostly paved, making journeys a lot quicker than they used to be. The turn-off for Tad Lo is 88km northeast of Pakse, just beyond the village of **Lao Ngam**. Buses will drop you at the turn-off where a congregation of restaurants and general stores crowds the mouth of the 1500-metre dirt road that leads to Tad Hang, the lower falls, which can be reached by tuk-tuk (5000K/person). When leaving, find a tuk-tuk to take you back to the highway, where you can pick up a morning bus to Salavan or Pakse.

High on a hill overlooking Tad Hang, but reachable on foot, perches the *Tad Lo Resort* (T031/214184; ❹), with thirteen rooms in an assortment of **bungalows**. Across the river bridge, *Saise* **guesthouse** has a couple of rooms with shared facilities in a raised house, plus some very pleasant en-suite ones in the "Green House" (it has a green roof) a few hundred metres upstream (both types 100,000K). It's the best

---

The Bolaven revolt

A chanting mob, two thousand-strong, descended on Savannakhet in April 1902, convinced by a holy man that any bullets fired at them would be miraculously transformed into frangipani flowers. Three times they attacked, and each time they were mown down by troops from France's "Garde Indigène". The rout, which left 150 dead, marked the climax of the so-called **Holy Man's Revolt**, which had its origins with the arrival of the French in 1893 and simmered on for many years afterwards in the highlands of the south.

The French brought with them administrative changes, increased taxation and reshuffled the traditional relationships that had guided life in Laos for generations. At first, resistance was textbook Lao. Villagers avoided direct confrontation, preferring to make their displeasure about the new order known through passive means: villages undercounted their populations, adapted a generally uncooperative attitude, or simply left. The first serious opposition didn't arise until eight years after the French employed gunboat diplomacy to wrest control of Lao territory from Siam.

When **Ong Kaew**, an Alak tribesman believed to possess supernatural powers, prophesied that "the end of the world as we know it" was nigh, he found willing listeners among midland tribes living along the plateau, chafing under increased taxes and *corvée* labour demands instituted by the French commissioner of Salavan. Sensing that Ong Kaew was gaining too much influence, the commissioner ordered the burning of a pagoda erected in the holy man's honour. This only served to increase support for Ong Kaew, and in April 1901, he and a band of rebels attacked the commissioner and his guard. Soon after, nearly all of the Bolaven region was in revolt.

By 1902, the revolt had spilled across the Mekong and briefly gained the support of older lowland Lao families, who felt threatened by the collapse of the social and economic order to which they were accustomed. After the disastrous march on Savannakhet, Ong Kaew and another Lao Theung leader, **Ong Kommadam**, whose son would later continue to resist the French and ultimately become a Pathet Lao leader, retreated across the Xe Kong as villages were burned and less fortunate leaders rounded up and executed. But the defeat at Savannakhet and renewed attempts by France to pacify the Bolaven region did little to dispel the holy man's popularity, and it took a new commissioner at Salavan, **Jean Dauplay**, to force Ong Kaew to surrender in 1907. Three years later, with the holy man's influence over the Bolaven inhabitants as strong as ever, Dauplay arrested Ong Kaew, who died "during a jail break" the next day. The revolt was effectively over.

Not all was lost during the insurrection. French authorities were careful to place more of the burden on lowland Lao when they raised taxes in 1914, and Ong Kaew had unwittingly sown the seeds for what the Pathet Lao would later claim to be the stirrings of Lao nationalism.

deal to be found in the area, especially the VIP rooms, which have balconies overlooking the river. Loads of cheap options have appeared back in Lao Ngam; the pick of the bunch is *Tim's Guesthouse* (☎034/211885; ❷), opposite the school library, which has a good selection of double and triple rooms with shared facilities. Downstairs there's a restaurant, internet access, a book exchange and bikes for rent.

There are plenty of options for **eating** – *Tad Lo Resort* has a relaxed open-air restaurant with good views of the Xe Set, but the food is no match for what's on offer at *Saise*'s huge oudoor restaurant right by the falls. Cheaper places worth trying include *Tim's Guesthouse* and, just over the road, *Jom*.

The remote provinces

Salavan, **Xekong** and **Attapeu**, cut off from the Mekong River Valley by the Bolaven Plateau and made remote by the rugged jigsaw of the Annamite Mountains, are some of the least-visited provinces in Laos. Until recently, poor infrastructure and the scars of war conspired to keep the region isolated. With the Ho Chi Minh Trail streaming across their borders, these provinces were victims of some of the heaviest bombing during the Second Indochina War. Villages were decimated, roads destroyed and in some places the dangerous litter of battle still lies about. Yet these factors kept the densely forested mountains of Attapeu and Xekong pristine until the beginning of this century. Today, intense **logging** along the Vietnamese border is turning parts of this once rich ecosystem into a moonscape. For the time being, however, the provinces are still home to a variety of wildlife and numerous ethnic minority villages.

Arcing around the **Bolaven Plateau**, these provinces can be seen in a convenient clockwise loop from Pakse. From Lak Sao-et (see p.252), 21km east of Pakse, head northeast for roughly 100km along well-maintained Route 20 towards Salavan, where bus connections are available for the bumpy 90km trip to **Xekong** via **Thateng**, the dusty northern gateway to the Bolaven Plateau. Just east of the plateau, uninspiring Xekong provides a jumping-off point for the pretty five-hour boat trip along the babbling Xe Kong to **Attapeu**, capital of Laos's southeasternmost province.

From Attapeu, it can be a rough haul back to Pakse up the eastern flank of the Bolaven and through the coffee plantations surrounding Paksong. Unfortunately, public buses have yet to start travelling impassable Route 18, the shortcut to Si Phan Don, which shadows the southern edge of the Plateau.

Salavan

Located on a flank of the former Ho Chi Minh Trail north of the Bolaven Plateau, Salavan province was held by the Royal Lao government until 1970, when an NVA push to consolidate control over the Trail drove the Royalists out. The provincial capital, also called **SALAVAN**, was, thanks to its proximity to the Trail, all but obliterated during the war by B-52 strikes. It wasn't until the late 1980s that rebuilding began; in the interim, the province was used as a re-education camp in which high-ranking RLA officers were given plots of land to till, many dying of malaria.

Today, Salavan town is a peaceful backwater, scorched in the hot season by desert-like winds. Many new buildings of permanent materials have replaced the rickety wooden structures that were the norm up until the 1990s, and nowadays you'd need a guide with knowledge of what the old town looked like in order to glimpse any evidence of Salavan's tumultuous history. Unless you are simply looking for a very out-of-the-way place to hang out, there isn't much reason to gravitate here, though the town can be used as a base to explore Mon–Khmer villages in the area.

In the early twentieth century, the French were looking for ways to make their newest chunk of Indochina profitable. Laos had become a disappointment when the grand scheme of using the Mekong as a trade link to China turned out to be impractical, but the French soon had other plans. Would **coffee**, which had been successfully introduced to Vietnam, also thrive in Laos? It seemed worth a try. Saplings were brought from the orchards around Buon Me Thuot in Vietnam and planted at varying degrees of elevation. From the banks of the Mekong on up to the Bolaven Plateau, rows of arabica and robusta were carefully nursed. After four years, the first harvest saw mixed results: coffee at lower elevations failed to fruit, but planters on the Bolaven were rewarded for their patience.

By the 1940s, **coffee plantations** covered the plateau. But then war and revolution intervened, and by the 1980s, the once painstakingly tended trees had gone wild. However, interest in Lao coffee has been rekindled over the last decade and the old plantations have benefited from foreign investment. A blight-resistant strain of arabica was recently introduced from Costa Rica, and the "Association des Exportateurs du Café Lao" is hoping to increase annual coffee production and make Lao coffee known to aficionados around the globe.

Although coffee made its way to Laos via Vietnam, the **coffee-drinking etiquette** and accoutrements of Laos have a flavour all their own. The tin-drip, used in Vietnam to filter coffee into a glass, is rare in Laos; the Lao favour pouring hot water through a sock-like bag filled with ground coffee. For more on Lao coffee, see p.38.

Practicalities

The daily buses that pull into Salavan's **bus station** connect the town with Pakse, Xekong and Paksong, with smaller buses and pick-up trucks heading off from here to the province's interior. Overly optimistic maps suggest the possibility of travelling north to Savannakhet province (through Toumlan to Muang Phin and through Taoy on to Ban Dong), but these roads, effectively taken out during the war, are now overgrown and lacking key bridges.

Salavan has a number of **guesthouses**, including *Silsamay 2* (**1**), on Route 20, near the bus station which offers rooms with a fan or air conditioning; other choices in town include the *Thipphaphone* (**2**) and, next door, the *Chindavone* (**1**).

A group of stalls at the town **market** sell Lao food and sticky rice. Nearby you'll find the **post office** and a branch of Lao Development **bank**, which exchanges cash and travellers' cheques.

The Xe Kong River Valley

The **Xe Kong** is one of Laos's great rivers, starting high in the Annamite Mountains from the eastern flanks of the 2500-metre-high Mount Atouat and flowing southwestward around the southern edge of the Bolaven Plateau. It enters Cambodia via the Xe Pian NBCA, eventually joining the Mekong River in that country, north of Stung Treng.

The main towns along the Xe Kong in Laos are **Xekong** and **Attapeu**, which are linked by a paved but bumpy road. If you're heading this way from Salavan, the first part of the journey involves a laborious climb through rich jungle and midland tribal villages up the steep curves of the Bolaven Plateau to **Thateng**, 40km away.

A dusty junction of threadbare markets and crooked wooden houses with thatch roofs, Thateng was where the French commissioner to Salavan, Jean Dauplay, "the father of Lao coffee", chose to settle in the 1920s. Sadly, Thateng's strategic location as the gateway to the plateau, a grip on which was considered key to controlling the bulk of the far south, made it a prime target for American bombs.

The town was basically wiped out, and although villagers returned after the war, the place is nowadays little more than an unappealing transit point.

Xekong

In 1984, a wide expanse of jungle was cleared of trees and graded flat in order to found the town of **XEKONG**. Created partly because the nearby town of Ban Phon was deemed no longer habitable owing to unexploded ordnance, Xekong, some 50km east of Thateng, is now the capital of a new province, created when Attapeu was divided in half. Xekong has some of a frontier feel but not much of interest, though intrepid travellers may be attracted by the prospect of a scenic journey downriver from here to Attapeu.

Three major branches of the **Ho Chi Minh Trail** snaked through the jungle surrounding Xekong, and consequently this area was one of the most heavily bombed in Laos. Animist tribal peoples living in the adjacent hills, under constant threat of attack from the sky, erected talismans above their huts to ward off falling bombs. Some of these strange war relics are still in place: rusting tail-fins from dud bombs have been arranged to form a protective X over thatched roofs, and, in at least one village, carved wooden miniatures of helicopters, looking like militaristic weather vanes, are mounted above the tribal meeting house. Some of these tribes produce **hand-woven textiles** that are highly sought-after by collectors. Decorative patterns feature traditional motifs such as animals and plants, alongside stylized fighter planes and bombs of obvious inspiration.

Despite the dropping of bombs and defoliants, the area is host to a surprisingly large and varied **wildlife** population. Herds of wild elephants regularly raid village rice barns, and tigers have been seen lapping at the pools below Tad Xe Noi, a waterfall 25km south of Xekong. Other rare species known to inhabit the wilds of Xekong include the Siamese crocodile and pygmy slow loris. There is even thought to be a small population of Sumatran rhinos deep in the jungled hills.

If you're ready to devote half your visa time to Xekong, prepare yourself for this cruel hitch: the astonishing amount of **UXO** that blankets this province makes exploration extremely dicey. Disposal teams have concluded that Xekong will be losing people to UXO for decades to come. Despite this, the average traveller has little to worry about if a few simple rules are followed. The number-one rule is to stay on well-worn paths, even when passing through a village. For more advice on UXO, see p.51.

As if the danger of UXO weren't enough, there is a disturbing beasty lurking in Xekong's waterways: the *pa pao*, an innocuous-looking blowfish with a piranha-like appetite and, according to locals, a particular fondness for lopping off the tip of the male member. The risk of losing a plug of flesh to a ravenous blowfish notwithstanding, the journey by **pirogue** down the stretch of river between Xekong and Attapeu (see p.258) is undoubtedly the best way to view this most inaccessible corner of southern Laos.

Practicalities

Buses to and from Pakse operate from the bus station, about 2km out of town. A handful of **tuk-tuks** await arriving buses and will ferry you into the centre for 5000K. Heading into town, you'll pass a branch of the Lao Development bank where you can **exchange cash** and travellers' cheques, and the **post office** and telecom building, where international calls can be made.

There aren't any fixed bus schedules as such (ask your guesthouse for the latest times) but a service that follows the Xe Kong south to Attapeu (15,000K) should leave the bus station at 8am, arriving in Attapeu about two hours later. Regular sawngthaews to Salavan (20,000K) and Pakse (25,000K) also leave here each morning.

Sekong Souksamlane (☏038/212039; ❷), near the post office, has decent if somewhat overpriced **rooms**. A cluster of cheap places to eat surrounds the hotel, and the hotel's **restaurant** cooks rather good Thai food at reasonable rates. The best place for **tourist information** (and delicious Vietnamese food) is *Phathip Restaurant*, just over the road.

Xekong to Attapeu by river

If you've made it as far as Xekong, the scenic **Xe Kong**, which meanders through little-visited countryside, provides a strong incentive to charter a motorized pirogue for the journey south to **Attapeu** – not cheap at $60–70, but well worth the expense. To find a boat in Xekong, follow the road that passes in front of the *Sekong Souksamlane* hotel south for 1km until you reach a boat landing on the riverbank, where you'll have to negotiate a price with the boatmen. Even if it's more expensive, go for one that can offer you a life jacket.

The pirogues make the journey to Attapeu through gentle rapids and past lushly forested riverbanks, where people living in the surrounding hills come to catch fish and bathe. The journey usually takes around five hours, but late in the dry season it can take seven, and at this time the shallow waters require passengers to walk short stretches of the journey along the bank. Although the fare doesn't rise at this time of year, captains limit the number of passengers to two, thereby increasing the price per person. Keep in mind that this river can be hazardous during high waters, and if you're not a strong swimmer you should probably give it a pass; more than one tourist has drowned on this journey.

During the Second Indochina War, US aircraft struck at the threads of the Ho Chi Minh Trail running parallel to the river, hoping to disrupt the endless tide of men and supplies streaming southwards. Bombs invariably wound up in the river and the resulting explosions sent scores of fish floating belly-up to the surface, unintentional war reparations quickly collected by villagers living amid a battlefield. Today's depleted fish catches are still blamed on the war, but more modern fishing equipment has surely had an impact, as has the use of explosives for catching fish, a technique that was utilized by Vietnamese soldiers during the war and remains part of the Cambodian fisherman's arsenal along some stretches of the river. One victim of such high-impact methods, the **Irrawaddy dolphin** (see p.250), until the 1980s a frequent visitor to Attapeu's maze of rivers in the rainy season, now rarely visits these waters.

Attapeu

A leafy settlement of almost twenty thousand people, most of whom are Vietnamese, Chinese or lowland Lao, remote **ATTAPEU** occupies a bend in the Xe Kong just south of where it is joined by the **Xe Kaman**. Access to the town is much improved, with daily buses plying the newly paved road that links it to Pakse, and it's a pleasant destination compared to the hot and dusty towns of Xekong and Salavan.

It was near Attapeu, the capital of Laos's southeasternmost province, that the Ho Chi Minh Trail diverged, with one artery running south towards Cambodia and the other into South Vietnam. But despite being the final staging point in Laos for North Vietnamese supplies, Attapeu somehow eluded the grave effects of war that wiped other southern cities off the map. That the town remains an oasis among rugged mountains perhaps reflects what some American military advisors mocked as the reluctance of the Royal Lao Army, who controlled Attapeu in the late 1960s, to engage their opponents in battle – a trait that prompted the Americans to nickname the Royalist troops "the Fastest Army Running", a moniker derived from the army's old French acronym FAR. When the Pathet Lao announced that they intended to take the city in April 1970, Royal Lao troops lived up to their reputation and fled. Five years later, the Pathet Lao made the entire province a **re-education camp** (see p.166), resettling political enemies and forbidding them to leave the province for years. The Pathet Lao perhaps thought it only fitting to punish opponents with a dose

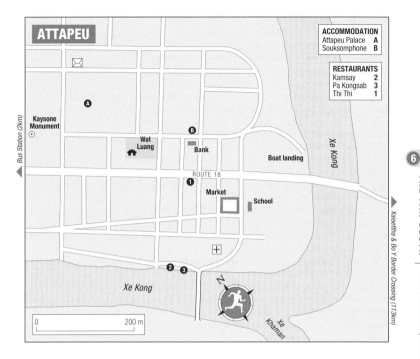

of what they had had to endure, living in the country's remotest areas during their Thirty Year Struggle; what better place than one which, even by nineteenth-century Lao standards, was known for its "extreme unhealthiness", as reported by French explorer François Jules Harmand, who visited Attapeu in 1877. This reputation festers to this day, with Attapeu registering the country's highest rate of malaria.

Such tumultuous history lends new currency to the old legend surrounding Attapeu's name. When the first lowland Lao immigrants to the region asked the indigenous people what the name of their town was, the latter thought the Lao were pointing to a pile of water buffalo dung, or *itkapu* in their language, and responded accordingly. With a slight change in pronunciation to accommodate the Lao accent, the town of "buffalo shit" was born.

The Town

Attapeu is no warehouse of tourist attractions: the way to enjoy this town is by leisurely wandering in its rambling red-dirt lanes, absorbing the easy-going pace and chatting with the genial residents. In the evening, head to the southern end of town, where the Xe Kong pauses to flow east to west, and the high riverbank invites you to catch a sunset over the river. The only real sight is Attapeu's main **wat**, which occupies a massive block in the heart of town. On the northern side of the compound, standing out among the gaudy modern temple architecture, there's also a handsome French-style monastery school building.

If you're arriving by bus on the newly built Route 18B, note the monument at the bus station, commemorating Lao–Vietnamese cooperation during the war. The monument, depicting Pathet Lao and NVA soldiers waving flags and Kalashnikov rifles aloft, is a near copy of the one in Muang Phin, Savannakhet province. Not surprisingly, it was built by the Vietnamese.

Practicalities

Arriving by **bus**, you'll find yourself next to a market (**Talat Noi**) on the northwestern outskirts of the city, 3km from the centre. If you're on the **express bus** from Pakse, don't get off here, as the bus may continue into town. Boats from Xekong dock at the **ferry landing**, just upriver from the bridge. A good point of orientation is Attapeu's only **bank**, a branch of Lao Development Bank, which is roughly in the centre of the town, and can be reached from the ferry landing by following the road into town.

Attapeu has one **hotel** and a handful of **guesthouses**. The block-like *Attapeu Palace* (formerly the *Yingchokchay Hotel*), in a huge compound (℡036/211204; ❷), has air-conditioned rooms with fridge and satellite TV, plus some very cheap, good-value fan rooms. Staff here can also help to arrange tours around Attapeu. The oldest of the guesthouses is the well-run but sometimes surly *Souksomphone* (❶), which has a range of rooms, some with private bathrooms; look for the modern building opposite the bank.

Attapeu's most reliable **restaurant** is Vietnamese-run *Thi Thi*, in the centre of town on Route 18, which does cheap traditional dishes. Other choices include *Kamsay* and *Pa Kongsab*, down by the riverside, but both are more about beer and karaoke than good food.

Moving on from Attapeu, an **express bus** leaves for Pakse at 6am, making the nonstop trip in a lightning-quick four hours. Otherwise you're stuck with the gruelling regular bus, which can take twice as long. Because most buses still can't travel on Route 18, public transport bound for Pakse has to go via Xekong and Paksong on the Bolaven Plateau – just tell the driver where you want to jump off. **Boats** to Xekong can be arranged through the owner of the *Souksomphone*; for more on this route, see p.258.

The Bo Y border crossing

A convenient new border crossing with Vietnam has opened up along the newly paved Route 18B, 113km east of Attapeu. Several minibuses leave from outside *Thi Thi* restaurant in Attapeu each morning, crossing the border at **Bo Y** after a winding, three-hour drive. By the time you read this, direct shuttle buses to the border may well be running from Attapeu's main bus station but for now, you'll have to buy a ticket that takes you all the way to Kon Tum, in Vietnam. Tickets to other Vietnamese destinations via Bo Y, including Da Nang and Hue, can be bought in Pakse. To cross into Vietnam, you must have arranged your visa before arrival at the border.

Travel details

Buses

Attapeu to: Pakse (4 daily; 4–7hr) via Paksong (2 daily; 5hr); Xekong (2 daily; 2hr).
Champasak to: Pakse (3 daily; 2hr).
Pakse to: Attapeu (4 daily; 4–7hr); Ban Saphai (hourly; 30min); Champasak (10 daily; 2hr); Chong Mek (every 30min; 45min); Muang Khong (5 daily; 3–4hr); Kiatngong (3 daily; 2hr 30min); Nakasang (6 daily; 3hr); Paksong (5 daily; 90min); Salavan (5 daily; 3hr); Savannakhet (4 daily; 6hr); Tad Lo (4 daily; 3hr); Thakhek (3 daily; 8hr); Ubon

Ratchathani (2 daily; 3hr); Vientiane (7 daily; 10–14hr); Xekong (2 daily; 2–5hr).
Paksong to: Attapeu (2 daily; 5hr); Pakse (hourly; 2hr).
Salavan to: Pakse (5 daily; 3hr); Taoy (1 daily; 4-5hr); Toumlan (1 daily; 2hr); Xekong (2 daily; 4hr).
Xekong to: Pakse (2 daily; 5hr); Salavan (2 daily; 4hr).

Flights

Pakse to: Savannakhet (3 weekly; 35min); Vientiane (at least 1 daily; 1hr 20min).

Contexts

Contexts

History

Laos as a unified state within its present geographical boundaries has only existed for little more than one hundred years. Its national history stretches back six centuries to the legendary kingdom of Lane Xang, a rival to the empires of mainland Southeast Asia until it splintered into a cluster of weak principalities dominated by their more powerful neighbours.

The beginnings

As long as forty thousand years ago, Laos was inhabited by **hunter–gatherers** who lived in relatively permanent sites and used tools made of stone, wood and bamboo, not terribly different from many of those still in use in rural Lao villages today. By 8000 BC, these peoples had become **farmers**, growing beans, peas and rice and domesticating animals. Excavations at a site in present-day northeastern Thailand reveal that copper and bronze work in the region dates back four thousand years – as early as anywhere in the world. **Ironworking** was the next step forward, and by 500 BC the inhabitants of the Khorat Plateau in northeastern Thailand were using ploughs with iron tips, pulled by water buffalo, to cultivate wet rice.

The **earliest indigenous culture** in Laos to have been investigated by archeologists was that of an Iron Age megalithic people that lived in what is now Xieng Khuang province on the Plain of Jars. These people built stone pillars which were positioned next to underground burial chambers, and large stone funerary urns to hold the ashes of their dead. The civilization is thought to have progressed from crafting the three-metre-tall stone slabs to the massive jars after the development of iron tools. Bronze objects as well as beads foreign to the region suggest that the civilization was a wealthy one and lay at the centre of trade routes to China, Vietnam and points south. However, very little else is known about this people and what became of them.

By this time, broad linguistic and cultural groups were beginning to emerge in Southeast Asia. Small villages were developing and between them there was regular communication and trade in such items as pottery, salt and metal tools. The early inhabitants of Laos and the surrounding parts of central and southern Indochina spoke Austroasiatic languages such as Mon and Khmer, while the ancestors of the lowland Lao spoke proto-Tai languages, and were still living in the river valleys of southeastern China. What is known about this group of **Tai** people comes mostly from documents written by their neighbours. Tai peoples described in early Chinese documents were valley- and lowland-dwelling subsistence farmers who typically cultivated wet rice and vegetables and, unlike the Chinese and Vietnamese, lived in houses built on piles. They reared water buffalo less for use as beasts of burden than as symbols of wealth and status or for use in ritual.

The **Tai villages** of the first millennium AD were probably much like the villages of rural Laos today, and would have consisted of a small cluster of households sharing labour during harvests. A need for mutual protection against outside forces most likely drove such villages together into larger units known as *muang* – a term which refers to both a group of villages and the central town in a network of villages.

With the lowlands to the east and northeast densely settled by Vietnamese and Chinese populations, the Tai peoples slowly **migrated** west and southwest into northern Laos and southern Yunnan, and eventually as far as Assam in northeastern

In the early days, when humankind grew unruly and refused to honour the gods, the **chief of the gods** flooded the earth. Three lords managed to survive the flood, floating up to heaven on a raft. They paid homage to the chief of the gods, and once the floods had subsided the lords returned to earth in the vicinity of Dien Bien Phu with a water buffalo, which helped them sow the rice fields in the plain. When the buffalo died, a large vine bearing three gourds grew from its nostrils, and from the gourds came shouts and cries. One of the lords pierced the gourds with a hot poker and a mass of people struggled out of the blackened holes. These were the **Lao Theung**, the Lao of the hillsides. Seeing their plight, a second lord cut more holes with a chisel and from these larger openings emerged the **Lao**. The lords taught the Lao how to grow rice and build homes, but when the population grew too big, the chief of the gods sent his son, **Khoun Borom**, to earth.

Descending to earth on an elephant with crossed tusks, Khoun Borom brought with him teachers and courtiers, teaching the Lao how to make tools and schooling them in the arts of dance and music. After a prosperous reign of 25 years, Khoun Borom sent his seven sons to rule over the Tai–Lao world. The eldest went to **Luang Prabang** and the others to Xieng Khuang, Chiang Mai, Xishuangbanna (in southwestern China), Ayutthaya and to regions of lower Burma and northern Vietnam.

India, displacing the sparse indigenous population of Austronesian and Austroasiatic groups and forcing them into the less desirable upland areas – where their descendants still live today. This migration is reflected in the Lao legend of Khoun Borom (see box, above). By the ninth century, the Tai were spread across upland Southeast Asia and surrounded by **Nanchao**, a well-organized military state located in southwestern China; a Vietnamese state on the verge of independence from China; Champa, an Indianized kingdom on the coast of Vietnam; Angkorian Cambodia; and the Mon and Pyu kingdoms of Burma.

Indianized influences

From the first century AD, Indian traders made their way east through Southeast Asia by land and by sea en route to China. Hinduized enclaves sprang up along the coast of Indochina and later, inland civilizations developed in Burma, Cambodia and Thailand. It was these classical **Indianized civilizations** along with individual Indian traders and travelling monks, rather than Chinese culture, that would shape the identity of the Lao, an influence evident today in the sharp difference between the Tai groups who underwent Indianization, became Buddhist and incorporated Pali and Sanskrit words into their languages, and those that did not.

The foundation of Buddhist civilization in Thailand and Laos was laid by a unique Theravada Buddhist cultural complex known as **Dvaravati**. This civilization grew up to dominate the Central Plain of Thailand for several centuries, although more as a cultural influence than an empire. Sites found across Thailand and Laos suggest Dvaravati was a prosperous, expansive civilization that flourished between the sixth and ninth centuries. The sites appear to have been most densely clustered around the lower Chao Phraya River Valley of Thailand, along what were regular routes of communication and trade, which contributed to the spread of Buddhism in the area. This is evidenced by the discovery of eleventh- and twelfth-century relics in Luang Prabang and near Phonhong on the Vientiane Plain, the earliest Buddhist statuary yet discovered in these parts of Laos.

The Khmer

By the end of the ninth century, Dvaravati's influence over central Southeast Asia was rapidly being eclipsed by the **Khmer Empire** of Angkor. At its height, this empire extended from its core of Cambodia and the southern half of northeastern Thailand into Vietnam, central Thailand and Laos, where the Khmer built dozens of Angkor-style temple complexes. As a result of this expansion, the Khmer gained control over important trade routes between India and China. The empire was held together by an extensive network of communications and institutions, as well as a system of highways linking key centres of the empire, traces of which are visible between Wat Phou and Angkor.

As the empire grew, Khmer governors, who were sometimes princes with ties to the royal house at Angkor, were placed in control of newly acquired areas, bringing with them tax collectors, judges, scribes and monks and ordering the construction of enormous religious monuments. The people then living in what is now southern Laos were probably predominantly Khmer as far north as Savannakhet, although by the eleventh and twelfth centuries, ethnic Tai made up a significant portion of the population on the fringes of the Angkor empire.

Early Tai principalities

The first record of contact between the Khmer empire and a Tai state occurred sometime after the seventh century near Chiang Saen in far northern Thailand, where a Tai state known as **Yonok** emerged along the Mekong River in the vicinity of Bokeo province. By the late tenth century, Buddhism was blossoming in Yonok, transforming the localized Buddhism into an institutionalized religious tradition with ties to the civilizations of the Mon and Ceylon. It was around this time that the Tai were beginning to move onto the lowland plains, suitable for extensive cultivation of rice.

Though the origin of the first Lao principalities is ill-defined to say the least, it appears that the first significant Tai centres in what is now Laos took root in the north, at Luang Prabang and Xieng Khuang, both of which are identified in legends as areas ruled by the sons of Khoun Borom.

By the thirteenth century, Luang Prabang, along with Chiang Saen, Jinghong (the Tai Leu capital located in Yunnan) and a Black Tai centre near the Da River in Vietnam, had emerged as one of the chief Tai centres of the Upper Mekong, an area settled by people who called themselves **Lao** and lived under the threat of invasion from Nanchao and Vietnam. A century later, Luang Prabang, then known as Xieng Dong Xieng Thong, had become but one of many small Lao principalities that existed on the fringes of two larger Tai states that had emerged: **Lan Na**, centred on Chiang Mai, and **Sukhothai**, the principality which is viewed as the cornerstone in Thailand's development. These states had capitalized on the collapse of the region's classical Indianized empires, Angkor and Pagan, their growth fuelled by large bases of rice land and manpower. Inscriptions from the Siamese *muang* of Sukhothai indicate that Lao rulers from Xieng Dong Xieng Thong were paying tribute to the Sukhothai by the late thirteenth century.

Yet even as the sun began to set on Angkor in the thirteenth century, the Khmer empire's most lasting impact on its still nebulous northern neighbour was to come in the form of a helping hand to the young exile who was to transform the petty Lao principalities scattered across Laos and portions of Thailand into a power in mainland Southeast Asia.

The rise of Lane Xang

Legends tell of a young prince named Fa Ngum, who belonged to the ruling family of Xieng Dong Xieng, being cast out of the fledgling Lao principality. But in 1351 he returned, backed by an army provided by the Khmer court at Angkor, and began fighting his way up the Mekong Valley atop a war elephant. After subduing the lower Mekong Valley, Sikhotabong (present-day Thakhek) and Kham Keut (near Lak Sao), Fa Ngum proceeded to the Plain of Jars where, with the aid of an exiled Phuan prince, he captured Muang Phuan, the capital of the principality of Xieng Khuang.

In 1353, Fa Ngum returned to Xieng Dong Xieng Thong, where he ascended the throne and began the reign considered the cornerstone in Laos's development. Fa Ngum called his new kingdom **Lane Xang Hom Khao**, the Kingdom of a Million Elephants and the White Parasol, a name signifying military might and royal prestige. For two decades he continued to expand Lane Xang, creating a decentralized state with hubs in Xieng Khuang, Sikhotabong and Vientiane. All three of these *muang* were virtually autonomous, but they each helped Lane Xang by contributing revenue and manpower – the greatest asset in a sparsely populated land.

With Fa Ngum and his Khmer queen, Kaew Keng Nya, came Cambodian monks and artisans, a new civil administrative system and a code of laws. It's fairly certain Buddhism also flourished during Fa Ngum's reign, growing further with the arrival of his second queen, Kaew Lot Fa.

Although Fa Ngum was a strong leader, after twenty years on the throne and following some internal strife, he was ousted by his ministers. In 1373 the succession passed to his only son, **Oun Heuan**, who ruled for 43 years, ushering in an era of peace during which the city flourished. Oun Heuan is remembered as Samsenthai or king of Three Hundred Thousand Tai, a name signifying the number of Lao men available to Lane Xang for labour and military service. After Oun Heuan's death, a period of bitter political infighting began – with eight kings in 22 years – which left the kingdom severely weakened.

The leading ministers of Lane Xang restored stability by offering the throne to the ruler of Vientiane, Vangburi (1438–79), the only surviving son of Oun Heuan. Whereas Fa Ngum had merely tipped his hat to Theravada Buddhism, Vangburi was a devout Buddhist. He took the Buddhist name Sainyachakkaphat upon his coronation and promptly appointed new abbots in key monasteries. Theravada Buddhism, slower to take hold east of the Mekong at first, now served to legitimize the rule of the kings of Lane Xang. In return for the king's patronage the monks taught that the king ruled because he possessed superior moral merit.

Sainyachakkaphat took pains to return Lane Xang to its former glory, but his rule was not to last. **Vietnam**, angered by Lane Xang's betrayal of the Vietnamese struggle against the occupying forces of China's Ming Dynasty and further provoked by a Phuan revolt against Vietnamese control over Muang Phuan, invaded Lane Xang in 1479. Five columns of Vietnamese troops swept through Xieng Dong Xieng Thong and Sainyachakkaphat, humiliated, abdicated and fled. The Lao king's younger brother, Souvanna Banlang, regrouped the Lao troops and eventually chased off the Vietnamese, whose final retort was the sacking of Muang Phuan on their way home.

Xieng Dong Xieng Thong's destruction proved to be a catalyst for Lane Xang's first golden age, a century when the civil administration was fine-tuned, striking temples were built and epic poems composed.

The kingdom of the Pha Bang

Souvanna Banlang's three successors – La Saen Thai (1486–96), Somphou (1496–1500) and Visoun (1500–20) – ruled over a peaceful and prosperous Lane Xang, their reigns marked by strengthened ties and an upswing in trade with Ayutthaya. The wealth generated by trade went into the adornment of Xieng Dong Xieng Thong. These rulers also reorganized the government, which served to make the kingdom more stable than it had ever been before.

Buddhism flourished, under **Visoun** in particular, as monks took up residence in the city and the monasteries became centres of literary culture, where sacred Pali texts were studied. It was also during his reign that the Lao Buddhist world-view came together. Visoun ordered the composition of the *Nithan Khoun Borom*, which brought together legends concerning the origin of the Lao, Khoun Borom and the founding of Xieng Dong Xieng Thong – complete with grand stories of Fa Ngum's deeds – and placed these tales within the framework of Theravada Buddhism. Arguably, Visoun's most important act was bringing the **Pha Bang** to Xieng Dong Xieng Thong from Vientiane in 1512, a defining event in the development of Lao identity. The golden Buddha image, installed at Wat Visoun, became the palladium of the ruling dynasty and the symbol of unity and power of the kingdom itself.

Whereas Visoun and his immediate predecessors had ruled over a peaceful state concerned primarily with domestic affairs, Visoun's son Phothisalat and grandson Setthathilat had major ambitions for Lane Xang, which they saw as being the equal of Ayutthaya. **Phothisalat** (1520–47) was a man driven by profound piety. He gave generously to the monastic order and left his mark on the spiritual life of Xieng Dong Xieng Thong when, in 1527, he broke with local traditions and banned the practice of animism, ordering the destruction of associated religious buildings. In pursuit of his expansionist aspirations, Phothisalat established a wide network of regional relations, which included taking a Lan Na princess as his queen. He chose to reside at Vientiane, which had the advantage of being closer to the trade routes linking Lane Xang with Vietnam, Ayutthaya and Cambodia. Vientiane was also closer to the population centre of the expanding Lao world: with the downfall of Angkor in the previous century, the Lao had begun to shift into the middle Mekong Valley and onto the Khorat Plateau where the land was flatter and more fertile.

Phothisalat's aggressiveness contributed to the souring of relations with Ayutthaya. Tensions between the neighbours flared up over the now weakened state of Lan Na; Lane Xang prevailed, and Phothisalat's son **Setthathilat** (1548–71) assumed the throne at Chiang Mai in 1546. He quickly hurried home, however, after the death of his father, who was crushed beneath his elephant during a display of his riding skills. In his hasty departure, Setthathilat nonetheless managed to pilfer Lan Na's talismanic Emerald Buddha, the sacred **Pha Kaew** that today is the palladium of the ruling line in Bangkok.

The Burmese invasions

Setthathilat was only 14 when, in 1548, he assumed the throne of Lane Xang. But the young king's hold over Lan Na gradually slipped away, as internal disputes in Chiang Mai and the rise of a powerful Burmese kingdom in the west dashed hopes of a greater Lao state unifying Lane Xang and Lan Na. Wary of the growing **Burmese threat**, Setthathilat reacted defensively. In 1563, he officially moved his capital to Vientiane and quickly set about building brick ramparts around the city. In deference to Xieng Dong Xieng Thong, the Pha Bang was left behind and the city was renamed after the revered image, while the Emerald Buddha was placed in the newly constructed Haw Pha Kaew in Vientiane.

Lane Xang managed to forge an alliance with Ayutthaya, but the Tai states proved no match for the armies of the Burmese warrior-kings who reduced Lan Na, Ayutthaya and Lane Xang to vassalage in a matter of a decade, and sacked Vientiane in 1565. The invaders were eventually repelled by a guerrilla campaign led by the king. After reclaiming Vientiane, Setthathilat renovated That Phanom in Sikhotabong and built That Luang in the capital, in an effort to lift the morale of his vassals in the central Mekong; they had misgivings about being ruled by a royal line whose roots were in Luang Prabang, especially one that was taxing their resources by waging a costly war.

By the end of 1569, Lane Xang was the only Tai power remaining. Burma once again set its sights on Vientiane, which fell for the second time, and once again Setthathilat regained his capital – but this time the heavy demands on the *muang* of the central Mekong brought resentment to boiling point. Setthathilat was lured into a campaign against the mountain peoples of the south by the powerful ruler of Sikhotabong, and was never seen again. The king's downfall revealed a major weakness in Lane Xang: the monarchy still depended on the loyalty of its vassals, but the latter no longer felt any strong allegiance to the king or to Lane Xang. With the death of Setthathilat, Lane Xang plunged into turmoil as the Burmese retook Vientiane and extended their rule to the Vietnamese frontier. By the early 1580s the kingdom was in such disarray that no king sat on the throne for nearly a decade. It would take half a century for Lane Xang to recover.

Sourinyavongsa and the Golden Age

The decisive character who returned stability to Lane Xang and eventually ushered in its **Golden Age** was Sourinyavongsa (1637–94). Although rarely seen in public, he was a popular king who ruled over a peaceful and prosperous kingdom. The **first Europeans** to reach Lane Xang, a mission from the Dutch East India Company led by Gerritt van Wuysthoff and a party of Jesuits, arrived during Sourinyavongsa's reign to find a flourishing Buddhist kingdom whose wealth was poured into the construction of religious monuments and the monastic order. Monks – more numerous than the soldiers of Germany, as one visitor observed – came from as far as Cambodia and Burma to Vientiane, which had emerged as a regional centre of Buddhist studies.

Sourinyavongsa ensured his reign was peaceful by aligning Lane Xang with neighbouring powers through marriage, although he did not hesitate to resort to force when necessary – after all it was a violent struggle among relatives that won him the throne in the first place. When the ruler of Xieng Khuang refused to offer his daughter in marriage to Sourinyavongsa, Lane Xang invaded Xieng Khuang, seizing the woman in question and taking several thousand captives, who were resettled near the capital. Thereafter Xieng Khuang paid regular tribute to Vientiane and was forced to break off its relationship with Vietnam. Sourinyavongsa took the daughter of the Vietnamese emperor as a concubine and established the boundaries between the two states in a treaty with Vietnam which identified all people living in houses on piles as Lao subjects and all living in homes that rested on the ground as Vietnamese. The frontier with Ayutthaya remained unchanged, with both countries respecting the border established by Setthathilat between the Mekong and the Chao Phraya rivers. Lane Xang was left holding sway over the northern and eastern portions of the Khorat Plateau.

Sourinyavongsa avoided the bitter rivalries that contributed to the downfall of Setthathilat, by striking a balance between the regional interests of the kingdom. He appeased the powerful families of the central Mekong by dividing the powers of state among three chief ministers – the minister of the palace conducted foreign relations and ran the royal secretariat; a second commanded the army and oversaw Vientiane; and a third, the viceroy, the powerful ruler of Sikhotabong, ruled the south.

While the new balance of power provided the stability Lane Xang needed to flourish, no provisions were made to maintain that stability after the king's death. In the end, the kingdom paid the price for Sourinyavongsa's stern brand of justice: the king had executed his only son for adultery, leaving no obvious heir to the throne when he died in 1694. Once again there was a political crisis, but this time around, the country's three regions went their separate ways.

The division of Lane Xang

In 1698, Vientiane was taken over by **Setthathilat II**, a Lane Xang prince who returned from exile in Vietnam to establish a new kingdom. Very soon, however, **Setthathilat** had trouble on his northern flank. Sourinyavongsa's grandsons – Kingkitsalat and Inthasom – had fled Vientiane to Chiang Hung (present-day Jinghong in Yunnan) some years before and sought assistance from their mother's relatives in Sipsong Pa Na. With the aid of a cousin, the princes raised an army, captured Luang Prabang in 1706 and soon after marched on Vientiane. Setthathilat appealed for help from Ayutthaya. The king of Ayutthaya negotiated a division of the territory at the bend in the Mekong, south of Paklai, making Kingkitsalat the first ruler of an independent Luang Prabang kingdom, and leaving Setthathilat to rule over Vientiane.

Meanwhile, in the south, a new ruling house had emerged at **Champasak**. The prince, sometimes said to be a long lost son of Sourinyavongsa, assumed the throne as King Soi Sisamouth in 1713. Thus the new ruling lines of each of the three major principalities, Luang Prabang, Vientiane and Champasak, could claim, however tenuously, some link to Fa Ngum and, by extension, to Khoun Borom. Family ties notwithstanding, it didn't take long for these isolated principalities of inland Southeast Asia to be at each other's throats, making these weak states easy prey for their larger neighbours. The rivalry between Luang Prabang and Vientiane was particularly bitter, deteriorating further when a second wave of Burmese invasions swept across the Tai world in the 1760s and forces from Vientiane aligned with the invaders and helped sack Luang Prabang.

Ayutthaya, which had flourished since the last wave of Burmese invasions, was next. The Burmese breached the walls and took the city in 1767, razing everything to the ground and hauling off tens of thousands of prisoners. The city was abandoned, but with remarkable speed the Siamese built a new kingdom, one that was to succeed at the expense of the Lao states.

The rise of Siam

Under the charismatic leadership of King Taksin, a military genius, the **Siamese** quickly rebuilt their kingdom downriver from Ayutthaya near Bangkok, and within a decade had retaken its territory, conquered Lan Na, and were prepared to expand to the east to secure its perimeter. Taking advantage of a peaceful Burma and a distracted Vietnam, twenty thousand Siamese soldiers set out towards Vientiane in 1778.

A second army of ten thousand swept east through Cambodia and, after conquering first Champasak and then Sikhotabong, turned north and marched on Vientiane. Here, the two Siamese forces met before the ramparts of Vientiane and were joined by a battalion from Luang Prabang bent on revenge. The city fell, and hundreds of prisoners, including the royal family, were dragged back to Siam and forcibly resettled on the plains north of the Siamese capital. The two Buddha image palladia of Lane Xang, the Pha Bang – which had been relocated to Vientiane by Setthathilat II in 1705 – and the Pha Kaew, were hauled off as well and enshrined in Thonburi (that part of Bangkok west of the Chao Phraya River). By reducing Champasak and Vientiane to vassal states and bringing Luang Prabang into an unequal alliance, Siam had extended its empire to the Annamite Mountains and forced the Lao world to adjust to a predominantly Bangkok-centred existence for the next century.

Anou's rebellion

The captured Lao princes returned to Vientiane as vassal kings, beginning with Nanthasen (1782–92). He brought with him the Pha Bang, which the Siamese king had decided was bad luck for his kingdom. Nanthasen didn't waste time in rekindling the old conflict with Luang Prabang, which his forces conquered in 1792. But Siam was wary of allowing any of the Lao vassal states to improve their position at the expense of another, and so recalled Nanthasen. He was replaced by Inthavong (1792–1804), the elder brother of the accomplished general Anou, who served as viceroy and led Lao armies to fight in the name of Siam in battles with Burma. By the time of Inthavong's death at the turn of the century, Vientiane had begun to pay tribute to Vietnam and, when **Anou** (1804–28) was chosen to ascend to the throne, he immediately notified the Vietnamese.

Siam became increasingly alarmed by Vietnam's growing influence, and, worried that Vietnam had its eye on Champasak, decided to run the risk of turning Anou into a powerful, and potentially dangerous, vassal by appointing Yo (1819–27), Anou's son, to the Champasak throne. Anou, who envisioned restoring Lane Xang to its former glory, made good on Bangkok's fears. On the pretence of coming to Siam's aid in the event of an attack by the British, who had by this time established a presence in Burma, Anou's and Yo's troops advanced across the Khorat Plateau early in 1827, and by late February had come within a few days' march of Bangkok. However, Anou misjudged the strength of the Siamese, who struck back fiercely, capturing Yo and sacking Vientiane. Anou fled to Vietnam. When he returned to Vientiane with a small force several months later, fighting broke out which resulted in Anou's capture. Siamese forces destroyed every building in the capital, save for Wat Sisaket, and dragged the entire population back to Thailand, where they were resettled. Vientiane was abandoned to the jungle; it was still in ruins when French explorers arrived four decades later. Anou was the last Lao ruler to attempt to liberate the former territories of Lane Xang.

During the decades that followed Anou's defeat, Siam and Vietnam jockeyed for control over the fragmented Lao *muang*. By force and diplomacy, Siam depopulated the area east of the Mekong, particularly in south central Laos, leaving a wasteland of burned villages and rice fields. Only Luang Prabang managed to stay intact. **Xieng Khuang** represented the greatest source of conflict in the struggle, effectively operating as a back door for a Siamese invasion of Vietnam.

By the middle of the nineteenth century, the Lao territories had become a buffer zone between the two powers. Siam was dominant in the Mekong Valley; the Vietnamese held sway in the east; joint control was exercised over what was left of Muang Phuan. This balancing act was soon upset, however, by **marauding Chinese**, remnants of Chinese rebellions, who swept through the northern Lao territories on horseback in the 1870s and 1880s. Siam, its position in Laos endangered by the incursions, launched a series of military expeditions. The last of these campaigns backfired, leading to the sacking of Luang Prabang and eventually to Siam's loss of Laos to the French.

French conquest

As the nineteenth century wore on, French governments became increasingly imperialistic. With Britain threatening to dominate trade with China, France saw Vietnam, and by extension Laos, as a potential route into the resource-rich Yunnan region. By the time the Mekong Exploration Commission of 1867–68 set off from Saigon for Laos and Yunnan, **Cochinchina** (present-day southern Vietnam) was already a French possession. Interest in Laos, however, quickly waned after the explorers found that significant stretches of the river were unnavigable.

It wasn't until the 1880s, when French explorer **Auguste Pavie** began trekking across Laos in search of political alliances and trade routes, that interest in the country was rekindled. As vice-consul in Luang Prabang, Pavie was the chief advocate of France's extension of the Indochina empire to the banks of the Mekong. He won an important ally for France by rescuing the northern kingdom's ageing king Oun Kham almost singlehandedly when the city, left virtually undefended by the Siamese, was torched in 1887 by a White Tai leader from Sipsong Chao Tai, out for revenge against Siam. Pavie's effort led the king to state: "[Luang Prabang] is not a conquest of Siam. Luang Prabang, wanting protection against all attacks, voluntarily offered its tribute. Now through Siam's interference, our ruin is complete… we will offer tribute to France…"

The relentless efforts of Pavie, coupled with gunboat diplomacy in Bangkok, eventually forced Siam to relinquish its claim to all territory east of the Mekong in 1893, although not before nearly sparking a war between Siam, Britain and France. Britain and France eventually settled on the Mekong River as the boundary between British Burma and French Laos and agreed to guarantee Siamese independence in the Chao Phraya River Valley in order to ensure a buffer zone between the two Western powers.

French rule

For half a century, Laos was ruled as a **French colony**. The boundaries with Burma, China, and Vietnam that were adopted – essentially the limits of the Mekong watershed – were carved with indifference to the complex existing political structures and ethnic groupings. In short, the borders meant nothing to the peoples of Laos. After initially dividing the Lao territories into three regions administered from Vietnam, the French eventually settled on **Vientiane** as their administrative capital and split the country up into eleven provinces, with the kingdom of Luang Prabang as a nominal protectorate.

After France realized that the Mekong was a poor transport route and that explorers' claims of an Eldorado were but a pipe dream, Laos became the neglected backwater of its Southeast Asian acquisitions. Accordingly, the French presence in Laos was minimal. The French made do with limited administrative manpower by simply floating their administration on top of existing feudal court structures. The royal houses of Xieng Khuang, Champasak and Luang Prabang – Vientiane's ruling line had been eliminated after Anou's defeat – were preserved, although France reduced the status of the rulers of Xieng Khuang and Champasak to that of governors and reserved the right to approve the successors to all three houses. Outside the cities, the French established an administrative system that pitted various ethnic groups against one another, effectively deflecting resentment away from themselves.

In order to cover the cost of administration, France imposed heavy **taxes** on opium, alcohol and salt, levied a head tax on males between 18 and 60, and required all adult males to perform unpaid *corvée* labour. Often required to walk days to work sites far from their villages, while supplying their own food, villagers sometimes responded by simply clearing out of an area altogether, returning once the project was completed. Such measures provoked **revolts**, some led by messianic religious figures, with the first large uprising beginning on the Bolaven Plateau in 1901 (see box, p.254). It seems these disturbances were more in response to central government intrusion into rural life and the disruption of old orders than they were specifically anti-French. It's telling, however, that most of these uprisings occurred among upland peoples, upon whom the French made harsher demands and for whose customs they showed less respect. Later, these revolts were construed as forerunners of the nationalist Lao Issara and Pathet Lao movements.

While explorers' reports that Laos was teeming with **natural resources** proved overly optimistic, the French did manage to exploit, among other things, tin deposits near Thakhek and teak trees, which were cut and floated down the Mekong, and introduced coffee. France's chief agricultural exports were cardamom from the Bolaven Plateau area and, from the highlands of Xieng Khuang, **opium**, a product that was later allegedly used by the CIA and the Pathet Lao to finance their respective war efforts.

Trade was in the hands of Chinese merchants, as it had been for centuries. Goods followed traditional routes from Laos and the west bank of the Mekong across the Khorat Plateau towards Bangkok and away from French Vietnam. The same Chinese merchants who exported cardamom, sticklac and benzoin, skins and ivory to the trading houses of the Siamese capital were already importing cheap British and German products by the time the French established themselves in Laos.

With trade flowing towards Bangkok, minimal exports and a depleted population providing an insufficient tax base, the colony remained dependent on **federal subsidies**. The French hoped to remedy these problems by building roads and, eventually, a railway from the Vietnamese coast – a project derailed first by the Great Depression and then by World War II – and by encouraging mass Vietnamese migration, in order to tackle the age-old problem of too much land and too few people. Had it not been for World War II, the French may well have succeeded in making the Lao a minority in their own land, in which case Laos might not exist today.

For all its talk of the "civilizing mission" of their particular brand of imperialism, France appeared to have no mission in Laos, other than to deny territory to the

Hill tribes of Laos

The Lao Soung (literally, the "high Lao") are comparative newcomers to Laos, having migrated from China at the beginning of the nineteenth century and settled on the only land available to them, at elevations over 1000m above sea level. Among them are the country's most colourfully dressed ethnic groups, including the Hmong, Mien, Lahu and Akha. For many visitors, the opportunity to visit a hill-tribe village is the highlight of a trip to Laos. Despite the prevalence of Western clothing these days, most villages appear not to have changed for centuries.

Hmong girls in traditional dress ▲

Tribal vendors at Muang Sing morning market ▼

The Hmong

Most numerous among the Lao Soung are the **Hmong**, their clothing some of the most colourful to be found in Laos. The ethnic group (within which a number of sub-groups, known by the colour of their clothes, ie **Red Hmong** and **Black Hmong**) are particularly known for their silver; Hmong babies receive their first silver necklace at the age of one month, and by the time they are adults they will have several kilos of **silver jewellery**, most of which is cached until special occasions such as Hmong New Year. Interestingly, their written language uses Roman letters – though it's hardly surprising considering it was devised by Western missionaries.

As many Hmong fought on the side of the Royal Lao Government during the war, the tribe has been **persecuted** since the Revolution; pogroms caused many to flee for refugee camps in Thailand, from where some were able to make their way to the USA and France. The recent deportation of thousands of Hmong from **Thailand** back to Laos received international criticism. Within Laos,

Akha women, Muang Sing ▼

Hill-tribe treks

Slow to assimilate to the relatively modern ways of the lowland Lao, the hill-tribe communities offer a glimpse of traditional Southeast Asian lifestyles. Visiting a hill-tribe village through a trek enables visitors the privileged opportunity to experience this way of life first hand. The most popular centres for hill-tribe treks are Luang Namtha (see p.185) and Muang Sing (see p.190), though if you're looking to get a bit more off the beaten track then it's well worth making the slog up to Phongsali (see p.180) for its burgeoning trekking opportunities.

Hmong use of slash-and-burn agriculture has given the government an excuse to **resettle** them at lower elevations. Tight controls on the media mean that unrest among the Hmong and Lao military drives against them are rarely reported.

The Lahu

The **Lahu** inhabit areas of northwestern Laos, as well as Thailand and Burma. A branch of the tribe known as the **Lahu Na**, or **Black Lahu**, are known first and foremost for their hunting skills. Formerly they used crossbows but now they manufacture their own muzzle-loading rifles which they use to hunt birds and rodents. Old American M1 carbines and Chinese-made Kalashnikov rifles are used to bring down larger game, and **Lahu hunters** are sometimes seen at the side of the road displaying freshly killed wildlife for sale, though the practice is increasingly less acceptable in the eyes of both government and local people.

The Mien

Linguistically related to the Hmong, the **Mien** also immigrated into Laos from China, but their culture is much more Sinicized; the Mien use **Chinese characters** to write and worship Taoist deities. Like the Hmong, they cultivate **opium**, which they trade for salt and other necessities that are not easily obtained at high elevations, and are known to be astute traders. It's estimated that nearly half the country's Mien population fled after the communist victory. Today Sayaboury province, northwest of Vientiane, has the largest population of Mien in Laos.

The **costume** of Mien women is perhaps Laos's most exotic, involving intricately embroidered pantaloons worn with

▲ Lahu people at home

▼ Mien women sporting woolly boas

Akha villiage, northern Laos ▲

Akha people work the fields ▼

a coat and turban of indigo blue. The most striking feature is a woolly red boa, attached to the collar and running down the front of their coats.

The Akha

The **Akha** are another of the highlands' stunning dressers. Catching a first glimpse of the Akha women's **distinctive headgear** – covered with rows of silver baubles and coins – is one of the highlights of many a Lao visit. Speakers of a Tibeto–Burman language, the Akha began **migrating south** from China's Yunnan province to escape the mayhem of the mid-nineteenth-century Muslim Rebellion. This was followed by another exodus after the Chinese communist victory in 1949 and again during the Cultural Revolution. They now inhabit parts of Vietnam, Burma (Myanmar) and Thailand as well as Laos, where they are found mainly in Phongsali and Luang Namtha provinces.

Akha villages are easily distinguished by their elaborate "spirit gate". This gate is hung with woven bamboo "stars" that block spirits, as well as crude male and female effigies with exaggerated genitalia. The Akha are **animists** and, like the Hmong, rely on a village shaman and his rituals to help solve problems of health and fertility or provide protection against malevolent spirits. The Akha raise dogs as pets as well as for **food**, but do not eat their own pets; dogs that will be slaughtered for their meat are bought or traded from another village.

The Akha are fond of **singing** and often do so while on long walks to the fields or while working. Some songs are specially sung for fieldwork but love ballads and a sort of "Akha blues" – songs about struggling through life while surrounded by rich neighbours – are also popular.

British. Elsewhere in Indochina, the French built schools, universities, a railway network and an extensive highway system, and though they did construct a skeletal highway system linking Laos with Vietnam and rebuilt monuments destroyed by the Siamese in the early 1800s, few improvements were made to Laos's educational or healthcare systems.

World War II

The initial fallout from events in Europe in 1940 was the **Japanese occupation** of Laos. Vichy France was left responsible for the administration of Indochina and gave the Japanese the right to move and station troops throughout the region. Sensing an opportunity to avenge its defeat of 1893, Siam, renamed **Thailand** in 1939, seized the west-bank territories of Xainyabouli and Champasak, leaving the Lao angry with both the Thai for encroaching on their territory and the French for failing to defend the country.

To counter the appeal of Thai nationalist propaganda, the French encouraged a weak **nationalism** among the Lao elite. They nurtured a renaissance of literature, theatre, music and dance, while supporting patriotic rallies and the creation of a national development programme. Schools were built, the healthcare system improved and the first Lao newspaper was published. Colonial officials raised concerns that these steps were arousing dangerous sentiments; they were to be proved right, although it would be left to the Japanese to shatter the illusion of French power and provide the spark for Lao independence.

In March 1945, the Japanese staged a pre-emptive strike to neutralize French forces in Indochina, imprisoning French soldiers and civil servants, and proclaiming an end to France's colonial regimes. Japanese forces reached Luang Prabang the following month and made Sisavang Vong, the pro-French king, declare independence, forcing his hand by hauling off the crown prince to Saigon. Somewhat less reluctantly, **Phetsarath**, who could trace his family line back to Anou, the last king of Vientiane, became prime minister. The eldest of three remarkable brothers who would profoundly affect Lao history, Phetsarath was now the second most powerful political figure after the king.

Free Laos

Nationalists across Indochina moved to take advantage of the power vacuum created by the end of World War II and **Japan's surrender**. In Laos, an independent-minded Lao elite formed a government which became known as the Lao Issara, literally "**Free Laos**", while next door Ho Chi Minh proclaimed the establishment of the Democratic Republic of Vietnam.

The rapid awakening of the Lao elite after years of French rule left them factionalized, with support split between opposition to the Japanese and opposition to the French. A power struggle ensued as King Sisavang Vong welcomed the return of the French and Phetsarath reaffirmed the independence of Laos and declared the union of the Kingdom of Luang Prabang and the territory of Champasak in a single, independent Kingdom of Laos. The king repudiated Phetsarath by dismissing him as prime minister and viceroy on October 10, 1945.

In response, the newly constituted **Lao Issara government** deposed the king two days later. This new government, which based itself in Vientiane, contained some of the key figures who would dominate politics in Laos over the course of the next few decades, including Phetsarath's younger brothers Souvannaphouma and Souphanouvong, both educated in Paris. Before joining the new government in Vientiane as Minister of Foreign Affairs and Chief of the Liberation Army, **Souphanouvong** was flown to Hanoi by an American general, where he met with, and earned the support of, Ho Chi Minh. He returned with a contingent of Viet Minh soldiers – the first instance of Vietnamese armed support for a Lao nationalist movement – and swore to continue the struggle until an independent Laos had been won.

The **Potsdam Agreement** marking the end of World War II failed to recognize the Lao Issara government. Under the terms of the agreement, the Japanese surrender was accepted by the British to the south, who facilitated the return of French occupation forces. In March 1946 French forces, along with their Lao allies, made their way slowly up the Mekong Valley. Lao Issara volunteers, led by Souphanouvong and assisted by the Viet Minh, resisted the French near Thakhek, but the French successfully reoccupied Vientiane in April 1946 and Luang Prabang three weeks later. Thousands of Lao Issara supporters and Vietnamese fled to Thailand, where Prince Phetsarath established a government-in-exile in Bangkok. Although Souphanouvong repeated US President Franklin Roosevelt's statement that the French should not be allowed to return to Indochina, the United States and Britain did not offer the Lao Issara support.

The Kingdom of Laos

In 1947, the newly constituted **Kingdom of Laos** began to take shape. Prince Boun Oum of Champasak, who had helped the French in the south, renounced his claim to a separate southern kingdom, strengthening the French position in Vientiane and paving the way for Laos to be unified under the royal house of Luang Prabang. The territories west of the Mekong were restored, elections for a Constituent Assembly were held and a new constitution proclaimed. The members of the new government, which was a decidedly pro-French body, were drawn from the elite that had benefited from the French presence all along. The government lacked cohesion, however, and the king opted to remain in Luang Prabang rather than move to Vientiane.

The French by now were increasingly bogged down in their struggle with the **Viet Minh,** which had erupted in December 1946 and would become known as the First Indochina War. What had begun as a police action had rapidly become a costly "war without borders" that was to last eight years and cost the lives of 93,000 on the French side and an estimated 200,000 Viet Minh supporters. Vietnamese nationalists coordinated and participated in Lao Issara guerrilla raids, led by Souphanouvong, on French convoys and garrisons. The Viet Minh's influence over Souphanouvong took its toll on the unity of the Lao Issara, and by May 1949 the rift had become irreparable; Souphanouvong was removed from his post. In July, France appealed to moderate elements of the Lao Issara by conceding greater authority to the Vientiane government. The Lao Issara announced its dissolution. As Souvannaphouma, along with two dozen moderate Lao Issara leaders, returned to Vientiane on board a French transport plane, Souphanouvong set out from Bangkok on foot for Viet Minh headquarters. Meanwhile, the leader of the movement, Phetsarath, remained behind, refusing to return to Laos until 1957, when his title of viceroy was finally restored by the king.

The Pathet Lao

When Souphanouvong arrived at Viet Minh headquarters in Tonkin in late 1949, he was warmly welcomed by Ho Chi Minh, who had ambitious plans for him. Souphanouvong, who sought only arms and money, also received some advice from Vo Nguyen Giap, the legendary Vietnamese general who would later defeat the French at Dien Bien Phu. In the course of the meeting, Giap told Souphanouvong to keep away from towns, saying "Remember, those who rule the countryside rule the country."

While the moderate members of the dissolved Lao Issara joined the new **Royal Lao Government** (RLG) in 1950, Souphanouvong founded his own government, which saw itself as the successor to the Lao Issara. In August 1950, in a far corner of northern Laos, Souphanouvong presided over the **First Resistance Congress**, which was supervised by the Viet Minh. The Congress adopted a twelve-point manifesto, at the bottom of which appeared the notation "**Pathet Lao**", literally "the Land of the Lao". This became the name by which his resistance group was to be known. The manifesto called for a truly independent and unified Laos to be governed by a coalition government with the RLG, and the Pathet Lao pledged cooperation with the Vietnamese and Khmer in the common struggle against the French.

The Pathet Lao then focused on recruiting members in northern and eastern Laos. Cadres moved into remote villages, promoting literacy, building schools and organizing village militias. Kaysone Phomvihane directed the Committee for the Organization of the Party, which recruited new cadres, until the **Lao People's Party** was formally established in 1955.

The First Indochina War

By the early 1950s, the **First Indochina War** had engulfed the region. Chinese military aid flowed to the Viet Minh, while the United States, smarting from the fall of China to the communists, supported France. After the routing of the nationalists in China and the outbreak of the Korean War, the French could portray, with greater success, their struggle against the Viet Minh not as a colonial war but as a fight in defence of the "Free World".

For the Viet Minh, Laos was an extension of their battle against the French. Twice in 1953 they staged major invasions of Laos, seizing large areas of the country before turning them over to the Pathet Lao.

By this point, Souphanouvong had formally established the headquarters of the resistance government in **Sam Neua**, which lay at the heart of an extensive "liberated zone"; meanwhile in Paris, Souvannaphouma was pressing the French for complete independence. By the time this was granted in October 1953, however, Laos was a divided country, with large areas controlled by the Pathet Lao and the rest of the country under the RLG.

Taunted by the Viet Minh invasions of Laos, which France was obliged by treaty to defend, General Henri Navarre, the French Commander-in-Chief in Indochina, ordered the French Expeditionary Force's parachute battalion to establish a massive base in **Dien Bien Phu** in November 1953. Navarre reasoned that by creating a camp in this isolated valley along the traditional invasion route of Laos, he could force the Viet Minh into an open battle – while at the same time protecting Laos – and end the war in eighteen months. The war did end, but not quite as he expected. The Viet Minh encircled the valley and began a bloody assault that lasted 59 days and cost the lives of twenty thousand Viet Minh soldiers. The French were forced to surrender on May 7, 1954. Their efforts to restore the pre-World War II status quo in Indochina had collapsed.

The Geneva Conference

On May 8, the nine delegations attending the **Geneva Conference** called to discuss the situation in Korea shifted their focus to Indochina. The government in Vientiane was represented by Phoui Sananikone, the scion of Vientiane's leading family and a leader of the anti-Japanese resistance in northern Laos during World War II. The Viet Minh arrived with a young Lao by the name of Nouhak Phoumsavanh, who proposed that the Pathet Lao resistance government of which he was a member be represented as well. Phoui defended the sovereignty of the Vientiane government and the proposal was rejected. The conference's final declaration included Phoui's proclamation that the RLG would not pursue a policy of aggression nor would it allow a foreign power to use its soil for hostile purposes. The **Agreement on the Cessation of Hostilities** was signed on July 20 – by the Viet Minh and France – which in addition to a ceasefire also called for a regrouping of opposing forces, leading to elections in two years.

Although Laos was reaffirmed as a unitary, independent state with a single government, the Pathet Lao did manage to win de facto recognition as an insurgency group and were allotted the provinces of Phongsali and Hua Phan in which to regroup.

America intervenes

The **United States** had since 1950 been funding an estimated seventy percent of the French war effort in Indochina. In 1951, the US signed an economic aid agreement with the government of Phoui Sananikone which aimed to speed up the development of a free and independent Laos. After the 1954 Geneva Accords, which the US did not sign, considering them a sell-out to international communism, strengthening the anti-communist governments of Indochina became a priority for President Dwight Eisenhower's administration. The withdrawal of the French military left a power vacuum on the edge of a historically expansionist state, a worrisome state of affairs in the eyes of the United States.

As of 1955, the US was financing most of the Lao government budget and completely bankrolling the Royal Lao Army, countering the Viet Minh, which was shouldering the entire cost of the Pathet Lao's army. Feeling that the French were not taking their responsibility of training the Lao army seriously enough, the US skirted the terms of the Geneva agreement by training select officers in Thailand and by equipping and expanding the police force. Other funds went into churning out propaganda, building roads and communications networks, and propping up the kip. The Americans bought truckloads of the local currency above the black market rate, burned the notes and gave the government US dollars in exchange.

For the next eight years, the US spent more on foreign aid to Laos per capita than it did on any other Southeast Asian country, though the overwhelming majority of the aid was military. As US dollars poured into the country, the army grew increasingly powerful and existing rivalries between leading families were reinforced, with the clans more concerned with improving their social standing than exercising responsible power. Fretting over recent communist takeovers around the world, US policies were motivated by the fear of the so-called **Domino Effect**. As President Eisenhower prepared to turn over the helm to John F. Kennedy, he told his successor: "If Laos is lost to the free world, in the long run we will lose all of Southeast Asia."

The quest for unity and neutrality

After Geneva, the priority of the RLG was to regain control of the two Pathet Lao provinces so that elections could be held in accordance with the peace settlement. But when elections finally went ahead in December 1955, it was without the Pathet Lao, disgruntled at being refused its demands for changes to the electoral law and freedom for its front organization, the Lao Patriotic Front (behind which stood the Lao People's Party), to operate as a political party. The elections resulted in the formation of a government led by **Prince Souvannaphouma**, who entered into negotiations with his half-brother Souphanouvong in the belief that national unity and neutrality were the key to the preservation of the state. The two sides cut a deal in November 1957 to include two Pathet Lao members in a coalition government in exchange for the reintegration of Hua Phan and Phongsali into the rest of Laos.

Left alone, it seemed, the people of Laos could work out their problems, or so Souvannaphouma thought. However, when elections the following May gave leftist candidates 21 seats in the National Assembly, the US embassy and the CIA actively promoted the creation of the right-wing Committee for the Defence of National Interests, known as the CDNI, and withheld aid from Souvannaphouma's government, forcing its collapse in July. Power in Vientiane had shifted from the National Assembly to the American Embassy.

With the collapse of the government, any hope for a neutral, united Laos was rapidly disintegrating. After a right-wing government – led by **Phoui Sananikone** – took charge in August, the truce put in place by the Geneva Accords began to unravel. Civil war seemed inevitable. In January, claiming that a North Vietnamese invasion was imminent, Phoui demanded and received emergency powers for a year, effectively shutting the Pathet Lao out of Vientiane's political arena and opening the door for the Royal Lao Army to gain control of the Ministry of Defence. A ruthless and powerful military figure, **General Phoumi Nosavan**, assumed the post of vice minister of defence. The story goes that in 1949 he drew matchsticks to decide between staying on with Prince Souphanouvong in his alliance with the Viet Minh or travelling to Vientiane to cooperate with French forces. A decade later, no such indecision hampered Phoumi as he eagerly auditioned for the role of strongman. Immediately stepping up harassment of the Pathet Lao's political front, he did not disappoint the Americans.

After negotiations to integrate two Pathet Lao battalions into the Royal Lao Army stalled, one battalion slipped back to Hua Phan, where the communist forces were preparing to resume their insurgency. The government considered the leftist troops to be in rebellion and responded by arresting Pathet Lao leaders in Vientiane, including Souphanouvong. As skirmishes signalled a return to the battlefield, the country's two most powerful political figures, Prince Phetsarath and King Sisavang Vong, died within a fortnight of each other in October 1959.

Phoumi's coup and the growth of the Pathet Lao

Phoui's failure to rein in the increasingly powerful military had sown the seeds for his ousting. With a helping hand from the vehemently anti-communist CDNI, General Phoumi, by now in charge of the ministry of defence, staged a **coup** in December. His troops took to the streets of Vientiane under the pretext, yet again, of a Pathet Lao attack. Although Phoumi failed to take charge of the newly formed government, it was nonetheless controlled by the military and staunchly aligned with the US and Thailand. Rigged elections held in April left the leftists without a seat, much to the satisfaction of the US.

The **corruption** of the generals and politicians in Vientiane and the purge of communist cadres in the countryside gave the Pathet Lao propaganda machine ample material with which to win hearts and minds. With Souphanouvong biding his time in jail, Kaysone Phomvihane, as head of Pathet Lao military operations, expanded his control over the organization's leadership. Communist forces were active throughout most of the country, and by 1960, roughly twenty percent of the population was no longer under government control.

Although the Royal Lao Army generals were far too concerned with vying for influence to worry about the communists' successes in indoctrinating the rural population, the men guarding Souphanouvong and his comrades certainly took note. As the new government – one which was set on a show trial for the Red Prince – was taking shape, all fifteen Pathet Lao prisoners, along with their guards, slipped off in the night. Souphanouvong began his now legendary 500km march to Pathet Lao headquarters in Hua Phan.

The Laotian crisis

The Pathet Lao weren't the only ones fed up with the self-serving politicians and generals in Vientiane. In August 1960, a disgruntled 26-year-old army captain named **Kong Le** seized control of Vientiane, much to the surprise of the United States and the Cabinet, whose ministers were away in Luang Prabang. Proclaiming himself a neutralist, Kong Le called for an end to "Lao killing Lao" and an end to foreign interference in the affairs of the country. He then invited Souvannaphouma to lead a new government.

As Laos began to split apart, the Pathet Lao seized more territory. Phoumi regrouped what troops he could in Savannakhet, where he gained the backing of the CIA. Planes belonging to Air America, a civilian contract airline that was later revealed to be a front for the CIA, began flying into Savannakhet with arms and bundles of money.

In November, Phoumi's men, coordinated by American advisors and assisted by a group of crack Thai troops, began a march on Vientiane, as Moscow and Washington – both of whom saw Laos as an excellent place from which to control Southeast Asia – looked on. The Soviet Union began airlifting supplies to Kong Le's neutralist forces in the capital. Laos was now at the heart of a Cold War showdown.

By the time Phoumi's troops reached Vientiane in December, the neutralists had allied themselves with the Pathet Lao and the Viet Minh. With both sides reluctant to spill Lao blood, a sloppy battle ensued which was won by the rightists. The

Soon after Soviet aircraft began dropping weapons and supplies by parachute to Pathet Lao and neutralist forces stationed on the Plain of Jars in December 1960, a Central Intelligence Agency operative by the name of Bill Lair boarded an H-34 helicopter in Vientiane and flew off into the mountains of Xieng Khuang in search of **Vang Pao**, a little-known Royal Lao Army lieutenant-colonel. With Laos in the midst of a crisis that held the rapt attention of the world's superpowers, the 30-year-old Hmong officer was holding out against the communist forces who had taken over the Plain of Jars and the surrounding hillsides, an area heavily populated by Hmong. Lair and Vang Pao had been preparing for this meeting, albeit unknowingly, for a decade. The Texan had spent the better part of the 1950s training members of Thailand's national police in guerrilla warfare, a measure taken against the perceived threat of an invasion by communist China. Vang Pao, meanwhile, had been earning his reputation as a ruthless and clever soldier by leading raids against North Vietnamese forces stationed in Laos, first as a police officer and later as a member of a group of French-trained hill-tribe irregulars.

As retold in Second Indochina War correspondent Jane Hamilton-Merritt's *Tragic Mountains,* Vang Pao made clear in his meeting with Lair that the Hmong and the United States shared a common enemy: "For me, I can't live with communism. I must either leave or fight. I prefer to fight." In the cool of a hillside thatch hut, the seeds of the CIA's so-called **secret army** were sown. To Lair and Vang Pao, American and Hmong needs were a perfect fit. The United States provided weapons and training for the indigenous population, who were led by one of their own in a fight for their own cause.

The **Hmong** were naturals as guerrilla soldiers. Determined to defend their homeland, they knew the terrain and could run circles around the Pathet Lao and the North Vietnamese. After a three-day crash course in the weapons of modern warfare, Vang Pao's initial force of several hundred soldiers won their first battle, ambushing a curious band of Pathet Lao who had tracked the supplies descending from Air America planes by parachute. Operation Momentum, as the project was known, was a success. The clandestine army developed into an effective **guerrilla fighting force**, their numbers swelling to twenty thousand over the course of the decade. Hmong soldiers rescued downed American pilots, learned to fly fighter planes and bravely marched into battle, often trailed by their wives and children. Most importantly, Vang Pao's slapdash band of irregulars were all that stood between the Mekong and the North Vietnamese.

At first, US costs were low and Americans few and far between, a far cry from the battle next door in Vietnam. But a low-cost, home-grown war run out of the hip pocket of a lone CIA agent wasn't what the United States military had in mind for Laos. As the 1960s progressed, the war in Laos escalated, advisors flooded the American ranks, and the role of air power grew to criminal proportions, and with it the role of the Hmong. Although they were best at guerrilla warfare, the Hmong were increasingly involved in set-piece, conventional battles against a determined North Vietnamese force; an estimated 25 percent of the Hmong who enlisted to fight were killed in battle.

By 1968, Vang Pao's forces were no longer fighting for their homeland, they were fighting for the United States, pawns of the **war in Vietnam**. The institutionalization of the Laos war had reduced Operation Momentum to a bloated recruitment programme churning out war-weary Hmong mercenaries. Half a world away in Washington DC, former ambassador to Vientiane William Sullivan, questioned in Senate hearings as to whether the US had any responsibility for the well-being of Vang Pao and his people, made it painfully clear where the Hmong stood: "No formal obligation upon the United States; no."

neutralists retreated north and eventually joined Pathet Lao forces on the Plain of Jars. Souvannaphouma, who fled for Phnom Penh before the battle, was formally ousted as prime minister by King Sisavang Vatthana and replaced by Prince Boun Oum of Champasak.

But by March 1961, as a neutralist–Pathet Lao offensive got under way, President Kennedy announced American support for a **political settlement** involving the neutralization of Laos. This was an acknowledgement that America saw military victory as unlikely given the incompetence and reluctance to fight on the part of the Royal Lao Army, something that Kennedy sensed when he first met the diminutive Phoumi and commented, "if that's our strongman, we're in trouble". With Cuba, Berlin and numerous other hotspots on the radar, Washington worried about spreading itself too thinly. The president concluded his March 23rd speech on the "Laotian Crisis" saying: "All we want in Laos is peace, not war; a truly neutral government, not a Cold War pawn; a settlement concluded at the conference table and not on the battlefield."

The United States had already begun to hedge its bets, however. Lao army troops were training in Thailand, US army advisers had arrived with new weapons and a handful of planes, and the CIA launched Operation Momentum (see p.279), which established a **clandestine army** recruited from the Hmong.

Two months after Kennedy's speech, a **second conference** was convened at **Geneva**, but despite the determination of the Soviet Union and the US to neutralize tensions over Laos, it took a year and a decisive defeat for the Royalist army at Luang Namtha before the feuding Lao factions reached an agreement on the formation of a **second coalition government**. The second coalition, however, was a failure, dissolving after the April 1963 assassination of a neutralist cabinet member. Fearing arrest or assassination, Pathet Lao ministers fled the capital.

The tacit agreement

Following the second round in Geneva, Washington's priority was South Vietnam, where, by 1962, it already had ten thousand military advisers and support troops. By October 1962 American and Soviet military personnel had withdrawn from Laos, but only forty North Vietnamese had cleared the checkpoints, leaving an estimated five thousand troops in Laos.

The country was being drawn increasingly into the **Second Indochina War**, as North Vietnam and the United States undermined its neutrality in the pursuit of their agendas in Vietnam. Lao territory was a crucial part of the North Vietnamese war effort. They could not risk allowing the United States to use northern Laos, in particular the Plain of Jars, to threaten North Vietnam and they needed to control the mountainous eastern corridor of southern Laos in order to move soldiers and supplies to South Vietnam along the Ho Chi Minh Trail (see p.223). The US saw no option but to challenge North Vietnam's strategy. Eventually, all sides with a stake in Laos came to the same conclusion about the Geneva Accords: while they would have loved to point an accusing finger at the opposition's violations of the agreement, they had much more to gain by quietly pursuing their own agendas. So the right-wing Lao, the Americans and the Thais on the one side and the Pathet Lao, the North Vietnamese and their Chinese and Soviet backers on the other all tacitly agreed to pretend to abide by the accords, guaranteeing Laos's neutrality while keeping the country at war.

Even after the collapse of the second coalition government in 1963, patriotic Souvannaphouma was determined to keep the vision of a neutral Laos alive. After negotiations with the Chinese and Vietnamese failed, he returned to Vientiane and on April 18, 1964, he announced his plans to resign, prompting Phoumi's rightist rivals to launch a surprise coup the next day. But within a few days, the prince was back in power and the generals were out.

Excluded from the new government, the Pathet Lao went on the offensive, chasing Kong Le's remaining neutralists off the Plain of Jars and into an alliance with Vang Pao and his Hmong army. The communist offensive fitted neatly into what would become the standard seesaw pattern of fighting in northern Laos, in which each side went on the offensive when the season best suited them.

But in the spring of 1964, the communists came up against a whole new enemy: **airpower**. Single-prop T-28 aircraft hammered at communist positions, scaring off their soldiers who had never faced aeroplanes before. Within a matter of weeks, T-28 bombing runs were joined by US jets, which were sent over Laos as they happened to be in the neighbourhood. Once the bombing began, Washington apparently decided it wasn't such a bad idea. And although the bombing campaign would be reported for years by Pathet Lao and North Vietnamese radio, it would take five years before the United States public heard anything about it.

Escalation

In 1964, a new phase of the war in Laos began. With the US pushing hard for an **escalation of the bombing** in the summer, Souvannaphouma, prodded by the US embassy, declared that the North Vietnamese were using the eastern flank of Laos to send combatants and supplies to South Vietnam along what would become known as the **Ho Chi Minh Trail**. He then gave the go-ahead for what were euphemistically known as "armed reconnaissance" flights over Laos, permission that essentially became a blank cheque for the US to bomb wherever it pleased.

The war was intensifying next door in **Vietnam**, too. US President Lyndon B. Johnson, facing an election in November 1964, did not want to be the president who lost against the communists. After the USS *Maddox* came under attack off the coast of North Vietnam, US senators passed the **Gulf of Tonkin Resolution**, which became Johnson's justification for the Vietnam War. No such resolution was passed regarding Laos; after all, the country was "neutral".

When Ambassador William Sullivan assumed his post in Vientiane near the end of 1964, his assignment was to wage war while maintaining the fiction of the Geneva Accords, which he had personally helped to negotiate. He came to the Lao capital aware of US plans for Operation Rolling Thunder – a sustained carpet-bombing campaign against North Vietnam designed to go "after the manure pile" rather than simply swatting flies, as the Commander of the US Air Force, General Curtis Le May, eloquently put it. Even before the Vietnam operation began, Sullivan established his own programmes for Laos, called **Operation Barrel Roll** in the north and **Operation Steel Tiger** in the south.

Sullivan set the tone for the US campaign in Laos – ground troops were kept out (apart from reconnaissance missions and raids on the Ho Chi Minh Trail area) and military planes had to take off outside the country. The war took place in total secrecy. As British journalist Christopher Robbins wrote in *The Ravens*, based on interviews with pilots who fought in "the Other Theatre", "There was another war even nastier than the one in Vietnam, and so secret that the location of the country in which it was being fought was classified… The men who chose to fight in it were handpicked volunteers, and anyone accepted for a tour seemed to disappear as if from the face of the earth."

From 1964 until the ceasefire of February 1973, United States planes flew 580,944 sorties – or 177 a day – over Laos and dropped 2,093,100 tonnes of bombs – equivalent to one planeload of bombs every eight minutes around the clock for nine years – making Laos the most heavily bombed country per capita in the history of warfare.

The turning point: 1968

On March 10, 1968, communist forces overran a strategic limestone massif in Hua Phan which the US had crowned with a high-tech bombing guidance device that directed attacks on Hanoi and was guarded by Hmong troops. The **fall of Phou Pha Thi** (see box, p.163) underscored the lack of unified command that plagued the various US factions – the embassy, the CIA and the air force – responsible for fighting the Laos War.

According to Roger Warner in his book *Shooting at the Moon*, while some involved in directing the US war effort thought the US had erred by provoking the North Vietnamese with the installation of this direct threat to Hanoi's security, others argued that the North Vietnamese escalation in Laos was simply a part of the same intensive effort that produced the January 31 **Tet Offensive**, in which a combined force of 70,000 communists violated a truce to launch attacks on more than a hundred cities across South Vietnam. In a Washington reeling from Tet, which brought with it the popular perception that the communists were winning the war in Vietnam, President Johnson vetoed requests for a massive troop expansion, and on March 31 he suspended bombing north of the Twentieth Parallel to jump-start the peace talks in Paris that would grind on for five years. By the year's end the bombing had completely ended.

The suspension of bombing in Vietnam was terrible news for Laos, as the US Air Force's reaction was to send more planes over Laos than ever before. Swarms of planes circled the country, zeroing in on their targets with the help of a new breed of forward air controllers known as Ravens, introduced in the wake of the Phou Pha Thi disaster. These pilots, dressed in civilian clothes, flew single-engine Cessna propeller planes, with a hill-tribe translator in the backseat to communicate with ground forces, guiding up to three hundred American sorties per day. The early days of Operation Momentum, when the CIA quietly waged a grassroots guerrilla war, were a distant memory.

Nixon's presidency

In order to facilitate pulling out of Southeast Asia while saving face for the United States, President **Nixon** initiated a policy of "**Vietnamization**". This involved a gradual withdrawal of US forces coupled with an intensification of the air war and more material support, as well as pursuing communist sanctuaries with greater intensity in the hope that South Vietnam could hold its own against the North.

The first major test of this strategy was the United States' **invasion of Cambodia**, which lay at the end of the Ho Chi Minh Trail. Until 1970, Cambodia, under the leadership of Prince Norodom Sihanouk, had stayed neutral in the war. Neutrality for Sihanouk, however, meant allowing the North Vietnamese to operate on Cambodian soil and the United States to bomb the North Vietnamese with B-52s. On March 18, 1970, a right-wing pro-US general named Lon Nol replaced Sihanouk in a coup and, two weeks later, US and South Vietnamese troops invaded the regions of the country nearest South Vietnam.

The operation set off a political uproar in the US, and massive **anti-war demonstrations** spread across the country. Politically, the Cambodian "incursion", as it was termed, and subsequent protests prompted the US Congress to pass a measure forbidding the use of American ground troops in Cambodia and Laos. Had they not, US ground troops might have taken part in **Lam Son 719** (see p.223) – one of the most disastrous operations undertaken by the United States in the whole of the war. Backed by American air power, 20,000 South Vietnamese troops drove across the Annamite Mountains in the hope of cutting North Vietnamese supply lines near Xepon. The move proved catastrophic. Five thousand South Vietnamese were killed or wounded, 176 Americans died and more than one hundred US army helicopters were shot down, with an estimated six hundred more damaged. It became clear that even with massive US support, the South Vietnamese didn't stand a chance, pushing US policymakers closer to the realization that the war was a lost cause.

The US realized that as long as it fought in Indochina, it would continue to give the Soviet Union and China reason to cooperate. By July 1971, Nixon seemed ready to sacrifice South Vietnam – and by extension Laos and Cambodia – in order to create an opening with China.

On January 27, 1973, the United States, North Vietnam, South Vietnam and the Viet Cong at last signed the **Paris Accords**, under the terms of which a ceasefire was established and all remaining American troops were to be repatriated by April. In reality the accords would accomplish little more than smoothing the US withdrawal from Indochina.

The Pathet Lao takeover

Souvannaphouma wanted assurances from the Americans that the North Vietnamese would pull their troops out of Laos. But the Vietnamese had never acknowledged having troops in Laos in the first place and the US had already committed itself to a withdrawal. The North Vietnamese knew this left them in a position of power and decided to stay in Laos and Cambodia until a new government was established in Vientiane. When the Vientiane government and the Pathet Lao eventually signed an agreement of reconciliation, neither US nor North Vietnamese signatures were present.

Continued negotiations resulted in the formation of a **third coalition government** in April 1974, with leftists taking half the ministerial portfolios and the remainder going to the right. But when Phnom Penh and then Saigon fell to communist forces in April 1975, a complete communist takeover in Laos appeared a foregone conclusion.

By August 23, a band of fifty women soldiers had symbolically "liberated" Vientiane. Vang Pao was persuaded to leave Laos by the US, whose representatives were also pulling out. A mass exodus of Hmong towards Thailand followed; an estimated thirty thousand Hmong had died during the war.

Lowland Lao generals of the Royalist side usually cooperated with the new government. Thousands of civil servants and military officers went willingly to re-education camps (see pp.166–167) in remote corners of the country after being told these "seminars" would only last a few weeks.

The absence of right-wing figures opened the door to further Pathet Lao advances which culminated in a **National Congress of People's Representatives** on December 2, 1975, when the congress proclaimed the Lao People's Democratic Republic and accepted the abdication of King Sisavang Vatthana.

The Lao People's Democratic Republic

The **Thirty Year Struggle**, with its roots in the short-lived Lao Issara government, was over. The man in charge was the little-known party secretary-general **Kaysone**, who was named prime minister. The man who had been the face of the Pathet Lao all along, Souphanouvong, assumed the role of president, essentially becoming a figurehead – after all, it wouldn't do to have a communist country run by a French-educated prince.

Unlike their comrades in Vietnam and Cambodia, the Pathet Lao took power in a **bloodless coup**. After overthrowing the government of Souvannaphouma and abolishing royalty, the Pathet Lao named the prince and the king as advisors to the new government and demonstrated further flexibility by inviting the United States to maintain its embassy in Vientiane.

The Pathet Lao's goodwill ended there, however, as they continued to round up civil servants and military personnel with ties to the Royalists until as many as fifty thousand people were in **re-education camps** (see p.166). Many, on their release, left the country. By the mid-1980s Laos had lost ten percent of its population – including an overwhelming majority of its educated class.

Considerable problems faced the new government, which took over a country stripped of money and resources. The **economy** was now a shambles, crippled by the termination of US aid, runaway inflation and the closure of the border with Thailand – the country's primary source of imports, which resulted in severe food shortages. Thirty-five-thousand ethnic Vietnamese and Chinese – the traditional merchants of the country – boarded up their shops in Vientiane and crossed the Mekong. Intent on ushering in a socialist state, the Pathet Lao followed **Eastern bloc models**: they collectivized farms, centralized control of prices and nationalized what little industry there was. The government required long-haired teenagers to get haircuts and women to wear traditional skirts in an effort to develop Lao socialist men and women. Prostitutes and petty thieves were shipped off to re-education camps of their own on islands in the middle of Ang Nam Ngum.

As living standards declined within Laos and the number of refugees in camps in Thailand swelled, **opponents of the regime** found ready recruits. The Thailand-based Lao National Revolutionary Front produced anti-government propaganda and sent sabotage teams into Laos, while remnants of the Hmong secret army went on the offensive in northern Laos, capturing a town on the outskirts of Luang Prabang in March 1977. Fearing that opponents might rally around the figure of the king, the government arrested the royal family and banished them to Hua Phan, where the king, queen and crown prince died, something officially acknowledged only in 1990.

Vietnamese forces helped quell the Hmong revolt, and in July, Vientiane and Hanoi signed a 25-year **Treaty of Friendship and Cooperation** which formalized Vietnamese political, economic and military assistance, including the stationing of more than 30,000 Vietnamese troops in Laos over the next decade. Relations were also close with the Soviet Union, which sent hundreds of technicians and advisers to Laos, drawing it firmly within the Soviet sphere of influence.

The new thinking

By 1979, external and internal difficulties facing the new government forced it to re-evaluate its policies; as a result, its agricultural cooperative programme was suspended and a less rigid form of socialism was adopted. After ten years of power, in December 1985, Laos was still dependent on foreign aid and it remained one of the world's poorest countries. The time had come, in the eyes of Kaysone, for a change.

After overcoming opponents of reform, Kaysone was able to implement the **New Economic Mechanism**, approved by the Fourth Party Congress in November 1986, which essentially introduced a market economy. Without an upheaval among the party's leaders – many of whom had worked together since their days in the Indochinese Communist Party in the 1940s – the ageing hardliners of the Pathet Lao embarked on a series of reforms, generally known as *jintannakan mai* or the New Thinking, which was as thorough as anything to be found in Eastern Europe at the time. By the late 1980s, the centralized socialist economy had been largely dismantled. Farmers could own their own land and sell their crops at free-market prices, state-owned businesses had to make a profit or close their doors and wholly owned foreign investment projects, protected against nationalization, were authorized.

Political changes did not accompany the economic reforms, however. Local elections held in 1988 – the first since 1975 – and subsequent national elections in 1989 did provide some popular legitimacy for the government, but candidates were approved by the party prior to polls. And although the re-education camps were wound down, the government continued to deal strictly with **dissent**.

Discontent was eased when the economy opened up, raising living standards and making material goods more abundant. Government intrusion into people's lives was also reduced, and by the late 1980s, the Mekong was again a two-way street. Lao refugees were invited to return, and Western tourists began to visit the country.

In 1991, the Fifth Party Congress endorsed the long-awaited **Constitution**, which guaranteed basic freedoms and the right to private ownership of property. The congress served to indicate that the party was no longer above the law when one member of the politburo was demoted for corruption. Economic reform also received an endorsement, with the party replacing the communist red star in the national crest with the That Luang stupa and eliminating the word "socialism" from the national motto.

The 1992 **death of Kaysone**, who had led the communist movement since the inception of the Lao People's Party in 1955, presented a serious challenge to the regime, but a smooth transition, resulting in the appointment of **Nouhak Phoumsavanh** as state president and **Khamtay Siphandone**, the prime minister, as president of the party, ensured the government's political stability.

Regional integration

As communism began to collapse in Eastern Europe and Vietnam began to withdraw its forces from Laos, the government strengthened ties with Thailand and with other capitalist countries, notably Japan, Australia and Sweden. Cooperation with the United States in the search for missing US servicemen on

Lao soil and control of the opium trade improved the relationship with the United States, culminating in the re-establishment of full ambassadorial relations in 1992. With the collapse of the Soviet Union in 1991, Laos also began to smooth over difficulties with China which had arisen as a result of Vientiane's alliance with the USSR and Vietnam. China has in fact emerged as Laos's most important foreign military ally, as well as a powerful economic force on Laos's northern border. Thus, by the early 1990s, Laos enjoyed relatively good relations with all its border countries, allowing it to slip back into its familiar role of a crossroads between contending regional powers.

The Australian-financed **Friendship Bridge** to Thailand – opened in 1994 outside Vientiane – as well as membership in the **Association of Southeast Asian Nations** in July 1997 were two important signs that Laos had finally begun to shake off decades of isolation. But for the **Sixth Party Congress**, the Friendship Bridge to Thailand symbolized the way in which the New Thinking was being corrupted, as economic reforms brought a host of new problems, including corruption, gambling dens, brothels and increased crime. The conservative policies introduced by the congress indicated the party intended to slow the pace of reforms and would attempt to contain the fallout from "socially evil outside influences", in part by appealing to traditional Lao values.

Laos today

Economic reforms, with the accompanying social problems, increased official corruption and growing income disparity, represent a great challenge to internal order in the eyes of the party. The party clings to this view despite the fact that in the mid-1990s and again in the first few years of the new millennium, there was a slight upswing in insurgent activities, reportedly by the group known as the Chao Fa, perhaps owing to anger at government attempts to **resettle** highland groups. The official reason for resettlement was to put an end to opium cultivation and slash-and-burn agriculture, and bring far-flung villagers closer to hospitals and schools. The consequences in some cases have proved fatal for the highlanders, who have contracted valley-related diseases such as malaria.

In June 2006, former Minister of Defence **Choummaly Sayasone** took the reigns of power from Khamtay Siphandone. **Sayasone** is the first post-revolution leader of Laos that is not a member of the ageing old guard, but he appears committed to maintaining the status quo. With absolutely no possibility of a home-grown opposition leader coming to the forefront, the government is under little pressure to initiate political reforms.

Despite the prospect of rewards from the sale of power from hydroelectric projects to its neighbours, Laos continues to rank among the world's poorest and least developed countries. Indeed, the World Bank has said that Laos's social indicators are more akin to those of sub-Saharan Africa than they are to the rest of Southeast Asia. Roughly half the adult population is illiterate, access to safe drinking water is unreliable, and the country continues to be mired at the bottom of World Health Organization rankings. In the meantime, Laos continues to shrewdly manipulate international governments as well as non-governmental organizations in order to keep aid flowing in, while human rights abuses continue to be overlooked.

In late 2009, around four thousand Hmong were deported back to Laos from refugee camps in northern Thailand. The move was widely criticized by the UN, who were, along with the Hmong themselves, concerned that they might face retribution for their involvement in the second Indochina War. Following the deportations, there were reports of the Hmong refugees being forced into signing "confessions", and the majority of the refugees were sent to an apparently heavily guarded "resettlement area", with limited access to adequate food and supplies. At the time of writing, the true condition of these camps was unknown; for more information, contact Amnesty (⒲www.amnesty.org).

The future of Laos does look somewhat brighter. Tourism is growing apace, bringing with it much-needed investment, and trade links with Thailand have been strengthened by two further "friendship" bridges spanning the Mekong. In 2009, Vientiane hosted the 25th **Southeast Asian Games**, with the attention of international news teams giving the tourist industry an important boost in the aftermath of the global financial crisis.

Religion and belief systems

The multiplicity of belief systems in Laos mirrors the complexity of its ethnic make-up. Theravada Buddhism is the majority religion, practised by approximately two-thirds of the population, followed by animism and ancestor worship. The remainder practise Mahayana Buddhism and Taoism, and a small percentage of the population follow Christianity or Islam.

Buddhism

Lao legend has it that Buddhism came to Laos in the fourteenth century, but archeological evidence suggests that Buddhism existed in parts of what is now Laos as early as the eighth century. **Theravada Buddhism**, sometimes referred to as the "southern school" of Buddhism owing to its geographic spread, is prevalent in Sri Lanka, Myanmar (Burma), Thailand and Cambodia as well as Laos. The vast majority of lowland-dwelling ethnic Lao, whose numbers make up over half of the population of Laos, are adherents of Theravada Buddhism, as are other ethnic groups such as the Tai Leu, Phuan and Phu Noi, plus a fraction of the tribal Tai groups, such as the Phu Tai, Tai Daeng and Tai Dam. Lao-style Theravada Buddhism is a fascinating blend of indigenous and borrowed beliefs and rituals. During Laos's many years of vassaldom to the various kingdoms made up of lands that now lie within Thai borders, many outside religious beliefs and customs found their way into the Lao royal courts of Luang Prabang, Vientiane and Champasak and, from there, into the valleys of the interior via the tributaries of the Mekong River. The Hindu customs and beliefs that were adopted by the Thai after their sack of Angkor, in what is now Cambodia, were also passed on, in diluted form, to Laos.

Later, Chinese and Vietnamese immigrants brought with them **Mahayana Buddhism**, the so-called "northern school" of Buddhism. As the immigrants prospered and assimilated, the images of their gods found their way into urban monasteries. Go into one of these monasteries today and, alongside images of the Buddha, you may well see a representation of a Hindu god such as Ganesh or a Mahayana Buddhist deity such as Kuan Yin.

The ideological rift between the two Buddhist schools is as vast as the one that divides Catholicism and Protestantism. Theravada Buddhism is the more austere of the two and has been described as having an "every man for himself" philosophy, that is to say, each individual adherent is believed to be responsible for his or her own accumulation of merit or sin. Mahayana Buddhism is more of a "group effort", with adherents praying for divine assistance from *bodhisattva*, near-Buddhas who have postponed their enlightenment in order to serve as the compassionate protectors of all mankind.

For most Lao Buddhists, religion in everyday life revolves around the all-important practice of **making merit**, or *het bun*. This accumulation of merit is paramount to a Theravada Buddhist's spiritual strategy, a way to dilute the destructive effects of any sin that may have been accrued by bad deeds, while at the same time ensuring that the next incarnation will be better than the present one. Many of the holidays in the Lao calendar are associated with Buddhist festivals and give the visitor a chance to

Most ethnic Lao men become novice monks at some time in their lives, usually before marriage. Monks take **vows** to uphold no less than 227 precepts. These range from abstinence from sexual relations, alcohol and the wearing of any sort of ornamentation to more arcane rules such as a prohibition on urinating while standing upright (so as not to soil robes). Laos's history of social upheaval and a generally relaxed attitude towards rules, however, have meant that, especially in rural monasteries, not all of the precepts are strictly adhered to. For most Lao males, the time spent wearing a robe is short, usually no more than three months or so during the rainy season. Interestingly, a man who has yet to do time in a monastery is referred to as *dip* or "unripe", alluding to the fact that many Lao don't consider a man complete without some time spent in the monastery; before the advent of public schools, lessons in reading and writing at the monastery were about all the education the average Lao could hope for.

As the state religion, Buddhism enjoyed royal patronage up until the time of the **revolution**. In the years leading up to the revolution, the communists cleverly used Buddhist monks, many of whom were unhappy with widespread government corruption, as instruments for diffusing propaganda. Once the cause had been won, however, the communists moved to gain total control, banning the practice of alms-giving. This effectively made it impossible to remain a monk, as it is against Buddhist precepts for monks to cultivate plants or raise animals for food. The move backfired, however, as laypeople were shocked at the new regime's heavy-handed treatment of the monkhood and resented being deprived of any opportunity to make merit. Popular outcry forced the government to rescind the draconian measures, but only after large numbers of monks fled to Thailand or abandoned their robes and became laymen. Today, the study of Marxist–Leninist theory is still mandatory for all monks, but Lao Buddhism has made a strong comeback and economic reforms and liberalization have helped to increase the numbers of men in the monkhood to pre-revolution levels.

observe the practice of merit-making, whether it be ritually bathing Buddha images or donating new robes to monks. Making merit is accomplished most readily by giving **alms** to Buddhist monks and novices. This enchanting practice can be witnessed just after dawn, when barefoot monks solemnly walk through the neighbourhood or village surrounding their monasteries in order to collect offerings of food from laypeople. Merit thus acquired is believed to bring the giver good fortune in this life and the next, and also to dilute the destructive effects of sin that may have been accumulated. Male adherents may also make merit for themselves and their families by taking vows and becoming a novice monk for a limited period of time. Even more merit may be acquired by becoming an ordained disciple of the Buddha.

Animism and ancestor worship

Predating Buddhism in Laos, **animism** is the belief that natural objects – such as hills, trees, large rocks or plots of land – are inhabited by spiritual entities or possess supernatural powers. While the Buddhist Lao still harbour vestiges of these beliefs, some midland and highland tribal peoples are exclusively animist.

An easily recognized example of animism among Buddhists is the practice of erecting a **spirit house** on plots of land. Ordinarily found in a corner of a piece of property, a spirit house is the customary abode of the *jao bawn*, or spirit of the site, and resembles a miniature house or sometimes a model of Mount Meru, the Hindu Mount Olympus, atop a pedestal. The idea is to make the spirit house a more habitable place than the dwellings for humans located on the same plot of land; naturally, if the *jao bawn* is comfortable in its digs, it is less likely to cause trouble for people living in the vicinity. Offerings to keep the spirit of the site propitiated may include flowers, incense, candles or sweets. A much simpler offering to *jao bawn* that visitors may note is the practice of pressing spirit offerings of sticky rice against trees or rocks. Another manifestation of animism that can be readily seen is the **talaew**, a six-pointed star made from strips of bamboo and placed over doors and gates or in rice fields. The device is thought to bar evil spirits from entering and doing harm.

After the revolution, the communists discouraged many animist practices, such as the annual sacrifice of water buffalo in tribal villages in the south, believing that such worship wasted resources and held back the progress of the nation. As with Buddhism, animism quickly revived once official suppression was relaxed.

Ancestor worship in different forms is also practised by many of the highland tribes that migrated to Laos from China, including the Akha, Hmong and Mien. Practices vary, but all believe that the spirits of deceased ancestors have the ability to affect the lives of their descendants. The ancestors are thought to be rather helpless and dependent on the living for earthly comforts; they reward descendants who remember them with offerings, but can become harmful if neglected.

Other beliefs

The Mien also worship **Taoist** deities, painted images of which are traditionally displayed on the Mien altar.

Hinduism, or Brahmanism, was first introduced to what is now southern and central Laos by the Khmer, who adopted many Hindu traditions and beliefs from Indian traders who began arriving in the ports of Southeast Asia in the first century AD. While the Laos' recognition of Hindu divinities is minimal compared with that of their Thai cousins, two such deities, namely the multi-armed, four-faced **Brahma** and the green-skinned **Indra**, have become icons in the Theravada Buddhist pantheon and so are commonly depicted in Lao monasteries. Images of **Ganesh**, the so-called elephant god, can be found on the premises of some Buddhist monasteries and shrines, particularly in the south. The *shivalinga*, or stone phallus symbolizing the god **Shiva**, was commonly enshrined at ancient Khmer temples and, because many Lao Buddhist monasteries were built on top of ancient Khmer sites, the *shivalinga* and other bits of Khmer statuary are often found on Buddhist altars, particularly in the south.

Christianity arrived in Laos in 1642 in the form of an Italian Jesuit missionary but, according to his journal, he was far from successful. Not until the French colonial period did Christian missionaries scramble to make converts throughout Laos. A significant number of Laos's ethnic Vietnamese population is Catholic and the largest concentration of Catholics is found in southern Laos, particularly Savannakhet, which boasts the country's most elaborate Catholic church. Lao Christians also fared badly after the revolution. Because the communists saw Christianity as a "Western", and therefore potentially subversive, religion, missionaries were expelled and churches throughout the country were closed.

Arts and temple architecture

The vast majority of works of art created in Laos – sculpture, painting, architecture, even decorative motifs on jewellery – are inspired by Buddhism, with the important exception of Lao textiles. The motivation behind much Theravada Buddhist art relies heavily on the concept of making merit. Wealthy patrons looking to acquire religious merit and dilute an accumulation of sins can do so by commissioning the crafting of an image of the Buddha or by financing the building or restoration of any of the structures found in monastery grounds.

Owing to Laos's distance from lucrative trade routes and its tumultuous history, the patronage of the religious arts never reached the heights that were attained in neighbouring Cambodia, Thailand and Burma. Nevertheless, a style did develop that is distinctively Lao and, although the number of works which exhibit a high degree of refinement is rather small, Lao art makes up for it with a vigour and whimsy that rarely fails to charm.

Sculpture

The historic Buddha was a prince who gave up his wealth and birthright in order to pursue the "middle path" – a philosophy of moderation – towards enlightenment. Just before his death, the Buddha was said to have discouraged his followers from making images of him, saying that it was his teachings that should be worshipped, not a likeness of him. For a time after the Buddha's passing, Buddhists used **symbolic imagery** to recall the enlightened one. An empty throne or a royal parasol was sometimes depicted commemorating the Buddha's decision to abandon his life of luxury and seek the path to enlightenment.

However, human nature being what it is, adherents needed something more concrete. The **first images of the Buddha** were probably made several centuries after the Buddha's death. By that time, no living artist had actually seen the Buddha, but a list of physical traits said to be unique to the Buddha had been passed down. The result of this list of fairly rigid attributes is that Buddha images from all over Asia share much the same characteristics. Lao images are no different and many of their seemingly bizarre features, toes of equal length for instance, are due to the strictness with which the aesthetic canon has been followed. In much the same vein, the attitude of the Buddha's arms and hands, or *mudra*, are rich with **symbolism** and must be depicted accurately if they are to be understood. Most of these gestures correspond to Buddhist theory or to events that occurred during the Buddha's lifetime. Besides the standard gestures and poses, the Lao have invented a couple of their own. One is a standing Buddha with arms to its sides and fingers pointing downwards, known as the "Beckoning Rain" pose. Buddhas with this *mudra* are found only in Laos and parts of northern Thailand. A similar standing Buddha with arms crossed at the wrists is also a Lao-invented *mudra*, known as "Contemplating the Tree of Enlightenment". The most sacred Buddha image in the country, the Pha Bang (see p.126), is also a standing Buddha, this time with arms held out in a blocking gesture, known as the "Dispelling Fear" pose.

One *mudra* in particular is especially popular with the Lao. This is found on Buddhas sitting in a half-lotus position, with the left hand resting palm-upward on the image's lap and the right hand extended down and touching the earth with the fingertips. Known as "Victory Over Mara", this pose commemorates the historic Buddha's triumph over Mara the Tempter, a Satan-like figure that tried unsuccessfully to distract the Buddha from his path to enlightenment.

The best place to see sculpted images of the Buddha is on an altar in a Buddhist temple's main *sim*. Typically, a massive central image, usually constructed of brick and stucco, is flanked by numerous smaller images cast from bronze or carved from hardwood. In Luang Prabang, the Pha Bang undeniably gets the most attention, but the superb reclining Buddha enshrined in a small "chapel" at Wat Xieng Thong is perhaps the best example of Lao sculpture to be found in the country.

Temple architecture

Of all Lao architectural elements, the *that*, or **stupa**, is probably easiest for the visitor to appreciate. This is due mainly to the fact that it is at once readily recognizable and varied in design. The concept of the stupa – a monument atop a reliquary containing sacred relics of the Buddha – originated in India and spread throughout Asia. In each country where Buddhism took root, the local architects and artisans put their own ideas to work when designing a stupa, and thus the bell-shaped stupas of Sri Lanka have little in common stylistically with the multistoreyed "pagoda" stupas found in China and Japan. Vientiane's That Luang stupa, the national symbol of Laos, is a fusion of aggressive angles and graceful curves that make it quite different from designs predominant in neighbouring countries (although stupas in this style can also be found in the northeast of Thailand where ethnic Lao predominate). This design of stupa is probably the greatest single Lao contribution to Buddhist architecture.

Within a typical Lao wat there are a number of buildings serving different functions, but it is the **sim**, the structure in which the monastery's principal Buddha image is enshrined, that gets the most attention from Lao architects and artisans. Lao *sim* have two main styles: the **Vientiane style** owes much to the Bangkok school of architecture, while the **Luang Prabang style** shares characteristics with that of Chiang Mai in northern Thailand. From a distance, the difference between the two styles is easily discerned. The roof of a Vientiane-style *sim* is high and steep, while a Luang Prabang-style roof gently slopes nearly to the ground.

Variations on *sim* design were produced by the Phuan and Tai Leu ethnic groups. The rare **Xieng Khuang style**, once found in the province of the same name, is low and squat, designed to withstand the weather of the windswept Plain of Jars. The handiwork of the Phuan people, this style barely survived Laos's violent history – the only remaining example lies outside of the province at Wat Khili in Luang Prabang (see p.128). Examples of architecture produced by the Tai Leu are very similar to that found in the Xishuangbanna region of China's Yunnan province. The *sim* at Muang Sing's Wat Sing Jai (see p.193) is a picturesque example of the Tai Leu style.

Decorative features on the *sim* and other structures found at a Lao wat are in a variety of mediums. Carved wood, moulded stucco and, to a lesser extent, mirrored-glass mosaics typically ornament the exterior while, inside, detailed murals cover entire walls. Doors and windows of the *sim* are often made from teakwood, ornately carved with the figures of celestial beings or demons upon a background of stylized flames or floral forms known as *lai lao* – "Lao pattern". The structure's wooden pediments – triangular segments of the upper facade that support the roof – are another place to look for pleasing examples of *lai lao*, along with carved depictions of Hindu deities such as Kala and Indra atop Airavata. Many of these motifs have origins in ancient Khmer ornamentation, such as that found at Wat Phou in Champasak province. Lao stuccowork is sometimes gilt-covered and almost always looks better from a distance. The use of stucco for ornamentation was introduced to Laos by the Khmer or possibly the Mon, but the methods and designs of Lao stuccowork owe more to the Tai Yuan of what is now northern Thailand. Likewise, the use of mirrored glass also came to Laos via Thailand. The mosaics at Wat Xieng Thong are Laos's most famous example of ornamentation using this medium but the works are modern, having been created in the late 1950s. Lao murals are meant to be read like a story and those found on the walls of the *sim* usually depict one of the tales from the Jataka tales, the Lao version of the Ramayana (see p.304), or scenes of local life.

The Lao belief that religious merit can be made by **restoring** old monastery buildings ensures that nearly all Lao *sim* are restored every fifty years or so. The artisans who restore these buildings are under little pressure to be true to an earlier design. Indeed, it is believed that the more lavish the new design, the more merit is likely to be made by the patron who commissioned the restoration. The result is that much of the decoration on Buddhist buildings in Laos is nowhere near as old as the structure it adorns.

Textiles

The matrilineal society of the lowland Lao and tribal Tai meant that when a man married, he immediately set up house on the property of his new bride's parents. Sometimes this entailed leaving his home village and subsequently, when this couple's son came of age, he would do the same. With such a custom, men's roots in a village were never deep and this was reflected by their simple dress: it told almost nothing of a man's background. Women, on the other hand, were the heirs to a weaving tradition that reflected their ethnic and geographical origins. Techniques improved with each new generation and were passed on.

Each **ethnic group** had its own particular patterns and colours, which varied from village to village but were still recognizable as belonging to that group. Sometimes, as with the Tai Daeng, these variations were great – indeed, one could fill a hefty book with the myriad designs found in Tai Daeng weaving. According to experts, the "grammar" of a textile can be read to reveal not only the ethnicity of the wearer, but also her marital and financial status. Because all women in a village wove and wore similar patterns and a woman normally wore only what she herself had made, it was apparent at a glance who had mastered the art of weaving – a highly desirable skill in the eyes of young men looking for a prospective bride. Not surprisingly, a woman's most striking apparel was saved for festival days when all the young men from the village and beyond would be in attendance.

The many years of war in Laos had a predictable effect on textile weaving, with the heavy looms too heavy for fleeing refugees to take with them. By sad coincidence, peace in Laos was accompanied by the introduction of inexpensive, mass-produced textiles. The importance that Lao mothers once placed on teaching their daughters the secrets of the loom rapidly faded. As a result, antique pieces have become highly sought-after collectables, and museums as far afield as Australia have hired textile experts to scour Lao villages for examples of nineteenth- and early twentieth-century Lao weaving. In recent years, a few companies have been encouraging villagers to return to their traditional weaving with fair-trade and cooperative initiatives that gives both weaver and tourist the opportunity to benefit from the traditional skill.

Laos's ethnic mosaic

While many of Southeast Asia's nations are ethnically diverse, Laos is one of the few that is still visibly so. That is to say, it is one of the last countries whose minorities have not been totally assimilated into the culture of the majority.

In an effort at categorization, the Lao government officially divides the population into three groups. Which group an ethnicity fits into is determined by the **elevation** at which that ethnicity dwells; thus many unrelated ethnic groups may be grouped together if they reside at one elevation. This method of categorization may be seen as a tenuous majority's subtle means of proclaiming cultural superiority over its sizeable population of minorities while at the same time trying to bring them into the fold. In this section we discuss two of these three groups, namely the **lowland Lao** and the **Mon–Khmer groups** who live at somewhat higher elevations; the third group is covered by the separate colour section on the **hill tribes**.

The lowland Lao

The so-called **Lao Loum** (or lowland Lao) live at the lowest elevations and on the land best suited for cultivation. For the most part, they are the **ethnic Lao**, a people related to the Thai of Thailand and the Shan of Burma. The lowland Lao make up between fifty and sixty percent of the population, and are the group for which the country is named. They, like their Thai and Shan cousins, prefer to inhabit river valleys, live in dwellings that are raised above the ground, and are adherents of Theravada Buddhism. Laos is by no means the only place where ethnic Lao dwell. Most of Thailand's northeastern region is populated with ethnic Lao and, owing to internal migration patterns caused by economic factors, Bangkok has the largest concentration of ethnic Lao anywhere. This fact is not lost on the Lao of Laos who feel that history has deprived them of much of their original territory.

Of all the ethnicities found in Laos, the culture of the lowland Lao is dominant, mainly because it is they who hold political power. Their language is the official language, their religion is the state religion and their holy days are the official holidays. As access to a reliable water source is key to survival and water is abundant in the river valleys, the ethnic Lao have prospered. They have been able to devote their free time – that time not spent securing food – to the arts and entertainment, and their culture has become richer for it. Among the cultural traits by which the Lao define themselves are the cultivation and consumption of sticky rice as a staple, the taking part in the animist ceremony known as *basi* (see p.142), and the playing of the reed instrument called the *khaen*.

Akin to the ethnic Lao are the Tai Leu, Phuan and Phu Tai, found in the northwest, the northeast and mid-south respectively. The **Tai Leu** of Laos are originally from China's Xishuangbanna region in southern Yunnan, where nowadays they are known as the "Dai minority". In Laos, their settlements stretch from the Chinese border with Luang Namtha province, through Oudomxai and into Sayaboury; Muang Sing is perhaps the Tai Leu settlement visitors are most likely to encounter. The Tai Leu are Theravada Buddhists and, like the Lao, they placate animist spirits. They are known to perform a ceremony similar to the *basi* ceremony which is supposed to reunite the wayward souls of their water buffalo. They are also skilled weavers whose work is in demand from other groups that do not weave, such as the Khmu.

The **Phuan** were also once a recognized kingdom, but are now largely forgotten. The kingdom's territory, formerly located in the province of Xieng Khuang (the capital of which was formerly known as Muang Phuan), was at once coveted by the Siamese and Vietnamese. Aggression from both sides as well as from Chinese Haw bandits left it in ruins and the populace scattered.

The Phuan are Theravada Buddhists, but once observed an impromptu holy day known as *kam fa*. When the first thunder of the season was heard, all labours ceased and villagers avoided any activity that might cause even the slightest noise. The village's fortune was then divined based on the direction from which the thunder was heard.

The **Phu Tai** of Savannakhet and Khammouane provinces are also found in the northeast of Thailand. They are Theravada Buddhists and have assimilated into Lao culture to a high degree, although it is still possible to recognize them by their dress on festival days. The predominant colours of the Phu Tai shawls and skirts are an electric purple and orange with yellow and lime-green highlights.

The "tribal Tai"

Other Tai peoples related to the Lao are the so-called "**tribal Tai**", who live in river valleys at slightly higher elevations and are mostly animists. These include the rather mysteriously named Tai Daeng (Red Tai), Tai Khao (White Tai) and Tai Dam (Black Tai). Theories about nomenclature vary. It is commonly surmised that the names were derived from the predominant colour of the womenfolk's dress, but others have suggested that the groups were named after the river valleys in northern Vietnam where they were thought to have originated. These Tai groups were once loosely united in a political alliance called the **Sipsong Chao Tai** or the Twelve Tai Principalities, spread over an area that covers parts of northwestern Vietnam and northeastern Laos. The traditional centre was present-day **Dien Bien Phu** in Vietnam, known to the Tai as Muang Theng. When the French returned to Indochina after World War II, they attempted to establish a "Tai Federation" encompassing the area of the old Principalities. The plan was short-circuited by Ho Chi Minh who, after defeating the French, was able to manipulate divisions between the Tai groups in order to gain total control.

The **Tai Dam** are found in large numbers in Hua Phan and Xieng Khuang provinces, but also inhabit northern Laos as far west as Luang Namtha. Principally animists, they have a system of Vietnamese-influenced surnames that indicate political and social status. The women are easily recognized by their distinctive dress: long-sleeved, tight-fitting blouses in bright, solid colours with a row of butterfly-shaped silver buttons down the front and a long, indigo-coloured skirt. The outfit is completed with a bonnet-like headcloth of indigo with red trim.

Mon–Khmer groups

The ethnic Lao believe themselves and their ethnic kin to have inhabited an area that is present-day Dien Bien Phu in Vietnam before migrating into what is now Laos. Interestingly, there is historical evidence to support their legends. As the Lao moved southwards they displaced the original inhabitants of the region. Known officially as the **Lao Theung** (*theung* is Lao for "above"), but colloquially known as the *kha* ("slaves"), these peoples were forced to resettle at higher elevations where water was more scarce and life decidedly more difficult.

The **Khmu** of northern Laos are thought to number around 350,000, making them one of the largest minority groups in Laos. Speakers of a Mon–Khmer language, they have assimilated to a high degree and are practically indistinguishable from the ethnic Lao to outsiders. Their origins are obscure. Some theorize that the Khmu originally inhabited China's Xishuangbanna region in southern Yunnan and migrated south into northern Laos long before the arrival of the Lao. The Khmu themselves tell legends of their being northern Laos's first inhabitants and of having founded Luang Prabang. Interestingly, royal ceremonies once performed annually by the Lao king at Luang Prabang symbolically acknowledged the Khmu's original ownership of the land. The Khmu are known for their honesty and diligence, though in the past they were easily duped by the lowland Lao into performing menial labour for little compensation. Their lack of sophistication in business matters and seeming complacency with their lot in life probably led to their being referred to as "slaves" by the lowland Lao. Unlike other groups in Laos, the Khmu are not known for their weaving skills and so customarily traded labour for cloth. The traditional Khmu village has four cemeteries: one for adults who died normal deaths, one for those who died violent or unnatural deaths, one for children and one for mutes.

A large spirit house located outside the village gates attests to the Khmu belief in **animism**. Spirits are thought to inhabit animals, rice and even money. Visitors to the village must call from outside the village gate, enquiring whether or not a temporary village taboo is in place. If so, then a visitor may not enter, and water, food and a mat to rest on will be brought out by the villagers. If there is no taboo in effect, male visitors may lodge in the village common-house if an overnight stay is planned, but may not sleep in the house of another family unless a blood sacrifice is made to the ancestors. There is no ban on women visitors staying the night in a Khmu household as it is thought to be the property of the women residents.

The village common-house also serves as a home for adolescent boys, and it is there that they learn how to weave baskets and make animal traps as well as become familiar with the village folklore and taboos. The boys may learn that the sound of the barking deer is an ill omen when a man is gathering materials with which to build a house, or that it is wrong to bring meat into the village from an animal that has been killed by a tiger or has died on its own. Young Khmu men seem to be prone to wanderlust, often leaving their villages to seek work in the lowlands. Their high rate of intermarriage with other groups during their forays for employment has contributed to their assimilation.

Another Mon–Khmer-speaking group which inhabits the north, particularly Xainyabouli province, are the **Htin**. They excel at fashioning household implements, particularly baskets and fish traps, from bamboo (owing to a partial cultural ban on the use of any kind of metal), and are known for their vast knowledge of the different species of bamboo and their respective uses.

Linguistically related to the Khmu and Htin are the **Mabri**, Laos's least numerous and least developed minority. Thought to number less than one hundred, the Mabri have a taboo on tilling the soil which has kept them semi-nomadic and impoverished. Half a century ago they were nomadic hunter-gatherers who customarily moved camp as soon as the leaves on the branches that comprised their temporary shelters began to turn yellow. Known to the Lao as *kha tawng leuang* ("slaves of the yellow banana leaves") or simply *khon pa* ("jungle people"), the Mabri were thought by some to be naked savages or even ghosts, and wild tales were circulated about their fantastic hunting skills and ability to vanish into the forest without a trace. The Mabri were said to worship their long spears, making offerings and performing dances for their weapons to bring luck with the hunt.

Within the last few decades, however, they have given up their nomadic lifestyle and many now work for other groups, often performing menial tasks in exchange for food or clothing.

The Bolaven Plateau in southern Laos is named for the **Laven** people, yet another Mon–Khmer-speaking group whose presence predates that of the Lao. The Laven were very quick to assimilate the ways of the southern Lao, so much so that a French expansionist and amateur ethnologist who explored the plateau in the 1870s found it difficult to tell the two apart. Besides the Laven, other Mon–Khmer-speaking minorities are found in the south, particularly in Savannakhet, Salavan and Xekong provinces. Among these are the **Bru**, who have raised the level of building animal traps and snares to a fine art. The Bru have devised traps to catch, and sometimes kill, everything from mice to elephants, including a booby-trap that thrusts a spear into the victim.

The **Gie–Trieng** of Xekong are one of the most isolated of all the tribal peoples, having been pushed deep into the bush by the rival Sedang tribe. The Gie-Trieng are expert basket weavers and their tightly woven quivers, smoked a deep mahogany colour, are highly prized by collectors. The **Nge**, also of Xekong, produce textiles bearing a legacy of the Ho Chi Minh Trail that snaked through their territory and of American efforts to bomb it out of existence. Designs on woven shoulder bags feature stylized bombs and fighter planes, and men's loincloths are decorated with rows of tiny lead beads, fashioned from the munitions junk that litters the region.

The **Alak** and **Katu** have of late been brought to the attention of outsiders by Lao tour agencies who are eager to cash in on the tribal custom of sacrificing water buffalo, in a ceremony reminiscent of the final scene in the film *Apocalypse Now*. The Katu are said to be a very warlike people and, as recently as the 1950s, carried out human sacrifices to placate spirits and ensure a good harvest. The ethnic Lao firmly believe that these southern Mon–Khmer groups are adept at black magic, and advise visitors to keep a cake of fragrant soap on their person to foil the sorcery of tribal witchdoctors.

The environment

A landlocked state in the heart of tropical Southeast Asia, Laos covers a land area of nearly 237,000 square kilometres, a size comparable to that of England. Laos is dominated by rugged highlands cut by narrow river valleys and shares in two of Southeast Asia's most prominent geographical features: the **Annamite Mountains** and the **Mekong River**, with the Mekong picking up more than half of its water flow during its nearly 2000km journey through Laos.

With a heat and humidity typical of a tropical region, Laos's climate nourishes a natural wealth of wildlife that includes rare or endangered species. Early French explorers marvelled at the sheer beauty of Laos's landscape, as they dodged tigers and collected samples of strange and wonderful insects. Indeed, the country's former name, the Kingdom of a Million Elephants, boasts of these tropical riches. In the recent past, Laos has surprised the scientific world with a number of new species of plant or animal life discovered or rediscovered in the country's forests and rivers. Sadly, Laos's natural wonders have been greatly diminished since the late nineteenth century – there are at most a few thousand elephants roaming the country's frontiers today, and the forest continues to shrink each year. Despite the efforts of a handful of concerned international groups, the Lao government's efforts at **conservation** have been half-hearted and ineffectual. Lucrative **logging** and **mining** contracts have been awarded to Chinese and Vietnamese firms, bringing riches to government and military officials but leaving the environment much poorer as a result. Likewise, the **damming** of Lao rivers to generate hydroelectricity that can be sold to neighbouring countries is seen as a way for Laos to generate capital, but the ill effects that dams and the reservoirs behind them have on the environment are often ignored.

Agriculture

Agriculture plays a significant role in Laos's economy as the vast majority of people in Laos live off the land. Rice, as the cornerstone of the Lao diet, accounts for eighty percent of agricultural land. For the most part, farmers employ one of two cultivation systems when growing rice. In the lowlands, farmers generally practise the wet-field paddy system, while swidden cultivation (also known as shifting or slash-and-burn agriculture) is primarily employed in the highlands. Large level areas along the Vientiane Plain, in Savannakhet and in Champasak are perhaps the areas best suited for extensive paddy rice cultivation in the country, and these places have not surprisingly emerged as the country's population centres. Other crops include cardamom, coffee, corn, cotton, fruit, peanuts, soybeans, mung beans, sugarcane, sweet potatoes, tobacco and various vegetables.

Swidden cultivation techniques practised by the Lao Theung and Lao Soung date back thousands of years and vary from group to group, with some peoples living in permanent villages around which they rotate cultivation within a large swath of forest, and others shifting their settlements from hillside to hillside. Nearly all midland and upland groups rely on swidden rice cultivation. Given the destruction of vast tracts of forest every year due to this method (a sight that visitors to the north during the months of March to May cannot fail to notice), there is a move towards educating farmers and villagers in the hope that they can adopt less destructive methods – conversely, however, some say that this practice keeps the soil fertile and the forests in balance.

The Lao government has used shifting agriculture among tribal peoples, especially the Hmong, as a reason to forcibly **resettle** thousand of highland families. The stated policy is to protect forest habitats and to bring hill peoples closer to community resources such as hospitals and schools. While this may have been beneficial for forests, the effects on resettled peoples are often no less than disastrous.

The Mekong

With such a limited land base for agriculture, it's no surprise that **freshwater ecosystems** are of massive importance to Laos. The heart and soul of Laos's freshwater ecosystems is the **Mekong River**, the longest river in Southeast Asia, and, in terms of volume, the tenth largest in the world, carrying 475,000 million cubic metres to the sea each year. With the beginnings of its 4180km journey in a frozen stream high up in the Plateau of Tibet, the Mekong travels the entire length of Laos before slipping through Cambodia and fanning out into the "Nine Dragons" that constitute the river's delta in Vietnam. The Mekong is joined by fourteen major tributaries during the course of its 1993km journey through Laos. Nearly all the rivers and mountain streams in the country eventually find their way into the Mekong, as ninety percent of Laos drains into the river.

Rural life revolves around the Mekong River System, which encompasses everything from the myriad mountain streams to the flooded rice paddies to the river itself. It generates power, waters crops, provides a place to bathe and is an all-important source of fish. In most of lowland Laos, as well as in many parts of the highlands, fish and other aquatic animals provide more than seventy percent of the animal protein in people's diet. Nowhere in Laos is this more evident than in the country's southernmost tip, where every family fishes and every meal includes something from the Mother of Waters. It is in this region that the Mekong expands to attain its greatest width – 14km at the height of the rainy season – and journeys through the country's best known **wetlands**: Si Phan Don and the Khone Falls (see p.243).

Forests

The country is dominated by mixed **deciduous forests**, in which trees survive lengthy periods of minimal rainfall by shedding their leaves in order to conserve water. Tall, pale-barked **dipterocarps**, a group of tropical hardwoods prized for their timber, tower over these monsoon forests, ranging in height from ten to forty metres. Natural stands of teak, rosewood and mahogany were once common features of Laos's deciduous forests, though these much sought-after hardwoods, considered ideal material for building everything from furniture to the decks of yachts, have been substantially reduced in number.

Bamboo, hardly in short supply, thrives in Laos's monsoon climate and appears in more varieties in Laos than in any other country with the exception of two of Laos's neighbours, China and Thailand. Growing at astonishing rates during the rainy season, bamboo rules the understorey of the deciduous forests, surviving in soils too poor for many other types of vegetation and dominating secondary forests – those areas where a new generation of plants has grown up after forest has been stripped bare by swidden agriculture, rampant logging or the harsh excesses of chemical defoliants. Flexible bamboo is used by the Lao for making everything from houses to Laos's national musical instrument, the *khaen*, while bamboo shoots find their way into a variety of Lao dishes. Other, less common forest types in Laos include dry dipterocarp forests, noteworthy for their more open canopies and found along the arid plateaus of southern Laos; and rare old growth pine forests and semi-evergreen and hill evergreen forests, the latter soaked by frequent rainfall and possessing moss-covered forest floors and dense undergrowth.

Conservation zones and wetlands

CONTEXTS | The environment

In the early 1990s, the government of Laos established a system of **National Biodiversity Conservation Areas** throughout the country, which put under protection more than twelve percent of the country's total land area, one of the highest ratios in the world. However, that has not stopped the Lao government from leasing logging and mining concessions within NBCAs. Forests have been particularly damaged in the south along the Vietnamese border – where until recently never-before-seen species were turning up – and in the northeast.

As yet only a few parts of the conservation areas are accessible and open for tourism – such as the caves of the Khammouane Limestone NBCA near Thakhek; most are well off the beaten track. A survey of some of the more interesting areas follows.

Southern Laos

Flush against the Vietnam border in Khammouane and Bolikhamxai provinces and to the south of Lak Xao, the **Nakai–Nam Theun** is without question one of the world's more important biodiversity areas. Indeed, three of the last five large mammals to be discovered or rediscovered worldwide inhabit this area. A lost world of evergreen forests, savanna and jagged, mist-shrouded peaks, the Nakai–Nam Theun is one of the richest wildlife and forest areas remaining in Southeast Asia. It is best known for the discovery of the saola, a large mammal resembling a shaggy brown and white deer with spindly horns; and the giant-antlered muntjac and the black muntjac, as well as the rediscovery of the Indochinese warty pig.

Once a royal hunting reserve, this area is now the largest single "protected" area in Laos, extending over 3700 square kilometres, with an elevation ranging from 500m on the Nakai Plateau to mountain peaks of well over 2000m, and is home to at least eleven globally threatened large mammal species. Its forests provide habitat for most of the mainland Southeast Asia fauna, including such rare animals as tiger, lesser slow loris, clouded leopard – a small tree-dwelling cat which hunts birds and monkeys by night – Asiatic black bear and elephant. More than four hundred bird species, among them the endangered white-winged duck, crested argus, beautiful nuthatch and greater spotted eagle, have been recorded here, the highest diversity of any site surveyed in Laos. The area is also noteworthy for its forests, composed of stands of wet and dry evergreen, cypress forest, old growth pine, found only in parts of Southeast Asia, and riverside forest – all of which are regionally threatened habitats. Nakai–Nam Theun is also treasured for its four river systems. However, their hydroelectric potential now figures large in national development plans, which have consequences for the wildlife of the surrounding area, not to mention the livelihood of local people.

Further south, spectacular waterfalls plunge from soaring escarpments cloaked with pristine evergreen forests in **Dong Hua Sao**, a 910-square-kilometre zone to the east of Pakse and the south of Paksong, which encompasses a flat, upland area along the Bolaven – of immense floral and faunal interest – and the lowlands along the Plateau's southern flank. With its habitat further diversified by the presence of sandstone flats and wetlands, Dong Hua Sao is home to nearly 250 species of birds, including the rare Siamese fireback, green peafowl and red-collared woodpecker as well as primates, including the endangered douc langur and gibbons, sun bear and the world's largest species of wild cattle, the gaur, once a prized trophy among big game hunters during colonial times.

Shadowing the Laos–Cambodia border and spanning the southern stretches of Attapu and Champasak provinces, the **Xe Pian** is for the most part covered by semi-evergreen forest, interspersed with tracts of dry dipterocarp forest. Wetlands and riverine systems are also an important feature of the Xe Pian, which takes its name from the snaking Xe Pian River that bisects the reserve's eastern and southern flatlands. As home to eight threatened bird species, the protected area is of global significance for wildlife conservation and supports numerous lowland bird species as well as a wealth of migrants. Woolly-necked storks and nesting sarus cranes are both thought to inhabit the wetlands of the Xe Pian. Gibbons also fill the central forests of the Xe Pian with their unmistakable hooting, and villagers have reported seeing kouprey, the elusive grey forest ox whose global population is thought to number no more than three hundred, hog deer and Eld's deer. Black bears, sun bears, peacocks, leopards and otters, hunted for their skins which are sold to Cambodians, have also been spotted in the area, as have two rare river creatures: the Irrawaddy dolphin, which is said to still pay seasonal visits to the Xe Pian, and the Siamese crocodile, already extinct in most Southeast Asian rivers.

Just west of the Xe Pian lie two **wetlands** of regional significance, Si Phan Don and the Khone Falls. Here, the Mekong concludes its journey through Laos, swirling past the countless outcroppings of soil and rocks that constitute the "Four Thousand Islands" of the region's name. Considered the richest fishing grounds in Laos, Si Phan Don possesses large tracts of seasonally flooded forest, along the banks of the Mekong and on the dots of land in between, which constitute a crucial spawning ground for the unknown number of fish species inhabiting this portion of the river. At the southern tip of Si Phan Don – and the entire country for that matter – lie the Khone Falls, an 8km-wide series of channels composed of waterfalls and rapids flowing between rocky islands. The falls, which begin 5km north of the Cambodian border, are a vital passageway for the Mekong's many species of migratory fish.

The seasonally flooded islands here are also an important sanctuary for **birds** and represent one of the last nesting areas of the river tern, greater thick-knees and river lapwing, all of which appear as the water level begins to recede in January. The trees of the wetlands' flooded forests also provide perches for thick-billed pigeons, pied hornbills and green imperial pigeons and offer a welcome spot for blue-tailed bee-eaters to rest after one of their aerial insect chases. The area is also one of the rare places in Southeast Asia visited by red-headed and white-rumped vultures, whose numbers are on the decline owing to hunting and a shortage of food, caused partly by the fact that Laos now has fewer tigers, whose leftovers make a favourite vulture snack. Other rare or endangered birds making the rounds in the area are the grey-headed fish eagle, the woolly-necked stork and the giant ibis.

Beneath the surface, Laos's lower Mekong area possesses a stunning array of **fish species**, including giant golden carp, featherbacks, eels and freshwater rays that grow well over a metre in length, fish that climb the Khone Falls by sucking their way up the rocks with their lips and the mysterious *ba leum,* a fish weighing 200kg that fishermen attempt to snare with the entrails of dogs attached to a hook at the end of a 30m length of rope. Long the jewel of the Mekong, the blunt-nosed Irrawaddy dolphin is now critically endangered.

Central and northern Laos

East of Ang Nam Ngum and less than two hours' drive from Vientiane, centrally located **Phou Khao Khouay** is perhaps the most accessible of the conservation zones. In this often steep upland area large tracts of evergreen forests dominate the valleys and hillsides, while coniferous and scrub forests flourish in the thin soils masking sandstone bedrock formations at higher elevation.

In the far northern corner of northeastern Hua Phan province, elephants roam the bamboo forests of **Nam Et** protected area, more than half of which lies 1000m above sea level. Nam Et has been severely affected by shifting cultivation which has left the area with relatively little dense forest. It remains an important refuge for bears, endangered cats, such as the clouded leopard and tiger, wild cattle, and dhole, the rare, reddish wild dogs that hunt in packs. To the southwest of Nam Et, **Phou Loei**, occupying more than 1400 square kilometres in Luang Prabang and Hua Phan provinces, is one of the most important wildlife and evergreen forest conservation areas in northern Laos. Composed of rugged highlands, most of which are well over 1000m, and cut by the Nam Khan and Nam Xuang rivers, Phou Loei has a significant amount of bamboo forests and grasslands resulting from swidden cultivation – still the primary form of agriculture among villagers living in the area. Hunting and fishing with poison present further challenges to managing this NBCA, whose wildlife includes silver pheasants, banteng, hog deer, bears and cats, as do the creation of new settlements in far-flung areas noted for their pristine forests.

Environmental issues

In its rush to develop by capitalizing on key natural resources, primarily its wetlands and forests, Laos must come to terms with a number of critical, often interrelated, **environmental issues**. Perhaps the greatest source of concern for conservationists is Laos's many **hydroelectric dam** projects. It is no secret that dams have the potential to cause a serious negative impact on the environment, yet for Laos, the Mekong and its tributaries, with an estimated hydroelectric potential of more than 18,000 megawatts – more than half the river's total estimated potential – represent an alluring means for generating much-needed foreign exchange. Dams, in the view of the International Union for the Conservation of Nature, are not necessarily incompatible with conservation goals; instead, they represent a critical challenge to the integration of conservation and development objectives. No project better illustrates this than the $1.2 billion, 1070-megawatt Nam Theun 2 Dam, which began operation in spring 2010. The creation of the dam led to local villages being resettled (and which, some claim, still hasn't been adequately completed), and has undoubtedly impacted upon the Nakai–Nam Theun and other local conservation areas. Conversely, however, it is claimed that projects like this, through the amount of money and foreign investment involved, are better placed to help conserve the local environment – though as it's still in its infancy, it remains to be seen how much of this is true.

Laos's potential for hydropower development is inextricably linked to its forests, which protect the catchments that provide the water that ultimately generate the energy. **Deforestation** is a major problem, with the country's primary forest cover having steadily declined over the past five decades from an estimated seventy percent at the time of the French withdrawal from Indochina to roughly ten percent today. Laos's forests are threatened by the clearing of lowland forest for permanent agriculture, the use of chemical defoliants during the Second Indochina War, infrastructure development, shifting agriculture, new settlements and logging; large companies from Asian countries continue to win logging concessions from the government.

Developing and enforcing a set of regulations governing logging is a difficult task given the government's limited resources and the vast tracts of forest spread through the country; simply designating biodiversity conservation zones isn't enough to preserve the country's natural wealth.

Deforestation places increasing pressure on Laos's rural population, who rely on the forest for food, firewood, construction materials, herbs, medicine and a host of other things. The declining forests also threaten Laos's wildlife, which is already struggling to survive other intense pressures, including **hunting** and the **wildlife trade**. Despite the country's relatively low population density, the level of hunting has increased in recent decades, the result of the increased availability of guns and explosives, improved access to previously remote areas via newly cut logging roads and the exorbitant prices that rare and endangered species fetch on international markets. The gathering of forest products is also on the rise. While much of the wildlife trade is for local food consumption and use in traditional medicine, large quantities of wildlife and wildlife products are sold to Thailand, Vietnam and China. Thus, while posters and pamphlets warning villagers against hunting vulnerable species are visible in government offices and noodle shops throughout the country, elephant ivory, bear paws, pangolin scales, turtle shells, rare types of orchids and bird bills – all highly valued items in this cross-border trade – continue to find their way onto restaurant tables in Hanoi and into traditional medicines in Bangkok and Hong Kong.

Literature and myths

Classical Lao literature has its roots in the **Jataka** tales, a collection of 547 stories about the Buddha's previous lives. The tales recount the events and experiences which led to his incarnation as Siddhartha Gautama, the prince who sought the meaning of life and attained enlightenment. Penned in India and Sri Lanka, they spread with Buddhism to Southeast Asia.

Of more direct impact on Lao literature were an additional fifty tales that employed the same basic theme as the Jataka. Known as the **Panyasa Jataka**, these were perhaps composed by the Mon and abridged by the Tai Yuan of Lan Na, a kingdom centred around Chiang Mai in what is now northern Thailand. Contacts between Chiang Mai and Luang Prabang resulted in the Panyasa Jataka arriving in Laos where the stories were modified and expanded upon. Eventually the Lao versions came to differ significantly from the Tai Yuan versions, in that the former deviated from strict religious themes and became more entertaining, even to the point of having some sexual content.

Two types of story emerged: prose and poetic. Prose stories contained much Pali, the language of the Theravada Buddhist scriptures, and were written in a script called *phasa tham*, or Dharma language. These would have been comprehensible only to monks who had studied the language. Much more popular with lay-people were the poetic stories, written using the Lao script and containing mostly Lao vocabulary. As Lao is a tonal language, these poems did not rhyme as poetry composed in English sometimes does. Instead, tones and alliteration were used to produce a rhythm. Both types of stories were recorded by writing on the fronds of a certain kind of palm with a stylus, and some of the longer versions made use of hundreds of palm leaves. These surprisingly durable palm-leaf manuscripts were kept in a special library in the monastery grounds or sometimes in private homes.

The Ramayana

Of the Indian literature to become established in Southeast Asia, the Hindu **Ramayana** is by far the best known. This epic poem, with its host of vivid characters possessing comic-book hero attributes, arrived in Southeast Asia during its "Indianization" at the hands of Hindu traders. In the original, Hanuman, the King of the Monkeys, assists the god Rama in rescuing his wife Sita from the many-headed, multi-armed demon Ravana.

Once the Ramayana became established in Southeast Asia, however, it didn't take long for local variations to emerge. The inhabitants of Java, Bali, Burma, Cambodia and Thailand all composed their own distinct versions and eventually the story spread from coastal areas into the Indochinese hinterland. Although a version of the poem was well known to the Khmer who once inhabited what is now southern Laos, the Ramayana's introduction to the ethnic Lao came much later via Siam.

French colonization brought scholars who, perhaps because they were already familiar with the Khmer version of the poem, tended to overemphasize the Ramayana's significance to Lao literature, proclaiming it Laos's most important work. Later, Indian scholars, eager to aggrandize the influence of Indian culture in a country they considered an outpost of "Greater India", echoed French opinions. In fact, the Lao version of the Ramayana, known as **Pha Lak Pha Lam**, was never popular at the village level. Suitably modified to suit Lao tastes, it did, however, become a favourite of the Lao court. This popularity is reflected in depictions of the Ramayana in murals and reliefs found at Buddhist monasteries, especially those that were patronized by the monarchy.

Occasionally, the stories were copied anew, but there was no pressure on the scrivener, usually a monk, to remain true to the original. The result was literally hundreds of versions and variations of these stories that not only taught values but also contained a wealth of information about traditional Lao society. During certain festivals, villagers would gather at the local monastery or in a private home to hear the stories read aloud and in this way some favourites eventually emerged. The *Sang Sin Sai* in particular is felt by many Lao to be the pinnacle of Lao literature. As with all of these stories, the plot takes a back seat to the poetry itself and the author is obscure. Attributed to "Pangkham", the story is almost certainly the product of many authors and editors.

A tradition of oral folk tales known as **Xieng Miang**, after the name of the central character, were eventually transcribed as both poetry and prose. The stories seem to be almost the opposite of the Jataka-style morality tales: Xieng Miang is a lazy but clever trickster who enjoys outwitting authority figures, especially the king. In a typical exploit he covets the king's prized cat and so decides to kidnap it. Once he has the cat safely home, Xieng Miang teaches it to shun the fresh fish it is accustomed to by beating the cat every time it nears a fish placed on the floor. The cat soon learns to eat rice and when the king arrives to claim his cat, Xieng Miang "proves" it doesn't belong to the king by letting the cat choose between a plate of rice and plate of fish. Knowing that going near the fish will bring on a beating, the cat chooses the rice and the king goes home empty-handed. The stories of Xieng Miang remain popular today among Lao children, and work recently began on creating animated short films about the character, which is testament to its enduring popularity.

The present climate for Lao writers living in Laos has been described as "tricky". Laos is still rather **restrictive** in what it will allow to be published, but a few Lao writers manage to make social commentary without the government's approval by publishing in Thailand in the Thai language.

Books

As Laos is one of the least-known countries in Southeast Asia, it should be no surprise to find that books about it are hard to come by, to say nothing of quality works on the country. You're likely to have more luck searching for many of the titles listed below at an online bookstore such as ⓦwww.amazon.com, ⓦwww.powells.com or Thailand's ⓦwww.asiabooks .com than you would wandering the aisles of your local bookshop. While some books will need to be specially ordered, others will be easier (and sometimes cheaper) to find at bookshops in Bangkok, Vientiane or Luang Prabang.

In the book reviews below, the abbreviation o/p means "out of print"; titles marked 🎿 are particularly recommended.

Culture, society and environment

Sucheng Chan (ed) *Hmong Means Free*. Fascinating personal narratives by three generations of Hmong refugees from five different families, which describe their lives as farmers on the hilltops of Laos, as refugees in the camps of Thailand and as immigrants in the United States.

Brett Dakin *Another Quiet American: Stories of Life in Laos*. A very personal account of modern Laos by an American who lived in Vientiane during the 1990s.

🎿 **Natacha Du Pont De Bie** *Ant Egg Soup: the Adventures of a Food Tourist*. A wonderful foodie journey across the country, illustrated with excellent recipes that the author collected during her travels.

🎿 **Anne Fadiman** *The Spirit Catches You and You Fall Down: A Hmong Child, Her American Doctors,* and the *Collision of Two Cultures*. An excellent exploration of the sad, absorbing tale of Lia Lee, a severely epileptic child, born to a family of Hmong refugees living in California, who clash with their daughter's

Western doctors over how to treat the child's condition.

Stephen Mansfield *Culture Shock! Laos*. A cultural starter kit detailing how to avoid such faux pas as touching your spouse in public, pointing your foot at someone and eating your sticky rice with chopsticks. Mainly aimed at soon-to-be expats in Laos, with details on working in the country. Its tone is at times a little patronizing.

Phia Sing et al. *Traditional Recipes of Laos*. Not only is this one of the rare books explaining how to prepare Lao cuisine, it's the only book containing the recipes of the former royal chef and master of ceremonies of Luang Prabang.

Liesbeth Sluiter *The Mekong Currency: Life and Times of a River*. An earthy account of green issues along the Mekong corridor, in Laos, Cambodia and Thailand, Sluiter's book does an excellent job of presenting environmental concerns from the perspective of the fishermen and farmers whose livelihoods are sustained by the Mekong and its tributaries, though it's now in need of some updating.

Fiction and travellers' accounts

🎿 **Marthe Bassenne** *In Laos and Siam*. The evocative account of a French expatriate woman's 1909

journey up the Mekong River to Luang Prabang.

Colin Cotterill *The Coroner's Lunch*. The first of an enjoyable series of crime novels about Doctor Siri, the reluctant chief coroner, set in Vientiane after the end of the Second Indochina War. An often farcical thriller, Siri is an engaging narrator as he tries to expose the secrets of a number of mysterious deaths.

Louis Delaporte *A Pictorial Journey on the Old*. Volume three of the Mekong Exploration Commission's report is devoted to the exquisite illustrations of the artist who accompanied French explorers Francis Garnier and Doudart de Lagrée during their 1866–68 expedition.

Francis Garnier *Travels in Cambodia and Part of Laos*. The English translation of the first volume of the report by France's Mekong Exploration Commission, which set out from Saigon to find a back-door route to China via the Mekong, details the group's travels from Cambodia to Luang Prabang.

Francis Garnier *Further Travels in Laos and in Yunnan*. Volume two of the Mekong Exploration Commission's report focuses on the weary explorers' travels in Upper Laos and Yunnan, with entries on a Muslim uprising in China and Garnier's explorations of alternative trade routes.

F.J. Harmand *Laos and the Hill Tribes of Indochina* A cultural barbarian by today's standards, the French explorer nevertheless produced a valuable report on his late nineteenth-century journey through southern Laos, researching the region's natural history and searching for an overland route from Champasak to Hué. The account, which records funerary and religious customs of the highland tribal minorities of the Bolaven Plateau, also focuses on his encounters with the Phu Tai people of the Savannakhet region, and is liberally sprinkled with amusing and insightful anecdotes.

Henri Mouhot *Travels in Siam, Cambodia, and Laos* The account of the final journey of the legendary "discoverer of Angkor Wat", filled with his characteristically blunt observations of the people of Laos, from the tobacco-hungry infants to the uncouth court officials that he encountered on his journey to Upper Laos which resulted in his death outside Luang Prabang.

History

Jane Hamilton-Merritt *Tragic Mountains: the Hmong, the Americans, and the Secret Wars for Laos, 1942–1992* This impressive account of the Hmong, written by a Pulitzer Prize-nominated correspondent during the Second Indochina War, ranges from the personal to the political as it follows the Hmong from the battlefields to life after the war.

Victor T. King *Explorers of Southeast Asia: Six Lives*. Six different authors examine the journeys of various nineteenth-century European explorers, including Frenchmen Henri Mouhot and Francis Garnier.

Christopher Kremmer *Bamboo Palace: Discovering the Lost Dynasty of Laos*. A continuation of the author's earlier *Stalking the Elephant Kings*, which tracked his journey into remote Laos in search of the monarch who disappeared shortly after the communists took over in 1975. By interviewing a former inmate of Laos' re-education camps, Kremmer is able to piece together the last days of the royal family, some of whom perished due to harsh living conditions in the caves of Hua Phan province.

Alfred W. McCoy *The Politics of Heroin: CIA Complicity in the*

Global Drug Trade Laos, not surprisingly, figures prominently in this exhaustively researched, revised and expanded version of McCoy's landmark *The Politics of Heroin in Southeast Asia*.

Christopher Robbins *The Ravens: Pilots of the Secret War of Laos* (o/p). Although difficult to find, this book on America's secret war is well worth reading. Many of the details of America's secretive Laos operations during the Second Indochina War didn't come out until this gripping work by Robbins, a British journalist, was published in 1987. Based on interviews with American pilots who fought in Laos, this hard-to-find book is well worth tracking down.

Stan Sesser *The Lands of Charm and Cruelty: Travels in Southeast Asia* Among the five insightful essays in this superb book is a 53-page segment on Laos during the late 1980s and early 1990s. In presenting a well-observed account of the country as it struggles to rebuild itself after the war, Sesser mixes reflections on Laos's recent history with insights into the country's political leadership, culture and economic reforms. The book builds on articles Stesser originally wrote for *The New Yorker*.

Martin Stuart-Fox *A History of Laos*. Written by an Australian scholar who covered the Second Indochina War as a foreign correspondent, this work represents the best available overview of Laos's history, although it's extremely light on the country's early history.

Martin Stuart-Fox and Mary Kooyman *Historical Dictionary of Laos* A encyclopedia of key people and events in the history of Laos which, though expensive and difficult to find, is worthwhile for the many insightful nuggets of information tracked down by the authors, and the extensive bibliography.

Roger Warner *Shooting at the Moon: The Story of America's Clandestine War in Laos* Winner of the Overseas Press Club's award for the best book on foreign affairs, Warner's thoroughly researched and crisply written account of American involvement reads like an adventure novel. Letting tragic events speak for themselves, Warner brings to life the key players and significant events as he follows the secret war from its origins at the end of World War II to the American withdrawal from Indochina.

Language

Language

Language

ao belongs to the Tai family of languages, which includes Thai; Shan (Tai Yai), spoken in Burma (Myanmar); Phuan, spoken in Laos and parts of Thailand; and Tai Leu, spoken by the Dai minority of southern China's Yunnan province. Besides Lao and its "cousin" languages, such as Tai Leu and Phuan, sundry other languages are spoken within the borders of Laos. These include tongues belonging to the Mon–Khmer and Tibeto–Burman families of languages which are spoken by upland tribal peoples, as well as Vietnamese and Chinese spoken by immigrants from Laos's neighbouring countries.

French was once the second language of the educated and elite classes, and fluent French-speakers can still be found among older Laotians, usually an indication that they were once functionaries of the old royal regime. In recent years French has fallen out of favour; since economic liberalization came into effect, **English** has become the preferred foreign tongue among the younger generation, who are convinced that learning English is the key to obtaining a high-paying job in the tourism sector. During the 1980s, Lao students were sent to study abroad in fellow Soviet-bloc countries such as Poland, East Germany and Cuba, and hence it is sometimes possible to find a rusty Polish-, German- or Spanish-speaking Lao.

Travellers will find that getting around in urban areas can be done using basic English. Once out in the countryside, however, the situation changes, and visitors will have to make an effort to learn some Lao phrases to get by. Don't feel too put out – urban Lao sometimes experience similar problems when travelling in rural areas.

One of the greatest obstacles to building a nation that successive Lao governments have had to deal with is language. While Lao as it is spoken in Vientiane has official language status, there are pockets of Laos where no dialect of Lao, much less the Vientiane version, will be heard. With little money or resources to post qualified teachers to isolated villages, **Vientiane Lao** is simply not being learned in these areas. The Lao government has experimented with the somewhat drastic step of relocating tribal children to lowland towns where they live in huts in the school grounds and where, theoretically, they are exposed to language and lifestyles that will help them assimilate and become more "Lao". In the meantime, many of the non-Lao-speaking ethnic groups in rural areas will continue to live as they always have done, speaking their own tongue among themselves while maintaining a handful of Lao phrases to conduct trade or other dealings with the lowland Lao.

To fully understand the contemporary state of the Lao language in urban areas, it is necessary to look at how it relates to Thai. The spoken Thai of Bangkok and the spoken Lao of Vientiane are similar, as akin as Spanish is to Portuguese. As vassals of the Thai, the Lao absorbed a fair amount of Thai vocabulary, mainly through the Buddhist monkhood and channels between the royal courts. This shared vocabulary was, for the most part, taken from **Pali**, in which the scriptures of Theravada Buddhism were written. During the Lao civil war, Thailand sided with the Lao royalists. The communist victory and death of the Lao monarchy saw the end of flowery court language, but although the communist government temporarily suppressed Lao Buddhism, no direct attacks on Pali-derived vocabulary were mounted. Some aspects of everyday spoken and written Lao were targeted, however. In an effort to erase class divisions, the communist government discouraged the use of personal pronouns that flaunted status or begged servitude. A typical banned pronoun was "*doi kha noi*", which translates into English as "I" but which literally means "I, small slave".

After the revolution the Lao government also made official changes to the **Lao alphabet** in order to simplify it, as well as purge it of aspects that the communists felt were too similar to Thai. The Lao government's policies had, for a time anyway, the desired effect of levelling class divisions, and the simplified alphabet has no doubt made teaching the illiterate to read an easier task. However, the changes and simplifications have had an unforeseen effect on the Lao language. What the government didn't anticipate was the growing sophistication of the **Thai media** and subsequent boom in popularity of Thai films, television and popular music in Laos. Every day, tens of thousands of Lao tune in to receive a dose of Thai, with its stratified personal pronouns and honorifics. Even broadcasts of the Thai royal language, almost identical to the extinct Lao royal language, can be heard daily on the Thai television news. These factors have conspired to give the Lao something of an inferiority complex about their own language, and they often compare it unfavourably to Thai by saying that Thai sounds more "beautiful" and "polite" than Lao.

Transliteration

Visitors who travel between Laos and Thailand may notice the similarity in the scripts of the two countries. This is because the Lao script was actually based on an early version of written Thai. During colonial times, the French considered replacing the **Lao script** with an alphabet similar to *quoc ngu*, the Romanized script now used to write Vietnamese. The project was never implemented, as French influence was waning at the time, but devising the system presented quite a challenge. The Lao language contains sounds that don't exist in French, or any other Western European language for that matter, making transliteration an inexact exercise at best.

Imperfect as it was, the fledgling **French transliteration system** has had some staying power. The Lao seem comfortable with the French system, and many educated Lao prefer to have their names transliterated in the French manner, which serves to differentiate them from the Thai, who use a different system. Official maps of Laos produced by the Lao government use a modified form of the old French system. This can create problems for English speakers who assume that the system was created for them. But if you keep in mind, for example, that the Lao "ou" rhymes with the French "vous", not the English "noun", reading Lao place names shouldn't be a problem. The transliteration of place names in this book follows the modified French system used by the Lao National Geographic Service. For the transliteration of Lao words in the following section, a simplified version of the same system is used. This is not to say that travellers will find exactly the system in use throughout Laos: the Lao are quite cavalier when it comes to **consistency** in transliteration. In Vientiane, for instance, it is possible to see the Arch of Victory monument transliterated as "Patouxai", "Patousai", "Patuxai" and "Patusai".

Consonants

b as in big	ng as in singer (this combination sometimes appears at the beginning of a word)
d as in dog	
f as in fun	ny as in the Russian nyet
h as in hello	p as in speak (unaspirated)
j (or ch) as in jar	ph as in pill
k as in skin (unaspirated)	s (or x) as in same
kh as kiss	t as in stop (unaspirated)
l as in luck	th as in tin
m as in more	w (or v) as in wish
n as in now	y as in yes

Vowels

a as in autobahn	i as in mimi
ae as in cat	ia as in India
ai as in Thai	o as in flow
aw as in jaw	oe as in Goethe
ao as in Lao	u (or ou) as in you
e as in pen	ua (or oua) as in truant
eu as in French fleur	

Lao is a **tonal language**, which means that the tone a speaker gives to a word will determine its meaning. While the tone system may make some visitors despair of ever learning any Lao, mastering a handful of simple phrases will greatly enhance your travels in Laos. The Lao are always delighted by foreigners who make the effort to converse with them in their own language and will reciprocate with more than the usual graciousness.

Lao words and phrases

As a stranger you should remember to utter a greeting first when you meet someone. Questions the Lao commonly ask in conversation may seem personal to Westerners ("Are you married?") but this is simply an indication of the importance of the family in Lao culture. Questions in Lao are not normally answered with a yes or no. Instead the verb used in the question is repeated for the answer; for example: "Do you have a room?" would be answered "Have" in the affirmative or "No have" in the negative.

Greetings and small talk

Hello (said with a smile)	sabai di	No I can't	wâo baw dâi
How are you?	sabai di baw	I only speak a little Lao	khói wâo phasã láo dâi nói neung
Thank you (very much)	kop chai (lai lai)	Do you understand?	jâo khào jai baw
I'm fine	sabai di	I don't understand	khói baw khào jai
Can you speak English?	jâo wâo phasã angkit dâi baw	Where are you from?	jâo má tae sãi

I'm from England/ America/Australia /New Zealand	khói má tae angkit/ amelika/awsteli /nyu silaen	No, I'm not married	yáng baw taeng ngan
What's your name?	jâo seu nyãng	How many kids do you have?	jâo mí lûk ják khón
My name is....	khói seu	I've got two kids	mí lûk sãwng khón
How old are you?	jâo anyu ják pi	I don't have any kids	yáng baw mí lûk
How many brothers and sisters do you have?	jâo mí âi nâwng ják khón	Are you enjoying Laos?	thiàw méuang láo muan baw
Are you married yet?	jâo taeng ngan léu baw	I'm enjoying it very much	muan lãi
Yes, I'm married	taeng ngan lâew	Goodbye	lá kawn
		Goodbye (in reply)	sok di

Places and directions

Where are you going? (often used as a familiar greeting)	pai sãi	Where is the boat launch/pier?	thà heuá yu sãi
To the market	pai talat	Drugstore	hân kãi ya
To the guesthouse	pai bân phak	Post office	paisani
To the ... Hotel	pai hong haem...	Police station	sathani tamluat
To the boat launch /pier	pai thà heuá	Museum	phiphithaphan
To the bus station	pai khiw lot	Thai embassy	sathanthut thai
Will you go?	pai baw	Chinese embassy	sathanthut jin
How much will you go for?	pai thao dai	Vietnamese embassy	sathanthut wiatnam
		Is the ... far away?	... yu kai baw
One thousand kip per person	phù la phán kip	Is the airport far away?	doen bin yu kai baw
Where is the...?	...yu sãi	It's far	kai
Where is the guesthouse?	bân phak yu sãi	It's not far	baw kai
		Go straight	pai sêu sêu
		Turn right	lîaw khwã
		Turn left	lîaw sâi

Accommodation

Do you have a room?	mí hàwng wàng baw	How much per night?	khéun la thao dai
Do you have a double room?	mí hàwng sãwng tiang baw	Seven thousand kip per night	khéun la jét phán kip
Does the room have a fan?	hàwng mí phat lóm baw	Can you discount the price?	lút lakha dâi baw
Mosquito net	mûng	Where is the toilet?	hàwng suam yu sãi
Bathroom	hàwng nâm	How many nights will you stay?	si phak ják khéun
Toilet	suam	I will stay two nights	si phak sãwng khéun
Air conditioning	ae yen	Sorry, no discounts	lút lakha baw dâi
Blankets	phà hom	Can you clean the room?	het anamai hàwng dâi baw
Hot water	nâm hâwn		
Can I see the room?	khãw beung hàwng kawn dâi baw	Can I have the room key?	khãw kajae dae

Can I move to another room?	yâi hàwng dâi baw	Do you have a laundry service?	mí bawlikan sak phà baw
This room is full of mosquitoes	hàwng nî mí nyung lãi	Do you have bicycles for rent?	mí lot thip hâi sao baw
This room is too noisy	hàwng nî siãng dang		

Shopping

Is this for sale?	an nî khãi baw	Washing powder	sabu fun
How much?	thao dai	Toilet paper	jîa hàwng nâm
How much is this?	an nî thao dai	Candles	thian
I'd like to buy...	khói yak sêu...	Mosquito coils	ya kan nyung baep jút
Cigarettes	ya sùp	Flip-flops	koep tae
Medicine	ya	How much is this?	an nî thao dai
Antiques	khãwng kao	How much is it in dollars?	ngóen dawn khit thao dai
Souvenirs	khãwng thilaleuk	I only have kip	khói mí tae ngóen kip
Clothes	seuà phà	It's very expensive	phaeng lãi
Silk cloth	phà mãi	How much of a discount can you give?	lút lakha dâi thao dai
Do you have...?	mí...baw		
Do you have soap?	mí sabu baw		
Toothpaste	yã si khâew		

On the road

Does this vehicle go to...?	lot nî pai ... baw	How much to hire the vehicle /boat outright?	mão lot/héua thao dai
How much is it to go to...?	pai ... thao dai	Don't pick up any other passengers	baw tâwng hap phù doi sãn khon eun
How many hours will it take?	sai wela ják sua móng	Do you agree to the price?	tók lóng lakha baw
What time will the bus depart?	lot si awk ják móng	I agree	tók lóng
What time will we arrive?	si hâwt ják móng	I don't agree	baw tók lóng
Is this seat vacant?	bawn nang nî wàng baw	Please stop here	jàwt nî dae
It's vacant	wàng	Please stop so I can urinate	jàwt thai bao dae
It's taken	baw wàng	What's wrong with the vehicle?	lot pen nyãng
Can I hire the vehicle /boat outright?	mão lot/heuá dâi baw	Will we be parked here for long?	jàwt yu nî don baw

Emergencies and health

Help!	suay dae	I'm not well	khói baw sabai
Can you help me?	jâo suay khói dâi baw	I have a fever	khói pen khai
There's been an accident	mí ubatihet	I have diarrhoea	thâwng khói baw di
I need a doctor	khói tâwng kan hã mãw	I'm in a lot of pain	khói jép nák

Please take me to the hospital	song khói pai hong mãw dae	I lost my passport	pâm doen thang khãwng khói sĩã hãi
I've been bitten by a dog/snake	khói theuk mã/ngu kát	My pack is missing	kheuang khãwng khói sĩã hãi
Where is the toilet?	hàwng suam yu sãi		

Common answers to questions

I don't know	baw hũ	It cannot be done	baw dâi
There isn't/aren't any	baw mí	It's uncertain	baw nàe

Numbers

0	sun	21	sao ét
1	neung	22	sao sãwng
2	sãwng	30	sãm síp
3	sãm	31	sãm síp ét
4	si	32	sãm síp sãwng
5	hà	40	si síp
6	hók	50	hà sip
7	jét	60	hók síp
8	pàet	70	jét síp
9	kâo	80	pàet síp
10	síp	90	kâo síp
11	síp ét	100	hôi
12	síp sãwng	200	sãwng hôi
13	síp sãm	1000	phán
14	síp si	2000	sãwng phán
15	síp hà	10,000	síp phán
16	síp hók	50,000	hà síp phán
17	síp jét	100,000	sãen
18	síp pàet	200,000	sãwng sãen
19	síp kâo	1,000,000	lân
20	sao	2,000,000	sãwng lân

Days of the week and time

Sunday	wán thít	Morning	tawn sâo
Monday	wán jan	Noon	thiang wán
Tuesday	wán angkhán	Afternoon	tawn bai
Wednesday	wán phut	Early evening	tawn láeng
Thursday	wan phahát	Late evening	tawn khám
Friday	wán súk	Midnight	thiang khéun
Saturday	wán sáo	Next week	athit nà
Today	mêu nî	Last week	athit thi lâew
Yesterday	mêu wan nî	Next month	deuan nà
Tomorrow	mêu eun	Last month	deuan thi lâew

Next year	pi nà
Last year	pi thi lâew
Now	tawn nî

Later	theua nà
Just now	ta kî

A food and drink glossary

Useful phrases

êu ... dâi bawn nãi	Where can I buy...?
sêu ahãn dâi bawn nãi	Where can I buy food?
hàwng ahãn yu sãi	Where is a restaurant?
khãw laikan ahãn dae?	Do you have a menu?
mi…baw?	Do you have…?
baw phét	Not spicy
khói kin te phák	I am vegetarian
khói ao…	I would like…
khãw sék dae?	Can I have the bill?
khói baw dâi sang náew nî	I didn't order this
nî nyãng?	What's this?
sai/baw sai	With/without
baw sai nãm pa	Without fish sauce
khãw baep nân ján neung	I'd like a plate of that
khói kin sîn baw dâi	I can't eat meat
baw sai nãm tan	No sugar
baw sai nãm kâwn	No ice
soen sàep	Bon appétit
kâew	Bottle
mâi thu	Chopsticks
jawk	Cup/glass
sàep	Delicious
sawm	Fork
hãn kãi fõe	Noodle shop
buang	Spoon
hãn ahãn	Restaurant

Staples

bai hóhlapha	basil
boe	butter
hét	mushroom
hua phák bua	onion
hua phák thiam	garlic

jaew	sauce
jeun khai	omelette
kai	chicken
kha	galingale
khai dao	egg, fried
khào jâo	rice, steamed
khào ji	bread
khào niaw	rice, sticky
khing	ginger
kũng	shrimp
màk kheua	aubergine
màk len	tomato
màk phét	chilli
mu	pork
nâm kat	coconut milk
nâm pa	fish sauce
nâm tan	sugar
naw mâi	bamboo shoots
nok	bird
nóm sòm	yoghurt
pa	fish
pa dàek	fish paste
pét	duck
phák	vegetables
phák nâm	watercress
phák salat	lettuce
phõng sú lot	MSG
pu	crab
sìn ngúa	beef
tâo hû	bean curd
tôm khai	egg, boiled

Noodles

fõe	rice noodle soup
fõe hàeng	rice noodle soup without broth
fõe khùa	fried rice noodles
khào piak sèn	rice noodle soup, served in chicken broth

khào pûn	flour noodles with sauce
mì hàeng	yellow wheat noodles without broth
mì nâm	yellow wheat noodles

Everyday dishes and "drinking food"

kaeng jèut	mild soup with pork and vegetables
khào ji pateh	bread with Lao-style pâté and vegetables
khào ji sai boe	bread with butter
khào khùa or khào phát	fried rice
khào khùa sai kai	fried rice with chicken
khùa khing kai	chicken with ginger
khùa phák baw sai sin	stir-fried vegetables without meat
larp mu	minced pork
man falang jeun	chips
mũ phát bai hólapha	pork with basil over rice
pîng kai	grilled chicken
pîng pa or jeun pa	grilled fish
tam màk hung	spicy papaya salad
tôm yam pa	spicy fish soup with lemongrass
yam sìn ngúa	spicy beef salad
yáw díp	spring rolls, fresh
yáw jeun	spring rolls, fried

Fruit

lamut	sapodilla
màk hung	papaya
màk kîang	orange
màk kiang	rose apple
màk kûay	banana
màk lînji	lychee
màk mángkhut	mangosteen
màk mì	jackfruit
màk mo	watermelon
màk muang	mango
màk náo	lime/lemon
màk nat	pineapple
màk ngaw	rambutan
màk nyám nyái	longan
màk phom	apple
màk sida	guava
thulian	durian

Sweets

kalaem	Ice cream
khào lãm	sticky rice in coconut milk cooked in bamboo
khào niaw màk muang	sticky rice with mango
nâm wãn	sweets in coconut milk
nâm wãn màk kûay	banana in coconut milk

Drinks

bia	beer
bia sót	beer, draught
kafeh	coffee
kafeh dam	black coffee
kafeh net	instant coffee
kafeh hawn	hot coffee
kafeh (nóm) hawn	hot Lao coffee (with sweetened condensed milk)
kafeh (nóm) yén	iced coffee (with sweetened condensed milk)
lào-láo	rice whisky
màk kuay pan	banana shake
màk mai pan	fruit shake

nâm deum	water
nâm hâwn	water, hot
nâm kâwn	ice
nâm màk phâo	coconut juice
nâm sá	tea
nâm soda	soda water
nâm tâo hû	soy milk
nâm yén	water, cold
nóm	milk, usually sweetened condensed
owantin	Ovaltine (a chocolate drink)
sá jin	tea, Chinese
sá yén	tea, iced

Glossary

Akha highland ethnic group

ARVN Army of Republic of Vietnam, the defunct South Vietnamese Army

baht Thai currency, also a unit for measuring gold

ban house or village

basi animist Lao ceremony

bia sot draught beer

bombi type of anti-personnel bomb which explodes when touched

Brahma Hindu god

bun (or boun) festival

dawk jampa plumeria (frangipani) blossom, the national flower of Laos

devaraja god-king a Khmer concept of divine kingship

devata female divinity

don (or dawn) island

dvarapala guardian divinities at doors and gateways of Khmer ruins

falang white person, person of European descent

fōe Vietnamese noodle dish ("pho" in Vietnamese) found throughout Laos

hân kin deum casual eating and drinking spot

HCMT Ho Chi Minh Trail, series of trails used by the NVA to infiltrate South Vietnam

heua sa slow boat

heua wai speedboat

Hmong highland ethnic group

Indra Hindu god

jataka mythological tales of the Buddha's previous lives

jumbo three-wheeled motorized taxi

kataw a game similar to volleyball, but played without the use of the arms; also played in Thailand and Malaysia, where it's called *takraw*

kha slave; formerly used as a pejorative for hill tribes

khào rice

khào ji French bread

khào niaw sticky rice

khiw lot bus stand

Khmer Cambodian

Khmu an upland ethnic group

khwaeng province

kip Lao currency

lak kilometre, often used in place names

lam wong traditional dance

Lane Xang ancient Lao kingdom

Lao Loum lowland Lao, mostly ethnic Lao

Lao Soum highland Lao; hill tribes

Lao Theung speakers of Mon–Khmer languages who live at higher altitudes than the Lao Loum

lào hái rice wine sipped from straws out of a large stoneware jar

lào-láo strong alcoholic drink made from sticky rice

Larp minced meat dish

lintel horizontal beam or stone over a door or window

LNTA Lao National Tourism Administration

lustral water holy water used to bathe a Buddha image

makara mythical water monster

maw thiam spirit medium

Mien a highland ethnic group

muan fun, enjoyable

muang (or meuang) city or town

mudra hand and arm positions depicted in Buddhist and Hindu imagery

mukhalinga phallic-shaped stone symbolic of Shiva with an image of the god's face carved into it naga benevolent mythical water serpent (pronounced "nak" in Lao)

nam river

nam phu (or nam phou) fountain

NBCA National Biodiversity Conservation Area

ngeuak malevolent mythical water serpent

NTAL National Tourism Authority of Laos

NVA North Vietnamese Army

pa dàek fermented fish paste, used as seasoning

pa kha Irrawaddy dolphin

pa pao blowfish with a vicious bite found in southern Laos

pak mouth of a river

Pathet Lao communist guerrilla movement which gained control of Laos in 1975

Patouxai monument in Vientiane

Pha Bang a Buddha image belived by many to be the talismanic protector of the Lao nation

Pha In Hindu god Indra

Pha Lak Pha Lam Lao version of the Ramayana

Pha Phut the Buddha

Pha Phutthahup Buddha image

phi spirit or ghost

phu (or phou) hill or mountain

Phuan lowland ethnic group

pirogue narrow dug-out canoe

Ramayana epic poem of Indian origin (Pha Lak Pha Lam in Lao)

rishi hermitic ascetic

Royal Lao Army (RLA) army of the defunct Kingdom of Laos

sala pavilion with a raised floor and roof but no walls

samana re-education camp, derived from the word "seminar"

sawngthaew pick-up truck used for public transport

Shiva Hindu god

Shivalinga phallic-shaped stone symbolic of Shiva

shophouse Southeast Asian property, usually built in terraces and comprising a shop at ground level with residential areas above

sim building in a monastery housing the main Buddha image

sin women's wraparound skirt

Sipsong Chao Tai the Twelve Tai Principalities, a loose federation that once included parts of northwest Vietnam and northeast Laos

soi lane or alley

somasutra stone pipe for channelling lustral water

stupa Buddhist structure built to contain holy relics ("that" in Lao)

tad (or tat) waterfall

Tai ethnic Thai

Tai Dam lowland Lao ethnic group, found in Hua Phan and Xing Khuang provinces

Tai Leu lowland Lao ethnic group, found in northwest Laos

Tai Yuan northern Thai

talat market

Talat Sao Vientiane's morning market

thanon road or street

that Lao word for Buddhist stupa

tuk-tuk three-wheeled motorized taxi

ushnisha finial symbolizing enlightenment found on the crown of the head of Buddha images

UXO unexploded ordnance

Vishnu a Hindu god

wat Buddhist monastery

wiang (or vieng) town surrounded by wooden palisades

xe river (southern Laos only)

xieng town surrounded by brick or earthen ramparts

Travel store

Books change lives

Book Aid
International
www.bookaid.org

Poverty and illiteracy go hand in hand. But in sub-Saharan Africa, books are a luxury few can afford. Many children leave school functionally illiterate, and adults often fall back into illiteracy in adulthood due to a lack of available reading material.

Book Aid International knows that books change lives.

Every year we send over half a million books to partners in 12 countries in sub-Saharan Africa, to stock libraries in schools, refugee camps, prisons, universities and communities. Literally millions of readers have access to books and information that could teach them new skills – from keeping chickens to getting a degree in Business Studies or learning how to protect against HIV/AIDS.

What can you do?

Join our Reverse Book Club and with your donation of only £6 a month, we can send 36 books every year to some of the poorest countries in the world. For every two pounds extra you can give, we can send another book!

Support Book Aid International today!

 Online. Go to our website at **www.bookaid.org**, and click on 'donate'

 By telephone. Start a Direct Debit or give a donation on your card by calling us on 020 7733 3577

Book Aid International is a charity and a limited company registered in England and Wales.
Charity No. 313869 Company No. 880754   39-41 Coldharbour Lane, Camberwell, London SE5 9NR
T +44 (0)20 7733 3577   F +44 (0)20 7978 8006   E info@bookaid.org   www.bookaid.org

Visit us online

www.roughguides.com

Information on over 25,000 destinations around the world

- **Read** Rough Guides' trusted travel info
- **Access** exclusive articles from Rough Guides authors
- **Update** yourself on new books, maps, CDs and other products
- **Enter** our competitions and win travel prizes
- **Share** ideas, journals, photos & travel advice with other users
- **Earn** points every time you contribute to the Rough Guide
  community and get rewards

BROADEN YOUR HORIZONS

Small print and

Index

A Rough Guide to Rough Guides

Published in 1982, the first Rough Guide – to Greece – was a student scheme that became a publishing phenomenon. Mark Ellingham, a recent graduate in English from Bristol University, had been travelling in Greece the previous summer and couldn't find the right guidebook. With a small group of friends he wrote his own guide, combining a highly contemporary, journalistic style with a thoroughly practical approach to travellers' needs.

The immediate success of the book spawned a series that rapidly covered dozens of destinations. And, in addition to impecunious backpackers, Rough Guides soon acquired a much broader and older readership that relished the guides' wit and inquisitiveness as much as their enthusiastic, critical approach and value-for-money ethos.

These days, Rough Guides include recommendations from shoestring to luxury and cover more than 200 destinations around the globe, including almost every country in the Americas and Europe, more than half of Africa and most of Asia and Australasia. Our ever-growing team of authors and photographers is spread all over the world, particularly in Europe, the US and Australia.

In the early 1990s, Rough Guides branched out of travel, with the publication of Rough Guides to World Music, Classical Music and the Internet. All three have become benchmark titles in their fields, spearheading the publication of a wide range of books under the Rough Guide name.

Including the travel series, Rough Guides now number more than 350 titles, covering: phrasebooks, waterproof maps, music guides from Opera to Heavy Metal, reference works as diverse as Conspiracy Theories and Shakespeare, and popular culture books from iPods to Poker. Rough Guides also produce a series of more than 120 World Music CDs in partnership with World Music Network.

Visit www.roughguides.com to see our latest publications.

SMALL PRINT

Rough Guide credits

Text editor: Róisín Cameron
Layout: Ankur Guha
Cartography: Rajesh Chhibber
Picture editor: Sarah Cummins
Production: Rebecca Short
Proofreader: Karen Parker
Cover design: Nicole Newman, Dan May
Photographer: Tim Draper
Editorial: **London** Andy Turner, Keith Drew, Edward Aves, Alice Park, Lucy White, Jo Kirby, James Smart, Natasha Foges, James Rice, Emma Beatson, Emma Gibbs, Kathryn Lane, Monica Woods, Mani Ramaswamy, Harry Wilson, Lucy Cowie, Lara Kavanagh, Alison Roberts, Eleanor Aldridge, Ian Blenkinsop, Joe Staines, Matthew Milton, Tracy Hopkins; **Delhi** Madhavi Singh, Jalpreen Kaur Chhatwal
Design & Pictures: **London** Scott Stickland, Dan May, Diana Jarvis, Mark Thomas, Nicole Newman, Emily Taylor; **Delhi** Umesh Aggarwal, Ajay Verma, Jessica Subramanian, Pradeep Thapliyal, Sachin Tanwar, Anita Singh, Nikhil Agarwal, Sachin Gupta

Production: Liz Cherry, Louise Daly, Erika Pepe
Cartography: **London** Ed Wright, Katie Lloyd-Jones; **Delhi** Ashutosh Bharti, Rajesh Mishra, Animesh Pathak, Jasbir Sandhu, Swati Handoo, Deshpal Dabas, Lokamata Sahu
Online: **London** Faye Hellon, Jeanette Angell, Fergus Day, Justine Bright, Clare Bryson, Aine Fearon, Adrian Low, Ezgi Celebi; **Delhi** Amit Verma, Rahul Kumar, Narender Kumar, Ravi Yadav, Debojit Borah, Rakesh Kumar, Ganesh Sharma, Shisir Basumatari
Marketing & Publicity: **London** Liz Statham, Jess Carter, Vivienne Watton, Anna Paynton, Rachel Sprackett, Laura Vipond; **New York** Katy Ball; **Delhi** Aman Arora
Digital Travel Publisher: Peter Buckley
Reference Director: Andrew Lockett
Operations Assistant: Becky Doyle
Operations Manager: Helen Atkinson
Publishing Director (Travel): Clare Currie
Commercial Manager: Gino Magnotta
Managing Director: John Duhigg

SMALL PRINT

Publishing information

This fourth edition published January 2011 by

Rough Guides Ltd,
80 Strand, London WC2R 0RL
11, Community Centre, Panchsheel Park,
New Delhi 110017, India

Distributed by the Penguin Group

Penguin Books Ltd,
80 Strand, London WC2R 0RL

Penguin Group (USA)
375 Hudson Street, NY 10014, USA

Penguin Group (Australia)
250 Camberwell Road, Camberwell,
Victoria 3124, Australia

Penguin Group (NZ)
67 Apollo Drive, Mairangi Bay, Auckland 1310,
New Zealand

Rough Guides is represented in Canada by
Tourmaline Editions Inc. 662 King Street West,
Suite 304, Toronto, Ontario M5V 1M7

Cover concept by Peter Dyer.

Typeset in Bembo and Helvetica to an original
design by Henry Iles.

Printed in Singapore

336pp includes index
A catalogue record for this book is available from the British Library
ISBN: 978-1-84836-659-6

Help us update

We've gone to a lot of effort to ensure that the fourth edition of **The Rough Guide to Laos** is accurate and up-to-date. However, things change – places get "discovered", opening hours are notoriously fickle, restaurants and rooms raise prices or lower standards. If you feel we've got it wrong or left something out, we'd like to know, and if you can remember the address, the price, the hours, the phone number, so much the better.

Please send your comments with the subject line "**Rough Guide Laos Update**" to ⓔmail @uk.roughguides.com. We'll credit all contributions and send a copy of the next edition (or any other Rough Guide if you prefer) for the very best emails.

Find more travel information, connect with fellow travellers and book your trip on ⓦwww .roughguides.com

Acknowledgements

Emma Gibbs: A big *kop chai lai lai* to everyone who helped me along the way, including the numerous travellers I met in various places for their company, especially Ryan, for whiling away an evening with me in Muang Ngoi, and Theo, for letting me drag him around Phongsali's few "sights" and helping me to hunt down Lao food in a town full of Chinese restaurants. I'm especially indebted to the following people for their help: Karin Van Zyl, Cyril Boucher and Noynaly Phimmavong at *3 Nagas by Alila*, not least for one of the most fabulous meals I ate while I was away and their constant hospitality; Andrew and the rest of the team at *Lotus Villa* for providing me with a very happy first night in the country and invaluable advice; Lee Sheridan and everyone else at luang-prabang-hotels.com; Caroline Gayland at *Tamarind*; Eskil Sorensen and everyone at *Nong Kiau Riverside*; Markus Neuer at Tiger Trail; Hom at Tiger Trail, Nong Khiaw, for endless amounts of information, a brilliant hike and a much needed steam bath and massage; Klaus Schwettman and everyone else at Green Discovery; Vicky Legg at Orient Express;

Phillippe Bissig and the rest of the wonderful staff at *La Résidence Phou Vau*; Mario at *Lao Spirit Resort* for pointing me in the direction of bathing elephants, providing a good natter and the most restoratative of surroundings; Emma Hill and Tiggy Dean at Hill and Dean PR; everyone at *Amantaka*; Nathalie Pouliot at Luang Say for all her help, especially when the river was too low and scuppered all my plans, and for pointing me in the direction of her fabulous restaurant; and Sanya Vincent for his hospitality at *Auberge de la Plaine de Jarres*. Big thanks also to Róisín Cameron, for her excellent editing, and to Keith Drew for getting me out there in the first place. Finally, my biggest thanks have to go to Matthew, for putting up with my absence (again), and for his constant support.

Steve Vickers sends a big "kop chai" to Oudomsay Thongsavath, Lee Sheridan, Karin (thanks for waiting for me), Dale Witheridge, the party people of Vang Vieng, the inspirational people of Laos, everyone at Rough Guides, Kev, Dan, and his wonderful mum and dad.

Readers' letters

Thanks to all the readers who have taken the time to write in with comments and suggestions (and apologies if we've inadvertently omitted or misspelt anyone's name):

Davide Almerico, Stephen Almeroth, Jonathon Blair, Neil Farmiloe, Owen Gallupe, Tara Gujadhur, Chris Hall, Richard Hindle, Lee Hodgson, Inga and Conrad, Katie Junkin, Rebecca Kallis, Zach Leigh, Ukirsari Manggalani-Soepijono, Susan Motyer, Lauren Perkins, Joep van de Rijdt, Peter Shaddick, Zofia Sitarz, Brian Stoddart, Joost Verboven, John Wigham.

Photo credits

All photos © Rough Guides except the following:

Full page
Sunset along Mekong River in Vientiane
© William Zhang/Alamy

Things not to miss
01 Rice fields near the village of Ban Xieng Fa,
Phongsali Province © imagebroker/Alamy
04 Tad Fan Waterfall © Atmotu Images/Alamy
10 Scattered limestone rock formations in Vieng
Xay © Bert de Ruiter/Alamy
18 Nong Khiaw Village © Alex Bramwell/Alamy

Hill tribes of Laos colour section
Lahu people © Terry Whittaker/Alamy

Festivals colour section
Dancers at the That Luang Festival © Val Duncan/
Kenebec Images/Alamy

Great Stupa of Pha That Luang at full moon in
Makkha Bu Saa © Robert Harding Picture
Library Ltd/Alamy
Buddhist New Year © Chris Lees/Alamy
Buddhist New Year, Luang Prabang © Chris
Lees/Alamy
Launching of a Bang Fai rocket © imagebroker/
Alamy
Decorative boat for Awk Phansa © Jennifer
Dunlop/Alamy
Boat racing © Stephane Camus/Alamy
Lighting candles at the That Luang Festival
© infocusphotos.com/Alamy

Black and whites
p.146 Buddha statue at Wat Phia in the ruined
city of Xieng Khuang © Chris Hellier/Alamy

Index

Map entries are in colour.

Map symbols

maps are listed in the full index using coloured text

– – – ·	International boundary		🏯	Chinese temple
– – –	Chapter division boundary		⚲	Stupa/that
═══	Major road		⊙	Statue/monument
──	Minor road		♟	Museum
⫘⫘⫘	Steps (town maps)		✈	Airport
═■═■	Rail line		★	Bus/taxi stand
— —	Ferry route		⛽	Petrol station
⋯⋯	River		ℂ	Telephone office
───	Wall		@	Internet access
- - - - -	Path		ⓘ	Tourist information
♦	Point of interest		⊠	Post office
♦	Border crossing		⊞	Hospital
𖤘	Mountain range		⚓	Boat
▲	Mountain peak		)(	Bridge
☀	Hill		▭	Market
⚱	Waterfall		⬭	Stadium
∴	Ruin		▬	Building
⌂	Cave		⊞	Church/cathedral
♁	Temple/monastery		▦	Park/national biodiversity
♜	Mosque			

MAP SYMBOLS

So now we've told you about the things not to miss, the best places to stay, the top restaurants, the liveliest bars and the most spectacular sights, it only seems fair to tell you about the best travel insurance around